GIANTS VS. DODGERS

COVER PHOTOS

Front: Giants shortstop Brandon Crawford throws over the Dodgers' Howie Kendrick to complete a double play in the fifth inning June 12, 2016, at AT&T Park in San Francisco. *Photo credit: Associated Press/Ben Margot*

Back: Giants pitcher Madison Bumgarner and the Dodgers' Yasiel Puig stare each other down as first base coach Bill Hayes stands between them after Puig was thrown out at first base September 19, 2016, in Los Angeles. The Bumgarner-Puig feud has heated up the rivalry on several occasions. *Photo credit: Associated Press/Mark J. Terrill*

GIANTS VS. DODGERS

THE COAST-TO-COAST HISTORY OF THE RIVALRY HEARD 'ROUND THE WORLD

JOE KONTE

With Forewords by
Bruce Jenkins and Steve Dilbeck

SPORTS
PUBLISHING

Sports Publishing books may be purchased in bulk at special discounts for sales promotion, corporate gifts, fund-raising, or educational purposes. Special editions can also be created to specifications. For details, contact the Special Sales Department, Sports Publishing, 307 West 36th Street, 11th Floor, New York, NY 10018 or sportspubbooks@skyhorsepublishing.com.

Sports Publishing® is a registered trademark of Skyhorse Publishing, Inc.®, a Delaware corporation.

Visit our website at www.skyhorsepublishing.com.

10 9 8 7 6 5 4 3 2 1

Library of Congress Cataloging-in-Publication Data is available on file.

Cover design by Tom Lau

Print ISBN: 978-1-68358-044-7
Ebook ISBN: 978-1-68358-045-4

Printed in the United States of America

For my Dad,
who taught me how
to draw a throw
and other baseball strategy

CONTENTS

PART THREE: TRANSITION 1970–1989

PART FOUR: EPIC HOMERS 1990–2009

PART FIVE: NEW ERA 2010–2016

PART SIX: RIVALRY NOTEBOOK

FOREWORD:
DATELINE, SAN FRANCISCO

The Dodgers-Giants rivalry changed my life at a very impressionable age. It's the reason I became a sportswriter, a delightful job that makes you question whether you're really working. And it's still the highlight of a baseball summer, always making me feel like a little kid again.

Other than that, I don't have much to say about it.

I was 10 years old, living on the very northern edge of Los Angeles County, when the Dodgers and Giants moved West in 1958. My parents were top-flight musicians who spent so much time working in New York; we actually lived there for a couple of one-year spells when I was still traveling about by stroller. My dad had seen many games at Ebbets Field and the Polo Grounds, and a love of baseball was in his blood. I didn't inherit those musical genes, but sports gave us something to share—even if it meant witnessing ballgames at a comically inappropriate venue.

Memorial Coliseum was all about the Rams, USC and UCLA football, and the wondrous deeds of track and field. No one in his right mind would try to fit a baseball configuration into that place, but it was the Dodgers' only option before the unveiling of Dodger Stadium in 1962. The left-field line stopped cold at 250 feet (no choice; football seats there), so they erected a 42-foot screen to preserve the pitchers' sanity. I don't recall the exact distance to right-center, but it was roughly the next town. It seemed like 480 feet, and it probably felt even farther to a powerful left-handed hitter like Willie McCovey.

I loved the Coliseum, truth be told. What did I know? I'd never seen Ebbets or Wrigley or Fenway; this was my baseball palace. I'll never forget emerging from one of those long tunnels and into the sunlight, a gorgeous ball field before my eyes. It was 1958, the Giants were in town, and that would be my first exposure to the major leagues.

I can't remember the details, but I remember Willie Mays, Orlando Cepeda, Willie Kirkland, and Jimmy Davenport. The Dodgers badly needed to make an impression on Southern California, and wisely, they employed a number of great Brooklyn names, the likes of Gil Hodges, Duke Snider, and Carl Furillo, each near the end of a distinguished career. For history-minded kids like me, this was a crucial connection to the Dodgers' past, a window into their long and colorful history.

As I grew older, I began to resent the Dodgers' move from Brooklyn, at least on a peripheral level. I found it heartbreaking that they'd abandon their neighborhood ballpark and a passionate fan base that lived and died with the team. I got over that, of course. By 1959, the Dodgers were world champions and launching the golden era of Sandy Koufax, Don Drysdale, Maury Wills, and the Davis boys.

Many people recall Koufax's 1963 no-hitter as his masterpiece against the Giants, but for me, it came on August 31, 1959, at the crazy old Coliseum. Those Giants were so loaded, they had McCovey batting second, followed by Mays, Cepeda, and Felipe Alou—and Koufax struck out 18. This was a life-changing performance at the time, matching Bob Feller's record set in 1938—and the fact that it came against the Giants made it that much sweeter. Wally Moon was famous for his "Moon shots"—a left-handed hitter going the opposite way to clear that screen—and old No. 9 (the number I always sought in Little League) hit a three-run shot that night.

My perspective on life changed in the fall of 1966, when I left Southern California to attend UC Berkeley, and that included my relationship with the Dodgers. Suddenly, I was in Mays-and-McCovey country. The Dodgers lost that World Series in baffling fashion to the Baltimore Orioles—the end of a fabulous era, as it turned out. I began to take a hard look at sportswriting, and by 1972, as a young writer for the *Santa Monica Evening Outlook*, I learned that a certain detachment is required for covering sports properly. But the Dodgers weren't quite through changing my life. With the *Outlook's* beat writer taking a break, I was sent on a road trip through Chicago, St. Louis, and Pittsburgh to cover the Dodgers. That's when I knew, beyond question, how I wanted my life to unfold.

So many Dodgers-Giants moments come to mind over the span of my 40-year *San Francisco Chronicle* career: Joe Morgan's shot off Terry Forster, the emergence of Bobby Bonds, John Montefusco's swagger, titanic home runs from Mike Ivie and Brian Johnson, the fateful decision to pitch Salomon Torres, Tommy Lasorda's flamboyant walks toward the Candlestick dugout, Barry Bonds's epic at-bat against Eric Gagne, or just the simple pleasure of Jon Miller imitating Jon Ramsey—the legendary Dodger Stadium PA announcer—or doing a Vin Scully impression in Japanese (who even thinks of that?). One night, after a particularly discouraging loss to the Dodgers, the Giants broadcasters assembled for their nightly wrap-up and picked their "player of the game." Mike Krukow, particularly disgusted, picked a Giant who hadn't even played that night—anyone but a Dodger.

I'd try to recall all of the great moments, but why bother? That's the beauty of this book. In meticulous fashion, starting with the first official game between the franchises in 1889 and focusing intensely on the West Coast era, Joe Konte brings them all home. We owe him a debt of gratitude for his toil, surely a labor of love, and a work to be cherished by everyone who loves this little kids' game.

> **Bruce Jenkins** has written for the *San Francisco Chronicle*
> since 1973 and has been a sports columnist since 1989.
> He has covered 25 World Series.

FOREWORD: DATELINE, LOS ANGELES

My parents were extremely proper. They raised me to try to avoid using the word hate, to understand the nastiness and near vulgarity of the remark. So believe me, I understand exactly what I'm doing when I write:

I hate the San Francisco Giants.

There now, I feel better. That's always a nice exhale, a pleasant little release. That felt so damn good, I just have to write it again:

I *hate* the San Francisco Giants.

That's an instant smile. Sorry Mom and Dad, that'll give me Snoopy Happy Feet every time. There are few things as glorious in life as watching the Dodgers beat the living snot out of the Giants. Just makes everything feel right in the world.

I've witnessed most of this rivalry since both teams moved West, or at least since Walter O'Malley told Horace Stoneham to move and he played the good soldier. I believe his actual response was, "Yes, Mr. O'Malley. Immediately, sir!"

At least the Dodgers were from Brooklyn. The Giants were always the second team in New York, and now they're forever the second team in California. Embrace it. Actually, the A's have still won more World Series titles, so I guess the Giants really are the third team from California. Best keep an eye on those Padres.

I was six when the Dodgers moved to Los Angeles, and we were simply told the Giants were their rivals. I just went with it. I was young but had already learned to feel sorry for everyone in San Francisco. It had a great bridge and funky streets but had almost killed Clark Gable in that 1906 earthquake, and a kid doesn't forget things like that. Plus, all those poor people had to live in the shade all the time. Guess I was too young to grasp the concept of perennial fog.

A year after the Dodgers moved to Los Angeles, they won the World Series. Was that so hard? It took the Giants over 50 years to figure it out, and by then the Dodgers had won five championships. Blind squirrel and all.

In my youth, the Dodgers played in what remains one of the most beautiful ballparks in the world, while the Giants played in a freezing wind trap called Candlestick Park, an oddly configured multipurpose stadium where they handed out little pins to people who stayed the entire game that said something like, "I survived." Spent some of the coldest nights of my life at the 'Stick.

Comparing ballparks wasn't fair, but then little of the rivalry seemed that way in my youth. I'm pretty sure Sandy Koufax threw a no-hitter against the Giants every time he faced them. Plus, the Giants played in those pukey Halloween-colored uniforms. The colors of witches and goblins and, you know, just general evil. I couldn't figure out why anyone would actually choose to be a Giants fan.

But you could truly sense the rivalry then, and it didn't take Juan Marichal plunking John Roseboro over the head with a bat to cement it. Though, see, those Giants really are crazy.

Meanwhile, the Dodgers kept winning and the Giants kept doing something. Freezing I think. When the Koufax-Drysdale Era subsided, the Garvey-Cey-Lopes-Russell Era began. At Candlestick, they bought more blankets. The Dodgers won another title. They even won one in 1988, with a rather unspectacular team beating the mighty A's. That would be the same A's team that swept the Giants the next year. After a little timeout for another earthquake (still didn't get Gable).

Mostly I don't believe Dodgers fans think about the Giants unless they're playing them. The possible exception being the 2002 World Series when the Giants did the absolute unthinkable and turned them into Angels fans. It's kind of like Los Angeles and San Francisco. People in L.A. don't hate (ooh, that word again) San Francisco. We like it. Think it's a great place to visit. No one in L.A. is fixated on the Giants. Not one fan chanted "Beat S.F.!" when they won any of their five World Series for Los Angeles. Maybe if you spend your whole life under a gray cloud, an inferiority complex is to be expected.

As a sportswriter/blogger/columnist over the years, I've been fortunate to watch many of these classic Dodgers-Giants games in person. Like when Mike Piazza hit a hundred home runs to squash the Giant's title run in 1993 and Steve Finley hit the momentous grand slam to kill them in 2004.

In more recent times, Dodgers fans have had to suffer through Fox and Frank McCourt ownership, while the Giants were getting a terrific new ballpark and winning two titles in three years. Good for them, I guess. Most of us were running out of sympathy, and besides, a one-sided rivalry is no rivalry at all. Competition is at its best when both teams are good. Now Dodgers fans can return guilt-free to their more base instincts and to despising the Giants. Something about it just feels good.

Joe Konte's excellent *Giants vs. Dodgers* details in exceptional fashion all the big games and moments between the two teams, apparently some of which the Giants actually won. This is truly the greatest rivalry in baseball history, if not all American sports, and it's great to have a single source for all of it. The most shocking aspect to it is that someone didn't write it sooner.

The future holds only more, of course. Teams reveling in causing the other pain. Consider it baseball's natural order. Wouldn't change a pitch, a moment, or a single Don Drysdale sneer. I don't know if the famous story about Jackie Robinson choosing to retire rather than accept a trade to the Giants is true, but I like to believe it is.

Steve Dilbeck has covered sports in Southern California for more than 25 years, including seven years on the Dodgers beat. He has been a Dodgers blogger for the *Los Angeles Times* for nearly four years.

PROLOGUE

I saw my first Dodgers-Giants game on September 1, 1958. I was only seven years old, but I have proof. I still have the scorecard my Dad kept as we watched the game together at Seals Stadium. Forty years later, I sat in the stands at Candlestick Park as the Giants commemorated the 40th anniversary of the Dodgers-Giants opening game on the West Coast with an on-field celebration. As some of the players from that inaugural year were driven around the field in convertibles, waving to the fans, I saw not the faces of aging men but pictured them the way they were. These players were baseball gods to me when I first saw them as a kid. They played this game that I already loved on this beautiful green grass in front of other adoring fans. As I watched the parade of cars pass by, I wished I could have one more day, one more game, one more cloudless summer afternoon to watch Drysdale's fearsome sidearm delivery, Snider's sweet swing, Gilliam's skill at moving the runner over, Cepeda's powerful stroke to right-center, Davenport's quick hands at third, and Mays's blazing speed turning a single into a double.

If only I could make them all young again.

As a longtime San Francisco Bay Area newspaperman, a former sports editor, and a lifelong baseball junkie, I pondered how I could combine my experience and passion to fulfill that dream. That set me out on a mission to tell the complete story of the West Coast rivalry from the first Dodgers-Giants game on April 15, 1958, through the nearly 60 years since then. I embarked on a labor of love to research every game the teams have played against one another, as well as every season and offseason of the two clubs. There were many hours spent in the microfilm section of the library looking at all the reports on the games and the box scores, but it never came close to feeling like work. I've either watched on television or attended most of the more than 1,000 games between the clubs since 1958, so the research gave me a chance to relive for myself all the great memories of the games and players that make this such a rich rivalry.

While the focus of this book is on the clubs after they moved west, I knew that it would not be complete without addressing the New York and Brooklyn era and the legendary games and names that made Dodgers-Giants baseball one of the greatest rivalries in sports. My research into this period began with the first official Dodgers-Giants game in 1889, and continued through the final year on the East Coast in 1957. The book gives extra attention to the 1950s, since some of the same players from those teams made the trip to California. The year 1951 receives special emphasis, since it still stands as the greatest ever Dodgers-Giants season.

The total research project covering more than 100 years resulted in *Giants vs. Dodgers*. My goal in writing the book was to approach the subject right down the middle, not as a follower of one team, but as one who has appreciated the rivalry and who wished to show respect for it by recording its history. The book provides an historical context on the rivalry for the newer generation of Los Angeles and San Francisco fans, rekindles the memories of longtime followers of both clubs, and gives new insight into one of baseball's great traditions for the general interest fan of the game. Even those who have closely watched the rivalry since 1958 will be surprised at how much they don't know or have forgotten. For example, most fans young and old know that Giants pitcher Juan Marichal struck Dodgers catcher John Roseboro on the head with a bat in 1965. The widely held version of the story is that Marichal's violent act was solely in response to Roseboro throwing a ball back to the pitcher near Marichal's ear on that August day at Candlestick Park. However, a more extensive look reveals a far deeper picture of the events of that dark day to show that the tensions between Marichal and the Dodgers had been building since early in the season and were ignited with the threatening remarks made by the intimidating Don Drysdale. The Marichal-Roseboro clash came in game four of a draining series in San Francisco with the pennant on the line and the earlier trash talk between Marichal and Drysdale still reverberating. Other brawls and near-brawls also receive billing, starring such names as Frank Robinson, Roger Craig, Bill Buckner, Mike Marshall, and Eric Gagne, right up to the current feud between Madison Bumgarner and Yasiel Puig. The book even takes the reader back to 1958 for a look at the first beanball battle between the clubs, coming in just their sixth game against each other that year.

My research could have produced an encyclopedia, but my intention was to condense that mountain of information into a concise, chronological, and compelling look at the rivalry. It also was clear in the research that one season doesn't stand on its own—that what happens during a season was set up by what occurred in the season or two prior to it. That is the driving theme of the book, as it sets the stage for each season and weaves together storylines from one year to the next.

That approach not only gives context to the rivalry each year but also allows the book to serve as a vehicle for telling the stories of the teams and the players. For example, Sandy Koufax didn't just suddenly show up and win Cy Young awards every year, although his 18-strikeout performance against the Giants in 1959 gave a hint. The book notes his struggles with control before he became so dominant. Similarly, the book tracks the Barry Bonds saga from all-star to all-world as balls suddenly were flying out of the parks.

Telling the story of the individual teams also provided a way to show how the rivalry played out in a given year. No sports rivalry, be it the Yankees-Red Sox or any other, sees those teams battling each other for a championship each season. In fact, even in the top rivalries, the Giants-

Dodgers included, it is rare that the teams are at their best in the same year. That reality, however, also provides one of the most competitive moments of the rivalry—the spoiler role. If you count it up, you might find that the Giants and Dodgers have played more games where one of the teams had a late-season chance to spoil the title drive of the other than you would games where both teams were fighting for the crown. Those spoiler situations were blood-feud games. The book describes several of those developments where preventing the other team from clinching a postseason berth on your home field was akin to keeping a burglar from smashing through the front door of your house.

That was never clearer than in the pennant battle of 2004.

After Los Angeles lost to St. Louis in the National League division series that year, the Dodgers came on the field to congratulate the Cardinal players. The gesture of sportsmanship had to come as a surprise to the Giants, who only the week before saw the Dodgers and their fans dance on their graves as they were eliminated from both the division and wild-card race.

Dodgers closer Gagne was far from a goodwill ambassador when he discussed how his club looked forward to winning the division title by beating the Giants in the final series of the season. Said Gagne: "I want them to see us clinch. The good thing is that they're going to see us clinch against them. It's going to be amazing and a lot of fun, especially for the fans. They'll be able to see us do it against the hated Giants."

Gagne got his wish as the Dodgers clinched the title in Game 161 with a seven-run rally in the ninth inning against the Giants capped by a walk-off grand slam. The Giants had a chance the next day to tie for the wild card but needed Houston to lose. When the Dodger Stadium message board announced that the Astros won while the Giants and Dodgers were still playing, Los Angeles fans rubbed it in with some taunting applause in appreciation that San Francisco's season was over.

Of course, Giants players and fans would have demonstrated equal glee if the situation was reversed—that has been the essence of the 50-plus years of the West Coast rivalry. One can be sure that the Dodgers and

Giants will have more bench-clearing brawls, but it's also a good bet that the teams can go another half-century and not conclude a tensely fought game with a bench-clearing handshake.

While such heated moments help define the Dodgers-Giants competition, there are those seasons when the rivalry is more fizzle than sizzle, as both teams have down years. But even though the rivalry appears to be smoldering at times, it's always ready to reignite with one brush-back pitch, one game, one series, or one hot season between the clubs. The fans to this day need little excuse to get revved up. At a Giants spring training game in their home field in Scottsdale, Arizona, several men wearing Dodgers jackets paraded through the stands. The Dodgers weren't even playing, but it didn't prevent Giants fans from breaking into a resounding chant of "Beat L.A.!"

Some argue that the rivalry was stronger in the early years and that some of the luster has faded. There might be some validity to that claim, but it could be more the result of outside realities than what happens between the white lines. For one thing, there is no way to recapture the excitement of those first few seasons when major league baseball was new to Northern and Southern California. For another, there was no other dominant sport claiming to be the national pastime in the late 1950s and early 1960s, when newspapers ran standings on the front page of the sports sections and gave top billing to baseball over all other sports. Changes in the game also have had an effect. In the 1960s, players didn't switch teams as frequently, so year in and year out, the same cast would be on the field. That meant that tensions and incidents from one season might carry over to the next, adding to the anticipation of the teams' next meeting. That feeling is not as common today, as players jump from team to team more often.

The book tells the story of the transition to the West Coast by describing the clubs' final games in New York and Brooklyn in 1957 and analyzing the contrasting strategies the teams employed when they arrived for their first seasons in San Francisco and Los Angeles. The book continues on through the fascinating journey of five-plus decades of Dodgers-Giants baseball. There is the flashy beginning of Fernando-Mania and the quiet goodbye of Willie Mays, the beefs with umpires and official scorers, the fading of New York–Brooklyn legends and the emergence of new San Francisco–Los Angeles stars, the colorful antics of Dodger-hater John Montefusco and Dodgers icon Tommy Lasorda, the players who went from friend to enemy simply by switching uniforms of the two clubs, and the skippers who oversaw it all. There is the epic pennant race of 1962, the down-to-the wire battle of 1971, the Joe Morgan home run that devastated the Dodgers in 1982, the Dodgers' payback victory to eliminate the Giants in 1993, the Brian Johnson shot that propelled the Giants past the Dodgers in 1997, and the Steve Finley slam that ended the Giants' dreams in 2004.

There are extensive accounts of the 2010 through 2016 seasons, as the rivalry reached its most competitive era since the 1960s with the Giants winning three championships and the Dodgers capturing four consecutive division titles.

One of the most intriguing challenges in the book is the selection of a starting lineup and 25-man roster for one West Coast rivalry mythical game. The names chosen are not necessarily those with the best statistics but were chosen for how they might add fire to the game.

It has been 59 years since Ruben Gomez threw the first pitch to Gino Cimoli at Seals Stadium to begin major league baseball in California. It has been 19 years since that day at Candlestick when the aging men from that first year were paraded around the park. Some of those who played in the rivalry have passed on. Others are not in good health. Many are living on and thriving, some who are still in baseball in some capacity, some who are not. But whatever they are doing, and wherever they are, they are all young again, playing the game and thrilling the fans one more time in *Giants vs. Dodgers: The Coast-to-Coast History of the Rivalry Heard 'Round the World.*

Joe Konte

Part One

ORIGINS
1889–1957

1

BIRTH OF A RIVALRY:
1889–1890

It didn't take long for the rivalry to catch on. Sixty-nine years before the
Giants and Dodgers arrived on the West Coast, the early passion
of the rivalry began working its way into a revered place in
baseball history as the clubs met for the first time.

The New York Giants won their second consecutive National League pennant in 1889, edging out the Boston Beaneaters by one game. The Giants were paced by the pitching of 28-game winner Tim Keefe. The offense was led by Mike Tiernan, the league leader in runs and walks, and Roger Connor, the league leader in RBIs and slugging percentage. Beating the Beaneaters was no breeze, since the Giants had to contend with Boston workhorse John Clarkson, who won 49 games in 1889 while pitching 620 innings and throwing 68 complete games.

Brooklyn dethroned the American Association defending champion St. Louis Browns to capture that league's flag in 1889 by two games. Brooklyn was led by pitcher Bob Caruthers, who topped the league in

1889 in wins with 40 and shutouts with seven. The offense was sparked by Darby O'Brien, who was among the top three in the league in runs and stolen bases; and Dave Foutz, who was second in RBIs.

The stage was set for the first-ever official game between New York and Brooklyn as the clubs met for a best-of-11 championship series. The account of the series opener on October 18, 1889, by the *New York Times* left no doubt about the passionate feelings for the two clubs. "The rivalry between New York and Brooklyn as regards to baseball is unparalleled in the history of the national game," the *Times* wrote. "It is not confined to the players or attaches of the clubs, but the patrons take part in it."

A crowd of 8,445 was on hand for the first game in Brooklyn, and controversy was already erupting. The contest was umpired by a two-man crew, and New York fans raised objections when they found out that one of the arbiters was a lifelong Brooklyn resident.

Brooklyn jumped out to a 5–0 lead in the first inning, and after six, held a 6–5 lead. The Giants scored five in the seventh to go ahead 10–6. Brooklyn battled back, and as darkness began to settle in, scored four in the eighth to take the advantage, aided by two batted balls that landed safely when the Giants fielders couldn't see them. The umpires concurred that it was too dark to continue, so the game was stopped and Brooklyn declared the winner, 12–10. Hub Collins was the hero for Brooklyn with a homer, two doubles and a single.

The tide would turn as New York won the final five games to take the series 6–3 after going down three games to one. After the 1889 season, Brooklyn switched to the National League. The clubs played their first regular season game on May 3, 1890, won by Brooklyn 7–3.

With those games, a rivalry was born.

2

EAST COAST ERA: 1900–1957

*It still seems hard to believe that the New York and Brooklyn clubs would
have ever left. Their move to California in 1958 ended an era, but it
did not end the memories. The teams may be long gone, but the legendary
players, the thrilling moments, the historic ballparks and
the devoted fans have made the rivalry's East Coast era one of the
greatest stories in baseball.*

GIANTS TAKE COMMAND

You couldn't tell the team name without a scorecard. At least that
was the case with the Brooklyn (fill-in-the-blank) clubs in the
early years of the franchise. The team began play in the American
Association in 1884 as the Atlantics. In 1885, the named changed to
the Grays. When seven players got married in 1888, manager William
McGunnigle started calling the club the Bridegrooms. The name Trolley
Dodgers caught on in 1891, generated by the many trolleys that zipped
around Brooklyn. The team was known as the Superbas starting in 1899 during the managerial reign of Ned Hanlon. The name came from a Broadway
act called Hanlon's (no relation) Superbas. Wilbert Robinson, who managed the team from 1914 to 1931, was referred to as "Uncle Robbie." That
spawned the nickname Robins. The club was called any of these names up
to 1932, when the Dodgers name finally took hold.

New York fans had a far easier time on what to call their club. The team was created as the Gothams for its debut in 1883. That changed on June 3, 1885, when manager Jim Mutrie was so excited about a win over the Philadelphia Quakers that he cried out, "My big fellows! My Giants!" You could hardly blame Mutrie for his enthusiasm. Trailing 7–5 in the ninth, the Gothams rallied to tie it. In the 11th, the Gothams' Dude Esterbook singled. He was running on the pitch when Mike Dorgan ripped a liner to left that got past leftfielder Ed Andrews. Esterbrook never stopped running as the relay throw came home, and scored when he slammed into catcher Charlie Ganzel, knocking the ball loose. The 8,688 fans watching at Philadelphia's Recreation Park went home disappointed by the defeat, but unaware that they were witnessing history as Mutrie's "Giants" name became part of baseball history. One final reason for Mutrie to be proud of his team: The Giants finished with an 85–27 record, although they still fell two games short of the first-place Chicago White Stockings.

Brooklyn had a big finish to the nineteenth century and a big start for the twentieth century by winning the pennant both years. The team was sparked by "Wee" Willie Keeler (.379 in 1899, .362 in 1900), known for proclaiming, "I hit 'em where they ain't." The Giants, on the other hand, hit 'em where they were as they finished 42 games out in 1899 and 23 back in 1900.

The fortunes of the two teams then shifted dramatically.

From 1901 to 1939, New York won 13 pennants and four World Series championships. Brooklyn won two pennants, and was defeated in both World Series. New York's overall success translated into dominance over Brooklyn during that span. New York won its head-to-head match-ups against Brooklyn in 27 of those 39 years, with three seasons ending in ties. The Giants won their season series against Brooklyn 12 years in a row from 1903 to 1914. In 1904, New York won the series 19–3.

The Giants' early 1900s success can be tracked to one move on July 16, 1902, when they signed John McGraw as a player-manager. McGraw won his first game seven days later as New York defeated Brooklyn 4–1. McGraw took over a team that would finish 53½ games out in 1902, so there was room for improvement. When he stepped down in 1932, McGraw had won 10 pennants and three World Series championships.

The Brooklyn club couldn't have played any flatter than if it was run over by a trolley. The team had 11 consecutive losing seasons from 1904 to 1914, including finishing 55½ out in 1909 and 56½ out in 1905. The 1908 team lost 101 games.

Brooklyn found some of the same spark the Giants got from the McGraw signing when they brought on Robinson as manager in 1914. In 1916, he guided the club to the pennant. The Giants finished just seven games behind in fourth place, but were never in the race. Brooklyn's bid for its first World Series title was thwarted by the Boston Red Sox and their young left-hander Babe Ruth, who won Game Two 2–1 with a complete game, 14-inning gem.

The Giants made World Series appearances in 1905, 1911, 1912, 1913, 1917, 1921, 1922, and 1923. They won it in 1905 over Philadelphia and in 1921 and 1922 over the Yankees. Christy Mathewson tossed three shutouts to beat Philadelphia in five games. The Giants came back from a 3–2 game deficit to win the final three in a best-of-nine series in 1921. Giants pitchers limited the Yankees to 11 runs, and held Ruth down to a .118 average in a four-game sweep (one game was called because of darkness) in 1922. Despite those seven Giants pennants, none of them involved a race to the wire with their rivals. The only first-second finish for the clubs at the time came in 1920, when Brooklyn won the pennant, while New York was runner-up, seven games behind. The year marked the first one-on-one pennant race, at least for a time. Brooklyn was tied with Cincinnati for first place September 8, with New York 1½ games back. The Giants played out the schedule with a respectable 12–10 record, but Brooklyn went on a 17–4 run down the stretch to take the pennant. New York had only itself to blame as the club lost 15 of 22 games against Brooklyn.

Four years later, the rivalry got its first real race for the flag. Brooklyn entered 1924 with low expectations after three consecutive mediocre seasons. The Giants began the season flying high in quest of a fourth consecutive pennant. New York took charge again, and by August 9, led the National League standings while Brooklyn was 13 games behind in fourth place. Brooklyn then went on a 26–4 run while New York stumbled with a 8–15 stretch. In one of the most significant meetings of this early era, Brooklyn swept a three-game series from New York August 29–31. At the end of play September 4, Brooklyn and New York were tied for first.

Brooklyn slipped back into second, but stayed close. On September 22, Brooklyn defeated Chicago 2–1 to tie New York for first. New York was at 89–59 and Brooklyn, having played two more games, was at 90–60. The Giants won three straight against Pittsburgh, while Brooklyn split its next two games with Chicago. The Giants clinched the pennant on September 27 with a 5–1 win over Philadelphia behind Jack Bentley's four-hitter while Brooklyn fell to Boston 3–2. In the end, New York's 14–8 advantage over Brooklyn in head-to-head play made the difference.

It was a disappointing finish for Brooklyn, which combined solid pitching and offense. Dazzy Vance (28–6) and Burleigh Grimes (22–13) were an excellent pitching duo, and Zack Wheat (.375, 97 RBIs) and Jack Fournier (27 HR, 116 RBIs) supplied the bats. The Giants relied on an offense that led the league in batting average and home runs. George "High Pockets" Kelly was the hitting star with 21 homers and 136 RBIs.

Brooklyn's hopes for another pennant chase went dormant for the next 15 years. During that time, its highest finish was third place, and included 10 years of being in sixth place or worse. New York had three second-place finishes in the next eight years, but in 1933 won the pennant and the World Series, defeating Washington in five games.

FIGHTING WORDS

Perhaps it was the boldness that comes following a World Series championship year, but in the offseason, Giants player-manager Bill Terry delivered a stirring wake-up call to those sleeping Dodgers. While talking with some sportswriters in February 1934, Terry responded to a question from New York newspaper men about the status of the rival club by saying,

"Brooklyn? Are they still in the league?" It was the "slight heard 'round the borough." It earned him the wrath of Brooklyn fans, although they would have to wait seven months to gain revenge.

The Dodgers were headed to another dreary finish as the 1934 season neared the end, trailing the first-place Giants by 23½ games on September 26. The Giants, meanwhile, were involved in a tight race with St. Louis, which they led by one game. St. Louis had played two fewer games than New York, so when the Cardinals won their next two while the Giants had the days off, the clubs were tied with two games to go on September 29 and 30. The Cards would have two more against Cincinnati. The Giants would have two more at home against the Dodgers.

Brooklyn smelled blood.

September 29 was a gray, wet day at the Polo Grounds, and while the weather kept some Giants fans away, Brooklyn backers braved the elements in hopes that the Dodgers would spoil New York's bid for the flag. The Brooklyn fans saved their biggest jeers for Terry every time he came to bat, and the fired-up Dodgers defeated the Giants 5–1 behind the five-hit pitching of Van Lingle Mungo. The hard-throwing right-hander not only won his 18th game of the season, but had two singles, scored one run and drove in another. The victory was even sweeter for Brooklyn because the Cardinals downed Cincinnati 6–1 as Paul Dean won his 19th game. The Giants, who had been in first place since June 8, were now a game out as the season came down to its final day.

The weather cleared on September 30, and 45,000 showed up in New York, with many of the now enthusiastic Brooklyn fans returning for the kill. The Giants quieted their enemies in the grandstands by taking a 4–0 lead in the first inning. Brooklyn refused to yield, and with the game tied 5–5 in the 10th, the Dodgers scored three runs for an 8–5 win. The St. Louis game was still in progress, and while the Cardinals would eventually win, it didn't matter. The Giants were dead.

As much as the Dodgers played a part in eliminating the Giants, the Dean family also could take some of the credit. Cardinals workhorse Dizzy Dean blanked the Reds 4–0 on September 28, and after his brother Paul won the next day, Dizzy came back on one day's rest to shut out Cincinnati again 9–0 for his 30th win of the season.

In the jubilant Dodgers locker room, someone shouted out, "Brooklyn's in the league now. And how!"

As if that ridicule wasn't enough to sour Giants fans, the club then had to release the sad statement: "The New York Giants announce refunds will be made for World Series tickets within the next few weeks."

———

Despite the delight Brooklyn's fans got in helping New York lose the pennant, there had to be some envy over the Giants' success through the years. The Giants went on to win pennants in 1936 and 1937—though falling in the World Series both years—while the Dodgers struggled to even be competitive.

Just as McGraw's hiring as manager inspired New York, and Robinson's taking the helm ignited Brooklyn, the naming of the scrappy Leo Durocher as skipper in 1939 energized the sagging Dodgers. Brooklyn won the pennant with 100 victories in 1941, and followed that up with 104 wins in 1942. The Cardinals prevented a Dodgers repeat by winning 43 of their last 51 games.

The Giants failed to remotely contend through the 1940s while the Dodgers had three pennants and three second-place finishes during that time. The Giants might have packed all their frustration of the period into one shocking, though insignificant, game against the Dodgers on April 30, 1944. The Dodgers jumped out to a 2–0 lead in the top of the first as 58,068 watched at the Polo Grounds, but by the time the carnage was over, New York had walked away with a 26–8 trouncing. In fact, Giants batters spent much of the day walking as five Dodgers pitchers issued 17 bases on balls. When the pitches got close enough to hit, the Giants took their licks, finishing with 18 hits. Phil Weintraub drove in 11 runs, and Ernie Lombardi added seven more. Durocher might have made the best play of the day, getting ejected in the sixth inning so he wouldn't have to witness the debacle. Strangely, the day turned out to be a wash for New York because the Dodgers took the second game of the doubleheader 5–4, holding the understandably tired Giants offense to five hits.

The Dodgers' success from the 1940s into the 1950s coincided with their breaking baseball's color barrier with the arrival of Jackie Robinson in 1947. Robinson had just one hit, a bunt single, in his first nine plate appearances in his opening year series against Boston. His breakout game came April 18 against the Giants at the Polo Grounds. After popping out in the first inning to drop his average to .143, Robinson hit a solo homer in the third off Dave Koslo as 37,546 watched. He singled and scored in the eighth though New York came out on top 10–4. Outside the Polo Grounds, vendors sold buttons that said "I'M FOR JACKIE."

The Dodgers won the pennant in 1947, but lost in seven games to the Yankees in the World Series. The matchup provided two of the most memorable moments in the history of the fall classic. Yankees pitcher Bill Bevens was one out away from the first ever World Series no-hitter, leading 2–1 in the ninth of Game Four at Ebbets Field with Al Gionfriddo and Eddie Miksis on base. Pinch-hitter Cookie Lavagetto smacked a Bevens pitch off the right field wall to drive in both runs for a 3–2 win. In Game Six at Yankee Stadium, with the Yankees leading the series 3–2, but trailing on the scoreboard 8–5 with two outs in the sixth, Joe DiMaggio drilled an apparent game-tying shot to left field. Gionfriddo saved the game for Brooklyn by snagging DiMaggio's home run bid as the ball was going over the fence. The Yankees took Game Seven and the series the next day with a less-dramatic 5–2 victory.

In 1947, the Giants were nice guys who finished fourth, and club management was looking for a way to jolt the team in hopes of bringing back the long-forgotten glory days. The stunning shake-up occurred midway through the 1948 season when Durocher, linked to the Dodgers as a player or manager or both since 1938, was named manager of the Giants. Some New York fans swallowed hard at having a despised Dodger on their side, hoping Durocher's exuberance would incite their slumbering team. Some weren't buying it. Giants fan Charley Chefalo was quoted as saying, "That settles it brother. I'm through. I'll never enter the Polo Grounds again."

Durocher uttered his famous "nice guys finish last" comment, referring to Giants manager Mel Ott, in 1946 when the Giants finished in the cellar for the second time in four years. Durocher couldn't turn around his new club overnight, but his strategy of building a team that stressed speed and sound hitting over swinging for the fences started to evolve. Durocher's first full year was a disappointment as the Giants finished 24 games out, but he improved them enough in 1950 to finish five games back in third-place.

The Dodgers, now under the guidance of Burt Shotton, returned to the World Series in 1949 against the Yankees. Robinson became a dominant player in 1949. The winner of the MVP award led the league with a .342 average and 37 stolen bases. He was second in hits with 203 and RBIs with 124. He was third in runs scored with 122, doubles with 38 and triples with 12. The Yankees limited Robinson to a .188 average and shut down most of his teammates as they took the series four games to one. Brooklyn made another run at the World Series in 1950 with a late-season surge. Trailing first-place Philadelphia by nine games on September 18, the Dodgers won 13 of 16, and got to within one game of first going into the final day of the season. The Phillies turned back the Dodgers 4–1 to end the challenge. The Dodgers would make one of their most significant off-the-field moves in the postseason, naming Walter O'Malley president. One of O'Malley's first moves was to name Chuck Dressen manager.

The Dodgers, who were becoming almost perennial contenders, and the Giants, revived after a dead period of the 1940s, both appeared primed for a potential race in 1951.

BOBBY AND RALPH

Bobby Thomson, born in 1923 in Glascow, United Kingdom, was signed by the New York Giants in 1942. After serving in the military from 1943 to 1945, Thomson made his major league debut on September 9, 1946, playing third base against the Philadelphia Phillies in Shibe Park. Thomson gave a hint of his offensive talents by going two for four, with a double and two RBIs. In his first full four seasons, he hit 97 homers and drove in 342 runs. He slugged a career-high 32 homers in 1951 and knocked in 101. Thomson made the All-Star team in 1948, 1949, and 1952. He finished his career with a .270 average and 264 homers. On those statistics and honors alone, Thomson would have gone down in the history books as a solid Giant and an impressive run-producer.

Ralph Branca was a horse at 6-foot-3, 220 pounds, ready to take the hill as a starter or in relief. Born in 1926 in Mount Vernon, New York, Branca signed with the Brooklyn Dodgers in 1943. He made his major league debut on June 12, 1944, in a 15–9 loss against the Giants. Branca was the only bright spot on the mound that day, allowing just a run in 3⅓ innings of relief, as four other Brooklyn pitchers took the pounding. Branca would go on to make the All-Star team in 1947, 1948, and 1949. His biggest year was 1947 when he went 21–12 with a 2.67 ERA. He completed his career with an 88–68 record and an ERA of 3.79. On those statistics and honors alone, Branca would have gone down as a tough competitor who usually gave his team a chance to win.

The Giants and Dodgers were both expected to be contenders in 1951, and players such as Thomson and Branca were both expected to have important roles. But as the teams prepared for the first of what would be 22 meetings, no one could ever imagine that these two players were just 5½ months away from being linked to perhaps the most stunning moment in baseball history. Bobby Thomson would forever be known as the hero who hit the famous home run while Ralph Branca would suddenly become the unluckiest man on the face of the earth.

—∞—

Brooklyn jumped on New York, winning the first five meetings between the clubs in early 1951. Star power gave the Dodgers a 7–3 win in the first of a three-game series April 20 in New York as Roy Campanella drove in three runs, Robinson knocked in two, and Don Newcombe went the distance. Robinson delivered again in another 7–3 victory the next day, as he drove in three runs with a homer and double, and then scored a run when he stole third and came home on a wild throw. Robinson's heroics were nearly overshadowed by bad manners displayed by both clubs. The rough-housing began in the first inning when the Giants' Eddie Stanky knocked the ball out of Pee Wee Reese's hands on a stolen base attempt. The Dodgers' Rocky Bridges followed that up by bowling over Thomson with a block during a pickoff play at third base. Chris Van Cuyk decked Hank Thompson in the fourth, prompting Thompson to yell out his displeasure to the Dodgers pitcher. After Larry Jansen buzzed Campanella with two inside pitches, Giants catcher Wes Westrum and Campanella squared off. Umpire Augie Donatelli got in between them to avert any physical altercation. In the series finale, Carl Furillo broke a 3–3 tie in the 10th with a homer off Sal Maglie to give Brooklyn a 4–3 win and a sweep.

Brooklyn continued its streak by winning the first two of a three-game series just six days later at Ebbets Field. The defeats were the 10th and 11th in a row for the Giants, whose record fell to 2–12. Robinson's two-run homer helped the Dodgers win the first 8–4 and Duke Snider's two homers led the way in a 6–3 victory the next day. New York ended the losing streak in the final game, combining timely hitting with three walks to score six times in the first inning in an 8–5 win. While it was only April 30, the Giants already had dropped seven games back, while the third-place Dodgers were in a three-way fight for first with Boston and St. Louis.

The Giants overcame their miserable start to compile a respectable 37–30 record by the time the clubs met again for three games June 26–28 in New York. Brooklyn, at 40–22, had taken over first place. New York took two out of three, starting with a 4–0, three-hit shutout by Sal Maglie. The game marked the rivalry's debut of minor league sensation Willie Mays. The 20-year-old replaced Thomson in center field after he was called up from Minneapolis, where he was batting .477 in 35 games with eight homers and 31 RBIs. Expectations were high for Mays, as a press release announcing his arrival said, "No minor league player in a generation has created so great a stir as has Mays at Minneapolis." Mays made the Dodgers take notice quickly as he doubled in the first inning and came home on Westrum's single. Mays followed that up with a two-run homer the next day, but it wasn't enough as the Dodgers rolled to a 10–4 win on three-run homers by Andy Pafko and Snider. Monte Irvin brought the Giants back from a two-run deficit with a three-run homer in the eighth off Branca for a 5–4 victory in the third game.

Brooklyn began to put some real distance between itself and New York in the next two series between the teams. The Dodgers won all three games in Brooklyn July 4–5, including a doubleheader sweep. They repeated the effort August 8–9, and once again took both ends of a doubleheader. In the first series, Brooklyn overcame a clutch Thomson homer to break a tie in the top of the 11th by scoring twice in the bottom half for a 6–5 win. Branca threw a complete game victory in the second game for a 4–2 victory, aided by Snider and Gil Hodges home runs. The Dodgers made it a series sweep with an 8–4 win behind Newcombe's pitching and homers by Hodges and Pafko. The Dodgers delivered an apparent knockout blow to the Giants' season in the August series. A rainout August 7 necessitated an August 8 day-night pair. Brooklyn, which began the day with a 9½ game lead over the Giants, stepped on their foes for a 7–2 and 7–6 doubleheader sweep. Hodges, Snider, and Carl Furillo homered in the day game, and Billy Cox drove home the winning run in the night contest with a bases-loaded, line drive single off the wall in the 10th inning. Campanella hit two homers the next day, including a tie-breaking solo clout in the seventh for a 6–5 win. Brooklyn, at a dominating 69–35, had pushed New York 12½ games back. Things got even worse for the Giants, who fell 13½ games behind on August 11.

As September broke, there was a hint of a possible final month race. New York went 17–3 since the clubs last met while the Dodgers were 13–10 to trim the seemingly insurmountable lead to seven games. Yet, any thoughts of catching Brooklyn seemed remote because the Giants and Dodgers would only meet four more times. New York soundly showed its pedal was still on the metal with a two-game series sweep of the Dodgers on September 1–2 at the Polo Grounds. The Giants turned the opener into a "statement game." Maglie easily outpitched Branca, holding the Dodgers down in an 8–1 victory. Branca, coming off back-to-back shutouts, was pounded early. Don Mueller hit three homers and drove in five runs. The Giants indicated they were still feisty, as Maglie and Robinson traded words after a high and tight pitch that the Dodgers second baseman had to deflect with his hand. Almost as if to rub it in, the Giants pulled off a triple play in the fifth. With Furillo on at first and Cal Abrams at second, Reese smashed a liner to Alvin Dark at shortstop. Dark flipped the ball to Stanky at second, who then tagged Furillo for the third out.

Mueller drilled two more home runs the next day in an 11–2 win, matching a major league record with five homers in two successive games. Jim Hearn picked up his 14th victory with a six-hitter, and Thomson belted his 25th home run of the season. Brooklyn's lead was now five.

The Giants had not been able to cut into the Dodgers' lead as the teams got set to meet September 8–9 at Ebbets Field, and now stood 5½ games out. Newcombe kept the Giants at bay with a two-hit shutout in a 9-0 win in the first game. The Giants' stellar play took a downturn, as their pitchers were responsible for 10 walks, a hit by pitch and a wild pitch. New York, now in must-win desperation mode, came back the next day for a 2–1 victory as Maglie picked up his 20th victory. Irvin was responsible for the Giants' runs with a two-run homer off Branca in the fourth. With three weeks to go, Brooklyn still sat firmly in the lead by 5½ games.

The Giants kept chipping away as the season headed for its final week. New York cut Brooklyn's lead to 2½ games on September 24 with a dramatic 4–3 win at Boston as Stanky singled home Davey Williams to break a 3–3 tie in the ninth. September 25 became the most pivotal day of the season as Boston swept Brooklyn while New York downed Philadelphia 5–1, leaving the Dodgers only one game in front. Big innings buried the Dodgers in both losses. The Braves got to Branca and scored six in the first inning in a 6–3 win in the opener of the doubleheader as Warren Spahn picked up his 22nd victory. Carl Erskine was the victim in the second game as Boston scored six in the second inning in a 14–2 romp.

The clubs enjoyed an easy day amid their frantic battle on September 26 as both rolled to victories. The Dodgers scored four in the first and fifth, and seven in the eighth in a 15–5 trouncing of the Braves. Campanella led the attack with five RBIs. Jansen picked up his 21st win, and Irvin had a homer, triple, double, and four RBIs in a 10–1 eruption against the Phillies. As National League President Ford Frick began considering plans for a possible three-game playoff, a confident Durocher said, "We believe we are very much alive."

Whether it was pressure, frustration, or simply pennant race competitiveness, the Dodgers came unglued in a 4–3 loss to Boston on September 27 that trimmed their lead over idle New York to a half-game. With Boston's Sam Jethroe on at first and Bob Addis at third in the eighth, Earl Torgeson grounded to Robinson. He threw home, and Campanella tagged Addis, but umpire Frank Dascoli called the runner safe. The ensuing argument got so bad that Dascoli ordered the Dodgers bench cleared, and Campanella and pitcher Preacher Roe were later fined for their actions. A panel in the umpires' dressing room was splintered by a kick as Brooklyn players left the stadium, though it wasn't clear who was responsible for the damage. Most damaging to the Dodgers was that Campanella, who was tossed out of the game, didn't get a chance to at least tie it when his spot in the batting order came up with Reese on third in the ninth. Meanwhile, Frick's office determined with a coin flip that if a playoff was necessary, the first game would be at Ebbets Field and the next two at the Polo Grounds.

Brooklyn's sole possession of first place, which it had secured since May 20, ended in a 4–3 defeat to Philadelphia on September 28. The Dodgers lost a 3–1 lead in the eighth when Andy Seminick hit a two-run homer off Erskine. In the ninth, Richie Ashburn scored on a single by Willie Jones. After 152 games, it had come down to a two-game season with both teams tied.

It didn't take a baseball expert to see the pitching matchups for games No. 153 for the Giants and Dodgers on September 29 to predict that this day's contests would be determined on the mound. It was New York (Maglie 22–6) vs. Boston (Spahn 22–13), and Brooklyn (Newcombe 19–9) vs. Philadelphia (Robin Roberts 21–13). The showcase pitching showdown went to the Giants and Dodgers, as Maglie shut out the Braves 3–0 on five hits, and Newcombe blanked the Phillies 5–0 on seven hits.

The teams went down to the final day at 95–58. Jansen won his 22nd game with a five-hit performance as New York took its seventh straight with a 3–2 win over Boston. Thomson had a solo homer in the second, and Irvin and Mueller had RBI singles. With the Giants' victory in the books, all eyes were now on Shibe Park, where the Dodgers and Phillies were playing in a later game. Brooklyn trailed 6–1 after three, bounced back to trim the lead to 6–5, but faced an 8–5 deficit with six outs remaining. The Dodgers had let the surging Giants make up so much ground, but they weren't quite ready to surrender. Rube Walker's two-run double in the eighth scored Hodges and Cox, and Furillo's single brought home Don Thompson, who was running for Walker. It was now 8–8. Robinson saved the game for Brooklyn in the bottom of the 12th with a diving catch of a line drive by Eddie Waitkus with two outs and the bases loaded. Robinson took command again in the 14th with a two-out homer to left off Roberts, who was pitching in relief. Bud Podbielan, who got one out in the 13th to end the inning, gave up a leadoff single to Ashburn in the 14th, but retired the next three batters to earn the victory and preserve the 9–8 win. The regular season finale took four hours-thirty minutes to play, and featured 17 hits by the Dodgers and 15 hits by the Phillies. Next stop: game one of a three-game playoff at Ebbets Field.

The Giants were riding the momentum of a comeback for the ages and a seven-game winning streak, while the Dodgers were on life support after their draining marathon victory the day before as game one unfolded. Perhaps that explained why the Dodgers hit into four double plays while Giants starter Hearn limited them to five hits in a 3–1 win in the playoff opener October 1. Branca, who pitched 1⅓ innings the day before, was staked to a 1–0 lead on Pafko's solo homer in the second. Branca lost the lead for good in the fourth when he plunked Irvin, and Thomson launched a two-run homer to left. Irvin provided unneeded insurance with a solo homer in the eighth. Thomson could hardly have been more excited about his blast off Branca, saying, "It was a great feeling when I saw it traveling into the stands." An even greater feeling was ahead.

New York's bid for a ninth straight win and a World Series berth was soundly denied the next day through a combination of strong pitching, powerful hitting, and sloppy defense. Clem Labine quieted the Giants with a six-hit shutout as the Dodgers won 10–0 to send the playoff to a third and deciding game. A 13-hit Dodgers uprising included two-run homers by Robinson and Walker, and solo shots by Hodges and Pafko. The Giants' one legitimate chance to get in the game came in the third with two outs and the bases loaded, but Thomson struck out swinging on a 3–2 count. The stage was set for game three October 3: 23-game winner Maglie vs. 20-game winner Newcombe.

The Dodgers got out in front in the first as Reese and Snider walked with one out, and Robinson drove in Reese with a single. New York finally broke through against Newcombe in the seventh. Irvin doubled, Whitey Lockman made it safely to first on a sacrifice bunt, and Thomson's sacrifice fly to center tied the score at 1–1. Reese and Snider singled in the eighth to put runners at first and third, and Reese came in on a wild pitch. After an intentional walk to Robinson, Pafko reached base on an infield single that scored Snider. Cox singled to left to bring home a third run, and give the Dodgers a 4–1 lead.

New York's miraculous comeback seemed to be coming to an end as the Dodgers needed just three outs from Newcombe to close out the Giants. Dark gave the Giants hope with a leadoff single off the glove of first baseman Hodges. Mueller followed with a single to right, but Irvin popped out. Lockman smacked an RBI double to left, scoring Dark and sending Mueller to third. Mueller sprained his left ankle on the slide, requiring the Giants to take him off the field on a stretcher, and to insert Cliff Hartung in the game as a pinch-runner. During the delay, Dressen decided to summon Branca from the bullpen to pitch to Thomson. While Newcombe was tough and durable, Dressen reasoned that his starter was fading after having pitched nine innings four days ago and followed that up with 5⅔ innings the next day. Branca got a first-pitch strike, but Thomson sent the next offering on a line drive trajectory that cleared the left-field wall for a three-run homer. Giants 5, Dodgers 4, and the whole place went crazy. The bedlam of the Giants madly celebrating on the field was sharply contrasted with the shock on the faces of Branca and the other Dodgers. The contrast was equally evident on the streets, where crushed Brooklynites mixed with cheering New York fans.

The playoff win earned the Giants their sixth World Series matchup with the Yankees. The Giants got off to a 2–1 edge in the first three games, but the Yankees won the next two. Yankees outfielder Hank Bauer broke up a 1–1 tie in Game Six with a three-run triple off first-game winner Koslo. The Giants put some heat on the Yankees in the ninth. Singles by Stanky, Dark, and Lockman off reliever Johnny Sain loaded the bases with no outs. Yankees manager Casey Stengel sent in Bob Kuzava to replace Sain. Irvin responded with a sacrifice fly to Gene Woodling in deep left field that allowed the runners to advance to second and third. Thomson lofted another long fly to Woodling to bring home Dark and cut the score to 4–3. Sal Yvars, a backup catcher, drilled a line drive to right field, but Bauer made a tumbling catch to end the game and give the Yankees their third straight championship. It was a World Series with subplots. Rookies Mickey Mantle and Willie Mays were making their first World Series appearances. Mantle's series ended in a frightening manner when he injured his knee in the fifth inning of Game Two after stepping into a drainage ditch while chasing a fly ball hit by Mays. The Giants center fielder had a quiet series debut, going 4-for-22 without any extra-base hits. Game Six also would become the final game in the Hall of Fame career of the Yankees' Joe DiMaggio, who retired after the series. The matchup also would be the final subway series between the Yankees and Giants. The clubs wouldn't meet in the World Series again until 1962, when curiously, the series would once more end with a Giant lining out to the right side with the tying run on base.

—⁓—

Ralph Branca would never be the same. Branca appeared in only 63 games after 1951, with a couple of short stints for the Detroit Tigers and New

York Yankees. He attributed the shortened career to a back injury, not the emotional scars from the Thomson home run. After the homer, Branca was quoted as saying, "I guess we weren't meant to win it."

But maybe they were, if only Dressen had walked Thomson intentionally and taken his chances with Mays, who was in the on-deck circle. Thomson was having a career year, and had already homered off Branca in game one of the playoff. In that game Branca twice struck out Mays with men on base. In the fifth inning of game three, Newcombe struck out Mays after Thomson doubled. Thomson also was far more of a threat at that point of the playoff. Going into his last at-bat, Thomson was 4-for-9 in the three games with two doubles, a homer and three RBIs. Mays was 1-for-10 with no extra-base hits and no RBIs.

In their postbaseball life, Branca and Thomson linked up at autograph sessions, as the former Dodger was able to benefit from the celebrity that developed from his infamous pitch. Eventually, a newspaper article and a book said that Branca and the Dodgers were victims in an elaborate sign-stealing scheme by the Giants. Thomson denied knowing what Branca was serving on that famous day, but the accusations of a scandal are left simmering on the back burner more than 60-plus year later.

Bobby Thomson was a good player who became a legend of the game because of his "shot heard 'round the world." He followed that up with two productive seasons, with 24 homers and 108 RBIs in 1952, and 26 homers and 106 RBIs in 1953. As his career faded, he kicked around with the Chicago Cubs, Boston Red Sox and Baltimore Orioles. "The Flying Scot" died at the age of 86 on August 17, 2010, in Savannah, Georgia. An obituary in the *New York Daily News* quoted Monte Irvin, who said of his former teammate, "He was a great ballplayer, a great fella, and he was beloved by all the Giants fans and teammates."

Ralph Branca died at the age of 90 on November 23, 2016. The accolades poured in when news of his passing became known, but it was the words of Thomson from 2002, given after they had marked the 50th anniversary of the home run, that might have been the most poignant. Said Thomson of Branca, "As good and decent a man as God ever put on this earth." Never was that description more true than during Jackie Robinson's early days with the Dodgers. Robinson had to contend not only with hatred and bigotry from fans and players from other teams, but even most painfully from his own teammates. One exception was Branca, who formed an almost protective friendship with Robinson. The relationship continued after baseball, and when Robinson died in 1972, Ralph Branca was one of his pallbearers.

MOMENTS OF GLORY

The Giants started their 1952 matchup with the Dodgers right where they left off. After scoring four runs in the dramatic ninth inning in 1951, New York tallied five times in the first inning April 18 in Brooklyn in its first meeting of the season against the Dodgers. Brooklyn clawed back and trailed 6–4 going into the last of the seventh before overwhelming New York with the long ball. The Dodgers caught the Giants on homers by Pafko in the seventh and Robinson in the eighth. Pafko finished off New York with a homer in the 12th for a 7–6 win. Brooklyn continued its power surge the next day, slugging five homers in an 11–6 rout. Campanella, Pafko, and Snider had back-to-back-to-back homers in the seventh. Branca made his first appearance against the Giants since giving up *the* homer, but it's unlikely that people around the world were listening to the rematch as the Dodgers hurler held Thomson to an 0-for-4 day with one walk. Maglie prevented a Dodgers series sweep with a two-hit, 6–0 shutout in the third game.

A possible repeat of 1951's Giants-Dodgers classic season was taking shape early. The Giants entered a May 26–28 series a half-game behind Brooklyn and on a four-game winning streak. The Dodgers arrived having won their last eight games. Thomson set the tone with a two-run homer in the first, and the Giants went on to sweep the Dodgers and take a 2½ game lead. The May 28 finale marked the last game for now for Mays, who would report for his service in the Army the next day. The Dodgers had already lost Newcombe to the Army.

The Dodgers caught and passed the Giants, and when the teams prepared to meet August 5, Brooklyn had a 6½-game lead. In the event the Dodgers needed a reminder that a lead against the Giants in August isn't safe, New York played the August 5 game as if it was the final game of a three-game playoff. Brooklyn took a 4–0 lead in the top of the sixth on a grand slam by Hodges. The persistent Giants rallied to send the game into extra innings at 4–4. The Dodgers took a 5–4 lead in the top of the 14th, but the Giants answered with a game-tying run in the bottom half. Brooklyn scored in the top of the 15th, and New York was ready again. Bobby Hofman, who doubled, was at second with two outs. Robinson bobbled a Dusty Rhodes grounder to keep the Giants alive, and Thomson followed with a game-tying single. Mueller bounced a chopper in front of home plate, and by the time it came down, Rhodes had raced home from second for the 7–6 victory. The clubs split a doubleheader on August 7, leaving Brooklyn 5½ games ahead.

The Dodgers took control after that, and built a 10½ game lead over the Giants by August 26. New York again refused to die, going on a 15–4 run, and moving to within three games by September 17. There was no miracle this time, as the Giants were unable to get any closer. The Dodgers, despite dropping 14 of 22 games to their rivals during the season, held on to win the pennant by 4½ games. Brooklyn, still seeking its first ever World Series championship, took a 3–2 game lead against the Yankees. Snider, who had four homers in the series, hit two in Game Six, but the Dodgers still fell 3–2. The Yankees took Game Seven 4–2 to win their fourth straight World Series title.

Newcombe was still in the Army, but the Dodgers had plenty of firepower to annihilate the rest of the National League in 1953. Five regulars batted over .300. The numbers: Furillo (.344, 21 HR, 92 RBIs), Snider (.336, 42, 126), Robinson (.329, 12, 95), Campanella (.312, 41, 142), and Hodges (.302, 31, 122). The Dodgers were first in the league in runs, hits, home runs, and stolen bases. They were second in doubles and triples. The team had the third best ERA, with Erskine stepping up in Newcombe's absence to finish 20–6 with a 3.54 ERA. The Dodgers went 105–49, their most ever wins for a season. They spoiled the Braves move from Boston to their new home by finishing 13 games ahead of second-place Milwaukee. Brooklyn fans who attended just a few games might have thought the club was undefeated since it seldom lost at home, going 60–17. The Dodgers didn't dominate from the start, dropping in and out of first, and even falling three behind Milwaukee on June 24. They won four straight to take sole possession of first place June 28, and never looked back. The Dodgers pushed their lead to a high point of 13½ games on September 9. The second half of the season saw the Dodgers erupt in several almost flawless streaks. They won 15 of 17 from July 12 to 29; 13 straight from August 7 to 20; and 12 of 14 from August 27 to September 9.

The Giants responded to the loss of Mays to the Army by waving the white flag early. They were never in the race and finished 70–84, 35 games out of first place. The lack of competition in the standings between the Giants and Dodgers didn't mean that the clubs would pass on the opportunity to slug it out physically if the opportunity arose. That moment came during a 6–3 Dodgers win over the Giants at the Polo Grounds on September 6. Furillo, the league's leading hitter, took exception when Ruben Gomez hit him on the wrist in the second inning. Furillo got to first base, but then made a charge to the Giants dugout where he was met by Durocher. The pair wrestled until they were separated by other players. Both were ejected and Furillo broke a bone in his left hand suffered when someone stepped on it during the melee.

The Dodgers went roaring into the World Series with possibly their greatest team and high hopes they could win their first championship. Their familiar opponent, the 99-win Yankees who were seeking their fifth straight World Series title, had other ideas. The Yankees scored four runs in the first inning of the first game, and went on to take a 2–0 game lead. Brooklyn got the series to a sixth game, but Billy Martin topped off his red-hot play with a game-winning single in the bottom of the ninth for another Yankees title. Martin went 12-for-24 in the series with eight RBIs.

—◆◆◆—

Both clubs had one more moment of glory before their departure after 1957. The Giants won their fifth world championship in 1954, but it was particularly special because it was the first one since 1933. The Dodgers won their first-ever championship in 1955, ending their 0–7 record in the World Series. The teams took different routes to their title years. New York had to fend off a stubborn Brooklyn squad in 1954, which, led by new manager Walter Alston, stayed in the race for much of the season. Brooklyn dominated the league in 1955, winning the flag by 13½ games.

Mays quickly shed any doubts that his two-year stay in the military would affect his play. Mays gave the Giants an April 13 opening day 4–3 victory in 1954 with a tie-breaking home run in the sixth off Erskine. Newcombe bounced back from his two years of duty the next day by pitching a complete game 6–4 victory. New York flexed its muscles in an 18-hit, 17–6 romp on May 28 that featured six Giants homers, including four in the eighth. The Giants took control by sweeping a pair of three-game series June 29–July 1 and July 6–8 for a 6½ game lead. Brooklyn refused to disappear, and a three-game sweep against the Giants on August 13–15 put them just a half-game behind. The Giants bounced back by winning 24 of their next 34, and clinched the pennant September 20 before 26,982 at Ebbets Field as Maglie limited the Dodgers to five hits in a 7–1 victory.

The Giants and Dodgers closed out their final series of 1954 in a game that was meaningless to everyone except a 23-year-old left-hander making his first major league start. Brooklyn's Karl Spooner pitched one of the most electrifying games in rivalry history, throwing a three-hit shutout in a 3–0 victory while striking out 15. He struck out the side three times. Spooner's career would last just 31 games, but on September 22, 1954, he etched his name in Dodgers-Giants history although it was witnessed by a crowd of only 3,256.

The Giants' chances of ending their 21-year championship drought appeared dim, as they had to face a mighty Cleveland team in the 1954 World Series. The Indians won 111 games, and had a dominating pitching staff. The Giants hoped to counter on offense with Mays, who was coming off a season of 41 homers, 110 RBIs and a .345 average. Mays would bat a respectable .286 with four walks and three RBIs, but it was his spectacular rally-stopping catch of Vic Wertz's 450-foot blast to center field in Game One that is most remembered. The Giants swept the Indians, but a new drought was ahead. It would take the Giants 56 years to win another world championship.

The Dodgers flew out of the blocks in 1955, winning their first 10 games. The Giants handed them their first loss April 22 in a series that saw emotions get out of hand. Brooklyn, upset at some close shaves delivered by "The Barber" Maglie, responded in the fourth inning the next day when Robinson bunted to the right side. Robinson crashed into second baseman Williams as he covered first, which brought Dark charging over from shortstop to express his outrage at the play. Dark got his revenge in the fifth when he slid hard into third to knock the ball away from Robinson. The Dodgers won the game 3–1, but the rough play was a draw, as the bruised Robinson and Williams were unable to start the final game of the series. That game also turned into a slugfest, except it featured bats instead of brawls. The Giants amassed 18 hits, while the Dodgers had 12. The clubs were tied 5–5 after nine. New York scored six in the top of the 10th, and survived a five-run Brooklyn rally in the bottom half for an 11–10 win.

The series was the last lively one of the season between the clubs as the Dodgers took out any suspense early, building a 9½ game lead by May 10 with a 22–2 record. The teams had one notable moment May 28, and it again involved Robinson and Williams in less violent roles. Robinson lifted a short pop fly over the head of the second baseman with Furillo at first and Hodges at second and no outs in the fourth. Williams surprised the Dodgers with a running catch, and the Giants were able to easily get both runners out before they could get back to their bases for a triple play.

Most teams had trouble getting one out against the Dodgers, as the club never let up. Brooklyn built a 14-game lead by June 23 with a 49–16 mark, and pushed it to a season high 17-game lead by September 8. The

Dodgers were so good that they could party before a game and still win. The club clinched the pennant on the road, so the city decided to throw a victory parade when the players returned home in the afternoon on September 16 before playing the Giants that night. Thousands saluted their heroes, as the players rode in autos while wearing their uniforms. After the festivities, the Dodgers got back to Ebbets Field where they downed the Giants 4–3.

The Dodgers were beaten in their seven previous World Series appearances, so prospects were not bright when the Yankees showed up again in the 1955 fall classic. Brooklyn lost the first two games, but rallied for three straight wins. Among their victims was fourth-game starter Don Larsen, who got thrashed for five runs in four innings. The Dodgers dropped Game Six when Spooner, the young pitcher who once dazzled the Giants, got rocked for five runs in the first inning. Johnny Podres, helped greatly by a highlight reel catch in left by Sandy Amoros, shut out the Yankees on eight hits in Game Seven for a 2–0 victory and a long-awaited World Series title.

———

By the time the 1956 season reached its final stretch, Brooklyn and New York had clear, but contrasting, goals. The Dodgers were pursuing a second straight pennant, and the Giants were trying to avoid last place for the first time since 1946. Brooklyn helped its cause, and damaged New York's, by taking six of nine from the Giants during a period from August 31 to September 9. The Dodgers stayed in contention most of the year. They lost their sole possession of first place May 1, and couldn't get back to the top alone again until they took the lead by a half-game over Milwaukee on September 16. They were in and out of first after that until September 29, when they swept a doubleheader against Pittsburgh to take a one-game lead over the Braves with one to play. The Dodgers defeated the Pirates 8–6 the next day to clinch the flag, as Snider and Amoros slugged two home runs apiece.

The Dodgers stuck a dagger in the Giants early in 1956, and finished them off midseason. Robinson got the attack started in the clubs' first meeting on April 25 by stealing home to help Erskine record a complete game 7–2 victory. Erskine came right back to toss a no-hitter against the Giants in the teams' third meeting of the year May 12. An Ebbets Field crowd of 17,395 saw near perfection, as Erskine allowed just two walks. Robinson snared a liner by Mays at third base and right fielder Furillo chased down a smash by Daryl Spencer to preserve the gem. Brooklyn swept a doubleheader from New York on July 4, which helped push the already slipping Giants over the cliff. New York finished in sixth, 26 games behind the Dodgers. In all, the Dodgers won 14 of their 22 meetings with the Giants.

On September 9 at New York, Brooklyn won 6–1 behind a three-hitter by Don Drysdale in what would be Robinson's final game in the rivalry. Robinson, though hitless, once more demonstrated his many talents to still influence a game with a diving grab of Jackie Brandt's bid for a base hit in the seventh. Robinson would still have more ball to play in the World Series, but for now, one of the treasured names of the rivalry had played in his last Dodgers-Giants game.

Brooklyn found itself in a World Series rematch with the Yankees and Larsen, who was becoming a Dodger pushover. After roughing him up in the 1955 series, the Dodgers knocked him out during a six-run second inning in Game Two. The Dodgers went on to win 13–8 to take a 2–0 series lead. The loud start had a quiet finish for the Dodgers as they scored just six runs in the next five games. Brooklyn survived for a seventh game, but was blanked 9–0 by Johnny Kucks. The story of this World Series, however, would forever have only one headline. Larsen—beaten, bothered, and bewildered by the Dodgers in two previous out-ings—performed with perfect pitch in the historic Game Five by retiring all 27 Dodgers.

THE CURTAIN FALLS

By the halfway point of the 1957 season, the Giants and Dodgers were halfway to California. Giants owner Horace Stoneham faced declining attendance at the aging Polo Grounds and had promises of a new stadium from San Francisco Mayor George Christopher. Dodgers owner O'Malley couldn't complain about fan loyalty as Ebbets Field still drew good crowds, but he wished to build a more modern stadium and wasn't getting the cooperation he needed from local officials. National League owners already had voted unanimously in May to allow the Giants to move to San Francisco and the Dodgers to Los Angeles, although there were some conditions attached.

Word of those high-level maneuverings was devastating to the loyal followers of the clubs, who just couldn't imagine that their teams would abandon them. No moment said it more powerfully than the picture of a Giants fan sitting in the left field bleachers in the Polo Grounds holding a banner that read STAY TEAM, STAY.

The entire season was played under the distraction of a potential move. Commissioner Ford Frick even tried to calm the uncertainty that was building in just the second meeting of the Dodgers and Giants on May 10 by calling public discussion of franchise shifts "harmful to baseball." Frick's statement came as Christopher met with O'Malley and Stoneham.

Meanwhile, the teams continued to put on a show.

The clubs played like it was 1951 on May 11, 1957, going 15 hard-fought innings before Giants catcher Valmy Thomas ended the 4:59 marathon with a solo home run in the 15th inning off Don Bessent for a 6–5 victory. Al Worthington blanked the Dodgers on just three hits in seven innings of relief. The possibility of the clubs having one more shootout for the pennant on the East Coast was growing less likely by the time they next met for a May 24–26 series. Brooklyn took two out of three, putting them two games behind first-place Cincinnati, but the Giants had fallen eight games back. The Dodgers continued to take the upper hand, shutting out the Giants twice in a two-game series July 1–2. Drysdale blanked the

Giants on five hits for a 3–0 win, and Maglie followed with a four-hitter in a 6–0 victory. The ex-Giant Maglie joined the Dodgers in 1956.

Brooklyn entered an August 5–8 series against New York hoping to take advantage of its stumbling rivals and did so in a 5–2 win in the opener despite a four-hit performance by Mays. The Dodgers began the series trailing league-leading St. Louis by 3½ games, while the Giants were now 18 games behind. New York quickly dismissed Brooklyn's momentum by taking the next three. The Giants got their first win on Curt Barclay's five-hit 5–0 shutout, pounded out an 8–5 victory the next day and finished off their foes with a 12–3 rout spurred by homers from Mays and Hank Sauer. The Giants continued to ruin the Dodgers' title quest, winning two out of three in their next series August 13–15.

It was fitting that the final series between the clubs in Brooklyn would be upstaged by news of the pending move, because neither team could make any headlines with their play. The Giants hadn't been a factor all year, and the Dodgers were now seven games behind first-place Milwaukee. A legal bid for a restraining order to prevent the Giants from moving was in the New York State Supreme Court. Mayor Christopher said that progress was being made in shifting the franchise and assured that San Francisco would fulfill all of its obligations to the New York Giants. A crowd of 17,936 turned out September 1 to watch the final game between the clubs at Ebbets Field, highlighted by Mays's home run and triple to spark the Giants to 7–5 victory.

The teams got together five days later for their final series in New York on September 6–8. Podres threw a three-hit shutout in the opener and Roger Craig's 5⅓ innings of strong relief the next day gave the Dodgers successive victories. The teams capped off their East Coast rivalry before 22,376. The Dodgers struck first on a two-run homer by Jim Gilliam in the second inning. The Giants scored three in the fourth on Ray Jablonski's RBI triple and a two-run homer by Sauer, and made it stand up for a 3–2 win. Marv Grissom retired Amoros on a groundout to Danny O'Connell at second base for the final out. There was still about three more weeks of baseball, but the Dodgers had already established momentum for 1958. The club finished the final East Coast season by defeating the Giants 12–10 in their head-to-head series. The Dodgers won their season series against the Giants 14 out of the last 18 years from 1940 to 1957.

The clubs would have one last goodbye at their own parks before heading west. The Dodgers played their final game at Ebbets Field on September 24 before 6,702, defeating the Pittsburgh Pirates 2-0 on Danny McDevitt's five-hitter as the organist "entertained" the fans with such numbers as "After You're Gone," "Don't Ask Me Why I'm Leaving," and of course, "Auld Lang Syne." The scene was far wilder at the Giants' farewell game on September 29, the last day of the season. Just after Dusty Rhodes grounded out to Pirates shortstop Dick Groat for the final out in Pittsburgh's 9–1 win, many of the 11,606 fans at the Polo Grounds ran onto the field, determined to take home memories of the ballpark. As the players rushed to the safety of their locker rooms, souvenir-hunters ripped up home plate, the pitchers' rubber, and the bases, and grabbed the protective foam lining the outfield walls, signs, and patches of grass.

—⁓—

In 1973, songwriter Joe Raposo provided four tunes used on Frank Sinatra's classic album, *'Ol Blue Eyes Is Back*. One of them was "There Used to be a Ballpark." Raposo's lyrics are widely believed to be motivated by Ebbets Field, although others say the sentiments also hold true for the Polo Grounds. The Giants and Dodgers were well settled in their new locations by the time the wrecking ball smashed into the walls of Ebbets Field on February 23, 1960, and the Polo Grounds on April 10, 1964.

The demolition at Ebbets Field brought out 200 spectators and former Brooklyn players such as Roy Campanella, Ralph Branca, and Otto Miller, the catcher in the stadium's inaugural game in 1913. For those in attendance, some might have remembered the colorful antics that gave Brooklyn fans their special personality such as the "Dodgers Sym-Phony Band," a very loose group of musicians, and legendary fan Hilda Chester and the cowbell she loved to ring. For others, it was the sweetness of having been witnesses to baseball legends Vance, Snider, Hodges, Keeler, Robinson, Durocher, Grimes, Reese, Wheat, Herman, and many more.

The razing of the Polo Grounds happened so long after the Giants had left that it appeared anticlimactic. The last game played at the Polo Grounds, temporary home of the New York Mets for two years, drew just 1,752 in 1963. It was a cathedral that no longer had any worshippers. But that quiet, somber end cannot dim the history of one of sports' greatest sites. Center field played as far as 500 feet away at one time, compensated by down-the-line distances of only 280 feet to left field and 257 feet to right. The legends played there, too. There was Frisch, Mize, Ott, Terry, Hubbell, Mathewson, Mays, and many more.

With those lists of legends and the two historic sites where the games were played for nearly 50 years, it is easy to still feel the emotions of Raposo's words and Sinatra's voice 50 years after the wrecking ball broke so many hearts:

> How the people watched with wonder,
> How they laughed and how they cried,
> Yes, there used to be a ballpark right here.

Part Two

GOING WEST
1958–1969

3

MOVING IN: 1958–1959

"We used to hate them, and still do. It'll carry over if the Dodgers wind up in Los Angeles next season." Giants manager Bill Rigney was taking a moment to reflect on the rivalry as the clubs played against each other for the last time on the East Coast in 1957. Hate is a strong word, but there were few signs of love between the Dodgers and Giants in the early years on the West Coast.

CALIFORNIA, HERE THEY COME (1958)

The great metropolitan areas of Los Angeles and San Francisco of the late 1950s didn't necessarily require big league baseball to make them whole, but just about everyone out west seemed grateful and excited about the baseball gifts that were headed their way. Civic pride was high at both venues as opening day approached. The excitement and curiosity about the new Californians who had come from afar created a new sense of community for the big-city residents. It seems odd to say that nine men in baggy, flannel outfits could bring glamour and prestige to two sophisticated urban centers that already claimed to have those traits, but that was the case as the new fans and the historic clubs counted down the days to the first pitch.

The Giants and Dodgers packed different plans with them when they traveled to their new West Coast homes. The Giants, behind third-year manager Bill Rigney, opted for a youth movement, featuring rookies who would garner much playing time—first baseman Orlando Cepeda, outfielder Willie Kirkland, third baseman Jim Davenport and catcher Bob Schmidt. The hope was that the invigoration of youth and a mix of some holdover veterans from New York would be the perfect blend, built around the brilliance of center fielder Willie Mays. Pitching was a big question, as the Giants hoped that two key starters, Ruben Gomez and Johnny Antonelli, would return to their World Series championship form of 1954. Gomez, 17–9 with a 2.88 ERA that glorious season, had become erratic in 1957. The temperamental Antonelli, 21–7, 2.30 ERA in the title year, also had slipped.

The Dodgers management wished to let Los Angeles fans enjoy the old-time Brooklyn standouts, and brought out a team with fifth-year manager Walter Alston that resembled their 1955 world championship year. It included such illustrious names as Duke Snider, Gil Hodges, Carl Furillo and Pee Wee Reese. It was a plan that Dodgers owner Walter O'Malley would later question himself. The unsettled catching situation was something the Dodgers could not anticipate, as Roy Campanella was tragically paralyzed in a car crash during the offseason. The Dodgers hoped that a third-stringer, John Roseboro, might help at some point fill the void. Expectations were high for starters Don Drysdale and Johnny Podres, but the Dodgers also believed that veterans Don Newcombe and Carl Erskine, who both had arm trouble, had at least another good year remaining. Optimism surrounded a hard-throwing left-hander, Sandy Koufax, who fanned 122 batters in 104 innings in 1957 to lead the league in strikeout percentage.

The Dodgers' 1957 season, in which they came in third with an 84–70 record, marked the first time since 1948 that they finished lower than second. The Giants, following their World Series championship in 1954, had stumbled, finishing third in 1955, and falling to sixth place in 1956 (67–87) and 1957 (69–85).

On April 3, just 12 days before the West Coast opener, the Giants traded away Bobby Thomson for the second and final time. The architect of the historic pennant-winning home run in 1951, dealt away in 1954 and reacquired in 1957, was now gone for good. While not intended as so, the deal symbolized a cutting of ties from the six decades of New York–Brooklyn baseball.

PLAY BALL! (1958)

Tiny Seals Stadium might fit snugly into the vast outfield at the Polo Grounds. But now, it was at the center of the baseball world in the days leading up to the April 15 opener. The minor league park that would host the Giants-Dodgers inaugural game had undergone a $75,000 makeover. Seating was expanded from 18,500 to more than 23,000, better lighting was installed, and the yard received a thorough new paint job. National League President Warren Giles inspected the Seals Stadium field and declared it ready for major league play. On April 14, Commissioner Ford Frick, Giles, and Los Angeles Mayor Norris Poulson were among the dignitaries to participate in a parade from Seals Stadium to downtown. A motorcade carrying members of the Giants team was showered with 2,000 balloons, 10,000 orchids, and rose petal confetti. A Marine band marched ahead of the players, serenading spectators with "California, Here I Come."

The nation's sportswriters and broadcasters were staying calm and detached amid all the hoopla, picking World Series champion Milwaukee to repeat while predicting a fourth-place finish for the Dodgers and a fifth-place season for the Giants. While the forecasts would turn out to be sound, fan interest remained high throughout the 22 games the clubs played against each other in 1958 as the rivalry was reborn in San Francisco and Los Angeles.

The Giants turned the opener into a rout.

Ruben Gomez, making his first opening day start in six years with the team, dominated the Dodgers with a combination of fastballs and screwballs, throwing a six-hitter before 23,448. Don Drysdale was knocked out in the fourth inning as the Giants jumped out to a 6–0 lead. Rookie Orlando Cepeda homered in the fifth for a 7–0 lead, which was more than enough for Gomez as he blanked the Dodgers 8–0.

The *San Francisco Chronicle* was so moved by the victory that its banner page one headline screamed out: "WE MURDER THE BUMS."

The Dodgers picked up their first win of the new West Coast rivalry the next day 13–1 as Johnny Podres allowed just five hits and struck out a personal best 11 on a chilly 50-degree night. The *Chronicle*, clearly wanting to be objective in its reporting, came back the next day with another banner headline: "BUMS MURDER US." Youngsters Jim Davenport, with four hits, and Bob Schmidt, who homered, helped the Giants win 7–4 the following day to take the first series.

If the Polo Grounds could almost hide Seals Stadium inside its walls, the Coliseum could probably swallow it. The scene shifted to the massive Southern California site the next night, drawing a crowd of 78,672 to witness the debut of big league baseball in Los Angeles. In contrast, the Dodgers drew just 11,202 for their 1957 opener in Brooklyn. The Dodgers' 6–5 victory was almost lost in the postgame talk about the odd left field screen, standing 42 feet tall, but just 250 feet from home plate, a configuration made necessary in putting a baseball field in a football stadium. Hank Sauer of the Giants, who hit two homers, christened it by sending one of his shots over the screen. Said Pee Wee Reese, "There's no other park in the league like it." Carl Erskine got the win despite allowing 10 hits and four walks, his first victory over the Giants since he no-hit them on May 12, 1956, at Ebbets Field. In an emotional moment during the ceremonial pregame introductions, the fans' largest applause was given to their seriously injured catcher Roy Campanella, who was still in a hospital in New York.

—⁓—

Despite the excitement in Los Angeles following the Dodgers' home opener victory, early signs of the Giants' superiority were starting to show.

The Giants put together back-to-back 15-hit games the next two days to take the second straight series against their foes. Cepeda led the way in an 11–4 win by going three for four with three RBIs and a homer, and Danny O'Connell slugged two homers over the left-field screen the following day in a 12–2 romp. The Giants' offensive blitz at the Coliseum included 42 hits and seven home runs in three games.

San Francisco newspapers liked to write headlines referring to the Dodgers as "Dem Bums," and few Dodgers fans were asking for a retraction as the Giants juggernaut rolled over their rivals like roadkill on an L.A. freeway. The Giants piled up 42 runs while defeating the Dodgers four straight times in early May as the clubs played successive two-game series in San Francisco and Los Angeles May 9–10 and 12–13.

Willie Mays entered the series in San Francisco with just one homer for the season, prompting the Giants to film his swing to see how he could get his power back. Mays turned the film into a hit movie, slugging two homers and a double, and driving in five runs in an 11–3 victory. The Giants began the game in third place, a half-game behind Chicago and Milwaukee, while the Dodgers were mired in seventh place.

The Dodgers quieted the explosive Giants bats the next day, but still lost again, 3–2, as Don Taussig drove in the winning run in the ninth with a single. The Giants went back on the attack as the clubs went to Los Angeles for the next games, where San Francisco roared to 12–3 and 16–9 wins. Mays hit two homers, one a grand slam, for the first win. It was a particularly painful defeat for the Dodgers, who fell to last place. It got worse for the Dodgers the next day. The Giants compiled 26 hits as Mays went five for five with two homers, two triples and four RBIs. The victory moved the Giants into first place.

The early hopes of the Giants had faded, while the Dodgers' disappointment had continued by the time the teams next met for three games August 8–10. Since then, the Giants had fallen from first, and now trailed first-place Milwaukee by 7½ games. The Giants, who hadn't been in first since July 29, were amid a disastrous road trip in which they lost 13 of 18 games. The Dodgers were in seventh, 12½ games out. In the first game, won by the Dodgers 6–3, Drysdale went 8⅔ innings to beat the Giants for the first time this year in four decisions. Gomez, unbeaten in three previous games with the Dodgers, took the loss. The Dodgers' victory turned into an aberration, as the Giants resumed control the next two days with wins of 6–3 and 12–8. Sauer had two homers in the first victory and Davenport belted a pair the next day.

The glory days of Brooklyn seemed far removed as the Dodgers, after a season-long battering by the Giants, were given one last chance by the schedule-makers to save face. The clubs would meet nine times in seven days from August 29–September 4, but the long season would only grow more depressing for Los Angeles as the Giants took five of the first six games, including sweeps of two doubleheaders. In the first doubleheader August 30, a day-night affair, Davenport's two home runs keyed a 3–2 win in the opener, and Mays's two-run homer broke a tie in a 3–1 victory in the evening game. The day game drew 16,905 fans and 9,865 attended the night match-up for the largest single day San Francisco crowd of the season. Mays again took charge in the second doubleheader September 1, going five for five with a home run and two doubles in an 8–6 win in the morning game. The day almost turned into a triple-header as the Giants outlasted the Dodgers 6–5 in 16 innings in the second game.

Rigney, enthused after five straight wins over the Dodgers, brushed aside the fact the team trailed first-place Milwaukee by 7½ games, saying, "We can still catch them." His confidence didn't take into account the determination of Drysdale, who blanked the Giants on five hits in a 4–0 victory in Los Angeles on September 2. Gil Hodges homered in the fourth inning, marking the 10th straight year he hit 20 or more homers. The Dodgers came back the next day to further dampen the Giants long-shot pennant hopes with a 5–3 win. Sandy Koufax was brilliant in a long relief appearance, picking up his 10th win while allowing just one run and two hits in seven innings.

The clubs closed out their season matchups September 4. The Giants erupted for eight runs in the first inning, and went on to win their 16th game of the year against the Dodgers, 13–3.

The September 4 crowd of 12,441 pushed the attendance for Giants-Dodgers games at the Coliseum to 382,731, even topping the totals for games involving the world champion Milwaukee Braves. The remainder of the season went quietly, the Giants going 9–10 and the Dodgers 8–12. The Giants considered the season a success, improving dramatically from the previous two years in New York, and were optimistic about the future as the young players they threw into the lineup performed well. The Dodgers never could get adjusted to their unusual stadium. The left-handed hitting Snider, frustrated by the deep right-field dimensions, hit only 15 home runs after slugging at least 40 the last five seasons in Brooklyn. The pitchers, forced to contend with the short left-field screen, saw the staff ERA climb from 3.35 to 4.47. The Dodgers' 71–83 finish was their worst since Brooklyn went 63–91 in 1944. But the Dodgers were far from dead. In 1959, much of the same cast would return for a wild ride back to the top of the National League.

FIRST PENNANT RACE (1959)

The West Coast rivalry was less than a year old, but it was already time to change the battery.

Giants pitcher Ruben Gomez threw the first pitch in the 1958 opener to catcher Valmy Thomas with Dodgers outfielder Gino Cimoli at the plate. As the new season broke, they were long gone. On December 3, 1958, Gomez and Thomas were traded to Philadelphia. The next day, Cimoli was traded to St. Louis. While the transactions didn't represent a significant roster overhaul, they served as a reminder of how both teams were moving forward to establish their new identities. The Dodgers couldn't move forward fast enough. Los Angeles lost 21 of its first 31 games in 1958, and never recovered. On the other hand, the Giants gained confidence with their respectable 80–74 1958 record.

Regardless what improvements the Giants and Dodgers would make for the 1959 season, it remained clear that they would have to handle the Milwaukee Braves, who won the pennant in 1957 and 1958, and were everyone's favorite to repeat in 1959. It was one area where Los Angeles could have some hope. In 1958, the Dodgers finished above .500 against only one team, the Braves, with a 14–8 record. The Giants, meanwhile, had their most trouble with Milwaukee, winning just six of 22 games.

The Giants revamped their pitching staff in the offseason, engineering trades for starters Sam Jones and Jack Sanford, who would be paired with veteran Johnny Antonelli and youngster Mike McCormick to form a rotation with great potential. Stu Miller and Al Worthington, part-time starters in 1958, would now be able to concentrate on their bullpen duties. Key returnees from 1958 included Willie Mays, Orlando Cepeda, Daryl Spencer, Willie Kirkland, Jim Davenport, and Bob Schmidt.

The Dodgers were last in the league in ERA and batting average in 1958, but it was difficult to attribute it to a talent gap. Los Angeles had a lineup that included Duke Snider, Gil Hodges, Charlie Neal, Jim Gilliam and John Roseboro. The Dodgers also had high hopes for newcomer Wally Moon, acquired in the Cimoli deal. The pitching staff was anchored by Don Drysdale and Johnny Podres, who both appeared to have off years in 1958. The club would rely on a mix of possible starters, including hard-throwing, but out-of-control Sandy Koufax, who struck out 131 while walking 105 in 159 innings. One thing was certain as the season got under way: shortstop Pee Wee Reese wouldn't be part of things. Two days before the 1959 season opener, the 16-year Dodger was released. The Dodgers still felt comfortable at the position, relying on veteran Don Zimmer for now, but seeing promise in the speedy rookie Maury Wills. The Dodgers also had an added incentive to come back after a disappointing premier season in Los Angeles. Said manager Walter Alston: "That seventh-place finish undoubtedly hurt the pride of a team that's been up in the race for so many years."

—◦◦◦—

As the 1959 pennant race headed to September, the Giants and Dodgers had refused to wilt under the continued solid play by the Braves. On August 31, the first-place Giants led the Dodgers by a game, with Milwaukee 2½ back.

The clubs only had one series together in September, played in San Francisco, but it was historic in a way because it marked the first high-stakes series on the West Coast.

September 19: Strong pitching performances by Roger Craig and Drysdale gave the Dodgers a sweep of the day-night doubleheader, putting Los Angeles into a tie with the Giants while Milwaukee moved to within a half game. The doubleheader was necessitated by a rainout September 18.

Dodgers 4, Giants 1 (first game): Craig fired a six-hitter, while his counterpart, Antonelli, failed in his third attempt to get his 20th win of the year. The Dodgers scored all the runs they needed in the second, including one on a fluke play. Don Demeter and Wills singled, and Joe Pignatano drove in Demeter with a base hit. With Wills at third, catcher Hobie Landrith's routine toss of a pitch back to Antonelli went over the pitcher's head, allowing the Dodgers shortstop to score.

Dodgers 5, Giants 3 (second game): McCormick threw shutout ball for six innings in the night game, but the Dodgers knocked him out in the seventh with a five-run barrage, keyed by two-run doubles by Gilliam and Neal.

September 20 (Dodgers 8, Giants 2): The biggest game ever played at Seals Stadium turned out to be its last, as the Dodgers swept the series, moving a game ahead of the Giants with five to play. Snider put the Dodgers ahead 1–0 in the second with a home run, which would become the final one hit at the ball park in its 29-year history. The sweep was devastating for the Giants, who were unable to win a game despite going with their three top pitchers—Jones, Antonelli, and McCormick. While the Giants were just one game back, the loss pushed them to third place and created a tomb-like atmosphere in the San Francisco locker room. "Now let's see if we can come from behind," said manager Bill Rigney. Snider viewed the sweep as a measure of revenge, saying, "The Giants humiliated us last year, beating us 16 times. This was a must-win series for us, and we told ourselves to remember last year." The sweep gave the Dodgers a 14–8 record against the Giants for the year.

With three games to play Friday, Saturday, and Sunday (September 25–27), the Dodgers and Braves were tied at 84–67 with the Giants two down at 82–69. The Dodgers took the lead Friday with a 5–4 win over Chicago while the Braves fell 6–3 to Philadelphia. The Giants, who were idle, dropped 2½ games back. The Braves got back a share of the lead Saturday with a 3–2 win while the Dodgers were roughed up 12–2. The Giants blanked St. Louis to stay alive, but would need to sweep a doubleheader Sunday while the Dodgers and Braves would lose to earn a tie. The Giants dropped a pair as Los Angeles and Milwaukee won their games to force a three-game playoff. The Dodgers won the opener behind 7⅔ innings of shutout relief by Larry Sherry. In game two, the Dodgers, down 5–2 in the ninth, rallied to tie it and won it in the 12th. The Dodgers had completed a remarkable seventh-to-first place turnaround in one year, and capped it by defeating the Chicago White Sox in six games in the World Series.

HIT OR ERROR? (1959)

Poor Charles Park. He never broke the hearts of Giants fans with a ninth-inning homer. He never brushed back Willie Mays. But on June 30, 1959, the official scorer from the *Los Angeles Mirror-News* became one of the big early villains of the rivalry.

Giants pitcher Sam Jones ended up with a one-hitter and a 2–0 victory, but left the Coliseum convinced he was robbed of a no-hitter. With two out in the eighth, Jim Gilliam hit a slow bouncer over Jones's glove. Shortstop Andre Rodgers charged in but fumbled the ball and Gilliam reached first. Park ruled it was a hit. When Park approached Jones afterward, the nearly tearful pitcher wasn't in a forgiving mood, responding, "I didn't think it was a hit, no matter what you called it." Rodgers sided with Jones, saying he could have thrown Gilliam out had he fielded the ball cleanly. It was left to veteran Duke Snider to put the proper spin on the evening: "I've seen some cheaper ones than that called hits. There's no sentiment in baseball."

Jones, who no-hit Chicago on May 12, 1955, seemed determined to get another. Three weeks after the disputed scoring call, Jones took a no-hitter into the seventh inning against the Dodgers, but Gil Hodges broke it up with a single. Jones then threw a rain-abbreviated, seven-inning no-hitter against St. Louis in his last start of the season.

———

Park's call, a very difficult one indeed, did have the consequence of preventing a unique baseball moment since a San Francisco hurler has never no-hit Los Angeles. The Dodgers have tossed three against the Giants. Sandy Koufax hurled his gem in 1963, Jerry Reuss in 1980, and Kevin Gross in 1992. The Giants have to go all the way back to April 15, 1915, for their last no-hitter against the Dodgers, when Rube Marquard shut them down.

May 11, 1963: Koufax was the first Los Angeles pitcher to no-hit the Giants, reaching the record books in an 8–0 gem May 11, 1963. Koufax took a perfect game into the eighth inning before walking a batter with one out.

June 27, 1980: You could almost see this coming. The Dodgers had won all six previous games against the Giants in 1980, giving up just eight runs and tossing three shutouts. Reuss, who was on his way to an 18–6 year, also was near-perfect in his 8–0 win in San Francisco. Jack Clark was the only Giant to reach base, as he was safe on an error when shortstop Bill Russell's throw to first short-hopped Steve Garvey in the first inning. Reuss retired the next 25 batters.

August 17, 1992: Gross, whose 12 defeats were the worst on the staff coming into the game, tossed a no-hitter before 25,561 in Los Angeles. Gross, a target of much criticism, silenced all critics for at least a day as he struck out six and allowed base runners in only two innings while earning his sixth victory, 2–0. Jose Offerman, who led the majors with 32 errors, provided the big defensive play when he made a leaping catch of Robby Thompson's line drive in the eighth.

THE LONGEST DAY (1959)

One of the oddest days of the rivalry came on May 7, 1959. The Dodgers and the New York Yankees agreed to play an exhibition game this night at the Coliseum to honor as well as raise money for Brooklyn great Roy Campanella, who was partially paralyzed in a car crash following the 1957 season. But first, the Dodgers had to play their regularly scheduled day game, the first of a four-game series, in San Francisco. As soon as John Roseboro caught a foul popup by Andre Rodgers to secure a 2–1 victory, the Dodgers hurriedly departed Seals Stadium and headed for the airport with a police escort. Within three hours, the Dodgers were at the Coliseum ready to take on the Yankees, which some observers saw as a possible pre-view of the World Series. A phenomenal crowd of 93,103 showed up and the Yankees won the game 6–2, but the score was clearly overshadowed by the emotional tribute. A prolonged applause greeted Campanella's arrival on the field, and between the fifth and sixth innings, with the stadium lights dimmed, the fans lit matches and cigarette lighters in a moving salute to the Dodgers' beloved Campy.

The Dodgers then had to board a plane back to San Francisco to con-tinue the series. The Giants took advantage of their jet-lagged opponents the next day in a 9–3 win, but the Dodgers reawakened for successive vic-tories to take three out of four.

4

TENSE TIMES: 1960–1969

Mays, McCovey, and Marichal were on one side. Drysdale, Koufax, and Wills were on the other. The supporting cast on both the Giants and Dodgers wasn't bad either. It appeared a lock that top–level, exciting baseball would be played in the 1960s. The thing that was not predicted was how bitter—and violent—the rivalry could get.

BRIGHT OUTLOOK DIMS (1960–61)

Get the California champagne ready.

That task might have been on the to-do list of both clubs as the Giants and Dodgers led the league in optimism in the spring of 1960, and who could blame them for not already imagining a wild clubhouse celebration in the fall?

The Dodgers had high hopes after a thrilling pennant-winning playoff against Milwaukee and a World Series title. The Giants looked forward to success as they expected rookies or inexperienced players from 1958–59 to mature into champions and eagerly anticipated getting a big lift from the opening of their new ballpark. Fans who were disappointed that neither club could contend in 1958 saw the teams fight it out in a tense three-team race in 1959, and assumed that would become an annual occurrence.

However, those bright outlooks for 1960 were never able to supply enough wattage as the 1960 and 1961 seasons failed to live up to the hype.

The Dodgers in 1960 finished in fourth place, 13 games behind Pittsburgh, while the Giants were 16 games out in fifth. The Giants were so frustrated with their performance that they fired manager Bill Rigney on June 18 and replaced him with Tom Sheehan. The Giants had difficulty getting acclimated to their new ballpark and its gusty, chilly climate. Home run totals dropped, with Willie Mays going from 34 in 1959 to 29, and Orlando Cepeda from 27 to 24. The Giants, having learned about some of the peculiarities of Candlestick Park's winds after the first year, hoped to give their sluggers actual and psychological help by moving in the fences: from 397 to 365 feet in left center, 397 to 375 in right center, and 420 to 410 in center. Dodgers management didn't see the need for dramatic moves. The club already was slowly phasing out players from the Brooklyn years, but brought back the same rotation for 1961 that led the league in ERA.

Both clubs improved their records in 1961, but it wasn't enough to overcome a 93–61 Cincinnati team. The otherwise quiet period of the rivalry flared in September as the Dodgers tried to chase down the Reds. The Dodgers were 3½ games behind, while the Giants trailed by 7½ games as the teams met for seven consecutive games. Los Angeles swept a four-game home series over the Giants September 3–6 to get within a game of Cincinnati.

The Dodgers jumped on Mike McCormick for four runs in the first inning of the opener, and Gil Hodges added a solo homer in the fifth for a 5–0 lead. The Giants clawed back to cut the deficit to 5–4, but reliever Dick Farrell got Mays to pop up with the bases loaded and two outs in the ninth. Don Drysdale fired a two-hitter in a 4–0 win the next day. Tommy Davis stole home and Duke Snider ripped a two-run homer. Alvin Dark, who took over as Giants manager in 1961, admitted before game three that seven unnamed players had been fined a total of $1,000 for missing a 1:30 A.M. curfew in St. Louis two weeks earlier. Dark, finding humor in defeat, told reporters that after successive losses to the Dodgers, he told players to stay out later in hopes it might turn their luck around. The Dodgers, however, seemed the better rested team as Stan Williams stopped the Giants on four hits in a 4–2 victory. Home runs by Jim Davenport, Felipe Alou, and Cepeda knocked out Sandy Koufax, and helped the Giants to a 5–4 lead in game four. The Dodgers roared back with a five-run eighth for a 9–5 win and a series sweep.

Any Dodgers' hopes that the momentum of their sweep in Los Angeles would carry over to San Francisco ended quickly in the opener of a three-game series at Candlestick Park on September 8. The Giants knocked out 18-game winner Johnny Podres in the first as Mays launched a towering two-run home run to deep left and Cepeda added a solo homer. The Giants increased the lead to 6–0 in the second on a two-run homer by Davenport off Roger Craig, and went on to a 7–3 win. Mays had four hits the next day, including a home run in the seventh that knocked out Drysdale in a 9–6 Giants victory. Stu Miller pitched five shutout innings of one-hit ball in relief to continue his dominance over the Dodgers, while lifting the Giants to a 7–1 win and a series sweep. In the fifth, with Koufax pitching in relief, the Giants put it away on Cepeda's 40th homer of the season, a three-run blast to deep right-center field. During the season against the Dodgers, Miller had three wins, four saves, and just one loss. The sweep dropped the Dodgers four games behind Cincinnati with time running out.

Los Angeles finished the season with an 11–8 record, but it wasn't enough to make a run at Cincinnati, which clinched the pennant on September 27. The Dodgers had only themselves to blame, as they went just 10–12 against the Reds, with a three-game sweep by Cincinnati at the Coliseum in August proving to be a devastating blow. The Giants finished the year out with a 12–7 mark, but saw their once high hopes for the year come to a stark end on September 20 when they were officially eliminated before a tiny crowd of 8,890 at Candlestick Park.

The 1960 and 1961 seasons were disappointing for both clubs, but they seemed to have enough talent to remain confident that they would be back in the hunt in 1962.

The year 1962 would surely be special for the Dodgers even if they weren't competitive. The long-awaited opening of Dodger Stadium would come on April 10, 1962, against defending National League champion Cincinnati. The opening was a testament to the determination of Dodgers owner Walter O'Malley, who had to clear political and legal hurdles to make the stadium a reality. The 1961 Dodgers yearbook boasted that the stadium would be "the most modern, most comfortable and most convenient in all baseball," and the ballpark pretty much lived up to those words for years. The stadium drew raves from Dodgers and Giants players, although it would take San Francisco six games to get its first win there.

MUDVILLE (1962)

Maury Wills would start every at-bat with a mighty practice swing, as if he intended to send one over the scoreboard. But in reality, Wills's hits could be better tracked with a yardstick than a tape measure. His bunts, rollers, and chopped balls off home plate proved more frustrating to the opposition than a cleanup hitter's 420-foot blast to the bleachers.

The Dodgers shortstop burst onto the scene in 1960 with 50 stolen bases, and followed that up with 35 in 1961. Wills was the fly at the Giants picnic with his knack for buzzing around the bases without even the need of a base hit. The Giants got an early preview of Wills's brand of baseball in a game September 2, 1960, when he reached first on a walk, stole second, went to third on a fly ball, and came home on a balk.

By 1962, in the heat of a pennant race, the Giants had seen enough of the Wills-led Dodgers running game. On July 5, the Dodgers stole four bases, including two by Wills, to spark an 11–3 win. The next day, the Dodgers accused the Giants of using more than a fly swatter to slow down their game-stealing speedster. The Dodgers complained that sand had been piled up near first base, and questioned whether it was a plot to slow their running game. Dodgers manager Walter Alston, asked if the Giants had set a sand trap, replied, "I wouldn't know, you have to ask the guy who put it there or had it put there." Giants manager Alvin Dark innocently blamed the elements, theorizing that the tricky Candlestick Park winds blew the dirt onto the base path. At the end of the third inning, umpires ordered the grounds crew to remove the extra dirt and firm up the ground. A footnote to the bizarre day: the Dodgers failed to steal a base.

A month later, when the clubs met for the start of a three-game series August 10–12, the sand had turned to mud at Candlestick and the accusations of dirty play created the scene for what still stands as one of the wildest days in West Coast baseball.

—*m*—

The development of the 1962 season into a Giants-Dodgers classic could not have been predicted, though arguments could have been made that both teams appeared to have run-producing lineups and adequate pitching to compete.

The Giants' optimism came from a powerful 1961 offense—sparked by Orlando Cepeda's 46 homers and Willie Mays's 40, and a late-season revival of the bat of Willie McCovey—and a pitching staff that seemed to have had an off year that hid its potential. The Dodgers continued their roster transformation, moving out Brooklyn veterans Gil Hodges, Charlie Neal, and Roger Craig as they assembled a go-go, opportunistic offense that appeared capable of scratching out the needed runs for a pitching staff of strong arms.

The Dodgers looked to Frank Howard, projected as a starter, to provide the power that was missing in 1961 when the team's highest individual home run total was 18. Wills was expected to provide excitement on the bases. Outfielders Tommy Davis and Willie Davis showed promise with their bats and speed. Twenty-two-year-old Ron Fairly would take over at first. Infielder Jim Gilliam and catcher John Roseboro were valued as solid everyday players. The Dodgers had evidence that Sandy Koufax had conquered his control problem. In 1961, Koufax struck out 269 batters in 256 innings while walking 96. The four-man rotation would return, consisting of Koufax, Don Drysdale, Johnny Podres, and Stan Williams. Larry Sherry (15 SV, 3.90) and Ron Perranoski were expected to lead the bullpen.

Second-year Giants manager Alvin Dark was confident that his club, which won 15 of its last 22 in 1961, had become a smart, experienced team. Dark was so sure of his club that he made the decision at the end of the 1961 campaign to start 1962 with one set lineup. It would consist of an infield of Cepeda, Chuck Hiller, Jim Davenport, and Jose Pagan; an outfield of Harvey Kuenn, Willie Mays, and Felipe Alou, and catcher Ed Bailey. Dark's biggest challenge was how to get McCovey sufficient at-bats, since he was reluctant to pull Cepeda off first base. The Giants' rotation appeared to be well stocked with Juan Marichal, Jack Sanford, and Mike McCormick, along with 1961 starter-reliever Billy O'Dell and Billy Pierce, acquired in a trade with the Chicago White Sox. Stu Miller would be the key arm in the bullpen.

For the first time, because of expansion, the schedule would stretch to 162 games. But as it turned out, even that was not enough to decide the pennant winner.

———

The first-place Dodgers led the Giants by 5½ games as the teams met August 10 in San Francisco. The Giants took the opener of the three-game series decisively. O'Dell tossed a five-hitter, retiring 24 of the last 25 batters, Tom Haller drove in four runs, and Mays homered in an 11–2 victory. Curiously, despite a lack of rain in San Francisco, the base paths appeared to be saturated in water.

The next day's game got under way with Tommy Davis staking the Dodgers to a 3–0 lead in the first inning with a three-run homer off Pierce. In the second inning, Wills, Gilliam, and Alston complained that the infield had been deliberately watered down to slow the Dodgers' speed game, but umpire Bill Jackowski ruled the field playable. With the still upset Wills batting in the third, he stepped out several times while continuing to argue about the muddy base paths until plate umpire Al Forman ejected him. The Giants came back in the fourth to get within 3–2 on an RBI single by Alou and an RBI double by Davenport. In the sixth, Alou doubled down the right field foul line off Drysdale. Haller struck out, but then Drysdale's pitch struck Davenport, breaking his hand. O'Dell pinch ran for Davenport, but Drysdale struck out Pagan.

McCovey was brought in to pinch-hit for Pierce, leaving Alston with a tough decision. Alston, concerned about McCovey's success against Drysdale, went to the mound as left-hander Perranoski warmed up in the bullpen. Alston stuck with Drysdale, and on a 3–2 count, McCovey ripped the pitch three-quarters of the way up the right field bleachers. Miller held the Dodgers to one run over the final three innings in the 5–4 victory. Afterward, the Dodgers were still steaming. Wills, who was having no joy in "Mudville," noted that the puddles at first and shortstop were not an accident because the same thing happened the night before. "They were taking away half our attack by handicapping our speed," he said.

Soggy base paths greeted the Dodgers for the third straight game on August 12, and this time the umpires had seen enough. Jackowski, ruling the base paths were too waterlogged to play, called on the grounds crew, which poured two wheelbarrows of sand onto the dirt, delaying the game eight minutes. Once the game began, Marichal bogged down the Dodgers, limiting them to four hits while striking out eight as the Giants won 5–1 to pull off a critical sweep to move within 2½ games. Alou had three singles, finishing the series with eight hits and seven runs scored. Fairly's homer was the lone offense for the slumping Dodgers, who hit just .153 during the three games, which drew 123,384.

DOWN TO THE WIRE (1962)

This was the kind of pennant race Giants and Dodgers fans dreamed about when word came that the clubs were moving west. Brooklyn vs. New York had been replaced by Northern California vs. Southern California. It was smugville vs. smogville: Giants fans enjoyed ridiculing L.A. for its air quality, and Dodgers fans thought residents of "Frisco" (a demeaning reference itself) had an overinflated view of their city. However, as entertaining as the back and forth sniping between the two rival regions was, the debate was now shifting to the field as the clubs squared off for a four-game series September 3–6 in Los Angeles with the pennant race in full swing.

September 3 (Giants 7, Dodgers 3): Sanford's pitching helped the Giants win their first game of the year at Dodger Stadium, as he picked up his 16th straight victory, and 20th of the season. In the final series of the regular season between the clubs, the Dodgers hoped to pad their 3½ game lead while the Giants aimed to at least chip away at the margin. The Giants took charge of a 1–1 game in the third when Mays slugged a three-run homer off Williams with Hiller and Alou on board. Alou singled home two more runs in the fourth and Haller added a homer in the fifth. Mays's homer was his 42nd, his highest total since 1955. The reverberations from the "Mudville" series at Candlestick Park were still being felt. Some 3,000 duck calls had been sold for $2 each during the week, with fans encouraged to bring them to the games. In the parking lot outside the stadium, a Giants booster rubbed it in, having parked his water truck which carried the sign CANDLESTICK SWAMP WATER.

September 4 (Dodgers 5, Giants 4): The Dodgers took advantage of their speed in regaining their 3½ game lead over the Giants. Willie Davis scored from first on a Tommy Davis single in the fourth thanks to a Giants error, and Roseboro stole home after tripling in the fourth. Howard had an RBI double and Fairly drove in a run with a single. Pagan hit a two-run homer in the ninth to cut the lead to 5–4, but reliever Perranoski struck out Mays and Cepeda to finish off the Giants.

September 5 (Giants 3, Dodgers 0): Marichal carried a 3–0 lead into the sixth, but injured his right foot while chasing down a slow roller by Willie Davis. Bob Bolin came on to preserve the shutout, giving Marichal his 18th win of the season. Both teams got good news after the game about their star pitchers: X-rays on Marichal were negative; and Koufax, out for almost two months with a forefinger and hand condition, threw 20 minutes in the bullpen before the game and another six minutes of batting practice, and said he was feeling better.

September 6 (Giants 9, Dodgers 6): The Giants broke a 5–5 tie in the ninth with a four-run outburst before 54,263 in a contest Giants skipper Dark called "the biggest game I ever managed." The Giants had taken a 4–0 lead after three innings, but the Dodgers tied it with a four-run fourth, high-lighted by Howard's two-run homer. The Dodgers fell behind 5–4 in the eighth, but Tommy Davis tied it with a homer. In the ninth, Hiller's single and Perranoski's bad throw on Davenport's bunt put runners at second and third. Alou was intentionally walked and after two were out, Cepeda walked to force in one run, and Kuenn cleared the bases with a triple. The teams finished the regular season series knotted at 9–9, with the Dodgers now clinging to a 1½ game lead.

SUPER SUNDAY (1962)

The Giants and Dodgers were going in different directions as they entered the last day of the regular season. The Dodgers were clinging to a one-game lead, having lost five of their last six, and nine of their last 12. The Giants had won four of the last six. The Giants and Dodgers were play-ing in their own parks Sunday, September 30, but never had the 400-mile distance between the cities seemed so close. The Giants were dead-locked 1–1 in the eighth inning against Houston when Mays homered for what would be the game-winner. Mays homered in his first at-bat of the regular season on April 10 off Milwaukee's Warren Spahn, and now had repeated the effort in his last at-bat of the 162-game campaign. The Giants could not celebrate immediately, however, because the Dodgers could still wrap up the flag by defeating St. Louis. The Giants waited in their locker room, the Candlestick Park crowd stayed in their seats, and thousands of San Francisco Bay Area radio listeners were tensely tuned in to Giants announcer Russ Hodges as he relayed reports of the final inning in Los Angeles. With the Dodgers' Gilliam batting with two out and Los Angeles trailing 1–0, Hodges triggered bedlam over the airwaves when he yelled, "He popped to Javier. We've got a playoff!" The celebrating Giants were back in first place for the first time since July 7, while players in the Dodgers' quiet locker room could only wonder how their lead slipped away.

THREE DAYS IN OCTOBER (1962)

Eleven years after the epic 1951 playoff, the Dodgers and Giants were fac-ing off again in a best-of-three matchup to determine the National League champion. Similar to 1951, the Giants had the momentum after chasing down the Dodgers to force the playoff. Los Angeles was showing little sign of life, having gone the last 21 innings without scoring a run.

October 1 (Giants 8, Dodgers 0): Game one was all Giants. Mays slugged his 48th and 49th homers of the season, and Pierce shut down the Dodgers on three hits, 8–0, in San Francisco. Pierce struck out Howard three times and kept base-stealing king Wills from reaching first. Koufax pitched to only seven batters and departed in the second inning, allowing three runs and four hits.

The Giants scored two in the first on Mays's homer, following a double by Alou. Davenport homered in the second to make it 3–0. In the sixth, Mays and Cepeda homered off Sherry. The Giants loaded the bases on three walks in the eighth. Two scored on Pagan's double and another came in when Howard's relay took a bad hop. The condition of the Giants' infield once again became an issue when a Dodgers official complained before the game that it appeared overwatered. Umpire Jocko Conlan had the crew do some housekeeping around first base and the game went on without further discussion. The Dodgers' scoreless streak extended to 30 innings, with three straight shutouts. Said Ralph Branca, the former Dodgers pitcher who was an authority on painful defeats, "I think they're in trouble now."

October 2 (Dodgers 8, Giants 7): The Dodgers extended their scoreless streak to 35 innings, and trailed the Giants 1–0 through five as the playoff shifted to Los Angeles. Alou began the scoring in the second, driving in Cepeda with a double off Drysdale. The Giants seemingly took command in the sixth as they scored four times. Haller walked with one out and went to third on Pagan's double. Sanford put down a squeeze bunt, and when Drysdale slipped while trying to field it, a run came home. Run-scoring singles by Hiller, Davenport, and McCovey put the Giants up 5–0.

It looked like the Dodgers were done.

Sanford, a 24-game winner in 1962, struck out the side in the first. He allowed only two hits over the first five innings. But Sanford was pitching on two days' rest, having gone 5⅔ innings on September 29 as the Giants won their 100th game, and Dark was concerned he was tiring.

After Sanford walked Gilliam to lead off the sixth, Dark brought in the usually reliable reliever Stu Miller. Nine batters later, the Dodgers had put together a stunning rally. The sixth-inning numbers: 7 runs, 4 hits, 1 error, 2 walks, 1 hit by pitch, 1 stolen base.

Duke Snider greeted Miller with a double, and Tommy Davis ended the offensive drought with a sacrifice fly. Wally Moon walked and Howard singled home Snider. O'Dell replaced Miller, and gave up a single to pinch-hitter Doug Camilli to load the bases. Andy Carey was hit by a pitch to bring home the third run, and pinch-hitter Lee Walls cleared the bases with a double. Don Larsen came on to pitch, and got Wills to hit a grounder to Cepeda, but Walls scored when Haller couldn't handle the throw home for the seventh run. The Giants tied it 7–7 in the eighth on an RBI single by Bailey and sacrifice fly by John Orsino.

In the Dodgers' ninth, Wills drew a walk off Bob Bolin. Dick LeMay relieved him, and walked Gilliam during an at-bat in which he threw to first base eight times in an attempt to prevent Wills from stealing. Rookie Gaylord Perry was brought in, and pinch-hitter Daryl Spencer bunted the runners over. McCormick came in and walked Tommy Davis intentionally to load the bases. Fairly drove in Wills for the 8–7 win with a sacrifice fly to medium-deep center field.

After 164 games, the teams were even again.

October 3 (Giants 6, Dodgers 4): The Giants struck first, taking a 2–0 lead in the third inning. Kuenn singled with Pagan at third and Marichal at first. Pagan scored, and when Kuenn was caught in a rundown between first and second, Gilliam's throw hit him in the back, allowing Marichal to score. The Dodgers got one in the fourth on Howard's ground ball force out after Snider doubled and Tommy Davis singled. The Dodgers got two more in the sixth on Tommy Davis's two-run homer. Wills provided all the offense in the seventh, stealing second and third after a single, and scoring when Bailey's throw went into left field.

It was 4–2 Dodgers, top of the ninth.

The Giants, hoping to channel Bobby Thomson, had to be thinking three-run homer as they entered the final frame. And why not? If runners got on base, McCovey, Mays, and Cepeda might all get a chance to put the Giants on top with one swing. But instead of one decisive at-bat, the powerful Giants scratched and clawed their way to a four-run inning.

Pinch-hitter Matty Alou led off against Ed Roebuck with a single. Kuenn forced him at second, and McCovey and Felipe Alou walked to load the bases. Mays singled off Roebuck's glove to drive in Kuenn. Williams replaced Roebuck, and Cepeda greeted him with a sacrifice fly that brought McCovey home with the tying run. A wild pitch moved the runners up, and Bailey was walked intentionally to load the bases. Davenport walked to give the Giants a 5–4 lead. Perranoski took over for Williams, and Pagan hit a grounder that Larry Burright booted at second base, scoring Mays for the fourth run of the inning. Pierce retired the side in the ninth, getting Walls to fly out to Mays for the final out and giving the Giants a pennant-clinching 6–4 victory.

—⁓—

Back in San Francisco, fans went wild celebrating the city's first pennant. Roads were jammed to the airport as thousands attempted to welcome the team as it flew in. Thousands more showed up downtown at Powell and Market streets for an impromptu celebration. The dejected Dodgers, meanwhile, struggled to console themselves. Alston, bemoaning the loss of Koufax in mid-July due to a circulatory disorder in the forefinger of his pitching hand, could only wonder what might have happened if he didn't lose the left-hander, who had a 14–5 record including a no-hitter when he went down. Outside the Dodgers locker room, Los Angeles outfielder Moon, noting a postseason pot that had gotten away, asked the press to be patient with the players. "Give them a little more time to cool off; they've just blown $12,000."

The Giants and New York Yankees split the first two games of the World Series played at Candlestick Park. New York took two-out-of-three at Yankee Stadium, but the Giants forced a Game Seven with a 5–2 victory back home in Game Six. The dream ended for the Giants in their last at-bat as they trailed 1–0. McCovey, batting with runners at second and third and two outs, stroked a line drive that was caught by second baseman Bobby Richardson to end it. Despite the heartbreaking loss, the Giants had every reason to believe that more pennants were in the immediate future. But it would be nine years before the Giants could claim another title, and when they would get close, it would be the Dodgers who would stand in the way.

HIT RECORD (1962)

The wild Giants-Dodgers 1962 season inspired entertainer Danny Kaye to produce and perform a record that lives on as a classic. The brilliant Kaye was at his tongue-twisting best as he told the story of a mythical game between the rivals from the perspective of a Dodgers fan. It began with a four-run Giants first ("Orlando Cepeda, is at bat with the bases jammed . . . Orlando Cepeda, with a wham, bam, he hit a grand slam"). A Dodgers comeback is thwarted two innings later ("In the third, like a bird, we get two on and none away, and Fairly hits into a double play"). The frustration grows as Maury Wills tries to steal second in the sixth ("Maury goes, the catcher throws. At the bag, he beats the tag, that mighty little waif, and umpire Conlin cries, 'You're out'"). The big moment comes in the ninth as Kaye incorporates Giants pitcher Stu Miller, catcher Tom Haller, and second baseman Chuck Hiller into a bit as clever as "Who's on first?" The Dodgers cut the lead to 4–2 and with Willie Davis and Tommy Davis on the bases, the 6-foot-7 Howard bunts ("Cepeda runs to field the ball, so does Hiller, so does Miller, Hiller hollers Miller, Miller hollers Hiller, Haller hollers Hiller, points to Miller with his fist, and that's the Miller-Hiller-Haller-hallelujah twist"). Howard comes around to score amid the confusion for a 5–4 Dodgers victory. Perhaps Kaye's real genius was to make up a game that actually might top many real-life wacky contests the teams have played.

JUST MISSED 'EM

Fans in Los Angeles and San Francisco were lucky that most of the key players from Brooklyn and New York came west in 1958. One of the notable exceptions, and certainly the saddest, was Dodgers catcher Roy Campanella, whose career prematurely ended in a car crash months before the opener. The eight-time all-star might have been reaching his final years as a player, but his absence will always leave a void in the rivalry's West Coast history. Bobby Thomson, who played with New York in 1957, finished out his career with the Chicago Cubs in 1958–59 and the Boston Red Sox and Baltimore Orioles in 1960. Ralph Branca threw his last pitch in 1956, so there never was a chance for a California version of Thomson-Branca. Jackie Robinson's 10-year career came to end in 1956, depriving spectators at the Coliseum and Seals Stadium from seeing the legendary, six-time all-star. Of course, if Robinson had stuck around for the 1958 season, it probably would have been in a Giants uniform. The Dodgers tried to trade Robinson to the Giants on December 13, 1956, for pitcher Dick Littlefield and $35,000 cash. Robinson rejected the trade, choosing to retire instead.

BOYS OF AUTUMN

When Don Drysdale retired in 1969, his departure left only one player remaining from the New York–Brooklyn era: Willie Mays. The phasing out of the holdovers from New York and Brooklyn was about complete.

The start of that transition began in 1958. Several of the key players from the East Coast rivalry made it to the West Coast, but fans never got to fully appreciate their talents since their skills were diminishing by then. Shortstop Pee Wee Reese lasted only 59 games in 1958, hitting just .224 before his career ended. Reese was a 10-time all-star, and the leader of the Brooklyn teams while appearing in at least 140 games each season from 1941 to 1956. Duke Snider played seven more years after arriving in Los Angeles in 1958, and finished out his career with one-year stints with the New York Mets and the Giants. But the Snider that fans saw during those times was not the slugger Brooklyn fans had come to know, as he hit just 91 homers in those seven seasons. Snider's fame came during a stretch from 1953 to 1957 with Brooklyn when he hit 207 home runs. Gil Hodges had two good years left in him when he arrived in Los Angeles, belting a total of 47 home runs in 1958 and 1959, and helping the Dodgers to their first World Series championship on the West Coast. But Hodges's best years came in his 12 previous seasons with Brooklyn, when he hit 298 homers. By 1960, Hodges and Snider were part-time players as the Dodgers prepared for a youth movement with such names as Willie Davis, 21, Tommy Davis, 22, and Ron Fairly, 22. Brooklyn great Don Newcombe won 123 games from 1949–57, including three 20-win seasons highlighted by a 27–7 record in 1956. But Newcombe couldn't even survive the first year in Los Angeles. He was traded to Cincinnati in June of 1958 after going 0–6 with a 7.86 ERA, and won only 26 more games before retiring.

The Giants pulled off what would be a rewarding trade in 1961 when they sent two 1958 key players, one-time ace Johnny Antonelli and outfielder Willie Kirkland to Cleveland for Harvey Kuenn, who had hit .300 or higher in eight of the last nine seasons. The Giants bragged that their 1961 rookie crop was the best since 1958, featuring second baseman Chuck Hiller, catcher Tom Haller, and pitchers Jim Duffalo and Bob Bolin. The Dodgers appeared to be phasing out veterans by that year, as Snider, 33, and Hodges, 36, played in only 101 games each in 1960.

By the start of the 1963 season, Jim Gilliam was the only regular left from Brooklyn. Gone were such names as Hodges, Charlie Neal, and Carl Furillo. For the Giants, the only link remaining from New York was Mays. In fact, the Giants had nearly overhauled their roster from 1958, with only four players remaining from that club. The combination of the turnover and the pennant race of 1962 had pushed the East Coast era into the history books as the clubs moved forward to write new chapters in their West Coast homes.

ACES (1963)

Sandy Koufax pitched with the demeanor of a cold-blooded assassin, quietly mowing down a lineup with a lethal combination of heat and pinpoint accuracy with his breaking ball. Juan Marichal was a more flamboyant figure, displayed most prominently with his high leg kick and an assortment of pitches thrown from overhand to sidearm. When Koufax and Marichal took the mound for any Dodgers-Giants game, the intensity jumped up a notch. This was the case in 1963 as both aces were at the top of their games.

—⁓—

The Giants got an early hint of what was to come on September 3, 1958, when Koufax picked up his 10th win of the year with a long relief appearance in which he allowed just two hits in seven innings. Yet, Koufax's future hinged on whether he could get a handle on his control. In 1958, he struck out 131 in 159 innings, but walked 105. He walked 92 in 153 innings in 1959, and 100 in 175 innings in 1960, but also struck out a staggering 370 in those two years. Koufax showed the Giants a little more of his talent when he struck out 11 in a losing effort on May 26, 1959. The breakthrough game came a few months later against the Giants on August 31 when he struck out a record-tying 18 batters in a 5–2 win. Koufax struck out the side in the fifth, sixth, and ninth innings. He fanned Jackie Brandt and Jack Sanford three times, and got Willie Mays, Willie McCovey, Orlando Cepeda, Ed Bressoud, and Danny O'Connell twice. Koufax became only the second pitcher to strike out 18 batters in a nine-inning game in the 1900s, with Cleveland's Bob Feller matching the total 21 years earlier.

Koufax's 1962 season was cut short by injury, but he still had an impressive year at 14–7 with an ERA of 2.54, 216 strikeouts, and 57 walks.

Marichal quickly got attention when he threw a one-hitter against Philadelphia in his major league debut on July 19, 1960. The 22-year-old took a no-hitter into the eighth, when Clay Dalrymple broke it up with a single. Marichal was rolling with four straight wins until his first appearance against the Dodgers on September 5 when he was knocked out in the sixth after giving up four runs, six hits, and walking seven. Marichal followed up his 6–2 rookie season with a solid 1961 (13–10, 3.89) and 1962 (18–11, 3.36).

In 1963, both pitchers appeared on the brink of stardom as the Giants and Dodgers entered the season pondering a "what if" question over the winter. Los Angeles wondered if the 1962 pennant chase might have turned out different had Koufax not been sidelined for much of the stretch drive. It was hard for the Dodgers to feel they could have played any better. Don Drysdale won the Cy Young Award, Koufax led the league in ERA, Maury Wills was MVP, Tommy Davis won the batting crown and the team won 102 games, the third most in Dodgers' history (an impressive number even with the expanded schedule and playoff games). With the club returning mostly intact, and Koufax apparently over his finger injury, the Dodgers appeared ready for another run at the flag. The Giants, meanwhile, could only imagine the feeling of a World Series title if Willie McCovey's line drive had gotten by Bobby Richardson.

The Giants returned in 1963 mostly with the same cast of regulars and substitutes from the World Series team. The only real question seemed whether the Giants offense could repeat the powerful numbers of 1962, when the team led the league with 204 home runs and a .278 batting average.

The Dodgers made just one major move in the offseason, trading veteran starter Stan Williams to the New York Yankees for first baseman Bill Skowron. The move was made to add some power, but this team, while slugging a respectable 140 homers in 1962, was about speed and pitching. The club put on an electrifying show on the bases in 1962, with 198 stolen bases. Wills set a record with 104 steals, eclipsing the total of any other team in the league.

A rerun of 1962 appeared to be in store, but that baseball cliché, about pitching being 90 percent of the game, would gain some credibility. The 1963 season would be a year of the pitchers, and spark a competition between Dodgers ace Koufax, and Giants ace Marichal for supremacy in the National League.

—◦—

Koufax pitched against the Giants five times in 1963, going 4–1. Marichal would make six starts against the Dodgers, going 4–2. Each of those games helps tell the story of the 1963 season, starting with Koufax's near-perfect performance.

May 11 (Dodgers 8, Giants 0): Koufax no-hit the Giants before 55,530 at Dodger Stadium. He threw 112 pitches, 72 of them fastballs and struck out four. He walked Ed Bailey in the eighth on a 3–2 count for the first runner, and walked pinch-hitter McCovey in the ninth for the only other Giants base runner. The Dodgers built a four-run lead, knocking out Marichal in the sixth. Pitching lines: Koufax: 9 (innings pitched), 0 (runs), 0 (hits), 4 (strikeouts), 2 (walks); Marichal 5⅓, 4, 9, 5, 1.

May 24 (Giants 7, Dodgers 1): Koufax failed to survive the first inning as the Giants scored five times. The anticipated Koufax-Marichal rematch was over shortly after the opening bell. Cepeda doubled home three runners, and Felipe Alou followed with a two-run homer to left. Koufax got only one out. Marichal gave up just four hits and struck out 10. The Giants' victory prevented the Dodgers from pulling into a first-place tie. Pitching lines: Koufax: ⅓, 5, 5, 1, 2; Marichal: 9, 1, 4, 10, 1.

June 11 (Giants 3, Dodgers 0): McCovey broke up a pitching duel with a three-run homer off one of his favorite victims, Drysdale, as the Giants swept the two-game series, leaving them tied with the Dodgers for second, one game behind St Louis. Marichal, who ended up with a seven-hit shutout, helped himself with a single in the sixth. Chuck Hiller sacrificed Marichal to second and Felipe Alou got him to third with a single. McCovey, who had a history of success against Drysdale, sliced a home run into the left-field bullpen. Entering the year, McCovey had 19 hits against Drysdale in 35 appearances, with seven home runs. Marichal's pitching line: 9, 0, 7, 4, 0.

June 17 (Dodgers 2, Giants 0): Koufax handcuffed San Francisco on four hits while striking out nine. The Dodgers scored the game's only runs in the third when Skowron drilled a two-run double to right center field off Billy O'Dell. Koufax threw his sixth shutout of the season. Koufax's pitching line: 9, 0, 4, 9, 4.

June 19 (Giants 8, Dodgers 3): Marichal, who no-hit Houston four days earlier, won his seventh straight decision and 11th game of the year.

The Giants offense struck quickly as McCovey hit a two-run homer to deep right field off Drysdale in the first. As the teams adjourned their rivalry until their next meeting about two-and-a-half months away, St. Louis was in first, a half-game in front of the Giants and 2½ ahead of Los Angeles. A pennant race reminiscent of 1962 appeared to be in store, but that forecast didn't take into consideration the next 10 weeks of torrid Dodgers' baseball. Marichal's pitching line: 7⅔, 3, 6, 5, 2.

August 29 (Dodgers 11, Giants 1): Koufax, supported by a 15-hit attack, raised his record to 20–5 as the Dodgers rolled on before 54,978 in Los Angeles. The Dodgers had gone 41–24 since their last meeting with the Giants to lead San Francisco by 5½ games and St. Louis by 6½. Frank Howard drove in three runs with a home run and single, and Ron Fairly collected three singles and four RBIs. Koufax's pitching line: 9, 1 3, 7, 1.

August 30 (Dodgers 3, Giants 1): Drysdale followed up Koufax's gem with nine solid innings, shutting out the Giants for the last eight. The defeat dropped the Giants to third place as Marichal failed to get his 20th win of the season for the second time. A crowd of 54,849 pushed the Dodgers' home attendance for the year past the two million mark. Marichal's pitching line: 6, 2, 6, 6, 0.

September 6 (Dodgers 5, Giants 2): The Dodgers demonstrated that fundamentals, especially when combined with power and pitching, can be a lethal weapon as they continued their march to the pennant. Koufax won his 22nd game of the season, and Jim Gilliam and Howard had solo homers. But it was the methodical way in which the Dodgers scored their other three runs that highlighted one of the club's strengths. In the first, Gilliam singled, went to second on Willie Davis's sacrifice bunt, and scored on a single by Tommy Davis. In the third, Gilliam singled, was bunted to second by Willie Davis and scored on a double by Skowron. In the ninth, Gilliam walked, Willie Davis delivered his third sacrifice bunt of the game, and Tommy Davis brought the run home with another single. The loss pushed the Giants 10½ games out of first place, but St. Louis, having won nine of its last 10, was still hanging close at 5½ games back. Koufax's pitching line: 8, 2, 9, 8, 2.

September 7 (Giants 5, Dodgers 3): The Giants, falling fast, went to their biggest guns to pull out a victory. Marichal won his 21st game of the year, and the Giants unloaded on Drysdale. Mays tagged a two-run homer in the first, Cepeda hit one out in the fourth, and McCovey added a solo shot in the sixth. The Giants survived a rarity—as Mays dropped a fly ball by Tommy Davis for a two-base error that led to a run. The Giants, while realistically, if not mathematically, out of the pennant race, had allowed St. Louis to creep within 4½ games of the Dodgers. Marichal's pitching line: 9, 3, 9, 8, 2.

The Dodgers, led by Koufax, went on to a 99-win season to win the pennant as they fended off a charge by St. Louis. On August 29, the Dodgers led St. Louis by seven games. The Cardinals won 19 of their next 20 to get within a game, but the Dodgers swept a series against the Cardinals to stop their momentum. The Dodgers clinched the pennant on September 24, and would go on to mow down the New York Yankees in four games in the World Series.

Koufax finished the season with a remarkable 25–5 record, 1.88 ERA, 306 strikeouts, and 11 shutouts. In the World Series, he allowed the Yankees just three runs while striking out 23.

Koufax was named National League MVP, and also won the Cy Young award.

Pitching hampered the Giants in 1963, as they finished 88–74, 11 games behind the Dodgers. The offense produced a league-leading 197 home runs, but the staff ERA of 3.35 was eighth, ahead of only the expansion New York Mets and Houston Colt .45s. Marichal wasn't to blame, as he compiled a 25–8 mark with an ERA of 2.41 and 248 strikeouts.

Koufax and Marichal had set the tone for greatness, and their performances over the next three years would cement their names in the legend of the rivalry.

BOILING POINT (1964–65)

Duck and cover.

No, this wasn't a safety tip on what to do should California be jolted by an earthquake. It was something that Giants and Dodgers batters needed to keep in mind whenever the teams got together.

Fans got an early taste of the bitter rivalry only six days into the 1958 season when the clubs engaged in their first West Coast–beanball flare-up, featuring Giant Ramon Monzant and Dodger Don Drysdale. The tension began early when Monzant's pitches decked Charlie Neal in the second and Gino Cimoli in the third. Drysdale responded by sending Monzant to the ground in the fourth. When Monzant threw high and inside to Gil Hodges in the Dodgers' half of the fourth, umpire Frank Secory summoned Dodgers manager Walter Alston and Giants coach Herman Franks, who was sitting in for an ailing Bill Rigney, for a peace conference which put an end to the incidents.

The battle over who owned the inside of plate would be a common theme early in the West Coast duels, but both teams seemed satisfied to even the score through quick retaliation instead of charging the mound and settling the matter with fists. On April 20, 1960, Drysdale plunked Willie Mays and Orlando Cepeda, and Mike McCormick responded by decking Wally Moon. On July 16, 1960, Jack Stanford threw a pitch in the second that sailed past the head of Stan Williams, who responded with a fast ball under Sanford's chin in the third. On September 6, 1962, Billy O'Dell decked Ron Fairly in the fourth after a Frank Howard home run. Drysdale followed up by knocking down Mays and Willie McCovey in the fifth, and O'Dell came back in the bottom half of the inning by brushing back Drysdale. Umpire Ed Vargo warned both benches, and again, the exchange stopped.

A common theme to the dust-ups was that Drysdale usually was involved. Drysdale, who stood at a menacing 6-foot-5 and seemed to arrive at the mound in a bad mood, used an intimidating sidearm delivery that motivated right-handed batters to keep their life insurance policies paid up.

In 1965, the Giants and Dodgers would engage in a blistering pennant chase in a year that would see remarkable individual performances on both sides. But the race for the flag would take second billing. Tension between Juan Marichal and Drysdale had been building, and on a Sunday afternoon at Candlestick Park, the West Coast rivalry would reach the boiling point.

—⁓—

The days leading up to the 1965 season gave no hint of the volatility that was ahead.

The Giants were coming off their second-best season in San Francisco (90–72), finishing three games out in a wild four-team race in 1964. The Giants nearly won the crown despite a number of key injuries and reported conflicts between manager Alvin Dark and some players. Herman Franks was taking over for Dark, inheriting a club that led the National League in homers in 1964, and that boasted a one-two starting punch of Marichal (21–8, 2.48 ERA) and Gaylord Perry. Marichal, who missed some turns because of back spasms in 1964, improved his career record to 83–39, the best winning percentage of any contemporary starting pitcher. On offense, the Giants looked to the bats of Willie Mays, Jim Ray Hart, and Orlando Cepeda, though he was suffering from knee problems in the spring, and Willie McCovey, who was slowed by an assortment of ailments in 1964. Despite concerns about Cepeda's knee, Giants management was feeling so good about the team that the only issue was whether the club would try to fill a void for a left-hander. Otherwise the Giants seemed content to hope for a better break on injuries and sit back and watch the sluggers dent the fences.

The Dodgers had more cause for alarm based on their nose dive to sixth place in 1964. The club fretted over a power outage that saw its home run total drop from 110 in 1963 to 79 in 1964, but the Dodgers were built on pitching and speed, and the combination again held promise for the new season. The Dodgers shed their top power hitter, Frank Howard, in a seven-player trade with the Washington Senators to bring in left-handed starter Claude Osteen, whom the club saw as a key member of the supporting cast for the Sandy Koufax (19–5, 1.74 ERA) and Drysdale (18–16, 2.18) show. The team was relying on a comeback by Tommy Davis, who had batted .346 in 1962 and .326 in 1963, but fell to .275 in 1964. Center fielder Willie Davis (42 stolen bases) and shortstop Maury Wills (53 stolen bases) were the sparks in the club's running game. The Dodgers led the National League in stolen bases every year since they moved west, and there were no indications they would relinquish that position this year.

Drysdale wasted no time in keeping Giants batters from digging in too deeply early in the 1965 season, as he twice sent Mays sprawling with high and tight pitches in the first game between the teams in Los Angeles on April 29. Marichal, who took the loss in the 2–1 defeat, didn't respond. Instead, Bob Bolin delivered the payback in the eighth when he hit Drysdale with a pitch. The two pitches that knocked down Mays sparked some tough talk, as Marichal threatened to retaliate against Drysdale when the two pitchers were scheduled to hook up the next weekend in San Francisco. Drysdale, denying he tried to hit Mays, replied, "If Marichal throws at me, or hits me, he better get me early. If he gets me, I'm going to get four Giants, and they won't be .200 hitters either."

Marichal's comments, which prompted Drysdale's response, would prove to be ominous, as he explained he was growing tired of the Dodgers right-hander brushing back Giants hitters. "For the five years I've been here, I've seen too much of this," Marichal said. "Next time, if he's pitching against me and comes close, we'll see what happens. He'll get it, and real good too."

National League President Warren Giles took the comments seriously, especially with Drysdale and Marichal scheduled to meet in the second game of a three-game series in San Francisco just six days later. Before the series, he warned both clubs about following through on the beanball threats. The potential confrontation never materialized, as a groin injury prevented Marichal from taking his turn. There were no brush-back incidents, although the Candlestick Park crowd booed Drysdale throughout the game. Drysdale and Marichal were matched up twice in June, but the war of words had quieted.

The stage was set for a face-off as the Giants and Dodgers got ready for a four-game series starting August 19 at Candlestick Park. Milwaukee led the Dodgers by a half-game and the Giants by one. Advance ticket sales were the highest for a series since the park opened. The clubs, tied 5–5 after nine innings, went to the 15th before the Dodgers posted three runs for an 8–5 victory in the four-hour, 11-minute struggle. The Dodgers outhit the Giants 20–7. The next day, Mays hit a two-run homer to lead a 5–1 victory. The third game of the series marked another epic battle. Wes Parker broke up a hard-fought contest with a two-run homer in the 11th inning as the Dodgers won 6–4 to move back into first, a half-game over Milwaukee, and 1½ in front of the Giants. The dramatic third game set the stage for the series finale on Sunday, with Marichal going against Koufax. Koufax, asked about the potential showcase matchup, shrugged it off, saying, "Who knows, it may be flop." Koufax turned out to be half-right. It would not be a pitching duel, but the day certainly would not be forgotten.

It was Sunday, August 22, game four of the high-stakes weekend with 42,807 in attendance. Marichal decked Wills and Ron Fairly in their first at-bats. In the third inning, while batting against Koufax, Marichal reacted angrily when he felt John Roseboro deliberately whizzed the ball past his ear when the catcher threw it back to the mound. Words turned to action, and in the ensuing scuffle, Marichal's bat hit Roseboro in the head, resulting in a two-inch gash. It took 14 minutes to settle down the wild scene as players from both teams came onto the field. Marichal was ejected and Roseboro had to leave for medical treatment. Mays, credited by even the Dodgers for helping restore peace, then figured in the key offensive blow of the game. After two were out, Jim Davenport and McCovey walked, and Mays launched his 38th home run of the season to put the Giants in front 4–2. Ron Herbel, in relief of Marichal, allowed just one run in 5⅓ innings for a 4–3 victory.

Afterward, both players gave their versions. Marichal: "He tried to hurt me. He hit me in the ear with the ball when he threw it back to the pitcher." Roseboro: "I have no love for that man and I don't believe in turning the other cheek. It's just not right to use a weapon on a man." When asked what Marichal's penalty should be, Roseboro replied, "He and I in a room together for 10 minutes." Other Dodgers called for the Giants pitcher to be banned from baseball. Alston, responding to a question about his thoughts on Marichal, said, "I don't think you want the comment I would give you about a character like that." The incident resulted in an eight-game suspension and $1,750 fine for Marichal. Roseboro calmed down the next day, saying he would not hold grudges, although he later would file a $110,000 damage suit against Marichal. Teammates reacted angrily over the penalty. Wills called it "a joke." Pitcher Bob Miller added, "If you went out on the street and hit a man with a bat, you'd get 20 years."

Even without the Marichal-Roseboro clash, the 1965 pennant race would have been a memorable one. As the teams entered their final series of the year, a two-game meeting September 6 and 7, the Dodgers led Cincinnati by a game and the Giants by two. Marichal's normal turn in the rotation would have put him on the mound against the Dodgers, but league president Giles banned him from pitching in Los Angeles for this series. Marichal responded by pitching on two days' rest, beating Chicago 2–0 on September 5 for his 20th win of the season. The Giants swept the two-game series to move into first place by two percentage points over the Dodgers, with Cincinnati a half-game back and Milwaukee one game down.

The Giants appeared destined to win their second West Coast pennant, holding on to first place from September 7 to September 28. But the Giants created an opening by losing seven of their last 12 games. The Dodgers, who trailed the Giants by 4½ games on September 15, and with no more head-to-head battles on the schedule, won 15 of their last 16 games to clinch the pennant on the second to last day of the season. The Dodgers closed out the year with one of the most dominating pitching performances in history. In the Dodgers' last nine games, in which they went 8–1, they allowed only five runs while recording five shutouts.

During the 15–1 stretch, eight of the wins came on shutouts. For the third straight year, the Dodgers would have the lowest ERA in the National League at 2.81. In the end, the Dodgers again depended on a devastating combination of pitching and speed, as Koufax and Drysdale combined for 49 victories, and Wills stole 94 bases. The club went on to greater glory in the World Series, defeating the Minnesota Twins in seven games, with Koufax throwing two shutouts in four days.

HIGH EXPECTATIONS (1966)

The first meeting of the season between the Giants and Dodgers featured an unusual matchup: the defendant vs. the plaintiff.

The anticipation of what might happen when Juan Marichal, John Roseboro, and the Dodgers would meet for the first time since the 1965 bat episode provided extra interest in the 1966 season. But even without the lingering effects of that incident, the clubs entered the year with high expectations that the real battle of 1966 would be the one for the National League flag.

Peace was at hand in that first game May 3 as Marichal threw a four-hitter in an 8–1 victory, although Roseboro still had a lawsuit pending against the Giants pitcher.

The Dodgers were victims of a milestone Willie Mays clout the next day in a Giants 6–1 win. Mays slugged his 512th career homer off Claude Osteen, putting him ahead of Mel Ott. The Candlestick Park wind, a daily nightmare for the Giants, haunted the Dodgers in game three as the Giants took a sweep with a 9–8 win when Willie Davis couldn't handle a swirling line drive by Jim Ray Hart in the 10th inning. Mays, an expert on the subject, provided some consolation to Davis, saying, "Whatever he said about the wind, believe him. ... I couldn't even explain to you what it was doing."

Behind the scenes, rumors hinted that a trade of Orlando Cepeda was in the works. Three days later, on May 8, the Giants traded their slugger to the St. Louis Cardinals for left-handed pitcher Ray Sadecki.

Another red-hot pennant race was developing when the clubs met for a three-game series in late August. Sandy Koufax fired a four-hit shutout for a 4–0 victory in the opener, winning his 21st game of the season as the Dodgers captured their sixth straight before 42,647, the largest Candlestick Park night crowd since 1960. Afterward, Koufax discussed his pain, saying, "My elbow still hurts when I'm throwing the curve, and at this stage of the season, I have to keep taking my turn."

Willie McCovey double-crossed the Dodgers to spark a 4–2 win the next day. With the Giants trailing 2–1 in the sixth, Mays singled and the Dodgers went into their shift for McCovey, shading fielders to the right side. McCovey then stroked a run-scoring double to left. Pennant fever heated up game three, which the Dodgers won 5–2. Don Sutton decked Mays with one pitch and took a hard slide into second base that upset the Giants. Gaylord Perry responded by hitting the Dodgers pitcher in the wrist, and Sutton followed that up with a pitch that sailed over Perry's head. The Dodgers were now within a game of the Giants and Pirates.

San Francisco won two out of three in the clubs' final head-to-head series of the year in early September, leaving Pittsburgh in first with the Giants a half-game behind and the Dodgers 1½ back. In the third game of the series September 7, Koufax went seven innings, allowing two runs and five hits, while striking out seven, but was unable to get his 23rd win of the season. It would be Koufax's last game against the Giants.

An eight-game winning streak put the Dodgers in first, 3½ games ahead of Pittsburgh and four in front of the Giants on September 16. The Giants got within two games with two to play with Pittsburgh eliminated. The Giants defeated Pittsburgh, and would have faced Cincinnati for a make-up game the next day had the Dodgers lost a doubleheader to Philadelphia. The Dodgers dropped the opener 4–3, but came back to win the nightcap 6–3 to clinch the pennant.

The World Series was a letdown for the Dodgers, as their pitching was victimized by poor defense and lack of offense. The Baltimore Orioles swept the series, as the Dodgers scored just two runs, losing the final three games by shutouts.

The disappointing ending symbolized a turn for the worse that was about to rock the Dodgers. In the last five years, Los Angeles won three pennants, two World Series, and just missed a fourth postseason bid in the 1962 playoff loss to the Giants. But in 1967, the Dodgers would experience their worst finish in the modern era. Maury Wills, Jim Gilliam and Tommy Davis would be gone by opening day. But the biggest blow came on November 18, 1966, when Koufax announced he was retiring because of his painful arthritic left elbow, complaining of "too many pills, too many shots."

It had been a tumultuous year for Koufax. Don Drysdale and Koufax proposed a joint contract in the spring for $1 million, which they would split over three years. The pitchers missed most of spring training, with Koufax finally settling for about $125,000 and Drysdale getting about $105,000.

From 1963 to 1966, Koufax went 25–5, 19–5, 26–8, and 27–9. His ERAs during that span were 1.88, 1.74, 2.04, and 1.73. Over the four years, he threw 31 shutouts and struck out 1,228. He won three Cy Young's and an MVP.

Koufax was a prime force that allowed the Dodgers to outlast the Giants in the 1965 and 1966 pennant races. Mays, upon hearing the news of the retirement, confirmed the intense competition Koufax provided, saying, "Sandy and I had some good battles, he on the mound and me at bat. I know we both enjoyed them. I'll miss him, but it won't hurt my batting average."

THE '60S FADE AWAY (1967–69)

As the 1960s came to a close, the Giants and Dodgers appeared nostalgic for the era as they together sang, "Where Have All the People Gone?"

The Giants were having trouble rallying their fans with the chant "We're No. 2," after finishing second from 1965–1969. The Dodgers could only dream for a finish that high, after plunging from first-place seasons in 1965 and 1966 to years in which they ended up eighth (1967), seventh (1968), and fourth (1969).

Fans of both teams were responding with yawns that translated into a slump at the gate. Giants attendance declined from 1.6 million in 1966 to 1.2 million in 1967, and dropped below 900,000 the past two years. Dodgers' attendance soared to 2.6 million in 1966, but had gone down since. The club drew 1.6 million in 1967, 1.5 million in 1968, and 1.7 million in 1969.

The start of the Dodgers' downfall coincided with the retirement of Sandy Koufax. The Dodgers entered the 1967 season in the unusual position of having to rebuild their roster, the first time they had to contemplate an overhaul since arriving at Los Angeles 10 years ago with an overload of veterans and facing the challenge of bringing in younger players to take over. The Giants, who came up empty-handed despite winning at least 90 games the last three seasons, hoped to take advantage of the Dodgers' apparent vulnerability. From 1964 to 1966, the Giants won 278 games, six more than the Dodgers, and yet had only a fourth place and two sec-ond-place finishes to show for it while the Dodgers won two pennants. The Giants' combination of power and pitching made them one of the favorites in the National League in 1967. Four of the eight starters were coming off impressive home run years: Willie Mays (37), Willie McCovey (36), Jim Ray Hart (33), and Tom Haller (27). Juan Marichal (25–6) and Gaylord Perry (21–8) both had big years.

The Giants pounced on their weakened rivals in 1967, beating them in 13 of 18 contests. They finished 18 games ahead of Los Angeles, their widest margin since the move west. The Dodgers had their fewest victo-ries for a season (73) since 1958 (71), when the schedule was eight games shorter. The club finished 28½ games out, its worst deficit since finishing 42 behind in 1944.

The Don Sutton-Willie Mays confrontation of 1966 resurfaced in 1967. With both clubs out of the pennant race on August 28, and only 11,762 in the stands, it seemed an unlikely game for fireworks. In the fifth with two on, Sutton hit Mays, drawing a glare from the Giants star. After one run was in and with the bases loaded again, Sutton uncorked a wild pitch. Tom Haller scored from third and Mays, who was on second, dashed for home. Sutton, who ran in to cover home, arrived there the same time as Mays, who crashed into him to score. Sutton brushed Mays back in the seventh, but there was no further retaliation as Perry blanked the Dodgers 7–0 on three hits.

The Dodgers' plunge in 1967 also had something to do with the loss of Maury Wills. During a postseason trip to Japan by the Dodgers, Wills left the team without permission, saying he was heading back to Los Angeles for treatment of an ailing right knee. When Wills instead turned up at a Honolulu nightclub playing a banjo on his knee, the Dodgers decided to deal him. The move left the Dodgers without the offensive spark that had defined their offense since Wills moved into the starting lineup in 1960. From 1956 to 1959, Mays led the league in stolen bases. Wills assumed the stolen base crown in 1960, and would hold it for the next five years. Wills's replacements, Gene Michael and Dick Schofield, would steal one base each in 1967.

While the Giants easily disposed of the Dodgers in 1967, and finished 91–71, the St. Louis Cardinals dominated with a 101–60 mark to ruin any San Francisco pennant hopes. The Cardinals also would handily take the flag in 1968.

—␣␣—

In a quest to fill the Wills void for the 1968 season, the Dodgers acquired Minnesota shortstop Zoilo Versalles, along with pitcher Jim Grant, in a trade that involved giving up catcher John Roseboro, and pitchers Ron Perranoski and Bob Miller. In a move to add power, the Dodgers purchased Rocky Colavito from the Chicago White Sox.

With the Dodgers still trying to restart their team, the Giants saw the opportunity to break out of their rut of second-place finishes, and shoot for the NL flag.

The Giants' rotation appeared to be a strong point. An injury-plagued Marichal, who failed to win at least 20 games for the first time in five years, was expected to return to top form. Perry's 15–17 record wasn't a true reflection on his season, as he pitched as effectively as in 1966 when he won 21 games. Mike McCormick, returning to the team in an offseason trade in 1967, was the big story as he captured the Cy Young Award with a 22–10 year.

The schedule makers must have known something. The Giants and Dodgers were not slated to meet after September 1. While that normally might deprive fans of a chance to watch tense head-to-head competition down the stretch, in this case it mercifully avoided a late-season mean-ingless match-up. The only suspense was whether the Dodgers could avoid finishing in the cellar. The Dodgers managed to tie for seventh with Philadelphia, four games ahead of 10th-place Houston. The Giants fin-ished at 88–74, nine behind the Cardinals.

The mostly uneventful 1968 campaign had one shining moment for San Francisco. Bobby Bonds, a 22-year-old minor league standout who was hitting .367 with Phoenix in the Pacific Coast League, was brought up to the big team to experience his major league baptism against the Dodgers on June 25. He grounded out in his first at-bat and was hit by a pitch in his second trip. The Giants loaded the bases in the sixth on a single by Ron Hunt, a double by Jesus Alou, and a walk to McCovey, and two scored when Mays and Hart drew walks. Bonds then placed his name in rivalry memories by launching a pitch off reliever John Purdin over the left-field fence. It was a rare moment. The last player to hit a grand slam in his first game was Philadelphia's William Duggleby, who performed the same feat in 1898. Duggleby's day might have even topped that of Bonds and the Giants, who won 9–0. Duggleby, a pitcher, got the victory, and hit his grand slam in his first at-bat. The victim: The New York Giants.

In 1969, a 90-win Giants season wasn't enough, as they fell to a scorching finish by Atlanta. The Braves won 20 of their last 26 games, including a 10-game winning streak that culminated in their title-clinching victory.

The Giants dominated the Dodgers in head-to-head competition for the second time in three years, taking another season series 13 to 5.

While neither club could be labeled as a powerhouse, both felt they had legitimate chances to compete in the West in 1970 as long as no other team took control of the division. McCovey (45 HR, 126 RBIs, .320), coming off his best year, and Bonds, starting to fulfill the predictions, provided two solid reasons for optimism on offense for the Giants. Marichal (21–11) and Perry (19–14) gave the club two reasons to be hopeful about the pitching. The Dodgers had one consistent theme to their opening day lineup since arriving in Los Angeles: Somebody new would be at third base. In the 12 previous seasons, 11 different players had started the opener at that position. This season's designee would be 20-year-old Steve Garvey. Garvey, along with outfielders Bill Buckner, 19, and Willie Crawford, 22, were part of a youth movement. The team's rotation appeared strong, led by 20-game winners Osteen (20–15) and Bill Singer (20–12), and Sutton.

The Giants and Dodgers often viewed the road to postseason as traveling through San Francisco or Los Angeles. But as the '60s faded away, the times were changing, and the path to success was about to move to Cincinnati where players such as Pete Rose, Johnny Bench, and Tony Perez were building a baseball machine.

—◊◊◊—

One thing was certain. The Dodgers would be entering the 1970s without one of their all-time performers. It was evident that Don Drysdale was hurting on April 22, 1969, in what would be his last game against the Giants as he took an uncharacteristic beating, allowing five runs and seven hits in 4⅔ innings. The last Giant he would face was Mays, who singled. Drysdale, who had come to spring training optimistic about his health, had one win in four starts, having allowed 15 runs, 26 hits and five home runs in 20 innings. Said a frustrated Drysdale: "I can't get my arm up. Maybe something can be done with it, but right now, it's just very simple. I don't have it and I'm not throwing very hard."

By August, there was no alternative. The right-hander, no longer able to effectively compete, would retire. Drysdale, 33, in his 14th season, left the game holding club records for victories, innings pitched, strikeouts and shutouts. Dodgers owner Walter O'Malley noted the historic significance of the loss, saying, "Among the players, Drysdale is the last tie to Brooklyn. It is a nostalgic wrench to see him go. He is one of the superstars."

STREAKERS (1968, 1988)

The streaks remain memorable today as part of rivalry trivia: Two phenomenal pitching accomplishments, two games 20 years apart, and two calls by umpires that kept the streaks alive.

In 1904, Chicago White Sox hurler Guy White threw five straight shutouts. No other pitcher had matched that, but on May 31, 1968, Don Drysdale had a chance. Drysdale brought his streak of four shutouts to a game against the Giants before 46,067 fans at Dodger Stadium hoping to see some history. The Dodgers scored individual runs in the second, third, and eighth, and the Giants cooperated with Drysdale's bid, trailing 3–0 in the ninth. The Giants appeared certain to break the streak when they loaded the bases with none out on a walk to Willie McCovey, a single by Jim Ray Hart, and another walk to Jim Marshall, but then came one of the most controversial calls in the teams' West Coast competition. Dick Dietz had a 2–2 count when Drysdale's breaking pitch hit him on the left shoulder, sending the Giants catcher heading toward first and pinch runner Nate Oliver down the line from third. Home plate umpire Harry Wendelstedt had a different interpretation of the apparent hit by pitch, however, calling it a ball because he said Dietz had not tried to get out of the way. Dietz, joined by third base coach Peanuts Lowrey and manager Herman Franks, erupted into screaming fits, with Franks's being sufficient enough to get him thrown out of the game. When play resumed, Dietz popped out to short left field, pinch-hitter Ty Cline grounded to Wes Parker, who forced Oliver at home, and pinch-hitter Jack Hiatt popped to Parker, putting Drysdale's name in the record book next to a guy named Guy White. Drysdale would eventually extend his scoreless streak to 58⅔ innings.

—⁓—

The Giants were already eliminated from contention on September 23, 1988, and the Dodgers were coasting to the division title, but the first of this three-game series was far from meaningless. Orel Hershiser had thrown four straight shutouts and had a streak of 40 scoreless innings, raising speculation as to whether he could match Drysdale's mark. At issue in this game: Could Hershiser make the Giants one of his victims and would it take another unusual call to keep the streak alive? The answers: Yes and yes. Hershiser fired a five-hitter and an umpire's call canceled out a run. In the third inning, Brett Butler was at first and Jose Uribe at third with one out. Ernest Riles hit a double-play grounder to Steve Sax, who threw to shortstop Alfredo Griffin for the force at second, but Griffin threw wild to first when Butler slid into him, allowing Uribe to score. However, umpire Paul Runge ruled it was a double play, taking away the run because he said Butler illegally interfered with Griffin. Atlee Hammaker matched Hershiser through seven innings. The Dodgers finally broke through in the eighth on Mickey Hatcher's three-run homer for a 3–0 win and Hershiser's 23rd victory of the season. Hershiser was now closing in on Drysdale's mark, and would surpass him with 59 scoreless innings.

Part Three

TRANSITION
1970–1989

5

NEW GENERATION:
1970–1979

The 1960s period of the rivalry could rely on the momentum from the late 1950s in Brooklyn and New York to keep the fires burning. But as the 1970s dawned, players from that time were mostly retired, requiring the rivalry to rebuild with a new generation of talent.

SEPTEMBER TO REMEMBER (1970–71)

Giants 14, Dodgers 10.

It would have been one of the most memorable games of the rivalry, but the fact that the Giants and Dodgers were playing for second place instead of first on September 23, 1970, robbed the contest of its drama. The Giants, trailing 8–0 after six innings, scored nine times in the seventh. San Francisco held a 10–9 lead in the bottom of the ninth, but the Dodgers managed to score and send the game into extra innings. The Giants scored four in the 10th to put the game away. Each club used 22 players, and the Giants outhit the Dodgers 15 to 14. Dick Dietz's grand slam in the seventh was the game's big blow. The result left the clubs tied for second, 14 games out of first.

The Reds could be blamed for trying to make the rivalry irrelevant. Cincinnati's spectacular 102–60 year in 1970 would turn out to be the Giants and Dodgers biggest concern. In the 1970s, the Big Red Machine would eventually win six division titles, post three 100-plus win seasons and five 90-win years, make four World Series appearances, and win two championships.

The Reds' dominance would have a big impact on the clubs, but the Giants and Dodgers still had one more real battle in 1971 before Cincinnati's run, and the stakes this time would be first place.

The Dodgers had fallen fast since their back-to-back pennants in 1965 and 1966, and even though they were respectable in 1970 with a second-place finish (87–74), they were still 14½ games behind Cincinnati. While the Dodgers continued to possess their traditional speed, leading the league in 1970 with 138 stolen bases, they had a league-low 87 homers. Pitching problems prevented the Giants (80–76) from making a serious run in 1970, as they were tied with Montreal for the worst ERA.

San Francisco looked forward to seeing what manager Charlie Fox could do with the club in a full season. Fox, who took over early in 1970, guided the team to a solid 67–53 mark. The Giants were getting desperate for a title, having come up empty since 1962.

—⁓—

The Giants roared out to an eight-game lead over the second-place Dodgers before the teams' first meeting of the year in mid-May 1971, and entered the series with a 25–9 mark. The Giants remained relentless throughout most of the season, and the Dodgers could only cling to contention. By September 6, the second-place Dodgers trailed the Giants by eight games, and faced the need to sweep their five remaining games with the Giants to have a chance.

The drama began September 6–8 in a three-game series at Los Angeles, and continued in a two-game series September 13–14 in San Francisco.

September 6 (Dodgers 5, Giants 2): The Dodgers were sparked by Steve Garvey's 400-foot, two-run homer, and Maury Wills's more modest 345-footer. It was just Wills's third homer of the season, but his second in two days. Don Sutton struck out 10 in seven innings, and Jim Brewer kept the Giants scoreless over the last two innings.

September 7 (Dodgers 9, Giants 3): Giants starter Ron Bryant lasted just 19 pitches and failed to record an out as the Dodgers took a 4–0 lead in the first and Claude Osteen made it hold up with a five-hit performance. Run-scoring singles by Willie Davis and Dick Allen, an RBI double by Manny Mota, and a sacrifice fly by Wes Parker gave the Dodgers the quick lead. The Giants cut the margin to 4–3 in the fifth, but Garvey drilled a two-run homer off Don McMahon in the sixth to put the Dodgers back in control. The Giants lost for the fourth straight time, and had now dropped five consecutive games to the Dodgers.

September 8 (Dodgers 3, Giants 0): The Giants' frustration at being unable to put away the surging Dodgers culminated in a fiery argument as Los Angeles swept the series, extending its winning streak over San Francisco to six games and moving within five games of the lead with 19 to play. The Dodgers picked up one run in the first on Willie Crawford's RBI single, and two in the third highlighted by Wes Parker's run-scoring triple, and then relied on the dominating pitching of Bill Singer. Singer had a streak of 20 consecutive outs going into the ninth when he walked Ken Henderson and Jim Ray Hart. Brewer, in relief, walked Willie Mays to load the bases, but got Bobby Bonds to ground out to Garvey, who stepped on third, and threw to first to barely get Bonds for a game-ending double play. Bonds slammed his helmet to the ground, and stayed around to argue the call.

September 13 (Dodgers 5, Giants 4): In a wild, bitter game evoking memories of the bat incident of 1965, the red-hot Dodgers built a 5–1 lead, and hung on for a victory that drew them to within two games of the fading Giants. The Giants entered the crucial series having lost seven of their last eight games, while the Dodgers had won six straight, and 11 of the last 13. The victory also marked their seventh straight over the Giants. Home runs by Allen, Crawford, and Willie Davis helped the Dodgers to a 5–1 lead after five innings. The Giants got three back in the seventh on Hart's homer, Dave Kingman's RBI double, and a throwing error that allowed a run to score.

The fireworks were a carry-over from the previous week, when Singer decked Mays with a pitch, and from a July game when Bill Buckner and Juan Marichal nearly came to blows. Singer plunked Mays in the first inning, and Chris Speier in the fourth. In the fifth, Marichal responded with a pitch under Singer's chin. One out later, Buckner was hit on the elbow. Buckner, holding the bat up, walked toward Marichal, as Giants catcher Russ Gibson stepped between them. The dugouts and bullpens emptied, and before order was restored, umpire Shag Crawford, who was working at home plate during the Roseboro-Marichal 1965 confrontation, ejected Marichal and Buckner. Jerry Johnson, a Giants pitcher, then got thrown out after giving the choke sign and yelling at umpire Crawford. Wills joined the list of ejected players in the seventh, when he argued too strenuously that Bonds should be called out for interference in a play at first base.

September 14 (Dodgers 6, Giants 5): Pinch-hitter Mota doubled with the bases loaded in the ninth as the Dodgers rallied for their eighth straight win over San Francisco, pulling them to within one game of the Giants with 14 games to play. The Giants had now seen an eight-game lead nearly disappear within nine days. The loss spoiled a big day for Bonds, who slugged two home runs and drove in four.

The Dodgers saw their momentum halted following the two-game sweep of the Giants as they lost four straight. Neither club could take charge in the remaining two weeks. The race went down to the final day September 30 in a situation reminiscent of the tense curtain-closer in 1962 as the Giants held a one-game lead. The Dodgers did their part, defeating Houston 2–1, but Marichal fired a five-hitter as the Giants defeated San Diego 5–1 to win the West.

The Giants lost their NL championship series to Pittsburgh three games to one after winning the opener. The excitement of the division race boosted attendance at Candlestick Park, as well as at Dodger Stadium. The Giants drew more than a million for the first time since 1967, and the Dodgers reached two million for the first time since 1966.

RESPECT

It is said that some fans in San Francisco didn't warm up right away to No. 24. Maybe there were some unfortunate cultural or social issues at play in those reactions, but if you truly were a fan of the art of baseball, Willie Mays was your masterpiece.

The 1967 season provided the first hint that Mays might be on the decline. Hampered by injuries and illness, Mays hit the fewest home runs (22) since his rookie year of 1951, excluding his 1952 season abbreviated by military service. His average of .263 was the lowest in his career for a full season, and his 92 strikeouts were his highest one-season total. The Dodgers organization might have recognized that Mays was on a downward trend. In the final game of the season between the clubs at Los Angeles, the Dodgers paid special tribute to the 36-year-old Mays. Appreciative fans applauded as the scoreboard message board listed his accomplishments while saying, "We'll always remember that there was never a more exciting player than Willie Mays."

Even in the enemy's park, Mays had earned respect through his power, speed, and defense, combined by an unmatched enthusiasm for the game. With the game on the line, and every play possibly affecting a pennant race, there was no stopping Mays on the bases or in the field. In a high-stakes game at Los Angeles on September 7, 1966, Dodgers fans could only watch in amazement. In the 12th inning, Mays walked and rookie Frank Johnson singled to right field. When right fielder Lou Johnson relayed the ball to infielder Jim Lefebvre, Mays broke for home. Lefebvre's throw and Mays arrived at the same time, but Mays's collision with catcher John Roseboro jarred the ball loose, giving the Giants a 3–2 win. Asked later if the third base coach tried to stop him, Mays laughed. "Man, I wasn't paying attention to him," he said.

It didn't take long for Mays to make his impact on the West Coast rivalry. In a four-game stretch against the Dodgers in early May 1958, Mays carried the Giants to four straight victories with a dominating display. His line: AB 17, R 10, H 12, RBI 15, D 1, T 2, HR 7.

The concern expressed in 1967 about Mays's demise was a bit premature. He came back with a respectable 1968, and even after a clear drop-off in 1969, still posted numbers in 1970 (28 HR, 83 RBIs, .291) that would be the envy of many younger players. But as the Giants and Dodgers gathered for their first meeting of the season in 1971, Mays took time to reflect on the history of the duel between the clubs, noting the importance of the series even though it was still early in the year. "It dates back to the New York–Brooklyn era," Mays said. "The rivalry was intense and genuine and it has carried over into this era. There's so much pride involved. We try as hard against all the other clubs, but somehow, some way, we feel all of the bad breaks, or sloppy games or mistakes—if any—will be forgiven by the fans if we beat the Dodgers."

Those words would have credibility and poignancy in any situation based on Mays's 20 years of experience in Giants-Dodgers battles. But what would make them even more significant is that while he didn't know it at the time, Mays was participating in the rivalry for the final season.

On September 14, 1971, the 40-year-old Mays batted in the ninth with two outs, a runner on second, and the Giants trailing 6–5. The Dodgers' 48-year-old reliever, Hoyt Wilhelm, struck out Mays on a 2–2 pitch. It marked Mays's last appearance in the rivalry. The Giants wouldn't play the Dodgers again until May 22, 1972, 11 days after he was traded to the New York Mets.

RED ALERT (1972–73)

Any leftover excitement from the Giants-Dodgers 1971 pennant race was dulled on April 1 during spring training when the players went on strike over pension and health benefits. The strike would end April 13, resulting in a 155-game season in 1972. The labor strife also might have presented the Giants ownership with a diversion, as it grew desperate to deal for a starting pitcher, and began to quietly realize that the best trade bait might be its aging center fielder, Willie Mays. The Giants pulled the trigger May 11, sending Mays to the New York Mets for pitcher Charlie Williams and $50,000 cash.

The Dodgers made the biggest offseason noise, acquiring Frank Robinson in a six-player deal with Baltimore. The trade came on the same day that the Dodgers said farewell to another power hitter, Dick Allen, who was sent to the Chicago White Sox for two players, including pitcher Tommy John. The addition of John appeared to give the Dodgers one of the league's strongest rotations, including 20-game winner Al Downing, Don Sutton, Claude Osteen, and Bill Singer.

The Giants had much of the same cast returning for 1972 with one notable exception as the Giants made a significant exchange of pitchers, sending Gaylord Perry to Cleveland for left-hander Sam McDowell. Veterans McDowell and Juan Marichal were expected to share the top billing on the otherwise young staff.

An overlooked factor to the Giants' 1971 success was their improved speed and the Dodgers' declining speed. The Giants stole 101 bases in 1971, their most in San Francisco. For the first time on the West Coast, the Dodgers, with 76, had fewer stolen bases than the Giants. More remarkable was that Willie Mays, at age 40, stole 23, more than any other Dodger, and only three fewer than the 25-year-old Bobby Bonds. In his last full season in the rivalry, the amazing Mays had once again found a way to leave his mark.

While the Giants beat out the Dodgers by a game in 1971, it was still difficult to claim bragging rights against their California rivals. The Dodgers won 12 of 18 against the Giants, their best record in the head-to-head series since 1959, and entered the season having won eight straight against San Francisco.

The 1972 season would have little suspense. The Giants stumbled early, and by the time they played their first game against the Dodgers with

Mays no longer on the roster on May 22, they were 10½ games behind first-place Los Angeles and Houston. By the start of July, the Dodgers had slipped seven games behind the Reds.

The Giants had their worst season in San Francisco. It was the farthest they had finished out of first, 26½ games, since they ended up 35 out in 1953 in New York, and the fewest games they had won (69) since coming west. The attendance matched the grim record, with the 647,744 total the lowest in San Francisco, a shocking drop from the 1.1 million in 1971.

One could not fault power hitters Robinson, Willie McCovey, Bonds, or Dave Kingman for not trying to keep the spirit of Mays from remaining part of the rivalry, as each had key moments in Dodgers-Giants games in 1972. Robinson belted two homers in an 8–5 Dodgers win May 23, and also had key homers to help the Dodgers to victories May 29 and May 30. Bonds belted a pivotal three-run homer in a 12–11 win over the Dodgers August 2, made a rare unassisted double play from the outfield May 31, and scored the winning run in the 10th inning September 2 when he came home from second on a groundout. McCovey crashed a grand slam off Sutton on July 2 in a 9–3 Giants win. Kingman had a grand slam in a 9–8 Giants win May 22, and a three-run homer in an 8–5 win over the Dodgers July 1.

Meanwhile, National League champion Cincinnati showed that its drop-off in 1971 was a fluke, as the Reds roared to the 1972 NL West crown.

—⁓—

Pitching was the anchor that brought the Dodgers their early success, and as the 1973 season neared, it was pitching again that appeared ready to return them to the top. The Dodgers, already strong in that department, believed they added the final piece of the puzzle on November 28, 1972, when the club acquired former 20-game winner Andy Messersmith in a seven-player deal that sent Frank Robinson and Singer to the California Angels.

Messersmith got a quick taste of the rivalry August 3 while hurling a three-hit shutout. In the ninth, Messersmith objected to an inside fastball by reliever Elias Sosa. He set off a bench-clearing incident by walking toward the mound before McCovey cut him off. Later, Messersmith observed, "People aren't the best of friends on these ball clubs."

The Giants rocked the Dodgers' pennant drive with a three-game sweep September 3–5. The Giants scored 10 runs in the last three innings in the opener for a come-from-behind 11–8 win. The Dodgers managed only one hit in a 3–1 defeat the next day, and Jim Barr tossed a six-hitter in a 7–0 win in game three.

The Dodgers would improve their record by 10 wins in 1973, finishing 95–66. The Giants would bounce back with a record of 88–74. The improvements weren't enough, however, as Cincinnati rolled to a 99–63 mark. The Dodgers inability to handle powerful Cincinnati (5–9 in 1972, 7–11 in 1973) made the difference.

The Reds gave notice with their 100-victory season in 1970 that the bar had been set high in the NL West. The Reds' success had altered the landscape of the rivalry. In the 1960s, the Giants and Dodgers could look at each other as the team to beat. But from 1970 to 1979, the road to postseason glory required a stop in Cincinnati.

CHANGING OF THE GUARD (1974)

Juan Marichal was in Boston. Willie McCovey was in San Diego. Willie Davis was in Montreal. With three transactions prior to the 1974 season, the last three members of the 1962 Dodgers-Giants pennant race were gone. Another page in the rivalry had been turned.

Marichal, suffering from back problems, began fading in 1972 when he went 6–16, and followed that up with an 11–15 mark last year. After 14 years, 238 victories and six 20-win seasons, the 35-year-old Marichal's Giants career came to an end as he was sold to Boston.

Upon the announcement that McCovey, 35, had been traded with Bernie Williams to San Diego for 24-year-old pitcher Mike Caldwell, manager Charlie Fox said, "McCovey has given the Giants a great many years of great service, but there comes a time when you have to give way to the young people." McCovey, with 413 homers and 1,165 RBIs, wasn't buying it, and thought he had several years left despite his constant knee ailments. The trade, however, didn't surprise him. Said McCovey, "When Willie Mays was traded, I knew I was expendable. Nobody was untouchable."

Willie Davis, 33, a major component of Dodgers teams built around speed and pitching, was traded to Montreal for relief pitcher Mike Marshall. Davis led or was among the Dodgers team leaders in a number of categories over the years such as hits, runs, total bases, doubles, triples, and stolen bases.

The changing of the guard for the Giants was obvious, as they fielded a starting lineup of 20-somethings with the exception of 30-year-old Tito Fuentes. The outfield appeared as solid as any in baseball, with Bobby Bonds—coming off a 39-homer, 96-RBI year—and Garry Maddox and Gary Matthews. The Giants rotation received a big blow when 24-game-winner Ron Bryant suffered a severe laceration to his side in an offseason swimming pool accident, forcing the club to open the year with him on the disabled list.

The Dodgers had been realigning their infield over the last couple seasons, and on June 23, 1973, started for the first time together Steve Garvey at first, Davey Lopes at second, Ron Cey at third, and Bill Russell at shortstop. The Fab Four would take the decision out of filling out a lineup card and remain together for the next eight years.

On May 25, the Dodgers began one of their strongest runs of success over the Giants. Garvey, getting his first shot at being the full-time first baseman, was showing signs of breaking out. He had four hits, including his 11th home run of the season, raising his average to .337 with a league-leading 42 RBIs as the Dodgers won 9–5. Garvey also was warming up to the competition against the Giants in his full-time role, saying after the game, "Everybody on the club gets keyed up. This is some rivalry. You just can't let up no matter how many runs you score. Something always seems to happen."

The Dodgers were keyed up enough to defeat the Giants in 11 of 13 matchups starting with the May 25 game.

The Dodgers outscored the Giants 80–46 over the 13 games, and had a stretch of three consecutive walk-off wins. The Dodgers rallied in the eighth from a three-run deficit June 21, and won it in the 10th on Bill Buckner's home run. Jimmy Wynn homered to tie the score 2–2 in the ninth the next day, and Joe Ferguson delivered the game-ending blast in the 10th. Los Angeles got the sweep as Ken McMullen drove in the winning run with a bases-loaded single in the ninth.

While the Dodgers had long ago helped bury the Giants, Cincinnati was very much alive. On September 12, the final Dodgers-Giants game of the season, Al Downing fired a two-hitter and the Dodgers banged out 15 hits for an 11–0 win and a two-game sweep, yet still couldn't prevent the persistent Reds from gaining ground as they won a doubleheader to get within 3½ games of first. Los Angeles got a break as Cincinnati lost two out of three to San Diego and three out of four to the Giants. The Reds wouldn't go away, however, with successive three-game sweeps over Houston and the Giants. But on October 1, the Dodgers defeated Houston 8–5 while Cincinnati fell to Atlanta 7–1 and the Dodgers ended eight years of frustration by clinching their first title since 1966. The trades that brought Marshall and Wynn helped the Dodgers overcome a serious elbow injury to Tommy John, who was 13–3 at the time. The Dodgers went on to defeat the Pittsburgh Pirates three games to one for the pennant, but lost the World Series to Oakland in five games, as A's pitchers limited Los Angeles to just 11 runs.

After a one-year comeback in 1973, the Giants resorted to their grim 1972 form as they ended up 30 games behind. The Dodgers' 102 victories, the club's most in the regular season since the move west, left them optimistic about a repeat in 1975, but again, it would be Cincinnati that would present a daunting challenge.

Two offseason transactions would draw attention. One was a blockbuster that would involve the Giants swapping Bobby Bonds for the Yankees' Bobby Murcer. The other was done in a much quieter way, yet still was equally startling. On March 15, 1975, a 37-year-old veteran right-hander was signed by the Dodgers as a free agent. Juan Marichal was going to be wearing Dodger blue.

FORGIVENESS

It was as if the Hatfields had invited a McCoy to dinner.

That was the reaction when the Dodgers announced during spring training in 1975 that they had signed Juan Marichal as a free agent. Los Angeles, desperate for a fourth starter because of the injury that shelved Tommy John, hoped that Marichal might still possess some of the skills the club had witnessed throughout the 1960s. Dodgers fans sent angry letters to the newspapers and front office, wondering why the team would accept "the most hated Giant of them all," a title bestowed on him since his bat came in contact with John Roseboro's skull on a summer day in 1965 at Candlestick Park. But somehow, in 1975, it was difficult for Marichal, the Dodgers organization, and even some of the fans to continue the 10-plus years' feud.

Marichal, in the final stage of his career, was ready to forget, saying of Roseboro, "I do not have anything against him. We can be friends right now." And when he walked onto the field at Dodger Stadium, applause was heard among a few boos. Marichal had two bad starts, getting knocked out in the third inning by Cincinnati and in the fourth by Houston.

On April 17, 1975, Marichal ended his comeback bid and retired from baseball. Had he tried one more time, his next start would have been against the Giants. A final tribute to Marichal came from an unlikely source, a Dodgers catcher. "He is one helluva nice guy," Joe Ferguson said. "I hated to see it happen this way. It became a matter of pride to him and he didn't want to push anymore. I only wish I had the privilege to catch him in his prime."

MOUTH THAT ROARED (1975)

The intense rivalry was appearing ready to go on hiatus by the end of 1974, and perhaps for the next few years because of the different directions the clubs appeared to be headed. Such prognostications would have been correct, except for one thing. They overlooked the fact that down in the Giants farm system, a 23-year-old right-hander with a good fastball and a chip on his shoulder about the Dodgers would enter the scene for a memorable game late in 1974 and set off sparks throughout the 1975 season.

On September 3, 1974, the Dodgers were battling Cincinnati in a dramatic fight for first while the Giants sat 24½ games out. Dave Kingman's two-run single in the first gave the Giants the lead, but the Dodgers jumped on a wild Ron Bryant, who failed to retire a batter while giving up four runs, one hit, and three walks. Manager Wes Westrum brought in pitcher John "The Count" Montefusco, who had arrived from the Phoenix farm club only an hour before the game, for his major league debut. Before the day was through, Montefusco had pitched nine innings while giving up just one run in the 9–5 win, slugged a two-run homer, and emphatically declared his dislike for the Dodgers. Montefusco described how sweet the victory was, saying, "I wanted to beat the Dodgers. I hate the Dodgers. I'm from New Jersey and I'd always been a Yankees fan."

The 1974 season went as expected. The Dodgers went to the World Series, and the Giants finished 30 games out. Montefusco seemed to take it all personally. He picked up where he left off in 1975, defeating the Dodgers 3–1 in the first meeting of the clubs. Montefusco was seemingly on his way to another successful outing against the Dodgers nine days later, but was knocked out in a three-run sixth as the Giants fell 7–3. Montefusco blamed tiredness for his sixth inning collapse, saying, "If I hadn't, there was no way these guys were going to beat me. No way. And they knew it, too."

The mouth kept roaring, even trying to stir up some fireworks in a July 4 start against the Dodgers. Montefusco allowed eight hits and struck out 10 in out-dueling Andy Messersmith in a 1–0 victory. Afterward, Montefusco said, "This one was for Ron Cey. He said in the papers that I wasn't a good pitcher and that I wouldn't win 10 games. "Cey later denied making any such comment.

Montefusco provided some tension as well as comic relief in 1975, but it wasn't enough to inspire either team to greatness. Cincinnati, with 108 wins, finished 20 games ahead of the second-place Dodgers and 27½ in front of the Giants. Montefusco's 31 wins his first two full seasons of 1975–76 gave him some credibility, and kept him talking and infuriating the Dodgers. After beating Los Angeles with a 6–3 complete game on July 31, 1976, he said of Dodgers coach Tommy Lasorda, "I wanted to shut them out so I could shut up Lasorda. He's been all over my case. He's been saying I'll never beat them again." The Dodgers were finally growing weary of the talk, and after an intense 1978 game, they took their shots at Montefusco for engaging Reggie Smith in a stare-down while the Dodgers slugger took his time performing his home run trot. "He comes out with these statements like he's God," Dusty Baker said of Montefusco. Added Smith, "It's no secret I don't like the man."

Hampered by injuries which left him with a 7–16 record in 1979 and 1980, the Giants let Montefusco go after the 1980 season. Montefusco's fiery comments about the Dodgers, his bold predictions, and his early success on the mound added some color to the rivalry even when the Giants were stumbling. But his pitching performance never matched the boasts. In contrast, as Montefusco faded away in 1980, another young pitcher was about to make a mark not only on the rivalry, but on all the National League as well. But unlike Montefusco, Fernando Valenzuela would capture baseball's imagination not with his talk, but with his pitching flair and a devastating screwball.

GOING, GOING . . . STAYING! (1976)

Russ Hodges, the great Giants radio play-by-play announcer when they debuted in San Francisco, had his famous call, "You can tell it bye-bye baby!" Duane Kuiper, a member of today's Giants broadcast team, dramatically describes the moment with the words "Outta here!" Giants fans had to listen closely when they heard similar descriptions during several unsteady periods for the San Francisco organization just to make sure the announcers were saying it was the ball, not the team that was leaving the park. While Dodgers fans were told with the comforting voice of broadcast legend Vin Scully to "pull up a chair" and enjoy the game, Giants announcers over the years had to talk about the team pulling up stakes. The rivalry appeared to be on the verge of a breakup for a number of years as the Giants' owners, unhappy about the small crowds and Candlestick, came close to making their own call of "Going, Going, Gone!"

The four years of noncompetitive Giants teams and gloomy attendance totals from 1972–1975 put the California rivalry in jeopardy. Since winning the NL West in 1971, the Giants suffered through three under-.500 years, finishing out of first in the ensuing seasons by 26½, 11, 30, and 27½ games. Since drawing 1.1 million in 1971, attendance fell to just 519,991 in 1974, and 522,925 in 1975.

In January 1976, owner Horace Stoneham sold the club to the Labatts Breweries in Toronto. San Francisco bought some time when a court granted a temporary restraining order to put the move on hold. At the eleventh hour, a deal was made that led to San Francisco businessman Bob Lurie taking over ownership of the club. The Giants would stay in San Francisco, but there were few signs that the franchise was about to turn things around on the field.

The Dodgers finished 1975 with a disappointing, yet respectable 88–74 record, but "respectable" wasn't enough in this era of Cincinnati's "Big Red Machine." The Dodgers, looking for more production from their outfield, dealt away two-thirds of it, sending Jimmy Wynn to Atlanta in a five-player trade that brought Dusty Baker to Los Angeles, and trading Willie Crawford to St. Louis for infielder Ted Sizemore. The outfield opening led to a significant midseason deal that brought Reggie Smith to Los Angeles. The club would lose front-line pitcher Andy Messersmith, who had won 53 games in three years, as he became one of major league baseball's first free agents.

The Giants entered the season with mostly the same crew, although eventually half the regular lineup would change. A familiar face was at the helm for the Giants, as Bill Rigney, who managed the club from 1956 until his midseason departure in 1960, was brought back as the skipper.

The Giants may have been coming off two losing seasons and a narrow escape from seeing the franchise move to Toronto, but the optimism that is opening day brought out a big crowd April 9 and big talk as San Francisco's new ownership enjoyed its first victory. The crowd of 37,261, though limited by a municipal labor strike that saw picket lines outside the stadium, was the largest for a Candlestick Park opener since 40,960 showed up in 1966. Baker, in his Dodgers debut, homered in his first at-bat. The Giants came back to take the opener 4–2, and followed that up with 6–4 victory for a two-game series sweep.

The impossible dream of the Giants going from the brink of leaving town to a contender had turned into a nightmare by the time the clubs met for the next time on May 31. The Giants opened the four-game series with their third straight win over the Dodgers, breaking up a 1–1 game with a six-run 12th inning. However, the Giants had already collapsed while the Dodgers were in the thick of the division fight. The teams split the series, leaving the Dodgers tied with Cincinnati while the Giants were in fifth, 11½ behind.

The Dodgers would go on to a strong 92–70 season, but it again wasn't enough to overcome Cincinnati, which finished 102–60. The Giants and Dodgers would play a late September three-game series in San Francisco. In the final game of that series September 23, a 4–1 Dodgers victory behind Burt Hooton's three-hitter, only 3,149 witnessed the contest.

Lurie saved the Giants for the city, but the fans, accustomed to a string of mediocre teams, weren't ready to reward him yet as attendance inched up slightly to a still poor 626,868. There was little indication that a turnaround was imminent, though interest would pick up in 1977 thanks to the return of Giants fan favorite Willie McCovey.

BIG BLUE MACHINE (1977)

If it wasn't for umpire Ziggy Sears, Walter Emmons Alston never would have gotten an at-bat in a major league game. The 24-year-old Alston, on the roster of the 1936 St. Louis Cardinals, was summoned to replace

Johnny Mize after the first baseman was ejected for arguing with Sears. Alston struck out in his lone trip to the plate, and never got another big league at-bat.

Alston's time would come though, beginning November 11, 1953, when Walter O'Malley hired him to manage the Dodgers with one mission: Beat the Yankees in the World Series. Alston was already successful as a minor league manager with pennants in 1949, 1951, and 1952. It would take Alston only one year to accomplish the mission, as he guided the Dodgers past the Yankees for the 1955 championship. O'Malley saw the future pretty clearly when he hired Alston, saying, "I like to think you will be the man for a great many years."

On September 27, 1976, the reserved, professorial Alston announced he was stepping down after 23 years. In his place, the Dodgers chose the flamboyant Tommy Lasorda. It was like replacing a string quartet with the Rolling Stones. The music still was great, but louder and more unpredictable. It wouldn't take long for Lasorda to start himself up as he took the reins in 1977.

—⁓—

While the Dodgers were making their first managerial change since arriving on the West Coast, the Giants were making their eighth with the hiring of Joe Altobelli. Altobelli appeared to have the tougher challenge, as the Giants were overhauling their lineup after a third straight losing season while the Dodgers were mostly standing pat.

Shortstop Chris Speier was the only position player from the Giants' 1976 opening day lineup to start in the 1977 opener, and he would be traded to Montreal by the end of April. There was one familiar face, though, as 39-year-old Willie McCovey returned after a three-year absence, having spent most of the time away with San Diego and a short period with Oakland. Bobby Murcer was gone after only two years, traded to the Chicago Cubs in a five-player deal for third baseman Bill Madlock, the National League batting champion.

The Dodgers boasted a powerful rotation in 21-game winner Don Sutton, Doug Rau, Rick Rhoden, Tommy John, and Burt Hooton, with Charlie Hough in the bullpen. The club felt its hopes of overtaking Cincinnati, which won the pennant the last two years with 210 victories, was to get more punch in the lineup. While the Los Angeles team ERA in 1976 was 3.02 to Cincinnati's 3.51, the Reds topped the Dodgers in batting average by .280 to .251 and in home runs by 141 to 91. In a four-player deal designed to add power to the lineup, the Dodgers sent Bill Buckner (7 HR) to the Chicago Cubs for Rick Monday (32 HR). The Dodgers also signed 35-year-old slugger Boog Powell in a bid to strengthen their bench.

The Giants appeared desperate, as seen in their sudden excitement for spring training phenom Randy Elliott, a 25-year-old who had played just 27 major league games. Elliott's .547 average and 16 RBIs in the spring put him on the roster, but he would have no impact, playing in only 73 games. The real surprise would come in the performance of a former rookie phenom, as McCovey would stage a memorable comeback in 1977. The only surprise for the confident Dodgers would be if they didn't challenge and surpass Cincinnati, as their new skipper prepared to roll out his Big Blue Machine.

—◊◊◊—

Steve Garvey assured that the Lasorda era would get off to a successful start with a bases-loaded, two-run single in the seventh to help the Dodgers to a 5–1 opening day victory over the Giants on April 7 in Los Angeles. The clubs would meet six times in the first two weeks of the season, and the Dodgers already had the machine humming. After taking two of three at home, the Dodgers swept an April 15–17 series in San Francisco to extend their winning streak at Candlestick Park to eight games dating back to August 1, 1976. The Dodgers, having won five straight games and off to a 7–2 start, were in first place with a two-game lead, while the Giants had fallen four games back. The good start had Lasorda's enthusiasm running high, a fact noted by Garvey, who joked after the game, "Have you ever seen him at a loss for words? We're going to have to give him something to calm him down."

By the start of July, the Dodgers had taken command, and entered a four-game series in San Francisco with a 50–26 record. The Giants felt the Dodgers' furious charge, as Los Angeles outscored them 34–15 for a sweep of the July 1–4 matchup.

July 1 (Dodgers 10, Giants 5): The Dodgers battered four Giants pitchers for 17 hits. Ron Cey hit a two-run homer, Steve Yeager drove in a pair with a triple, and Garvey's two-run homer capped a three-run ninth to lock up the win.

July 2 (Dodgers 10, Giants 3): The Dodgers scored an early knockout with three runs each in the first and second innings to take a 6–0 lead and Hooton went the distance. Garvey drilled a three-run homer in the first, and in the second, Bill Russell drove in two with a triple.

July 3 (Dodgers 10, Giants 7): Cey led an 18-hit Dodgers' attack with a 5-for-5 day, including two doubles and four RBIs. The Dodgers had four-run outbursts in the first and sixth to take a 10–2 lead.

July 4 (Dodgers 4, Giants 0): Sutton tossed a three-hitter, as the Dodgers scored their runs on solo homers by Johnny Oates and Monday, and on two RBI singles by Cey, who went 11-for-17 in the series.

The Dodgers had never been as dominant over the Giants in their 20 years of the West Coast rivalry. The sweep improved the Dodgers' record against the Giants this year to 9–1, and extended their winning streak at Candlestick Park to 12. The Dodgers raised their record to 54–26 to lead Cincinnati by 10½ games. The Giants were now 20 games back in fourth place.

The Dodgers continued to bully the Giants in a mid-August series, taking two of three as Sutton rubbed sand in their face with a near no-hitter. Sutton's bid was ruined by Marc Hill's sharp single to left field with two outs in the eighth inning as the Dodgers coasted to a 7–0 win.

The Dodgers, refusing to give ground with an 11–6 record in September heading into a September 20–21 series in San Francisco, clinched the division crown on enemy turf in a 3–1 win behind the pitching of John. The victory marked the Dodgers' 13th straight win at Candlestick Park. The Giants, who entered the series 22½ games out, finally ended the Dodgers' Candlestick dominance with a 5–4 win the next day.

———

The Dodgers, with a chance for their third 100-win year in Los Angeles if they could sweep the final four-game series with Houston, won two-out-of-four for a 98-victory season and 10-game margin over Cincinnati. The Dodgers defeated Philadelphia in the NL championship series in four games, winning the final three after dropping the opener. In the World Series, the Dodgers battled the Reggie Jackson-led New York Yankees, but after a big 10–4 victory in Game Five to stay alive, they fell victim to Jackson's memorable three home-run barrage in Game Six.

Los Angeles had the lowest ERA in the league at 3.22. While the Dodgers' pitching success was not a surprise, their power output was shocking. They hit a league-leading 191 home runs, 100 more than in 1976. Garvey (33), Reggie Smith (32), Dusty Baker (30), and Cey (30) set a record for a team by hitting 30 or more homers.

Although the Giants experienced their fourth straight losing season, 1977 turned into a feel-good year because of the successful return of McCovey. The veteran slugger led the team in homers (28) and RBIs (86), and more remarkably, played in 141 games. Still, the Giants appeared to be going the opposite direction of the powerful Dodgers. But spurred on by a blockbuster spring training trade that would bring Vida Blue to the pitching staff, San Francisco would reignite the rivalry and their fans in 1978.

Meanwhile, the Dodgers' winning teams of the 1970s had quietly chopped away at the Giants' lead in the overall games played between the clubs since moving to California. The Dodgers had 14 wins against the Giants, the most they compiled against their rivals in one season since 1959. The Dodgers, who once were 29 games down in the head-to-head competition at one point, had closed the gap to seven games.

RENEWAL OF HOSTILITIES (1978)

It might be easier to do the tango solo than it is to have a rivalry where one of the teams is so far out of step. As the 1978 season approached, the rivalry was out of synch, mainly because the stumbling Giants couldn't keep up with the graceful performance of the Dodgers.

The Giants achieved a winning record (88–74 in 1973) just once since capturing the division crown in 1971. During that same six-year period, the Dodgers reached the World Series twice, and finished second three times. Last year's powerful Dodgers' team, under first-year manager Tommy Lasorda, took the suspense out of the pennant race early, winning 22 of its first 26 games. Meanwhile, the Giants dropped 15 of their first 26. The experts didn't give the Giants much hope this year, seeing Cincinnati and Houston as the Dodgers' main threats. The Dodgers would do their part again as expected, but they would run into a year of revival in San Francisco, as the surprising Giants renewed the hostilities.

A sign that this might not be another uneventful season for the Giants came on March 15 when they sent seven players and $300,000 to the Oakland Athletics to acquire pitcher Vida Blue. A less-sensational deal, though it would prove highly beneficial, was made about two weeks earlier when the Giants traded for San Diego first baseman Mike Ivie.

The Giants would not only compete, but also hold onto first place for nearly three months from mid-May to mid-August. While the Dodgers would move on to greater glory with a second-straight pennant, the Giants' turnaround, which more than doubled Candlestick Park attendance to 1,740,477, had pumped some life back into the rivalry.

Enthusiasm was high at both ballparks as the season got under way.

The Dodgers took a hard-fought two out of three in Los Angeles in the clubs' first series of the year May 19–21, leaving the Dodgers and Cincinnati a half-game behind San Francisco. The series drew 153,113.

The Giants took the opener 10–7 as Darrell Evans hit two homers and Bill Madlock belted a homer and drove in four to overcome a two-home run, six-RBI performance by Rick Monday. The Dodgers scored the winning run in the ninth in a 3–2 victory the next day on a controversial call. Randy Moffitt's pitch to Bill Russell with the bases loaded was ruled to have hit the batter's hand. Giants manager Joe Altobelli argued vehemently with umpire Joe West that the ball hit the bat. The Dodgers took the final game 4–1.

When the teams resumed play five days later on May 26 in San Francisco, Willie McCovey drove in five runs as the Giants won 6–1 for their fourth straight, giving them a 1½-game lead. The Giants also were turning Candlestick Park to their advantage, winning their 11th straight home game before a stadium record attendance for a night game of 43,646. The Dodgers came back the next day for a 3–1 win in front of 45,865, the largest ever Candlestick Park Saturday crowd.

The boisterous, record weekend crowds and a close division race had lit a fire under Giants fans, as San Francisco won a thriller on May 28 before 56,103. It was the largest ever baseball crowd at Candlestick Park. One of the Giants' most dramatic moments of the season came in the sixth, with the Dodgers leading 3–0. Terry Whitfield doubled, and Darrell Evans drove him home with a single. Jack Clark and Larry Herndon singled to load the bases, and pinch-hitter Ivie electrified the stadium with a grand slam off Don Sutton. The Dodgers came back in the seventh to tie it on Reggie Smith's two-run homer. In the bottom of the seventh, Evans drove in Whitfield with what would be the winning run with a single in a 6–5 Giants victory.

The Giants kept their momentum going, setting up a duel in which the clubs would play a home-and-away four-game series against one another in 11 days between August 3–13. The Giants, who entered the first series in first, a half-game ahead of Cincinnati and 2½ in front of the Dodgers, took the first two contests at Candlestick Park. The Dodgers relied on strong pitching in the next two games for a series split. Cincinnati took advantage of the draw to slip ahead of the Giants by .002.

The Dodgers put the pressure back on the Giants when they met four days later, winning 12–2 August 10 with a 16-hit attack, and 4–3 the next day on a bases-loaded walk to Billy North in the ninth inning. Madlock broke up a 2–2 tie in the sixth in the third game of the series with a home run off Tommy John, and Bob Knepper threw a seven-hitter to give the Giants a 3–2 win.

The clubs engaged in a classic battle in the series finale August 13. Clark's broken-bat single drove in the winning run in the 11th inning as the Giants earned a series split, leaving them with the one-game lead they held when they arrived in Los Angeles. Smith homered in the first to put the Dodgers in front, but the Giants scored four in the second on Jim Dwyer's two-run double and run-scoring singles by Clark and McCovey. Lee Lacy cut the lead to 4–3 in the fourth with a two-run homer, and Smith homered again in the fifth to make it 4–4. The Giants took a 6–4 lead in the 10th on Marc Hill's two-run, bases-loaded single, but the Dodgers tied it in their half of the inning on a run-scoring double play and Davey Lopes's bad-hop RBI single. In the 11th, Herndon doubled, setting up Clark's game-deciding base hit off Charlie Hough. The Giants' confidence was high following the 7–6 victory. Said Clark: "This was a big series to prove to the Dodgers and the rest of the league that we're for real."

The fans believed the rivalry was real. The four games in San Francisco drew 193,954, and the four in Los Angeles attracted 207,570.

The Giants' stretch run turned them more into an imitation contender while the fast-finishing Dodgers established themselves as the real deal. The Dodgers hurt the Giants chances by winning all four of the head-to-head games with San Francisco in September.

Los Angeles owed its NL West title to an astounding 30–10 record from August 5 through September 16. The Giants were eliminated September 23, and the Dodgers clinched the division the next day. The Dodgers, with an offense that led the league with 149 homers, and a pitching staff that finished first with a 3.12 ERA, defeated Philadelphia in five games in the NL championship series. The Dodgers downed the New York Yankees in the first two games of the World Series, but a pitching collapse led to them dropping four straight.

The Giants' poor play in the stretch allowed Cincinnati to pass them in the closing weeks, and ruin their chance for a second-place finish.

BRAGGING RIGHTS (1979)

With one exception, Dodger blue had ruled Giants' orange and black in the colorful 20 years on the West Coast.

Entering the 1979 season, the Dodgers had been more successful than the Giants since the clubs arrived in California with three World Series championships to San Francisco's none. Now, one more piece of business remained: They had never been able to overtake their rivals in head-to-head competition since dropping the West Coast opener. The teams were even at 2–2 after their first four games against one another in 1958. On April 19, the Giants took a 3–2 head-to-head lead against the Dodgers that they would not relinquish. The Giants went 16–6 against the Dodgers in 1958, but Los Angeles roared back in their first championship season in 1959 to go 14–8 against San Francisco. The Giants lost only one season series to the Dodgers from 1960 to 1970. The Giants began letting their edge slip away in the five years preceding 1979, as Los Angeles won 55 of 90 between the clubs from 1974 to 1978.

Dusty Baker took charge of the Dodgers' quest to take over bragging rights in 1979, as his team trailed by only two games in the overall series record with the Giants at the start of three-game series in Los Angeles in May. On May 29, Baker singled home the winning run in a 6–5 victory to pull the Dodgers within one. On May 30, the Dodgers turned a late 5–4 deficit into another 6–5 win on Davey Lopes's homer in the seventh and Baker's run-scoring double in the eighth to square the overall series at 201–201. On May 31, the Dodgers built an 11–4 lead after six, and held on for a 12–10 victory.

The Giants, after holding on to the series lead for 22 years and 395 games, finally let it slip away and now the Dodgers held the series edge, 202-201.

—⁓—

The Giants and Dodgers had reason to believe that 1979 would be a promising year.

The Giants, after four losing seasons, came back to life in 1978 to make a run for the NL West flag. The club would return much of the same lineup, most notably offensive threats Jack Clark, Darrell Evans, and Bill Madlock, and pitchers Vida Blue, Bob Knepper, and John Montefusco.

The Dodgers appeared to be firing on all cylinders as the season opened, and a third consecutive NL West title didn't seem to be out of reach.

On paper, a potential Dodgers-Giants pennant race seemed quite likely, but on the field, injuries and some disappointing performances plagued both clubs. The Dodgers' 79 victories in 1979 were the lowest by the club since 1968, and marked the first time since 1972 that the team didn't finish at least as high as second. The Giants' revival year of 1978 seemed like a distant memory, as the team won only 71 games, its lowest total since moving to San Francisco with the exception of the strike-shortened season of 1972.

The matchups between the teams were highlighted by a pursuit of Dodgers milestones by pitchers Don Sutton and Rick Sutcliffe. Sutton picked up his 2,487 strikeout in an 8–1 win over the Giants on August 5 to surpass Don Drysdale for the club's No. 1 spot. Sutton tossed his 50th shutout August 10 against the Giants, moving ahead of Drysdale in that category. In 1949, 23-year-old Dodgers rookie Don Newcombe compiled a 17–6 record. Now, 30 years later, the 23-year-old right-hander Sutcliffe moved to within one win of Newcombe's total as he won a 7–2 decision against the Giants. One week later, Sutcliffe tied Newcombe's mark during an 11–2 Dodgers' romp over the Giants.

The 1970s had been rough on the Giants, save for 1971's NL West title. Over the other nine years, the Giants' highest finish was third, and included six seasons in which they were under .500. The year 1979 might have been difficult for the Dodgers, but the 1970s were successful, with three World Series appearances. They had five second-place finishes and two thirds, and won 90-plus games five times. Only the phenomenal Cincinnati Reds and their remarkable run prevented the Dodgers from being the NL team of the decade.

6

HIGHS AND LOWS: 1980–1989

The ebb and flow of baseball was on display in the 1980s. The Dodgers and Giants experienced misery and magnificence. Both teams had shining triumphs and suffered dark defeats. It was a decade highlighted by Fernando-mania, a famous Dodgers-killing homer, a near riot, and the return of the Giants to the World Series after a 27-year drought.

STRETCH

If the Dodgers needed testimony to prove that Willie McCovey was an offensive threat, their first move could have been to subpoena Robin Roberts as an expert witness. The Hall of Fame hurler won 286 games and posted a 3.41 ERA in his 19-year career which featured six seasons of 20 wins or more. Just 29 days before the Dodgers would see the lanky slugger known as "Stretch," McCovey would make the veteran Philadelphia right-hander look like a September call-up as he went four for four in his major league debut on July 30, 1959.

McCovey became an immediate factor in the Giants-Dodgers early West Coast duels, doubling in a run in the first inning off Don Drysdale in his first game against Los Angeles on August 28, 1959. Through the next 21 years, with the exception of his stint with San Diego and Oakland, the feared left-handed batter would become one of the rivalry's top names. The memorable moments ranged from his pinch-hit three-run homer off Drysdale on August 11, 1962, to give the Giants a 5–4 win in the heat of that year's dramatic pennant race to his five-RBI day against Los Angeles on May 26, 1978, that helped the Giants increase their first-place lead. It would all come to an end for McCovey on July 6, 1980, against the Dodgers as he retired from the game in midseason, and appropriately, he would contribute to a San Francisco victory in his last plate appearance.

Nostalgia took over for the day at Dodger Stadium as retired baseball legends gathered for an old-timers game. Among the greats on hand were Willie Mays, Duke Snider, Joe DiMaggio, Hank Aaron, Bobby Bonds, Lou Brock, Maury Wills, and fittingly, Drysdale, a favorite McCovey victim. In 128 at-bats against Drysdale, McCovey had 43 hits, 12 home runs and 31 RBIs. McCovey's goodbye came in the eighth with the game tied 3–3. With one out, Jack Clark walked and Rich Murray singled him to third. Rick Sutcliffe was brought in to relieve Jerry Reuss, and McCovey was called up to pinch-hit, prompting a standing ovation from the crowd of 46,244. On a 1–1 count, McCovey lifted a sacrifice fly to center field to bring home Clark with the go-ahead run. The Giants eventually won 7–4 in 10 innings. McCovey attributed the warm ovation from Dodgers fans to his place in the history of the two clubs, saying, "I'm the last link to the heated rivalry that used to be. I'm one of the few that remembers those great games of the 1960s."

DOMINANCE (1980)

The problem with reflecting on the "good old days" is that it probably means the current days aren't going too well. Willie McCovey represented the "good old days" for Giants fans, and while his exit in 1980 provided sweet memories, it also was a bitter reminder of how the Giants had fallen from those consistently competitive seasons in the 1960s.

The Giants were coming off another grim year. The team's ERA of 4.16 in 1979 tied them for 10th in the National League, and the batting average of .246 ranked them 11th. The Giants finished under .500 for five of the last six years, making it clear that manager Dave Bristol, who got the job at the end of 1979, faced a challenge. Instead of a roster shake-up, however, the Giants would return with largely the same lineup in 1980.

The Giants felt they had assembled a run-producing outfield in Jack Clark, Larry Herndon, and Billy North. North also gave the Giants a top running threat. His 58 stolen bases were a San Francisco record, eclipsing the 48 by Bobby Bonds in 1970. Darrell Evans, now settled in at third base, gave the Giants needed power.

The Dodgers shook things up after their disappointing 1979 season. The roster included four rookies and three free agents. The Dodgers in 1979 were known more for power than pitching, a sharp contrast to the club's traditions. The Dodgers led the league in home runs for the third straight year with 183. The team ERA of 3.83, however, was seventh in the league. The Dodgers' reliable infield returned after flexing its muscles last season as Steve Garvey, Davey Lopes, and Ron Cey each hit 28 home runs. The club appeared loaded with potential starting pitchers, including the top three of Don Sutton, Burt Hooton, and Jerry Reuss.

As both teams looked for an improved year, a labor showdown was brewing. A strike was called on April 1, canceling the remaining exhibition games, with an agreement to open the season while setting a new strike deadline of May 22. The season went on uninterrupted, but the dispute would not go away, and eventually led to a midseason shutdown in 1981.

—⁓—

The Giants were amid their own shutdown when it came to facing the Dodgers. Los Angeles won the first seven contests between the clubs in 1980, giving the Dodgers 49 victories in their last 64 games against San Francisco dating back to the end of the 1976 season. The Dodgers added an exclamation point to that shocking run as win no. 49 came on a Reuss no-hitter.

The Dodgers outscored the Giants 32–8 in the seven victories, including two shutouts by Dave Goltz, and one each by Reuss and Sutton. The Giants' frustration at being dominated by the Dodgers was never clearer than in a 6–0 loss April 22 as Sutton and Garvey ganged up on San Francisco. Sutton tossed a four-hitter, and Garvey drove in four runs with a homer, single, and sacrifice fly. Bristol, upset with the team's focus after players twice lost track of outs, held a closed-door meeting. Hitting coach Jim Lefebvre pondered why his club couldn't handle Los Angeles, saying, "Right now, the Dodgers have to figure all they have to do is throw their gloves out there to beat the Giants, and that's going to be their attitude until we change it."

The Giants' season had been rendered meaningless in 1980 save for one last chance to disrupt a final push by Los Angeles for the NL West title. The stakes were high, at least for the Dodgers, as the clubs met in their final series of the season September 30–October 2 in San Francisco. Los Angeles trailed first-place Houston by two games with six to play, with those teams scheduled to meet in the season windup after this series.

September 30 (Dodgers 6, Giants 3): The Giants led 3–1 going into the ninth, but the Dodgers tied it on run-scoring singles by Pedro Guerrero and Garvey. In the 10th, with runners at first and third, Guerrero homered to deep right-center field on a 2–2 pitch off Gary Lavelle. Fernando Valenzeula got the win, pitching two scoreless innings while striking out four. The Dodgers remained two back as Houston also won.

October 1 (Dodgers 8, Giants 4): The Dodgers jumped on the Giants to take an 8–1 lead in the fifth sparked by the bat of Joe Ferguson, but remained two games behind victorious Houston as time was running out on their division title hopes. Ferguson had six RBIs, a triple, and home run.

October 2 (Giants 3, Dodgers 2): Vida Blue spotted the Dodgers a 2–0 lead in the first on Garvey's two-run homer, but then pitched scoreless ball into the eighth. The Giants scratched out a run in the fifth on Blue's sacrifice fly to make it 2–1. In the eighth, with the bases loaded and two outs, Evans drove in a pair with a bloop single. Greg Minton and Al Holland shut the Dodgers out over the last 1⅔ innings. A victory by

Houston pushed the Dodgers three games down with three games left against the Astros, an uphill fight that the Giants appeared to relish. Said Holland, "This sure makes it tough on them now. They can just about kiss it goodbye, can't they?"

—⁓—

Holland seemed certain to have some good pitching years ahead of him, having led the Giants with 1.75 ERA for the year, but his days as a baseball analyst appeared to be in jeopardy. Holland's prediction that the Dodgers were out of it was clearly premature, as Los Angeles pulled off one of its most dramatic clutch efforts with a season-ending sweep of Houston to gain a regular season tie. However, the Dodgers' determined run ended in the one-game playoff to decide the division champion, as Houston triumphed 7–1 behind the six-hit pitching of Joe Niekro.

The Giants finished out their season quietly, dropping two of three to San Diego. The fan excitement they regained in their comeback 1978 season was diminishing, as attendance fell from 1.7 million that year to 1.4 million in 1979 and 1 million this year. Making matters worse, the Giants dropped 13 of 18 games to the Dodgers in 1980, six by shutouts. In the last four years, the Dodgers had a 52–20 mark against their rivals.

FERNANDO-MANIA

In 1980, the league—and the Giants—got a brief sample of the Dodgers' 19-year-old Fernando Valenzuela, as he went scoreless in 17⅔ innings of relief in 10 appearances after his late season call-up. The Giants got their first look at him on September 24 when he combined with two other relievers for 5⅔ innings of shutout ball to give the Dodgers a 5–4 victory. Six days later, Valenzuela got the win in relief against the Giants with two scoreless innings. Those performances were just a tease. In 1981, Valenzuela would become a big enough positive story for baseball to even help balance the negative consequences of a dark summer when a strike would jolt the game.

The Giants had the distinction of scoring the first run against Valenzuela on April 14, 1981. Valenzuela, who shut out Houston in his first game of the year, blanked the Giants through seven innings. In the eighth, Larry Herndon doubled and Enos Cabell singled him home, ending Valenzuela's scoreless streak that began last season at 33 innings. Valenzuela went the distance, allowing four hits and striking out 10 in a 7–1 victory.

The Giants also were there for the ending nine years later in San Francisco on September 30, 1990. The Giants rocked him in that game for eight runs and seven hits in four innings in what would turn out to be his final game with the Dodgers.

In between the early awe of his talent and the eventual sadness of seeing his decline, Valenzuela enlivened the rivalry because of his colorful approach, character, and competitiveness.

The Giants had some success against Valenzuela, preventing him from winning 20 games in two attempts in late 1982 as they rallied for two victories on September 25 and October 3, the latter being the famous Joe Morgan home run game. Often, the challenge of facing Valenzuela brought out the best in Giants pitchers. Mark Davis, a 22-year-old left-hander, got his first major league complete game in an 8–0 win over the Dodgers on July 30, 1983, and then came back six weeks later to stop Valenzuela and the Dodgers 1–0. Mike Krukow out-dueled Valenzuela for a 2–1 victory April 23, 1985, striking out 10. Dave Dravecky was up to the challenge on August 15, 1987, blanking the Dodgers 5–0 as the Giants offense got to Valenzuela early. Dravecky nearly repeated the performance April 4, 1988, throwing a three-hitter in a 5–1 win over Valenzuela. Mike LaCoss topped Valenzuela 3–1 on April 16, 1990, with a five-hitter.

While the Giants might have gotten the best of Valenzuela on some occasions, he also had his share of dominating moments. Valenzuela got his first shutout against the Giants, 5–0, on April 27, 1981, and even supplied some offense with three hits and an RBI. He tossed a two-hit shutout in a 5–0 win May 28, 1983, to stop a seven-game losing streak to the Giants at Dodger Stadium. Valenzuela often needed little support to win, as evident by his 1–0 gems against the Giants on April 30, 1984, and April 13, 1985. The Giants battled Valenzuela on September 27, 1986, thwarting his bid for his 21st victory of the season. Valenzuela came back seven days later to get No. 21 in a five-hit, 2–1 performance over the Giants.

Valenzuela also was a major factor in getting the Dodgers into the post-season in 1981 (13–7, 2.48), 1983 (15–10, 3.75) and 1985 (17–10, 2.45).

By mid-1988, the Dodgers had growing concerns about Valenzuela, with some wondering if his 255-inning per year average was catching up to him. The Giants experienced the possible overworking of Valenzuela in a game against the Dodgers on April 23, 1986, when he went the distance in a 6–4 victory while throwing 163 pitches. Valenzuela went on the disabled list for a time in 1988, and finished the season with a 5–8 record. Valenzuela had his second straight losing season in 1989, going 10–13. His ERA climbed to 4.59 the next year, and as spring training got under way in 1991, his future was uncertain.

Manager Tommy Lasorda, speaking candidly amid spring training rumors that the club was trying to trade Valenzuela, said, "In no way is Fernando a lock to make this team." On March 28, the Dodgers declared that Fernando-mania was officially over as he was given his release. Valenzuela, 30, was 23–26 with a 4.02 ERA over the last two years, and injuries had chipped away at his effectiveness. But to his many admirers, the reality that he might now be a tired-armed pitcher was quickly dismissed. Instead fans looked back at his 141–116 career record, his eight straight victories in his major league debut in 1981, his six all-star nods, his quirky one-of-a-kind delivery and perhaps most of all, his dramatic rise from being the youngest of 12 kids in a town in Mexico to becoming one of the game's most popular players. The Dodgers would find another arm, they always did, but they could never find another Fernando.

DIVIDED THEY STAND (1981)

The intriguing stories that shaped up for 1981—such as the historic debut of Giants manager Frank Robinson—were on the back burner as the season opened under the threat of a strike. A strike date of May 29 was set early in spring training. The strike date would be extended, but a settlement could not be reached, resulting in a two-month shutdown from June 12 until August 10.

Robinson, the National League's first black manager, inherited a team in disarray, as the Giants were coming off two dreadful years in which they won only 146 games. The Giants were ready for a shake-up. Starters John Montefusco and Bob Knepper were traded away. Doyle Alexander of Atlanta was added to the rotation. Enos Cabell came over from Houston to take over first base. Terry Whitfield and Mike Ivie were gone and Jeffrey Leonard and Jerry Martin were acquired in trades to shore up the outfield. On February 9, the Giants took a chance by signing 37-year-old free agent second baseman Joe Morgan, figuring that his veteran leadership might help.

The Giants hoped that the new bats would add needed support to their only two threats—Jack Clark and Darrell Evans. The Giants offense was sorely lacking in 1980: Their 80 homers were a San Francisco low and the fewest in Giants history since 1926. Their 573 runs were the fewest since the club came west, and their .244 average was last in the league.

The Dodgers lost veteran starter Don Sutton to free agency, but the routinely pitching-rich club still appeared strong with a rotation of the big three in Jerry Reuss, Burt Hooton, and Bob Welch, along with Fernando Valenzuela.

The Dodgers' coming season would be remembered for a variety of things, including the strike, Fernando-mania and a stellar postseason. But it would also go down in club history as the year when the inseparable infield of Steve Garvey, Davey Lopes, Ron Cey, and Bill Russell played their last game together. On February 8, 1982, Lopes would be traded to the Oakland A's, as the Fab Four, which had been together since 1973, began its breakup.

A shutdown was looming as the clubs met in late April. The Dodgers swept a three-game series in San Francisco, but the Giants bounced back with a pair of victories in a three-game set in Los Angeles. The Dodgers now held a three-game lead over Cincinnati, with the Giants in fourth, six games back. The April 29 game would be the last in the first half between the teams.

The dispute over what compensation a team should get when it loses a free agent in the reentry draft led to the strike, effective with the games of June 12. The strike was settled almost two months later, with play scheduled to resume August 10. Major league baseball decided to split the season, giving the first half NL West title to Los Angeles, whose 36–21 record put them a half-game ahead of second place-Cincinnati. The Giants, at 27–32, finished 10 games back in fifth place. The new season would mean a second chance for the Giants after their uninspiring first half.

As the Giants and Dodgers gathered September 7 to meet for the first time since the shutdown, San Francisco, at 16–10, was in second, trailing first-place Houston by 1½ games. Los Angeles and Atlanta were two games back. The Dodgers put a damper on the Giants' second-half title quest with 5–1 and 4–0 wins in the first two games of the series. Cey slugged a two-run homer in a three-run third inning in game one. Hooton, Alejandro Pena, and Dave Stewart combined for a three-hit shutout the next day, as Cey and Dusty Baker drilled two-run homers. The Giants avoided a sweep with an 11-inning, 6–3 victory.

The Giants, playing rare meaningful games in September thanks to the split season, had their sights set on a sweep as they met the Dodgers for a three-game series two weeks later. The Giants had dropped a devastating five of six games against first-place Houston since the last Dodgers series. As of September 22, the Giants were in fourth, 4½ games behind the Astros with 13 games to play. The Giants took the first game 5–2, getting a big break when Larry Herndon's line drive to right field got under Rick Monday's glove, resulting in a two-run inside-the-park home run. Fred Breining's three scoreless innings of relief helped the Giants to an 8–4 win in the second game. The Dodgers erupted with a 15-hit attack for a 7–3 win in game three, leaving the Giants 4½ games behind Houston with 10 to play.

The Giants won their next four to stay in contention, but then dropped two in a row, and Houston, refusing to give way, eliminated San Francisco on October 1. The Giants' 29–23 second half gave them an overall 56–55 record, only the second time since 1973 that they had a winning mark.

The big question facing the Dodgers in the postseason would be whether they could regain their prestrike momentum. In the second half, with a postseason already secured, the Dodgers were just 27–26. The Dodgers started out flat in their best-of-five division series against second-half winner Houston, losing the first two games while scoring just one run. The Dodgers bounced back with remarkable pitching, winning the next three while allowing the Astros only two runs in 27 innings. Pitching was the difference in the best-of-five league championship series, as the Dodgers won in five games while allowing Montreal only 10 runs and compiling a team ERA of 1.84. In the World Series against New York, the Dodgers overcame a 2–0 deficit to win four straight, and again, pitching was a key as the Yankees managed only three runs in the final two games.

Despite the divided season, 1981 had proved successful for the Dodgers as well as the Giants. The Dodgers, of course, had won a championship and would appear to be among the favorites for next season as well. For the Giants, the split year allowed them to build some confidence under new manager Robinson. The Giants bounced back to make a legitimate run for the division title in the second half. It was a momentum that would carry over into 1982, when the Giants and Dodgers would fire up one of the most exciting seasons of the rivalry.

JOLTIN' JOE (1982)

Joe Morgan wrote his ticket to Cooperstown during his eight years with Cincinnati from 1972 to 1979. He hit .288, and had 220 doubles, 27 triples, 152 homers, 612 RBIs, and 406 stolen bases. He was MVP twice and won five Gold Gloves. Morgan posted good numbers over his nine years with previous employer Houston, but his talents blossomed after being traded to the Reds after the 1971 season. Of all the skills Morgan possessed, one that stood out was his ability to hit in the clutch. That was never more apparent than in the 1975 World Series against Boston. Morgan drove in Cesar Geronimo with a bases-loaded single in the bottom of the 10th inning to win game three 6–5. He delivered again in game seven, scoring Ken Griffey with a base hit in the top of the ninth to break a tie and give the Reds a 4–3 victory and a world championship.

Clutch would become the word that defined the future Hall of Famer's 1982 season with the Giants, and it was the Dodgers who would painfully witness it firsthand.

———〰———

Following the strike-induced split season in 1981, which wiped out 713 games over three months, produced four division winners, forced an extra round of playoffs, and left bitterness among owners, players, and fans, baseball hoped for a return to normalcy in 1982. For the Giants and Dodgers, the season ahead had all the signs of what had become normalcy with the two clubs: Los Angeles was accustomed to winning and San Francisco was accustomed to losing. In the last five years, the Dodgers made three World Series appearances, and tied for the best division record another year only to lose a one-game playoff. The Giants' highest finish during that period was third place. As the 1982 season unfolded, there were few indications that the games between the teams would have great meaning, or that a fight to the finish was about to occur.

The Dodgers began the year with their championship team nearly complete. The pitching staff, which had the second lowest ERA at 3.01 in 1981, returned all five starters. The Dodgers roster was seen as so strong that there was no place for Mike Marshall, who won the Triple Crown in the Pacific Coast League in 1981 with 34 homers, 137 RBIs, and a .373 average.

The Giants entered the offseason in a house-cleaning mood. By March 30, 1982, San Francisco had dealt away its entire five-man rotation, and Giants management was being forced to deny that it had given up on the season before it began.

While the pitching staff remained unsettled, the Giants saw promise on offense, especially with the addition of 22-year-old rookie outfielder

Chili Davis and ex-Dodger Reggie Smith, obtained in free agency. Jack Clark and Darrell Evans also provided a solid threat.

While many other Giants would contribute to the club's return to respectability in 1982, Morgan would be the most remembered name of either team in the season's monumental race. Morgan haunted the Dodgers throughout the year. His home run off Fernando Valenzuela on April 25 got the Giants on the board in an eventual 6–3 San Francisco win. He picked up his 1,000th career RBI to help the Giants to a 6–2 victory July 28. His solo homer broke a tie and propelled the Giants to a 4–2 win on August 14.

Morgan continued his contributions when the clubs met for a crucial three-game series in Los Angeles September 24–26.

September 24 (Giants 3, Dodgers 2): The first-place Dodgers, hoping to knock the Giants out of the division race, were victimized by a stubborn San Francisco bullpen. The Dodgers entered the series with a three-game lead over Atlanta and a four-game lead over the Giants. Evans's single drove in Davis to break a 2–2 tie in the eighth. Al Holland and Greg Minton combined to shut out the Dodgers without a hit over the last five innings. Los Angeles had now lost four of its last five, prompting Morgan to offer some prophetic words, "The Dodgers had a chance to put it away this week. Now we have a chance to make it interesting."

September 25 (Giants 5, Dodgers 4): Davis and Morgan delivered run-scoring singles in the eighth to overcome a 4–3 deficit as the Giants closed the gap to two. The Giants trailed 3–2 in the seventh when Morgan tied it with an RBI triple. Bill Russell knocked in his third run of the game with an infield single in the Dodgers' half of the inning for a momentary lead.

September 26 (Giants 3, Dodgers 2): The Giants sloshed their way to a three-game sweep in a contest delayed three hours by rain, bringing San Francisco and Atlanta to within one game of the Dodgers. The Dodgers dropped their fifth straight. The Giants tallied all their runs in the fifth, as Morgan walked, stole second and scored on Clark's double, followed by a two-run homer by Evans. Giants manager Frank Robinson played the game under protest, complaining about the soggy conditions, which drew a pointed retort from Dodgers manager Tommy Lasorda: "Who's qualified to decide when it's too wet, Frank Robinson?"

Five days later, the division title fight would shift to San Francisco for the last weekend of the season with the Giants and Dodgers trailing first-place Atlanta by a game.

October 1 (Dodgers 4, Giants 0): For seven innings, Dodgers pitcher Jerry Reuss, who would allow just three hits the entire game, and the Giants' Fred Breining engaged in a tense, scoreless duel before 53,281, the largest crowd of the year at Candlestick Park. In the eighth, Steve Sax walked, and after one was out, Dusty Baker singled and Steve Garvey walked to load the bases. Robinson visited the mound, but though he had reliever Holland ready in the bullpen, he stayed with Breining. Rick Monday silenced the crowd by launching a grand slam to right for all the runs needed in a 4–0 win. An Atlanta victory put the Giants on the brink of elimination.

October 2 (Dodgers 15, Giants 2): The Dodgers kept their title hopes alive with a devastating offensive display. The attack included 17 hits and three home runs. Meanwhile, a victory by Atlanta officially ended the Giants' season.

October 3 (Giants 5, Dodgers 3): Ron Cey put the Dodgers in front 2–0 in the second inning of the regular season's final game with a home run off Bill Laskey following a single by Garvey. The Giants tied it in the second, scoring on a bases-loaded walk and a double play. While the game was in progress, Atlanta lost to San Diego, meaning the Dodgers could tie for the division crown and force a playoff with the Braves with a win. Tommy Niedenfuer replaced Valenzuela in the seventh with the score tied 2–2 after he was removed for a pinch-hitter. Niedenfuer allowed a single to Bob Brenly and a double to Champ Summers to put runners on second and third before striking out Minton. Terry Forster was brought in, and struck out Jim Wohlford for the second out.

It was now up to Mr. Clutch.

Giants fans had arrived at Candlestick ready to party entering the final three-game series, with visions of an on-field celebration and a pennant during the weekend. Monday's grand slam in Friday's game dimmed their spirits. The Dodgers' offensive assault on Saturday turned out the lights. But for the Giants, the party wasn't over. After Friday's crushing defeat, the Giants' tough-talking manager described the backup plan should his club be eliminated, "We've got two ballgames left," Robinson said. "If we can't do it, they won't either."

Morgan made Robinson's promise stand by drilling a Forster slider over the right field fence as the crowd erupted, and the Giants held on for a 5–3 win.

—∾∾—

The teams had come back from the dead to challenge Atlanta, and while both were heading to the offseason without a title, their emotions were a contrast. For the Dodgers and their high expectations, it was nothing but frustration. But for the overachieving Giants, the ending provided satisfaction. Robinson, while still disappointed his team didn't win the division, couldn't hide his excitement at bursting the Dodgers' bubble, saying, "I don't know if there's a next best thing, but if there is, this was it."

On December 14, Morgan and Holland were traded to the Philadelphia Phillies for pitchers Mike Krukow and Mark Davis and a minor leaguer. Morgan and the Phillies would reach the World Series in 1983, defeating the Dodgers in the NL championship series. But for all the glory Morgan enjoyed, both before and after his two-year San Francisco stay, Giants fans—and perhaps even Morgan himself—would always believe that the jolt that eliminated the Dodgers in 1982 was his ultimate blow. Said Morgan: "Of all the homers I hit, I might remember this one a little more."

SMACKDOWN

Most of the Giants-Dodgers brawls or near brawls involved bean balls. But in 1983, the clubs found a new way to light the fuse.

Steve Howe had established himself as the anchor of the Dodgers bullpen in 1982 behind one of baseball's most potent rotations, compiling a 7–5 record with 13 saves and a 2.08 ERA. In May of the 1983 season, it was announced that Howe, who had previously undergone treatment for cocaine use, suffered a relapse and was put on the disabled list as he headed back into rehabilitation. Howe was 2–0 with seven saves and a 0.00 ERA at the time.

Howe returned by the time the clubs next met two months later, and pitched a scoreless inning in relief in a 2–1 Dodgers victory in the first game of a doubleheader July 31. Giants manager Frank Robinson had complained to the umpires that Howe was using a sticky substance on the baseball. When Howe looked into the Giants' dugout in the ninth, Robinson made a gesture to his nose, which the Dodgers interpreted as mocking Howe over his cocaine problems. Dusty Baker had to be restrained as the Dodgers were infuriated with Robinson. Later, Robinson pleaded not guilty, but shot back at the angry response from the Dodgers, saying, "If (Howe's) got a guilt trip, that's his problem, not mine. If they want a piece of me, I'm not hard to find."

MOVING ON (1983)

Together, they had nearly 60 years of major league experience. Last year, they helped their clubs battle for the NL West flag down to the last weekend.

"They" were the Giants' Joe Morgan, 38, and Reggie Smith, 37, and the Dodgers' Steve Garvey, 33, and Ron Cey, 34. Smith, the ex-Dodger, was around for only a year, but brought needed power and a winning attitude to the Giants. Morgan, while his skills might be diminishing, proved he could still play. Garvey and Cey, as part of the Dodgers' now legendary infield, were still producing, accounting for 40 home runs and 165 RBIs between them in 1982. But as the Giants and Dodgers prepared for the 1983 season, all four were gone: Morgan and Cey in trades, and Smith and Garvey through free agency. For Giants manager Frank Robinson and Dodgers skipper Tommy Lasorda, at least one key part of the puzzle for the new season would be who would step up to the plate, literally and figuratively, to replace the combination of veteran savvy and offensive output.

As the Dodgers faced the new year, it was difficult not to still be haunted by the last one. The Dodgers would do little to compensate for the loss of Garvey and Cey. Instead, they were satisfied to rely on mostly the same lineup, the return of a solid pitching staff and two rookies with big minor league credentials. Greg Brock would take over at first base and Mike Marshall would start in right field, with slugging outfielder Pedro Guerrero moving to third base. Outfielder Dusty Baker and shortstop Bill Russell, both 34, would now become the senior citizens of the lineup. The rotation would again be led by Fernando Valenzuela, Bob Welch, Jerry Reuss, and Burt Hooton.

The Giants experienced one of the most uplifting third-place finishes in their history in 1982. They had their first winning season in four years; went 9–9 against the Dodgers, the first time they had not dropped a season series to their rivals since 1976; and eliminated Los Angeles from the division race on the final day of the season. The first question about the Giants was how they could replace the production of Morgan and Smith, who both hit above .280 and combined for 32 home runs and 117 RBIs. The answer would be to hope for big output from outfielders Jack Clark, Chili Davis, and Jeffrey Leonard, and first baseman Darrell Evans.

—⁓—

The clubs were heading in opposite directions as they met for the first time on April 18 in San Francisco. The Dodgers entered the series 8–3; the Giants were 3–9. Pitching woes were costing the Giants, who had already lost games by scores of 16–13, 12–3 and 10–2. Los Angeles continued its early season surge with a 4–3 win, but its control over the Giants was about to slip.

San Francisco won six of its next eight games against the Dodgers. However, the Giants were not as successful against their other opponents, and sat in fifth place, 12½ behind Atlanta on July 31. The Dodgers were 5½ games out.

The Giants never could get into the race, but they continued to harass the first-place Dodgers, sweeping them September 16–18 in San

Francisco while limiting them to just one run in the first 26 innings of the series. In the final game, the Giants rocked Reuss for four quick runs on Joel Youngblood's two-run single in the first and two-run homer in the third. The Giants took a 6–0 lead into the ninth. The Dodgers finally broke through for three runs against Mike Krukow, but the Giants held on for a 6–3 win. The Dodgers expressed surprise and frustration at how the Giants rallied against them. Said Guerrero: "They play us like it's the damn World Series."

The inevitable occurred in the next meeting of the teams September 30 in Los Angeles. The Dodgers defeated the Giants for only the fifth time in the season, but it wasn't necessary as the Dodgers clinched the division title in midgame when second-place Atlanta fell to San Diego. The Dodgers were leading 3–0 in the sixth when the Atlanta game ended, triggering a celebration among the club and the crowd at Dodger Stadium.

—⁓—

The Dodgers' postseason ended quietly as they scored just eight runs while losing three out of four to Philadelphia in the NL championship series. The division title still was satisfying as the club showed it could move on after the departure of longtime stars Garvey and Cey. While the defense might have been weakened by the pair's absence, their replacements held their own offensively. Brock's average of .224 was disappointing, but his 20 home runs were more than Garvey hit in the last two seasons. Guerrero brought more production to the third base position, and his move to the infield made way for slugger Marshall to join the lineup.

The season was a letdown for the Giants after their title run of 1982, though fans largely stuck with the team as attendance increased slightly to 1.2 million. The Giants' batting and pitching statistics nearly mirrored those of the previous years, bolstering the theory that the club missed the leadership of Morgan and Smith. The Giants would try to bring back some of that experience the next year with the signing of Dodgers' castoff Dusty Baker. Baker's departure from Los Angeles was bitter, but the Giants were happy to welcome him and his lifetime .280 average and 221 home runs. Baker would have a respectable year with the Giants, and would eventually return to guide the club during one of its most exciting and successful eras. But for now, in the Frank Robinson era, things were about to go downhill for the Giants. The club's struggles would hit bottom over the next two years, and Robinson would pay for it with his job.

MISERY (1984)

The year 1984 was so bad for the Dodgers and Giants that not even Big Brother could stand to watch.

The Dodgers won only 79 games, just the fifth time (excepting the 1981 strike year) since moving west that they had won fewer than 80. They were tied for last in the league in batting average, last in runs, and eighth in home runs.

The Giants lost 96 games, eclipsing their San Francisco mark of 91 in 1979. It was the most defeats of any Giants team since manager Mel Ott's club went 55–98 in 1943. The last-place finish was the worst for the franchise since 1946. Mike Krukow was the only Giants pitcher with double-figure wins (11), and even he didn't have a winning record (11–12). None of the starters had ERAs under 4.00.

The Giants suffered the ultimate blow of clinching last place against the Dodgers in a 4–3 loss in 11 innings September 29. Rob Deer broke up a 2–2 tie in the seventh with a home run, but Pedro Guerrero's RBI single in the bottom half of the inning evened the score again. Rafael Landestoy's bases-loaded single brought in the winning, and doomed the Giants to sixth place.

Giants owner Bob Lurie added to the fans' misery, announcing he was putting the club up for sale. While he wanted to find a buyer who would keep the team in San Francisco, the decision opened up the possibility that if a local buyer couldn't be found, the team could be gone. "It has become apparent that we can no longer continue as we have. Despite the efforts of all of us, the financial losses continue to grow," he said. Some viewed Lurie's statement as a ploy to pressure city officials to get a new stadium, but regardless of his motives, the chaos didn't bode well for the coming season.

PENTHOUSE TO CELLAR (1985)

With the rivalry a victim of another noncompetitive Giants' season, a minor eruption August 18 in San Francisco served as a reminder that the history of tension could surface even in quiet times.

The Dodgers led 1–0 through seven, scoring on a throwing error by shortstop Jose Uribe. Bob Brenly tied it in the eighth with a homer off Orel Hershiser, who then hit two of the next three batters. One of them was starter Mike Krukow, who was forced to leave the game with a sore wrist. The Giants won it in the 10th when Dan Gladden singled off Tom Niedenfuer to drive in Ron Roenicke. Giants fans harassed Hershiser for plunking the Giants players, and the Dodgers pitcher received a police escort to make sure he got safely down the right-field line to the clubhouse. The Giants' Chili Davis could only marvel at the passions that remained despite the clubs' opposite records: "When it's L.A., we have a certain level of intensity I wish we had all year. We play other teams with half the intensity we play these guys."

———

Both clubs were looking for a bounce-back year in 1985. The Dodgers hoped to do it with their pitching. The Giants hoped to do it with their hitting and a new manager.

The Dodgers, with the league's second lowest ERA last year, entered the season with a sound rotation. Their most effective pitcher from 1984, Alejandro Pena, underwent surgery on his right shoulder in February, and was figured to be lost for the season. The club still had five solid starters: Fernando Valenzuela, Bob Welch, Hershiser, Rick Honeycutt, and Jerry Reuss. The Dodgers, in search of more productive offense, were running out of patience with Greg Brock, the Steve Garvey heir apparent, and were looking at possible replacements at first. Pedro Guerrero was the one constant, though the Dodgers couldn't decide whether he should be a third baseman or outfielder.

The Giants' team batting average of .265 was the highest since the 1962 pennant-winning club hit .278. The team boasted perhaps the best young outfield in the league in Davis, Jeffrey Leonard, and Gladden. Catcher Brenly performed solidly in his first year as a regular. One big bat that would be missing belonged to Jack Clark, who got his wish for new scenery through a trade to St. Louis. The Giants filled their leadership void in the dugout with Jim Davenport, one of their most popular past players. Frank Robinson's reign as skipper came to a crashing end on August 4, 1984, as he was replaced by interim manager Danny Ozark with the team in last place with a 42–64 record.

The Dodgers had a history of coming back strong following a down year, leaving observers to ponder whether 1984 was a fluke or a trend. For the Giants, there had been too many down years followed by more of the same, leaving little room for optimism. The club hoped the change of managerial styles from Robinson to Davenport would change the course. But the Giants were destined for another dark year in the cellar while the Dodgers would be enjoying the view from the penthouse.

The clubs split their first six games in April, but their seasons were heading in different directions. By the time the teams resumed competition for a three-game series July 29, the Giants had stumbled while the Dodgers were sprinting toward a division crown. The first-place Dodgers held a 4½ game lead over San Diego. The Giants were 18½ out in last place.

With about two weeks to go, the Dodgers were trying to hang on to first and the Giants were trying to avoid losing 100 games for the first time in franchise history. Since the clubs had six more games against one another, each would have a say on whether the teams would accomplish their goals. The Giants entered the September 20–22 series fresh off a shake-up that saw manager Davenport replaced by Roger Craig and Al

Rosen hired as general manager. The Giants proved to be the spoilers in the series opener, scoring three in the seventh to overcome a 3–2 deficit. Chris Brown drove in two with a pinch-hit single and Brenly brought in another with a base hit. The Dodgers were now 4½ games ahead of second-place Cincinnati. The Dodgers put an end to any Giants' momentum before it could get started, as they banged out 16 hits in an 11–2 win the next day and followed that up with a 5–3 victory.

Los Angeles won the opener of a September 27–29 series against San Francisco 6–2 five days later, putting the Dodgers' magic number at six and the Giants' "tragic" number at six. The magic number referred to the number of Los Angeles wins and Cincinnati losses needed for the Dodgers to clinch the division. The tragic number referred to the defeats needed by the Giants to reach 100 losses.

The Dodgers continued to show no sympathy, sweeping the series with victories of 3–1 and 7–2. Starters Reuss and Welch had strong successive outings, and the bullpen blanked the Giants for five innings over the two games.

The Dodgers clinched the division crown on October 2 as Cincinnati lost to San Diego while the Dodgers were in the fifth inning of their game against Atlanta. Hershiser got his 19th victory as the Dodgers won 9–3 before 32,042 celebrating fans. The joy of an outstanding 95–67 season came crashing down on October 16 in Los Angeles. The Dodgers went up 2–0 in the seven-game NL championship series against St. Louis, only to drop the next three. In game six, Jack Clark hit a three-run homer off Niedenfuer in the ninth with the Dodgers leading 5–4 to end Los Angeles's World Series dream. Tommy Lasorda chose to pitch to the ex-Giants slugger even though there were two outs and first base was open, triggering a debate that lasted all offseason about why the Dodgers didn't walk him.

—∿—

The Giants came down to the final day of the season with a 62–99 record. On October 6, they fell 8–7 to Atlanta for their 100th defeat.

Despite the dubious distinction of being the only Giants club in franchise history to lose 100, the season ended in belief that better times might be ahead. The late-season shake-up that saw Craig named manager and Rosen tapped as general manager provided an immediate lift. Rosen, vowing to turn the Giants around, distributed a letter to fans at Candlestick Park at the final game against Los Angeles, saying, "The main point I want to make is that I've been a winner all my life, and I'll make the Giants a winner." His closing line: "Beat the Dodgers." It was bold talk from someone who was only on the job three days, but it was a promise that he would fulfill.

RISE AND FALL (1986)

The Giants began the 1986 campaign with a new attitude, some fresh faces and a desire to at least see some improvement. The Dodgers returned with the same winning attitude, mostly familiar faces and high hopes for another pennant run. The two clubs would indeed go off in two directions—one ready to rise, the other to fall. But surprisingly it was the Giants, who had not posted a better overall record than the Dodgers since 1971, who would find success.

The Dodgers entered spring training in 1986 carrying the emotional scars from their stunning elimination in last year's National League championship series, and began the season with a physical scar that they would not recover from. In an exhibition game three days before the start of the season, Pedro Guerrero ruptured a tendon in his left leg. The devastating injury would mean that the Dodgers would be playing most of the season without their top hitter, who had a .320 average with 33 homers and 87 RBIs in 1985.

Despite the loss of Guerrero, the Dodgers were still favorites based on a combination of offense, pitching, and experience. Mike Marshall and an improving Greg Brock could supply the power. The rotation shaped up as the league's best, with Orel Hershiser, who went 19–3 with a 2.03 ERA in 1985, Fernando Valenzuela, Bob Welch, Jerry Reuss, and Rick Honeycutt. Tom Niedenfuer, despite allowing the backbreaking postseason home run to Jack Clark, was still viewed as the foundation of the bullpen.

While not exactly a rallying cry, the Giants could open the season reasonably assured that it couldn't get any worse than 1985. The Giants scored the fewest runs and had the lowest batting average in the league. The highest individual average was Chris Brown's .271. Scott Garrelts led the staff in wins with nine. The Giants were also reeling from the effects of a disastrous trade prior to the 1985 season that sent Clark to St. Louis for David Green, Gary Rajsich, Dave LaPoint, and Jose Uribe. Only Uribe remained with the club. Clark, meanwhile, helped lead St. Louis to the World Series.

There was still some optimism because of the duo of manager Roger Craig and general manager Al Rosen. Craig's baseball savvy and "humm-baby" enthusiasm, and Rosen's sharp recognition of talent appeared a good match. One of the first major decisions was to turn over half the infield to rookies with no AAA experience. Will Clark took over at first and Robby Thompson started at second.

While the offense showed promise, the Giants faced an unsettled situation with the rotation. The top three starters would be Mike Krukow, Garrelts, and Vida Blue. Krukow was slowed by an injury in 1985 and Atlee Hammaker was starting the season on the disabled list.

—⁓—

The teams got off to a wild start in their first meeting of the year April 11. The Dodgers staged a roaring comeback, only to have it spoiled because of continued bad luck over intentional walks and guys named Clark. Los Angeles, haunted all offseason because of Tom Lasorda's decision to pitch to the Cardinals' Jack Clark in the NL championship series, this time saw a decision to not pitch to the Giants' Will Clark backfire.

The Giants rolled up an 8–1 lead after six innings. A three-base, bases-loaded error by Ken Landreaux and a three-run homer by Jeffrey Leonard did most of the damage. The Dodgers bounced back with four in the seventh on Landreaux's sacrifice fly and Franklin Stubbs's three-run blast. In the ninth, the Dodgers tied it on a Stubbs RBI single and a two-run double by Mike Scioscia. In the 12th, Candy Maldonado doubled with one out. Dan Gladden singled, but Stubbs threw Maldonado out at home, with Gladden taking second. Lasorda walked Clark intentionally, but Brad Gulden followed with a run-scoring single for a 9–8 win.

The Giants won four of their first six April games against the struggling Dodgers. By April 23, Houston led the Giants by a half-game with the Dodgers in last place, six games out. Although the Dodgers might not be going anywhere this season, they appeared committed to making sure the Giants didn't either as they swept a three-game series in late July in Los Angeles. Spurred by strong starting performances by Hershiser, Valenzuela, and Welch, the Dodgers held the Giants to four runs and only 15 hits in the series, and recorded 31 strikeouts. The Giants now trailed first-place Houston by 4½ games, while the Dodgers were in fourth, 7½ back.

When the clubs met again two weeks later for a three-game series August 15–17, the second-place Giants were trying to stay close to Houston, which held a five-game lead. The Dodgers were in third, nine games back. Krukow got the Giants off to a good start in the opener, striking out 12, and winning his 12th game of the season. The Dodgers bounced back to take the next two games as the Giants continued their trend of showing promise, but being unable to seize control.

The clubs still had six games to play as they met for a series September 26–28, but the season was already officially over. Houston clinched the division title with a punctuation mark, as Mike Scott no-hit the Giants the previous day. The September 26 game was delayed because of rain for almost two hours after two innings with no score. Dodgers starter Hershiser, with little incentive at this point, didn't return. Eighteen-game winner Krukow, motivated by a chance to win 20, did return. The result was a strong eight-inning performance, as Krukow gave up just three hits and struck out eight to earn his 19th victory in the 3–0 win.

The Giants pounded Valenzuela the next day for eight runs and nine hits in five innings in an 8–3 win. The Giants got a series sweep in the third game, but the Dodgers didn't make it easy for them. It took five hours-forty-five minutes, 16 innings, 52 players, 14 pitchers, and 25 hits. Giants reliever Greg Minton doubled in the 16th, and after an intentional walk to Clark, he scored on Bob Brenly's single for the 6–5 victory.

In a season-closing series in San Francisco, Valenzuela fired a five-hitter October 4 for a 2–1 victory and his 21st win as the Dodgers fought to avoid finishing last. With one game to play, the Dodgers were 73–88, San Diego 73–88 and Atlanta 72–88.

Krukow closed the season with his 20th win the next day, but the Dodgers avoided last place thanks to the Atlanta Braves. Krukow went 6⅓ innings, giving up two runs and seven hits, while the Giants rocked Hershiser for six runs in the seventh in an 11–2 romp. The Braves fell to Houston 4–1, leaving the Dodgers a half-game out of last place.

The Dodgers' win total of 73 was their lowest in a non-strike year since they lost the same number in 1967. The spring training injury that sidelined Guerrero for most of the season set the tone, as injuries mounted among the club's regulars. Hershiser, Welch, and Reuss, who combined for a 47–17 record in 1985, went 23–33. The Dodgers, believing that the injuries and pitching slump were a one-year fluke, would go into next season with much of the same roster. It would turn out to be a decision that led to another poor year.

The Giants had nowhere to go but up after their disastrous years of 1984 and 1985. While a third-place finish normally would not be something to boast about, the improvement provided confidence in the new leadership in the front office and on the field.

MARSHALL LAW (1987)

As the Giants and Dodgers prepared for the 1987 season, their fates appeared to rest more on who had the best medical plan.

The Dodgers' Mike Marshall, who led the league with 17 homers in the first half of 1986, was sidelined for most of the second half with a back ailment. Shortstop Mariano Duncan, hobbled by knee, ankle, and foot injuries, played just 103 games, saw his batting average dip, and committed 25 errors after a solid rookie season in 1985. Third baseman Bill Madlock appeared in just 111 games, going on the disabled list twice. Catcher Mike Scioscia spent a month on the DL with an ankle injury. Pedro Guerrero was attempting a comeback after his leg injury.

Fifteen Giants had undergone some type of surgery in the past year. Among the notable injuries were Will Clark's wrist, which put him out for about 40 games in his rookie 1986 season, third baseman Chris Brown's shoulder, and second baseman Robby Thompson's knee.

But on an April night at Candlestick Park in 1987, it was a bruised ego that triggered one of the hottest main events since the teams moved west.

The preliminary bout was held on April 20 in a hard-fought game eventually won 4–3 by the Giants. Tempers flared when Giants pitcher Mark Davis hit Marshall with a pitch and the Dodgers' Orel Hershiser brushed back Jeffrey Leonard. Umpire Dave Pallone warned both benches. The teams went back to their neutral corner, and played the remainder of the game in peace.

The truce only lasted 24 hours.

Leonard got the next night's game going with a homer for the Giants in the first, but the Dodgers picked up two in the fourth on Franklin Stubbs's two-run homer, and three in the fifth on RBI singles by Guerrero, Sciosia, and Stubbs. The Giants roared back in their half of the fifth on Clark's run-scoring triple and Leonard's two-run blast, and tied the game in the sixth on Chris Speier's home run. The Giants grabbed a 7–5 lead in the seventh on a passed ball and Speier's RBI single. The Dodgers scored three in the ninth to take an 8–7 lead on an RBI single by Sciosia and Stubbs's second two-run homer of the game.

The Giants bounced back in the ninth to tie it at 8–8 on doubles by Randy Kutcher and Harry Spillman, and the bell was about to ring for the 10th inning.

Mike Ramsey walked and stole second. Giants manager Roger Craig had Scott Garrelts walk Guerrero. Marshall, feeling he was being snubbed since Craig would rather take a chance pitching to him, homered, and responded by gesturing toward the Giants manager while circling the bases. An angry Craig came out of the dugout, and players from both teams gathered on the field. Garrelts's next pitch sailed over the head of Alex Trevino, resulting in both benches emptying. Giants fans behind the visiting third-base dugout screamed at the Dodgers and beer was tossed toward the players. Some Dodgers had to be restrained from climbing into the stands. One fan was arrested, and the game finished with police officers and stadium guards securing the Los Angeles dugout. The Dodgers received a police escort to their clubhouse down the right field line following their 11–8 win.

Craig, who later received an apology from Marshall, said earlier, "That was a bush league thing to do. This is the big leagues. I don't know where he's been." Dodgers manager Tommy Lasorda, while agreeing Marshall was out of line, was irate about the fans. "That's a disgrace," he said.

The next day, Trevino got revenge with his bat, stroking a two-run double to give the Dodgers a come-from-behind 5–3 victory. Security was increased, but the game went on without incident, although Marshall drew boos when he pinch-hit in the ninth.

—⚬—

The clubs had a three-month cooling off period as they didn't meet again until late July. The Giants were now fighting Cincinnati with the Dodgers turned into spectators. On July 29, the first-place Reds led the Giants by 2½ games, while the Dodgers were nine games out in fifth place. The Giants had a new look since the April series, having engineered a seven-player deal with San Diego July 5 that brought pitchers Dave Dravecky and Craig Lefferts, and outfielder Kevin Mitchell to San Francisco. The Giants, sensing a legitimate shot at a division title, made their second significant deal of the season on July 31, acquiring pitcher Don Robinson in a trade with Pittsburgh.

The Giants continued their roll in a mid-August three-game series with the Dodgers, using two sterling back-to-back pitching performances to win two out of three. Dravecky continued his success against the Dodgers with a four-hit, seven strikeout performance on August 15. It was his second shutout as a Giant, with four of his eight career shutouts coming against Los Angeles.

Mike LaCoss followed Dravecky with a 10-inning three-hitter for a 1–0 victory. Bob Welch nearly matched him, tossing four-hit, shutout ball through eight innings. The Giants broke through in the 10th when Chili Davis singled with two outs, and came home when Eddie Milner doubled into the left field corner off Tim Leary. The Dodgers had now gone 22 innings without scoring a run. The Giants ended the series still even with Cincinnati, but were on the verge of their third major deal of the summer, which resulted in Pittsburgh's Rick Reuschel joining the pitching staff on August 21.

The Dodgers would take three out of the remaining five games between the teams to capture the head-to-head matchup 10–8, but the Giants were heading for the postseason with their first 90-win season since 1971. The division crown, which they clinched on September 28, marked the first Giants' title since 1971, and capped a strong final two months. The Giants, who trailed first-place Cincinnati by five games on August 7, went on a 33–15 tear to clinch.

The Giants were on the brink of their first World Series appearance since 1962 after taking a 3–2 lead in their National League Championship Series against the St. Louis Cardinals. Dravecky and Robinson limited the Cardinals to a run and five hits in game six, but the Giants were blanked 1–0. St. Louis jumped out to a 4–0 lead in the seventh game, and the Giants' World Series hopes ended in a 6–0 defeat.

Still, Giants general manager Al Rosen's deals had paid off. Dravecky was 7–5 in 18 starts, Reuschel 5–3 in nine starts, Robinson 5–1 in 25 relief appearances, and Lefferts 3–3 in 44 games out of the bullpen. Mitchell slugged 15 home runs and hit .306. The Giants' 205 homers were the most by the team since 1962.

While the Giants could hail the season as a success despite the disappointing loss to St. Louis, the Dodgers could only ponder what went wrong. The team finished at 73–89 for the second straight year, attendance had fallen short of three million for the first time since 1979 (not counting the 1981 strike year) and there were already rumors about a roster shake-up.

TRUE GRIT (1988)

When John Wayne took a bullet during one of his westerns, it just made him more determined. That was the story of the Dodgers' 1988 season as the wounded Kirk Gibson would cowboy-up, get back in the saddle and ride off into the sunset with a World Series trophy.

Gibson's performance would become a scene-stealer that would make Wayne proud, since the script for the 1988 season had the Giants in a rare starring role, while the Dodgers were expected to receive second billing. The Giants, having bombed in the standings and at the box office for too many years, entered 1988 confident that they were ready for an Oscar-winning year. The club went from a 100-loss season in 1985 to an 83–79 mark in 1986 and a division-winning 92–70 season in 1987. It appeared the Giants, with much of the same cast returning, had a solid chance to reach baseball's ultimate stage in October. The Dodgers, meanwhile, had gone from Broadway to the basement in two years. A sequel to their 95-victory division title season of 1985 didn't seem likely.

The Giants' positive outlook was bolstered because of their sudden success against the Dodgers. The Giants finished ahead of the Dodgers in 1986 and 1987. It was the first time since the Giants' division-title year of 1971 that they had a better record than their rivals. They had to go back to the 1967–69 seasons to find a time when they finished ahead of the Dodgers for at least two consecutive years. The Giants also battled the Dodgers to an 18–18 tie in head-to-head competition in 1986–87, reversing a trend of mostly Los Angeles domination that began in the early 1970s.

The Giants were excited about seeing the dividends of their midseason deals of 1987 play out over a full season in 1988. Pitchers Rick Reuschel,

Dave Dravecky, Don Robinson, and Craig Lefferts would now be available from day one, as would power-hitting Kevin Mitchell. The lineup appeared solid with the bats of Will Clark, Candy Maldonado, and Robby Thompson, along with the addition of free agent Brett Butler. The health of the rotation was the only snag. Reuschel, 38, had shoulder problems in the past, Dravecky had a history of elbow problems, and Mike Krukow was hoping to revert to his 20-win form of 1986 after injuries limited him last season.

The Dodgers were not sitting by idly after their back-to-back flops. The club hadn't had more than two consecutive losing seasons since a six-year stretch from 1933–38, and management was ready for a shake-up to get the team back on track. A trade on December 11, 1987, had major repercussions on the bullpen, rotation, and infield. Starter Bob Welch, a 15-game winner, was traded in a three-team, eight-player deal that brought relievers Jay Howell and Jesse Orosco, and shortstop Alfredo Griffin to the Dodgers. Ex-Dodger Don Sutton was signed as a free agent, and was expected to join a starting staff led by Fernando Valenzuela and Orel Hershiser.

The headline-grabbing offseason acquisition was still to come, as the Dodgers on January 29 signed free agent Gibson. The Dodgers expected Gibson to add determination and grit, as well as offense, to the roster. Gibson, who had hit 103 homers in the last four years, had one downside, having missed games since 1980 with a variety of injuries. Former Detroit teammate Alan Trammel demonstrated some vision when he analyzed what the Dodgers got in Gibson, saying, "He thrives on late-inning pressure situations. He's going to strike out with the bases loaded, but he's also going to come through with some of those big hits."

The addition of Gibson had some observers comparing the power in the Dodgers lineup with that of the 1978 version when four players hit at least 30 homers. This year's team would have long-ball threats in Pedro Guerrero, Mike Marshall, John Shelby, and Franklin Stubbs.

The combination of the Dodgers' offseason moves, coupled with the Giants' revitalized roster from last year, triggered speculation as the clubs prepared to meet on opening day that they could both be in a fight through-out the season. The incident in 1987 when Marshall set off both the crowd and manager Roger Craig with some post-home run theatrics had revved up the rivalry. Ron Perranoski, former Dodgers pitcher and current pitch-ing coach, saw some of the sparks returning, saying, "I wouldn't say it's quite the way it was. But it's close. It's been rekindled."

The Dodgers got off to a big start on opening day in Los Angeles on April 4 as Steve Sax hit Dravecky's first pitch for a homer. Unfortunately for the Dodgers, their offensive output stopped there as the Giants left-hander allowed only two hits the rest of the way for a 5–1 win.

Sax's clout turned out to be a good sign for the Dodgers, who jumped out to an early lead in the NL West. That quick start was turning into a potential runaway as the Dodgers built a lead of six over Houston and seven over the Giants as the clubs met for a four-game series in San Francisco, including a doubleheader July 26.

Candlestick Park's history of poor fan behavior during Dodgers-Giants single games should have been enough of a warning that a doubleheader could double the trouble. Hershiser and Terry Mulholland were locked in a 1–1 tie after six innings in the opener. Rick Dempsey put the Dodgers in front with a two-run homer in the seventh, and Los Angeles added four more in the ninth for a 7–3 win. The teams battled to a 5–5 tie after nine innings in the second game. In the 11th, Stubbs doubled, went to third on a groundout and scored the winning run when Scott Garrelts was called for his second balk of the day. The ensuing argument led to the ejection of Craig and pitcher Krukow, who was tossed out when he expressed his displeasure from the bench. The rhubarb almost escalated into a riot, as fans threw objects onto the field, leading to the ejection from the park of about 100 people and the arrest of 18 others. The incident prompted Dodgers Executive Vice President Fred Claire to complain the next day to the Giants and the league office.

Little was resolved on the field as the teams split the series, but a big swing in the standings was about to shake up the race.

An instant division battle had developed as the clubs hooked up for a four-game set in Los Angeles August 12.

August 12 (Dodgers 7, Giants 3): The slumping Dodgers now led Houston by only 1½, while the surging Giants pulled to within 2½ games. The Dodgers took the opener of the four-game showdown before 48,744 as Tim Leary pitched a strong 8⅓ innings and broke up a 3–3 tie in the sixth with a sacrifice fly. Guerrero added insurance in the seventh with a solo home run.

August 13 (Dodgers 2, Giants 1, 11 innings): Leary's bat came through for the second straight game to give the Dodgers an 11-inning victory. The Dodgers scored in the sixth on Guerrero's double and Marshall's base hit. The Giants tied it in the eighth on Clark's RBI single off Jesse Orosco. The Dodgers loaded the bases with two outs in the 11th, but because of a depleted bench caused in part by two earlier ejections, they were forced to use Leary as a pinch-hitter for Alejandro Pena. Leary singled home Stubbs with the winning run.

August 14 (Giants 15, Dodgers 4): The Giants scored eight times off Hershiser in two innings and went on to collect a total of 20 hits. Three Dodgers' errors, two by Hershiser, opened the way to a four-run first.

August 15 (Dodgers 1, Giants 0): The Dodgers got shutout pitching from Tim Belcher and reliever Orosco. The Dodgers scored the game's lone run in the fourth off Robinson on singles by Marshall and Shelby and a sacrifice fly by Stubbs. The victory put the Dodgers 2½ games ahead of Houston and 4½ in front of the Giants.

The possibility of a late-season division battle faded, and by the time the clubs met again, on September 23 in San Francisco, the Giants were eliminated from contention and the Dodgers were coasting to the division title. Los Angeles took the first two games of the September 23–25 series to put themselves on the brink of clinching, but the Giants put the party on hold. Giants rookie Steve Cook pitched a two-hit shutout to deny the Dodgers a chance to clinch the division title. The Dodgers still had a seven-game lead with seven games to play, but Giants manager Craig was satisfied that the celebration wouldn't be held in San Francisco, saying, "You know it's going to happen, but you don't want to see it before your fans at your park."

The Dodgers wrapped up the title September 26 with a victory over San Diego.

The clubs had three mop-up games remaining. The Dodgers took the first two, and then fell 1–0 October 2 as Don Robinson tossed a three-hitter. The Dodgers had more to concern themselves with than a season-ending shutout. They were about to enter the postseason with key injury questions involving Valenzuela's shoulder and Gibson's left hamstring, which he aggravated two days ago against the Giants. Gibson for certain was not about to count himself out, saying, "I can't walk. This is the most sore it's been. It's been frustrating, but I'm not going to give up by any means."

The Dodgers defeated the New York Mets in a hard-fought seven-game series to win the NL championship. The club went on to win its fifth World Series since moving west, defeating the Oakland A's in five games. Dodgers pitchers held the bashing A's to a .177 average. The series, however, revolved around one memorable moment.

Gibson had experienced World Series glory in 1984 by slugging two home runs, driving in five, and scoring three runs for a Game Five victory against San Diego that gave Detroit the championship. But even that heroic outburst couldn't compare with his one-swing miracle against the A's. The ailing Gibson limped to the plate to pinch-hit against Dennis Eckersley in the bottom of the ninth in the opener with the score tied, leaving most to wonder how he would make it to first even if he made contact. Gibson solved that problem by getting enough of the barrel on the ball for a game-winning homer so he could circle the bases at his own speed.

The Dodgers, who had overcome key injuries during the year, had good reason to savor their 5–2 victory in Game Five to win the series. What the organization didn't know is that it would have to savor that victory for the next 15 years, as the Dodgers would not win another postseason game until 2004.

Despite the fourth-place finish, the Giants didn't see a need to overhaul the team, which featured sluggers such as Clark and Mitchell and a promising pitching staff. But before the Giants could look to a fresh start for 1989, they first had to cope with grim news. On October 7, Dravecky had a cancerous tumor removed from his left arm. The Dravecky story would play itself out during the 1989 season, providing inspiration and heartbreak, as the Giants went on an emotional roller coaster ride in a bid for their first World Series berth in 27 years.

DROUGHT ENDS (1989)

The Dodgers began the season as a vulnerable defending champion, giving the Giants hope they could come back after a disappointing 1988.

Los Angeles knew it couldn't live off last year's accomplishments as the 1989 season dawned. Gibson (25 HR, 76 RBIs, .290) was remarkable in 1988 despite nagging injuries. He had the highest average among regulars, led the team in walks, runs, doubles, and homers, and had the second-best totals in hits, RBIs, and stolen bases. But he entered the season hampered by knee and shoulder problems that threatened to severely limit his playing time. There also were big questions about Fernando Valenzuela, whose arm troubles ruined his season and raised concerns about his effectiveness for this year. The Los Angeles pitching staff, while coming off a season with a league second-best in ERA, didn't appear as formidable as those of past years. Hershiser (23–8, 2.26) was the obvious exception, having not allowed a run since August 30, 1988.

The Dodgers pulled off another Gibson-like deal in the offseason, acquiring seven-time all-star Eddie Murray in a trade with Baltimore. The club gave up little in the trade for the 32-year-old three-time Gold Glove first baseman. Murray, with 333 home runs and 1,190 RBIs, was expected to fill the power void at first that had been lacking since Steve Garvey departed.

The Giants slugged their way to the division title in 1987 with 205 homers, but dropped to 113 in 1988. Though the offensive numbers faded, the club was confident the lineup would bounce back if Will Clark, Kevin Mitchell, and Candy Maldonado met expectations. Staff leader Rick Reuschel would be followed by a revamped rotation as Don Robinson and Scott Garrelts, who combined for 97 relief appearances in 1988, would be shifted to full-time starting roles.

If the pitching held up and the offense returned to its 1987 form, the Giants again appeared to be a strong contender for another division crown. The Dodgers, as defending champions, could not be counted out, but it seemed a stretch to hope that Hershiser and Gibson would repeat their Superman seasons.

—◦◦◦—

The Giants and Dodgers sluggers took control in the first six games between the clubs. Murray belted a grand slam to highlight a five-run ninth inning to spoil the home opener April 10 for 53,015 fans at Candlestick Park. The Dodgers also got solo home runs by Mike Marshall and Gibson in the 7–4 victory. Clark responded the next day with a home run, two doubles, and five RBIs to pace an 8–3 win. Mitchell smacked a three-run homer in the first inning in game three, and four Giants pitchers made it stand up for a 3–1 win.

Murray drove in three runs as the Dodgers topped the Giants 8–2 in the opener of a three-game series April 21 in Los Angeles. Mitchell took an intentional walk personally, and then delivered the game-winning hit in the ninth in response to lift the Giants to a 5–4 win in game two. Clark was walked intentionally to get to Mitchell, who singled in the go-ahead run. Mitchell admitted later that seeing Clark walked ahead of him was frustrating. "I get tired of that, too. I go up with more confidence when that happens." Game three belonged to Clark, who went five for five, with three

RBIs, a double and homer, but it wasn't enough as the Dodgers took the series with a 10-inning, 7–6 win. The Giants now held a half-game lead in the division, with the Dodgers in fourth, one game back.

As the clubs prepared August 1 for their first series in more than three months, the Giants were in a race for the division crown and the Dodgers were stuck in fourth place. The Giants held a one-game lead over second-place Houston, and the Dodgers were 12½ games out. But while the Dodgers were coming to grips with the fact that there would be no first-place repeat, they were in position to play spoiler, since the schedule-makers had them playing 12 more against the Giants in the final two months.

The Dodgers would go on to win four of six games the teams played in the first two weeks of August, culminating in a tense contest on August 13 in San Francisco.

The stakes were not very high, with the Dodgers trailing the Giants by 12 games, but for one day, the teams played a game reminiscent of their tense battles when first place was on the line. A crowd of 53,821, the third largest to watch a Giants-Dodgers game at Candlestick Park, was drawn by an old-timers game, but got a good show from the current editions of both clubs. The Dodgers, trailing 2–1 in the eighth, tied it on Willie Randolph's RBI double. In the 12th inning, pinch-hitter Mike Sharperson's sacrifice fly off Robinson gave the Dodgers a 3–2 win. Dodgers manager Tommy Lasorda moved up Hershiser one turn in the rotation so he could pitch against the Giants, and used his closer Jay Howell for four innings. Remarked Lasorda afterward, "Hell yes, this was a big win. We had to win this one." In the old-timers game between 1978 versions of the teams, the Giants beat the Dodgers 3–2, highlighted by Dusty Baker's two-run homer. The Giants continued to lead the division, with Houston three games behind.

New York Giants manager Bill Terry and Brooklyn Dodgers manager Burleigh Grimes get together before the teams meet at Ebbets Field on April 20, 1937. Terry's 1934 quip about Brooklyn—"Are they still in the league?"—fired up the Dodgers, who got revenge by ending the Giants' pennant hopes that year. *Photo credit: Associated Press*

Brooklyn's Jackie Robinson goes down as a pitch from New York's Sal Maglie hits him in the hand with the bases loaded September 1, 1951, as New York catcher Wes Westrum and umpire Lee Ballanfant look on. Robinson and Maglie exchanged words after the high inside pitch. The Giants rolled to an 8–1 victory. *Photo credit: Associated Press/Ray Howard*

Bobby Thomson drills "the shot heard 'round the world," a three-run pennant-winning homer off Ralph Branca in the ninth inning at the Polo Grounds on October 3, 1951. Thomson's clout gave the Giants a 5–4 win over the Dodgers in the third game of a playoff. *Photo credit: Associated Press*

Branca pretends to choke Thomson in 1991 at a ceremony commemorating the 40th anniversary of Thomson's famous home run. Reports have surfaced since then that Thomson might have been tipped off about the kind of pitch Branca threw by an elaborate sign-stealing scheme. *Photo credit: Associated Press/Marty Lederhandler*

San Francisco Mayor George Christopher, second from right, talks with Dodgers owner Walter O'Malley, left, New York Giants owner Horace Stoneham, right, and San Francisco Supervisor Francis McCarthy, second from left, on May 10, 1957. Talks were under way to bring the Giants and Dodgers to California. *Photo credit: Associated Press/Harry Harris*

San Francisco celebrates the arrival of major league baseball in the city with a parade April 14, 1958, just one day before the Giants and Dodgers began play in the new West Coast rivalry. *Photo courtesy of the San Francisco Chronicle.*

The former minor league ballpark, Seals Stadium, joins the big leagues as the San Francisco Giants and Los Angeles Dodgers play their inaugural West Coast game April 15, 1958. A crowd of 23,448 watched the Giants defeat the Dodgers 8–0. *Photo credit: Associated Press*

The huge Coliseum is shown before the first pitch as the Giants and Dodgers get ready to play the Los Angeles opener on April 18, 1958. The Dodgers sent the crowd of 78,672 home happy with a 6–5 win. The Coliseum was known for its odd left field dimensions, with a 42-foot-high fence just 250 feet from home plate. *Photo credit: Associated Press*

Giants manager Alvin Dark and Dodgers manager Walter Alston meet October 1, 1962, as the clubs prepare for a best-of-three playoff to determine the National League champion. *Photo credit: Associated Press/Sal Veder*

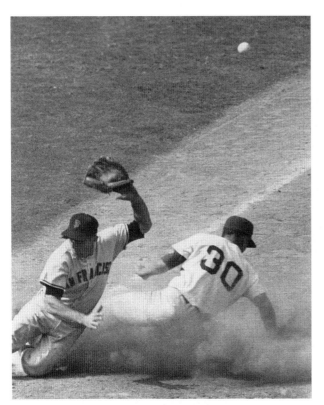

Dodgers speedster Maury Wills slides into third base for his 104th stolen base of the season as Giants third baseman Jim Davenport reaches for the throw during the third game of the playoff on October 3, 1962. During the season, the Dodgers accused the Giants of watering down the base paths to slow Wills down. *Photo credit: Associated Press*

The Giants celebrate after rallying to defeat the Dodgers 6–4 in the third game of the playoff in Los Angeles on October 3, 1962, to win the pennant. *Photo credit: Associated Press*

Dodgers ace Sandy Koufax holds a ball signifying his second career no-hitter after a near-perfect performance against the Giants in an 8–0 victory May 12, 1963, at Dodger Stadium. It might not have even been Koufax's best game against San Francisco—in 1959, he struck out 18 Giants in a 5–2 win. *Photo credit: Associated Press/Harold Filan*

Giants pitcher Juan Marichal swings his bat at Dodgers catcher John Roseboro as pitcher Sandy Koufax tries to intervene August 22, 1965, at Candlestick Park. Roseboro suffered a gash on his head, and Marichal was ejected and subsequently suspended. *Photo credit: Associated Press/Robert H. Houston*

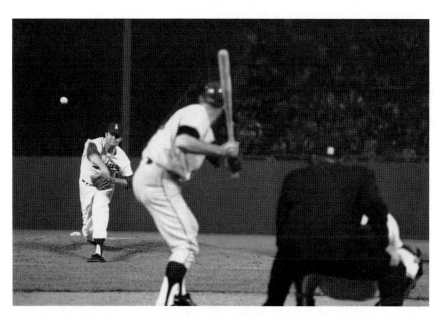

The Dodgers' Don Drysdale pitches to the Giants' Jim Davenport on May 31, 1968, in Los Angeles as he tries for a record-tying fifth consecutive shutout. Drysdale matched the mark with a 3–0 victory, but a controversial call in the ninth inning that kept the streak alive prompted a furious argument from the Giants. *Photo credit: Associated Press*

Beloved by Giants fans and despised by Dodgers fans, Juan Marichal threw the rivalry for a loop when he finished his career wearing a Dodgers uniform in 1975. Marichal makes his Dodgers debut on April 7, 1975, in an exhibition game against the California Angels. *Photo credit: Associated Press*

Mike Ivie is congratulated after his grand slam, which helped beat the Dodgers on May 28, 1978. Ivie's blast lives on as one of the most dramatic home runs hit by the Giants against their rivals. *Photo courtesy of the San Francisco Chronicle.*

Giants pinch-hitter Willie McCovey drives in Jack Clark with the go-ahead run in the eighth inning on July 6, 1980, in his final at-bat at Dodger Stadium. McCovey, a major figure in the rivalry for years, retired after the game. *Photo credit: Associated Press*

Joe Morgan knocked the Dodgers out of the pennant race on the final day of the season October 3, 1982, with a three-run homer in the seventh to give the Giants a 5–3 win. The Dodgers had eliminated the Giants the previous day with a 15–2 rout. *Photo courtesy of the San Francisco Chronicle.*

Above, left: Dodgers reliever Steve Howe reacts angrily after Giants manager Frank Robinson made a gesture to his nose, thinking the move was a reference to his problem with cocaine use. The angry response from the Dodgers nearly sparked a brawl. *Photo courtesy of the San Francisco Chronicle.*

Giants catcher Brian Johnson celebrates as he rounds the bases after a 12th-inning game-winning home run against the Dodgers on September 18, 1997. Johnson's clout was the biggest Giants home run against the Dodgers since Bobby Thomson's blast in 1951. *Photo courtesy of the San Francisco Chronicle.*

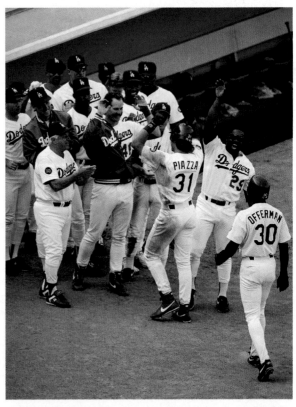

Right: Dodgers manager Tommy Lasorda and his players celebrate after eliminating the Giants from the pennant race with a 10–1 thrashing October 3, 1993. The Dodgers viewed the win as a payback for 1991 when the Giants ended their post-season hopes. *Photo credit: Associated Press/Jeff Robbins*

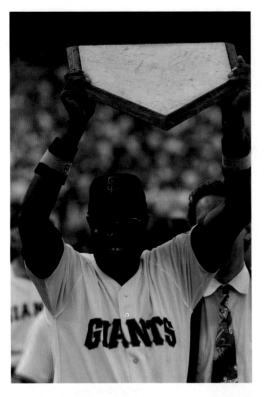

Dusty Baker holds home plate after it was dug up at the end of the last game at Candlestick Park on September 30, 1999, against the Dodgers. Los Angeles won the final game 9–4. *Photo courtesy of the San Francisco Chronicle.*

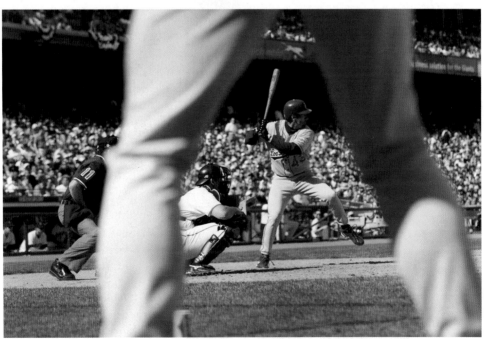

The Dodgers' Kevin Elster is at bat during the inaugural game at the Giants' Pacific Bell Park on April 11, 2000. The light-hitting Elster slugged three home runs to help the Dodgers spoil the Giants' opener 6–5. *Photo courtesy of the San Francisco Chronicle.*

Barry Bonds jumps on home plate after slugging his 500th home run on April 17, 2001, at Pacific Bell Park. The Dodgers were irked when the Giants went on to delay the game for an on-field celebration. *Photo courtesy of the San Francisco Chronicle.*

The Dodgers celebrate after Steve Finley crushed the Giants' pennant hopes with a walk-off grand slam October 3, 2004. Finley's blow might stand as the biggest Dodger home run against the Giants in the more than 100 years of the rivalry. *Photo courtesy of the San Francisco Chronicle.*

Los Angeles fans taunt the Giants' Barry Bonds with a "Got Juice" sign as he takes the field at Dodger Stadium on April 14, 2006. *Photo credit: Associated Press/Mark J. Terrill*

The Dodgers' Manny Ramirez circles the bases after homering against the Giants in the eighth inning in a 10–7 Los Angeles victory on September 20, 2008. Ramirez, who became an instant verbal target of Giants fans in the left-field bleachers at AT&T Park, led the Dodgers to the division crown in 2008. *Photo credit: Associated Press/ Jeff Lewis*

Players from both teams gather on the field at AT&T Park before the Giants–Dodgers game April 11, 2011, to urge fans to avoid violence while cheering for their favorite team. The unusual appeal followed the brutal beating of Giants fan Bryan Stow in the Dodger Stadium parking lot two weeks earlier at the opening game between the clubs. *Photo courtesy of the San Francisco Chronicle.*

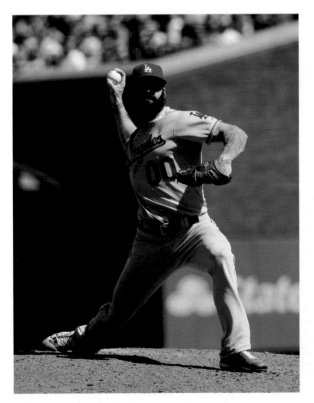

Dodgers reliever Brian Wilson throws a scoreless eighth inning against the Giants on April 17, 2014, in a 2–1 win over the Giants. Wilson, the former Giants closer, added spice to the rivalry with a postgame tantrum in 2013 directed at Giants executive Larry Baer because he hadn't received his 2012 World Series ring. *Photo credit: Associated Press/Jeff Chiu*

Giants outfielder Hunter Pence leads the celebration after the Giants defeated the Royals 3–2 in Game Seven of the World Series October 29, 2014, in Kansas City, for their third championship in five years. *Photo credit: Associated Press/David J. Phillip*

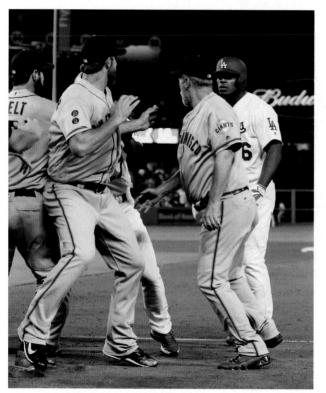

Giants pitcher Madison Bumgarner and the Dodgers' Yasiel Puig stare each other down as first base coach Bill Hayes stands between them after Puig was thrown out at first base September 19, 2016, in Los Angeles. The Bumgarner-Puig feud has heated up the rivalry on several occasions. *Photo credit: Associated Press/ Mark J. Terrill*

Dodgers ace Clayton Kershaw, top, joins the celebration after Adrian Gonzalez drove in the winning run against the Giants in the ninth inning September 19, 2016, in Los Angeles. The loss proved to be a backbreaker in the Giants' quest for the NL West crown. *Photo credit: Associated Press / Mark J. Terrill*

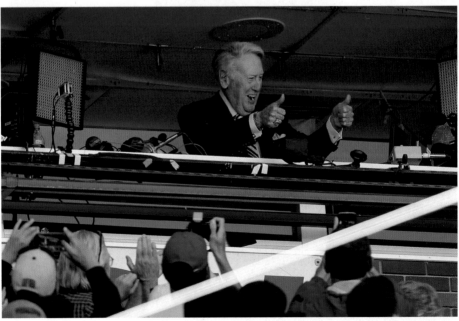

Vin Scully acknowledges the cheers of Giants fans who put aside the rivalry for a moment to salute the legendary broadcaster on October 1, 2016, at AT&T Park. The final series of the year between the clubs marked the end of his 67-year career as the voice of the Dodgers. *Photo credit: Associated Press / Jeff Chiu*

The Giants entered their final series of the year September 25–27 against the Dodgers with a magic number of two to win the West, making it possible that they could wrap it up in front of the Dodgers fans. Los Angeles catcher Mike Sciosica made it clear the Dodgers were not about to concede, saying, "None of us want them doing this on our field. Considering this rivalry, that's the last thing we want to see." Sciosia did his part, driving in four runs with a home run, two-run single and squeeze bunt in a 5–2 win September 25. Rookie Ramon Martinez hurled 8⅔ innings of four-hit ball while striking out 11 as the Dodgers again denied the Giants a chance to clinch the division crown the next day in a 2–1 win.

The Giants became Western Division champions on September 27, but the Dodgers savored the consolation prize. Tim Belcher fired a four-hit, 1–0 shutout, fanning 11 as the Dodgers swept the series. Meanwhile, San Diego lost its game in 13 innings after the Giants were already in the clubhouse, handing San Francisco the title. Said Belcher, "Averting a celebration on our field was a sweet, sweet thing."

———

It was an emotional ride over the last two months of the season for the Giants as they marched to the division title while seeing the comeback of pitcher Dave Dravecky end in tragedy. Dravecky pitched successfully on August 10 in his first game back since having a tumor removed from his pitching arm, but suffered a broken arm in his next start, ending his career.

The postseason was good for the Giants, at least to a point. The Giants defeated the Chicago Cubs in five games to win the NL crown, ending a 27-year drought since they appeared in a World Series. The Giants, facing an uphill battle against a tough Oakland A's pitching staff, succumbed quietly by scores of 5–1 and 5–0 to fall two games down. On October 17, a deadly earthquake just before Game Three put the series on hold. When the games resumed 12 days later, the A's finished off the Giants with a sweep. But the numbing finish of 1989 could not erase the fact that the Giants had turned around their sagging franchise in the final years of the 1980s.

The Giants' recent success didn't come at the expense of the Dodgers, who went 32–22 against their rivals over the last three seasons. Injuries to sluggers Gibson and Marshall slowed the offense, which had the 10th worse batting average and 11th lowest home run total in the league. While the Dodgers finished 1989 in fourth place, they could look back at the 1980s as a decade of success, with four division titles and two World Series championships.

Part Four

EPIC HOMERS
1990–2009

7

∞∞∞

SALUTING THE 'STICK: 1990–1999

Candlestick Park once was a venue for professional boxing matches with the ring set up in the infield. A Candlestick veteran might ask, "Who needs a ring to have a fight in this ballpark?" The Giants and Dodgers fought on that infield, fans fought among each other and sometimes the players and fans met halfway for a fight at the railing. The 1990s had its share of actual good baseball moments at the park, but it was the final salute to the 'Stick that brought back so many memories of a rivalry gone wild.

SLOW STARTS HURT (1990)

The teams' faithful were all in as the season neared. The Dodgers had a five-year streak of plus-3 million attendance from 1982–1986, and had flirted with that number the last three seasons. The Giants were experiencing their biggest attendance boom since coming west. Since the dismal total of 818,697 in the 100-loss season of 1985, the turnstiles began to turn more frequently as the team found success on the field. The Giants drew 2 million last year, the first time the club had reached that milestone in San Francisco.

Despite valid questions about both clubs, there was some thinking that the Giants and Dodgers could get the 1990s off to a fast start with a competitive pennant race.

But then someone locked the starting gate.

First, a labor dispute led to the players being locked out of spring training camp until March 18. A four-year contract was eventually worked out, regarding issues of minimum salary, pensions, and salary arbitration, but the season was delayed a week.

Second, the Cincinnati Reds returned to the spotlight. This was more like the Big Red "Wayback" Machine instead of the Big Red Machine because the club really hadn't been a legitimate contender since the 1970s.

Third, the Dodgers and Giants got off to slow starts. The Dodgers began the season 28–33, then posted a 58–43 record the rest of the way. The Giants had an early disappointing mark of 19–29, and then went 66–48. Cincinnati, which went 33–15 in the first two months of the season, held on to win the NL West.

To their credit, the fans stood by their men despite the disappointing years. The Dodgers' attendance went just over three million, and the Giants drew 1.9 million.

The fourth decade of the West Coast rivalry began with the Giants thinking they might be poised to shake the Dodgers' control over them. The Giants once provided an obstacle that Los Angeles had to detour around. Lately, the Giants had been merely a bump in the road that the Dodgers drove over on their way to success. The Dodgers took the head-to-head competition by 108–72 in the 1970s, and by 95–79 in the 1980s. The clubs entered the 1990 season with the Dodgers having had the series edge in five of the last six years.

The Giants had some hope, though, since they were coming off their most successful four-year run since 1968–71. They won 348 games from 1986–89, 31 more than the Dodgers during that time, and captured two division titles. The lineup that got them to the World Series was returning almost in full. Kevin Mitchell (47 HR, 125 RBIs, .291) and Will Clark (23 HR, 111 RBIs, .333) were the biggest offensive threats. The Giants continued to have high expectations that Matt Williams would make it a threesome of sluggers. Williams hit 18 home runs in 1989, but while he had shown progress in his first three years in the big leagues, he was still a question mark because of a weakness with breaking balls. The chances of a pennant repeat appeared to rest with the health of the pitching staff as injuries forced the Giants to have 15 pitchers start games in 1989.

The Dodgers appeared to be a club that was all pitching and no pop. The outlook for 1990 was a mirror of last season, when the team was 10th in the league in batting average at .240, and 11th in home runs with 89, while leading in ERA at 2.95. Kirk Gibson, who powered the lineup when he joined the club in 1988, had been rendered ineffective because of injury. He hit just .213 in 1989 while playing in 71 games, and would start the season on the disabled list as he tried to come back following knee surgery. The Dodgers did little to fill the Gibson void, leaving Eddie Murray as the only genuine home run hitter. The Dodgers hoped to get at least one more solid year from Fernando Valenzuela, but the rotation would suffer a serious blow when Orel Hershiser had to undergo reconstructive shoulder surgery a few weeks into the season.

While the Giants and Dodgers had a split decision in their first four meetings in April, Cincinnati was already moving in for an early knockout, leaving the Dodgers 4½ out in second place, and the Giants seven back in fifth.

The clubs entered their next matchup, a July 23–25 series, still looking up at Cincinnati, but from a longer distance. The Reds led the second-place Giants by 10 games and the third-place Dodgers by 13½. Los Angeles took two out of three in the seemingly meaningless games, but the division race was about to get new life.

Within one week, the Giants and Dodgers found themselves with a chance to get back in the race that had appeared to be nearly over. The Giants won six of seven, including a four-game sweep over Cincinnati, to close to 5½ games behind the Reds. The Dodgers won five of six, and were now eight games back.

When the teams met for five straight games from August 1–5, the outcome suddenly had some meaning. The Giants won the August 1 contest in Los Angeles, a makeup game from the delayed start of the season. The scene shifted to San Francisco the next four days, and an unexpected division race quickly stirred passions between Candlestick Park fans and the Dodgers.

John Burkett's strong pitching and defensive gems by center fielder Brett Butler and right fielder Dave Kingery in the eighth helped the Giants to a 3–1 win in the San Francisco opener. Los Angeles rocked the Giants with 17 hits for an 11–2 win the next day, though the Dodgers were more focused on rowdy San Francisco fans than on their own offensive assault. Back in the clubhouse, the Dodgers shook their heads over the harassment they said they received from the crowd. "It's not easy for us to win here," said Lenny Harris. "I've never seen fans get on a team like they get on us." Manager Tommy Lasorda, claiming that one fan tossed a hamburger at Gibson, was typically more direct, saying of the spectators, "They stand there behind our dugout and throw stuff and shout such obscenities. There are a lot of good fans, but they are overshadowed by all the bad ones."

The clubs split the next two games, leaving the Giants 4½ games behind Cincinnati while the Dodgers remained eight back.

—⁓—

Perhaps spurred on by their Candlestick confrontation, the Dodgers put themselves into contention with a second-half surge. The Dodgers, now in second, entered a September 21–23 series against the Giants 3½ games behind Cincinnati, while the Giants had fallen to third and were 6½ back. The Dodgers took two out of three, but a stubborn Cincinnati team refused to yield any ground.

The Dodgers needed a sweep of a three-game series in San Francisco September 28–30 to have any realistic chance of catching Cincinnati, but lost the opener 7–6 in the ninth on a wild pitch. The Dodgers were now five games out with five to play. The following day, Clark drove in three runs to help the Giants end the Dodgers' faint hopes of catching the Reds with a 4–3 win.

——∿∿——

The Giants in 1990 were hindered by an unsettled pitching staff with a 4.08 ERA. Six pitchers, including four starters, were slowed at some point by injuries. Williams showed he was worthy of the expectations, as he broke out for 33 homers and 122 RBIs in his first full-time season.

The Dodgers had to get along without the two stars of the 1988 championship year. Hershiser was lost for the year after undergoing surgery. Injury-riddled Gibson played just 89 games and produced just eight homers and 38 RBIs. The Dodgers' team ERA rose to 3.72. The Dodgers had bounced back from a dismal 77-win season in 1989, but the results in 1990 were not good enough to allow them to keep the status quo in the offseason. Changes were afoot, and before the first pitch of 1991 would be thrown, Gibson and Valenzuela would be gone, and slugger Darryl Strawberry and Giants outfielder Brett Butler would be signed. The Giants, meanwhile, would make a few additions, but with the big bats of Clark, Mitchell, and Williams returning, the club could make an argument that it was just a healthy pitching staff away from making a run for the division crown.

PAYBACK (1991–93)

Much has been written about the unwritten rules of baseball. The rivalry has unwritten rules of its own. Rule No. 1: Don't allow the other team to clinch a postseason berth on your field. Rule No. 2: Better yet, eliminate the other team from a postseason berth on your field.

As the first-place Dodgers tried to hold on to a two-game lead over the relentless Atlanta Braves in the final week-and-a-half of the 1991 season, the out-of-contention Giants had both rules in mind. The schedule-makers matched up the rivals for a pair of three-game series, at Los Angeles September 27–29 and at San Francisco October 4–6. The Giants were heading for a fourth-place finish, but after they downed the Dodgers 4–1 September 28, San Francisco reliever Don Robinson admitted the opportunity to make life miserable for their opponents was a motivation. "It will make our season if we knock the Dodgers out of it," he said. "It's all we've got going."

When the clubs met in San Francisco for the season-ending series, the Dodgers and Braves were locked at 92–67 with three games to play. Giants pitcher John Burkett seconded Robinson's motion. "I hate the Dodgers. I've been in this organization since 1983, and there's always been a rivalry, even in 'A' ball." Some Dodgers took exception to the Giants' desire to choose sides in the race, since they were in effect rooting for the Braves. Los Angeles outfielder Darryl Strawberry carried the case most bluntly, saying, "I find that kind of arrogant. If they don't want to see us up there at the top now, they should have beaten us when it counted for them."

One Giant took the debate a step further. Reserve outfielder Mike Felder was in his first year of the rivalry, yet he topped all the talk by having "Beat L.A." shaved into the back of his head before the series. Explained Felder, "We don't want them celebrating on our turf."

The Giants, 19 games out going into the October 4 game, quickly made it clear that they would make things difficult for the Dodgers. A two-run homer by Will Clark, and a solo shot by Matt Williams in the first inning gave the Giants a 3–0 lead, and San Francisco went on to a 4–1 victory. Meanwhile, Atlanta defeated Houston 5–2 to move into sole possession of first place. One day after the 40th anniversary of Bobby Thomson's homer, the Giants had again handed the Dodgers a devastating defeat. A lively crowd of 44,994 showed up the next day, some performing the tomahawk chop sign to show support for the Braves. Trevor Wilson was working on a two-hit shutout in the ninth when Atlanta posted a 5–2 victory over Houston. Giants fans began celebrating, as Wilson got the final out for a 4–0 win to end the Dodgers' season.

Dodgers manager Tommy Lasorda gave credit to the Braves, but took a shot at the Giants and their fans. "If they're happy they knocked us out of first, and they finished 20 (actually 19) games out, that doesn't show me too much."

Clark made it clear he would not be sending Lasorda a sympathy card, as he reveled in the Dodgers' agony of defeat. "This series salvages our season," Clark said. "We can look at ourselves and say, 'We're not a bad club. The Dodgers had a chance to win it, and we kicked their butts.'"

There would be more to say about the unwritten rivalry rules, and that would come just two years later.

———ᴧᴧ———

While spring training normally abounds with optimism for even the most helpless team, the Giants and Dodgers could make a reasonable case that both would have competitive years in 1992. The Dodgers were coming off two consecutive second-place finishes, though 1991 was clearly a disappointment after they allowed Atlanta, which they led by 9½ games at the All Star break, to pass them on the final weekend of the season. The Giants could look back at manager Roger Craig's first five full seasons, all of which were winning years and included two division titles and a World Series appearance, and conclude that 1991's fourth-place team merely had an off year.

Spring's optimism turned to summer's reality as both teams were playing meaningless games before August. When the clubs met for the first of a three-game series July 27 in San Francisco, the Giants were in fourth, 12 games back, the Dodgers were 17½ out in last place, and only 18,364 bothered to show up.

The cumulative team records in 1992 were even worse than 1984. Once again, the Giants played with uncertainty about their future because of the pending sale of the team by owner Bob Lurie and the possibility that the franchise would be moved to Florida. The uncertainty placed a pall over the year, and the teams' play matched the mood. In 1992, the Giants and Dodgers combined for their worst year since making the trip out west. As the 1992 season ended, the West Coast rivalry appeared to be over as the Giants looked as if they would be heading to Florida. As tragic as that sounded, one couldn't blame some fans, based on the 1992 results, if they said, "Who cares?" The clubs hit a collective bottom in 1992. The last-place Dodgers lost 99 games, the most since they dropped 101 in 1908. Attendance at Dodger Stadium was 2,473,266, the lowest for a nonstrike year since 1976. The Giants lost 90 games, the most since the 100-defeat season of 1985.

The grim play on the field matched the mood in San Francisco. The Giants would have one more homestand, drawing 45,630 on September 27 against Cincinnati in what was feared would be the final game ever in San Francisco. Police lined the field after the game, but there was no repeat of the Polo Grounds finale when wild fans invaded the diamond on a scavenger hunt for souvenirs. Instead it was a somber day of tears, sadness, and signs pleading for the Giants to stay. Giants manager Craig, who would be out as the skipper in 1993, took a more sentimental view after the possibly last San Francisco–Los Angeles game on September 20 at Candlestick Park. "This could be the final time these two teams play here," he said. "But it's pretty evident by the way the fans were into it today that the rivalry lives on."

It would live on. In almost rapid-fire succession, the club was purchased by a group of investors led by Peter Magowan, Barry Bonds was given $43.75 million to play left field and Dusty Baker was named the new manager.

—⁓—

The rivalry, energized by the Giants' moves, almost got physical in the early going in 1993. Williams tore the Dodgers apart in the clubs' first meeting of the year May 7 in San Francisco, going four for five with two RBIs, a double and a triple in an 8–5 victory. The next day, the hard-throwing, 21-year-old Pedro Martinez knocked down Williams with a pitch in the ninth. Giants reliever Mike Jackson evened the score the next inning by moving Jose Offerman off the plate. The pitch prompted some players to step onto the field, but they returned to their dugouts before any punches could be thrown. The Dodgers took two out of three in the series (5–2 in 12 innings and 6–4), which drew 140,034, but a good start kept the first-place Giants a half-game in front of Houston and 5½ ahead of Los Angeles.

The Dodgers continued to play the Giants tough, winning their next two series against San Francisco. That, however, was about the only thing going wrong for the Giants. San Francisco went 15–9 in April, 18–9 in May, 19–9 in June, and 18–8 in July for a 70–35 record that put them 7½ games up on Atlanta and 15 ahead of the Dodgers on July 31. The Braves refused to back down, and in what had become one of baseball's most extraordinary races, Atlanta stood at 101–57 and San Francisco at 100–58 as the Giants and Dodgers began a season-ending four-game series September 30–October 3 in Los Angeles. For the Dodgers, it was a chance to answer what they interpreted as Giants' trash talk from 1991.

September 30 (Giants 3, Dodgers 1): Bill Swift came through for the Giants, limiting the Dodgers to one run and two hits through seven innings for his 21st win of the season. Kevin Rogers and Rod Beck preserved the win with scoreless relief. The Giants scored two in the fourth on Kirt Manwaring's bases-loaded single. Dave Hansen singled home a run in the sixth. Williams tripled in the eighth and scored on Willie McGee's single as the Giants picked up a 3–1 win. Combined with Atlanta's 10–8 loss to Houston, the Giants and Braves were now tied with three games to go.

October 1 (Giants 8, Dodgers 7): Bonds hit two home runs and drove in seven runs to keep the Giants tied with Atlanta. The Dodgers took a 4–0 lead off Burkett after two innings. In the third, Darren Lewis tripled and scored on Clark's double. After Williams singled, Bonds launched a three-run homer to tie it. Clark's single and Williams's double put runners at second and third in the fifth, and Omar Daal came in to relieve Ramon Martinez. Lasorda chose to pitch to Bonds despite first base being open, and the decision proved costly. Bonds hit his second three-run blast to give the Giants a 7–4 lead. San Francisco held on for an 8–7 victory. Atlanta defeated Colorado 7–4 for the 12th straight time this season to stay even.

October 2 (Giants 5, Dodgers 3): The Dodgers were far more careful with Bonds than the previous night when he destroyed them, but they still paid a price for not pitching to him. The Giants' win, coupled with Atlanta's 10–1 rout of Colorado, put both teams at 103–58 with one game to play. The Giants took a tense 3–2 lead into the seventh. Clark singled, and this time, Lasorda decided to walk Bonds intentionally, but Dave Martinez followed with a two-run double. The Giants owed the crucial victory to their bullpen, after starter Bryan Hickerson had to leave the game when he was hit by a line drive in the third inning. Jeff Brantley, Rogers, Mike Jackson, and Beck combined to limit the Dodgers to one run the rest of the way for a 5–3 win. The Giants' spectacular season came down to the final day, one of the biggest games in franchise history, and there was some concern that the pitching-weary club would have to rely on 21-year-old Salomon Torres. The Giants won 14 of their last 17, and Torres took all three losses. In his last start, five days ago against Colorado, Torres gave up four runs, three hits, and two home runs in 2⅔ innings. However, Baker had no reservations, saying, "In our mind, he's the right guy for this situation."

October 3 (Dodgers 12, Giants 1): Revenge was in the air at Dodger Stadium. The Dodgers had the chance to crush the Giants' division title quest as San Francisco had done to them just two years earlier. Fans taunted the Giants with Braves' tomahawk chops over their dugout just as Candlestick Park fans had done in 1991. Lasorda, still fuming over that day, called his team together before the game, and one player was quoted as saying he told them "this game could make my year." With Atlanta a 5–3 winner over Colorado earlier in the day, the Giants needed to win to force a one-game playoff the next day.

The Dodgers went to work early against a wild Torres, building a 6–1 lead after five innings and going on to dash the Giants' hopes. Mike Piazza had two homers and four RBIs, and Raul Mondesi and Cory Snyder had two-run homers as the Dodgers totaled 14 hits. The ineffective Torres went 3⅓ innings, giving up three runs and five hits and walked five. Kevin Gross turned in a masterpiece, silencing the Giants' potent bats on six hits in a 12–1 complete game performance. Afterward, Lasorda basked in the payback the Dodgers delivered to the Giants. "I wouldn't call it revenge," he said. "Will Clark made some statements that were not apropos to the situation. You don't hear guys in this clubhouse popping off. We have those statements he made in 1991, and we remember."

—∿—

The Giants won 103 games, the club's most regular season victories since John McGraw guided them to the same number in 1912. Baker had a successful managerial debut, Bonds lived up to the hype with a .336 average and 46 home runs, and Burkett and Swift were 20-game winners. Attendance reached 2.6 million, the largest Giants home total since coming to San Francisco, but Candlestick Park would sit vacant during the postseason.

While the Giants were frustrated, it was hard to accept much blame for falling short after such a remarkable year. Instead, they could only admit that they were victims of an amazing finish by Atlanta. The Braves, 9½ games out on August 8, won 39 of their last 50 games. The Giants won 14 of their last 17, but the Braves would not back down.

The Dodgers were one of only three teams to have a winning record against the Giants in 1993, but while there was satisfaction in eliminating the Giants on the final day, there was little consolation that they could do no more than finish at .500.

BATTERY MATES, RIP

Roy Campanella, 71, died on June 26, 1993. In 10 seasons with Brooklyn, the eight-time all-star catcher hit .276, with 242 home runs and 856 RBIs. His career ended when he was severely injured in a car crash in 1958, a little more than two months away from the West Coast opening game against the Giants. Among the many who admired Campanella was Don Drysdale, who offered these words about his former battery mate: "You have to realize how strong a man he was just to survive, everything he had to endure since the automobile accident. It was just absolutely amazing."

Seven days later, Drysdale, who had gone into broadcasting, was found dead in his hotel room. The statistics tell a lot about the Hall of Fame pitcher: a 209–166 record in a 14-year career and a 2.95 ERA. He once threw 172 pitches and struck out 11 in a 13-inning, 2–1 win over the Giants in 1959. But even more than his numbers, Drysdale was remembered for his fierce intensity. Yet, he had the respect of most of those who faced him, so it was fitting that among those who praised him in death was former Giants manager Bill Rigney, who said, "I don't think there was any tougher competitor than the big guy with the game on the line."

Drysdale led the league in hit batsmen from 1958 to 1961. His high mark was in 1961 when he drilled 20. Giants batters spent much time diving and ducking from Drysdale's darts, a memory that still stuck with former Giant slugger Orlando Cepeda, who had his share of battles with the right-hander. Cepeda, speaking for many of those who faced him, said, "The trick against Drysdale is to hit him before he hits you."

LOST SEASON (1994)

It's never a good sign when the start of a season is more focused on the suits in the suites than the fans in the stands.

As the 1994 season opened, the usual optimistic baseball talk was being overshadowed by pessimistic boardroom talk. Owners, claiming losses, wanted a salary cap tied to revenue sharing, and there were no signs the players would back off their contract positions.

On the field, the prospects of a division title for the Giants and Dodgers improved dramatically in the offseason prior to the 1994 campaign, though it had nothing to do with any significant trades or signings for either team. Realignment created three divisions in each league, with the Atlanta Braves joining the new East Division. Atlanta won the last three NL West titles, compiling 296 victories.

The Giants hoped they could make a run at a crown with one of the best one-two punch combinations in baseball: Barry Bonds (46 HR in 1993) and Matt Williams (38 HR in 1993). The Dodgers, trying to bounce back after two disappointing years, thought they could contend with a solid rotation of Orel Hershiser, Pedro Astacio, Ramon Martinez, Tom Candiotti, and Kevin Gross.

With a players' strike threatening to disrupt the season and possibly force a shorter schedule, a midseason Dodgers-Giants series on July 25–27 in San Francisco took on the importance of a critical late September matchup. The Dodgers had slipped, and while their record fell below .500 at 48–50, it was enough to lead the division. The Giants, who were 9½ games out on July 6, were now just 1½ behind, with Colorado two back.

Eric Karros took charge of the opening game, going four for five with two homers and four RBIs in a 10–5 Dodgers win. The Giants came back the next day for a 12–5 victory as Williams hit his 37th homer. San Francisco, trailing 1–0 after seven in game three, scored four in the eighth for a 4–1 win to draw within a half-game of the Dodgers. The victory set the stage for a three-way battle for the NL West flag, featuring the Dodgers and Giants, and the Rockies, who were just one game behind Los Angeles.

The Giants took three of four from Colorado following the Dodgers series, while Los Angeles swept Houston. That left the Dodgers with a one-game lead over the Giants on July 31. The Giants then lost six straight, and the Dodgers went on to take a 3½-game lead on August 11 with a win over Cincinnati. The Giants bounced back to sweep Chicago, wrapping up the series with a 5–2 win on August 10. But on August 12, the players went on strike, and the failure to reach a settlement resulted in the cancellation of the season.

The stoppage couldn't have happened at a worse time. The July three-game series between the Dodgers and Giants drew 158,012 fans. Excitement was growing as the clubs were headed to their best battle for the title since the memorable 1982 season. Bonds and Williams were on their way to a season reminiscent of the 1961 Maris-Mantle home run derby. When play ended, Williams had 43 homers and Bonds had 37. Williams was on a pace to possibly match Roger Maris's 61, and Bonds had a shot at Mickey Mantle's 54. The clubs already had met 10 times, splitting those games. They only had three games left against one another, but in what would have been a scheduling gem, those contests would have been in Dodger Stadium in the final series of the season. One can only imagine the possibilities: The clubs tied for first, Williams going for his 61st homer, and the division title on the line.

Baseball had turned the potentially greatest year of the West Coast rivalry into a lost season.

BACK TO WORK (1995)

A truce in the labor war was declared April 2, 1995, so the teams could get back to business, but it wouldn't be business as usual. Opening day was delayed until April 26 to give the clubs time for spring training, and the season was reduced to 144 games.

Those fans willing to return to the ballparks would indeed need a scorecard to tell the players, as owners, citing losses from the strike, did some house cleaning. Gone from the Dodgers were pitchers Orel Hershiser, Kevin Gross, Roger McDowell, and Jim Gott, and outfielders Brett Butler and Cory Snyder. The Giants would move on without pitchers Bill Swift, John Burkett, Bud Black, and Mike Jackson and veteran outfielder Willie McGee.

The Dodgers appeared to have emerged from the rubble with a better outlook for the season. Ramon Martinez, Tom Candiotti, and Pedro Astacio would return in the rotation, and the club hoped 21-year-old Ismael Valdes and newly signed Hideo Nomo would fill in for the departed Hershiser and Gross. The Dodgers' roster had been evolving even without the strike, as shortstop Jose Offerman would be the only returning player from the opening day lineup of three years ago. The club had a core of power hitters in Mike Piazza, Raul Mondesi, Tim Wallach, and Eric Karros, who all posted good numbers despite the shortened season.

The strike and subsequent roster shake-up killed any momentum the Giants might have had following their 103-victory season in 1993. Prospects didn't appear bright for the new season because of holes in the offense and serious questions about the revamped rotation.

The Giants had the fearsome twosome of Barry Bonds and Matt Williams returning, but the remainder of the lineup was unlikely to scare any opposing pitcher. The Giants' .249 batting average was the lowest in the National League in 1994.

There were few doubts among baseball forecasters that the Dodgers would win the weak NL West in 1995. The club, with a 58–56 record before the 1994 shutdown, was the only team in the division to finish above .500.

———✳———

A rough collision at home plate indicated the clubs were ready to resume the rivalry following the strike, but the fans weren't so sure. The Giants, behind the pitching of Terry Mulholland, blanked the Dodgers 7–0 on May 1 before only 10,828 at Candlestick Park. Mulholland pitched seven strong innings, and the bullpen completed the shutout. The game nearly began with a brawl when Mondesi barreled into Giants catcher Kirt Manwaring as he was tagged out while trying to score from first on a base hit. Mondesi and Manwaring got up glaring at one another, prompting Mulholland to later remark about the near altercation, "Oh yeah, just like old times."

The teams put on another show the next day with one of the rivalry's most grueling contests. Nomo made his major league debut for the Dodgers, allowing one hit and striking out seven in five innings. Mark Portgual of the Giants was equally effective, giving up just three hits and striking out eight in seven innings. The game was still at 0–0 after 14 innings. The Dodgers broke through for three in the top of the 15th on an RBI single by Reggie Williams and a two-run double by Karros. The Dodgers were one out away from wrapping it up in the bottom of the 15th when Jeff Reed walked, Darren Lewis singled, and Robby Thompson homered to tie it. Bonds followed with a single, and Williams brought him home for the winning run with a double. The clubs combined to use 17 pitchers and 46 players in the five-hour, 16-minute game.

The Giants, with a surprising 28–25 record, were just a half-game behind first-place Colorado as the clubs met for four games in Los Angeles June 22–25. The Dodgers, after having lost 19 of their first 32 games, came back to sit two games behind the Rockies. Injuries were threatening to dismantle the Giants' good early effort. Williams went down with a broken foot on June 3 after getting off to a strong start.

The Dodgers took full advantage of the Giants' weakened state, first with their bats, then with their arms. Los Angles slugged five homers, two by Karros, for a 7–6 win in the opening game of the series. They followed that with solid pitching performances by Valdes, Nomo, and Candiotti for a four-game sweep, limiting the Giants to four runs in the last three games, and moving into a first-place tie with Colorado. The Giants had slipped into fourth, 2½ games back.

The Dodgers continued to fight it out with the Rockies, while the declining Giants were getting desperate. When the teams next met, for four games in Los Angeles August 4–7, the Dodgers were in second, 2½ games behind Colorado. The Giants were 9½ games behind. San Francisco shook up its roster two weeks earlier in a trade that sent pitchers Mark Portugal and Dave Burba, and outfielder Darren Lewis to the Cincinnati Reds for five players, including National Football League star Deion Sanders.

The Giants played the Dodgers tough, forcing Los Angeles to go 12 innings in game four to salvage a split. Karros broke up a 1–1 tie with a two-run homer in the 12th for a 3–1 win.

With Williams sidelined, the Dodgers made certain that Bonds, the only other main threat in the order, would not hurt them. Bonds was walked four times, three intentionally.

—⁓—

The Dodgers, in the thick of a division and wild card race through September, clinched the division crown on the next to last game of the season with a 7–2 victory over San Diego. The Dodgers entered their best-of-five division series match-up against Cincinnati with high hopes as they sent out their three top pitchers—Martinez, Valdes, and Nomo—and their combined 43–24 record. Cincinnati scored four runs in the first inning of the opening game off Martinez, and never looked back as they swept the Dodgers.

The quick postseason exit was a shock for the Dodgers, who appeared to have had the pitching and offense to make a serious run at the World Series. Despite the letdown, the club had to be considered among the favorites again next season. The exciting arrival of Nomo, Mondesi's establishment as one of the top young sluggers in the game, and the rising stature of Piazza as one of baseball's superstars cemented the good feelings.

Dreadful pitching and the injury that limited Williams to 76 games crippled the Giants. The midseason deal that brought Sanders to the Giants appeared to be more of a gimmick to spark fan interest in the post-strike times than a move crafted to strategically improve the club's outlook. The fans were looking for more substance, as home attendance fell to 1.2 million after reaching 2.6 million in 1993.

CONSTRUCTION ZONE (1996)

The Dodgers entered the 1996 season looking as if they might have built a dynasty, while the Giants looked more like a team under construction.

Last year ended in a division series debacle for the Dodgers, as the league's top pitching staff yielded 22 runs in the three-game sweep by Cincinnati. The Dodgers, though, could attribute the disappointment to more a case of catching a hot Reds team than an exposure of any weaknesses on the club. The Giants finished last in the division as its pitching staff collapsed. The pitching staff had an ERA of 4.86, second highest in the league, and gave up a league-high 173 home runs. Fortunately for the Giants, the San Francisco voters were willing to overlook the current foibles as they approved a proposal for a new ballpark in San Francisco. The club, which nearly left for Canada in 1976 and Florida in 1993, was going to stay put.

For the second straight year, the Giants would begin the season with an overhauled pitching staff. Mark Leiter and William Van Landingham, hampered by a rib injury in 1995, would be the only returning starters as the rotation added three new members.

An injury to Matt Williams added to the Giants' misery in 1995. Williams broke a bone when he fouled a ball off his foot on June 3 at a time when he was hitting .381 with 13 homers and 35 RBIs. The loss of Williams coincided with a slide by the Giants. There would be no slipping from Barry Bonds (33 HR, 104 RBIs, .294), though the absence of Williams might have affected his numbers.

The Dodgers were the NL West favorite for the second straight year, boasting a club with power, speed, and pitching. The pitching staff, which posted a 3.66 ERA in 1995, was among the best in the game. It consisted of starters Ramon Martinez, Hideo Nomo, Ismael Valdes, Pedro Astacio, and Tom Candiotti.

The team's potent offensive trio of Mike Piazza, Raul Mondesi, and Eric Karros would return. Delino DeShields (39 SB) and Mondesi (27 SB) also gave the Dodgers base-stealing threats. Los Angeles hoped that Brett Butler, who rejoined the club late last season after a stint with the New York Mets, would still be productive at age 39.

The Dodgers would embark on a quest for another postseason spot with manager Tommy Lasorda in charge, but would have to adjust in midyear under the new leadership of interim manager Bill Russell.

—⁓—

The teams split their first two games of the year on April 16–17, but the significance wouldn't be known until more than two months later. Lasorda stepped down July 29 after undergoing an angioplasty procedure on his heart, meaning that the two-game series marked his final time at the helm of a Giants-Dodgers contest.

It was only fitting that Lasorda's final rivalry series feature an old-fashioned Giants-Dodgers clash. The Dodgers jumped out to a 4–0 lead in the third on a DeShields's homer and two bases-loaded walks. Los Angeles put the game away with a four-run fourth highlighted by DeShield's two-run double. In the ninth, with the Dodgers leading 11–2, youngster Roger Cedeno stole second base. The breach of baseball etiquette by the Dodgers infuriated the Giants, who felt that was unnecessary considering the score. Manager Dusty Baker and other Giants screamed at Cedeno and Williams had to be restrained from going after him. Dodgers players, who gathered around Cedeno to escort him off the field when the game ended, were sympathetic to the Giants' complaints, but argued that the 21-year-old, in just his second major league season, was merely showing his inexperience.

The resumption of play after the All Star break July 11 saw the Dodgers trailing San Diego by one game in a red-hot division race, and the Giants fighting to stop a free-fall that saw them plummet into the cellar, 8½ games out. In a scheduling oddity, the clubs would play eight of their 13 games against each other in 11 days.

The Dodgers jumped on the Giants to win the first two of a July 11–14 four-game series in Los Angeles. The Giants countered with consecutive shutouts 7–0 and 6–0 featuring strong outings by starters Shawn Estes and Van Landingham, and late-inning help from the bullpen. But even with the split, the Dodgers moved into first, a game ahead of San Diego.

The Giants continued to play the Dodgers tough despite being 9½ games back to gain another split in a four-game series at San Francisco. The Dodgers, unable to take advantage of having the eight games with a struggling team, ended up where they began, a game behind first-place San Diego.

The Giants had long disappeared from the division picture, heading to their worst season in 11 years when the clubs next met September 24 in Los Angeles. Yet, Baker wasn't planning to concede anything as the clubs squared off in a three-game series in which the Dodgers had an outside chance to wrap up a playoff spot. "I don't want nobody to clinch against me," Baker said. The Giants manager was still smarting from the last day of the 1993 season when the Dodgers killed his club's postseason hopes. "I've got the rest of my life to pay them back for '93, Baker said, "and I've got a long memory." The first-place Dodgers entered the final six games of the season in control of their destiny, leading San Diego by a half-game, and having the advantage over Montreal in the wild-card race.

The Giants dropped two of three, but Baker achieved his goal of not letting Los Angeles clinch. The Dodgers now led San Diego by two, and those clubs would meet for a final three-game series in Los Angeles.

—⁓—

The Dodgers were swept, giving San Diego the division title, and putting wild-card Los Angeles in a first-round playoff against the pitching-rich Atlanta Braves.

The Dodgers went down quietly as the Braves swept them in three games. The Dodgers produced just five runs in the series. The sweep was made more painful because the Dodgers knew this was one of their best clubs in years. The team was well balanced, slugging 150 homers, stealing 124 bases and posting a league-best 3.46 ERA. It also was frustrating because the club had proved it could handle adversity when a sudden managerial change was necessitated because of the illness of Lasorda. The Dodgers, 41–35 at the time the club was turned over to Russell, went 49–37 the rest of the way.

The Giants had a losing record for the third straight year. The 94 losses were the third most by a San Francisco team. The pitching staff was even worse than in 1995, posting a 4.71 ERA, and surrendering 194 homers. The club's lineup also was in disarray. Williams, plagued by injuries, appeared in only 181 games the past two years. The Giants hadn't come close to finding a solid replacement for Will Clark at first base since he departed after the 1993 season. Second base also seemed to be a growing problem. Robby Thompson, after hitting .312 in 1993, tailed off drastically, in part because of injuries, and batted .209, .223 and .211 the last three seasons. The Giants countered those gaps in dramatic fashion during the offseason. On opening day of 1997, Williams would be gone, J.T. Snow would be at first, and Jeff Kent at second. The moves would get immediate results, and more significantly, set the stage for the Giants' most successful era since the 1960s.

SHOT HEARD 'ROUND CALIFORNIA (1997)

Giants catcher Brian Johnson seemed the unlikeliest of would-be heroes. He was a lunch-pail player, showing up for work every day ready to do the job, but not the guy who would stand out among the rest of the employees. He hit just 16 homers in 682 at-bats in his three-plus years in the big leagues as a part-timer with San Diego and Detroit before coming to San Francisco. He didn't lack athleticism, however, having thrown for 3,334 yards and 18 TDs while sharing the quarterback position at Stanford for three years. He also had experienced baseball success, participating with Stanford teams that won the College World Series two years in a row. But so far, glory had eluded him in the major leagues.

That would change in the heat of a Giants-Dodgers September pennant race.

—*m*—

The Dodgers entered the 1997 season as the team to beat in the NL West, while the Giants went into the year as the team most likely to get beat on. The Dodgers were coming off two straight years in which they made it to the postseason, and boasted a pitching staff and lineup that were among the strongest in the league. The Giants were coming off two dreadful fourth-place seasons and were mocked in the offseason for trading slugger Matt Williams. Of course, the Giants still had three-time MVP Barry Bonds, but even his bat (33 homers, 104 RBIs in 1995; 42 homers, 129 RBIs in 1996) could not change the club's fortunes in those years.

The most striking change for the Dodgers was that for the first time since 1977, Tommy Lasorda was not on the field with the team at the start of the year. Bill Russell was entering his first full season as manager after taking over for Lasorda during the 1996 season. The Dodgers saw few flaws in their lineup, with Brett Butler, speedy newcomer Wilton Guerrero and Raul Mondesi at the top of the order, setting the table for power hitters Mike Piazza and Eric Karros. The pitching, considered on par with the outstanding Atlanta Braves rotation and holders of the major league's lowest ERA in 1996 of 3.46, consisted of Ramon Martinez, Ismael Valdes, Chan Ho Park, Hideo Nomo, and Pedro Astacio.

Giants management, in particular new general manager Brian Sabean, faced months of criticism for the November 13, 1996, trade that sent popular third baseman Williams to the Cleveland Indians for second baseman Jeff Kent and two others. On November 26, Sabean pulled off a second deal, which received a positive reaction, bringing two-time Gold Glove first baseman J.T. Snow to San Francisco.

The Giants had a scare in the exhibition season when Snow was hit in the face with a pitch from Seattle's Randy Johnson, fracturing his right eye socket. Snow's remarkably quick and courageous recovery gave the Giants an unexpected lift—the team, which experienced grumbling from some players during 1996's dismal campaign, was brought together as the players rallied around their injured teammate.

The Dodgers, on the other hand, entered the season with significant cracks in team unity. The cultural and ethnic diversity of the roster apparently affected team chemistry, and led to an extraordinary clubhouse meeting in which pitcher Todd Worrell pleaded with his teammates to not allow the cliques that had developed to disrupt the club.

In San Francisco, Sabean's wheeling and dealing would pay off, and another trade for three pitchers on July 31 would revamp the team for the stretch drive. Sabean's detractors would back off on their criticism as the Giants kept winning. However, amid the headline-making deals, it was a routine trade on July 16, 1997, that would turn into gold, as the Giants acquired Johnson from the Detroit Tigers.

—⁓—

The Giants jumped out to a surprising 13–3 record, and entered the first series June 4–5 against the Dodgers 1½ games in front of Colorado and five ahead of Los Angeles. The clubs split the series, highlighted by Piazza's 454-foot home run in the Dodgers 5–1 win in game one. The Giants had extended their lead to 3½ games over Colorado and 6 games over Los Angeles when they began a stretch of playing eight of their 12 games against the Dodgers in 25 days beginning June 19. The Giants managed to split a four-game series June 19–22 to maintain the same lead, but the Dodgers were about to make a move. In a four-game series in Los Angeles July 10–13, the Dodgers won three. The Dodgers' third victory of the series drew them to within four games of the Giants. While the clubs would not be facing each other for another two months, the NL West had developed into an apparent two-team race, with Colorado having dropped 8½ games out.

———

In the 60 games since the Giants-Dodgers last meeting, a significant change had occurred. The Dodgers, with a 36–24 record over that period, had taken a two-game lead over the Giants as the teams prepared for a September 17–18 pair in San Francisco.

September 17 (Giants 2, Dodgers 1): The Dodgers carried the momentum into the series—riding a three-game winning streak while the Giants had lost four straight. Bonds quickly turned things around when he crushed a two-run homer in the first inning. The Giants' pitching made it stand up for a 2–1 win. Bonds's blast into the right-field upper deck off Park followed a walk to Darryl Hamilton. Mondesi ripped a home run to deep left off Kirk Rueter in the fifth. Rueter allowed just one run and four hits in seven innings, and Roberto Hernandez pitched two shutout innings to preserve the victory. Ten games were left to play, with a final, memorable battle about to unfold.

September 18 (Giants 6, Dodgers 5, 12 innings): The scoring the next day began on Otis Nixon's solo homer in the first. Glenallen Hill tied it in the Giants' half, following Bonds's triple with an RBI single. Snow made it 2–1 Giants in the fourth with a homer, and in the fifth, after singles by Hamilton and Bill Mueller, Bonds launched a three-run homer for a 5–1 lead. Karros's RBI single and Todd Zeile's run-scoring double in the sixth cut the lead in half, and Piazza's two-run single in the seventh off Hernandez tied it. In the 10th, with the score still at 5–5, the Dodgers appeared certain to break the game open against closer Rod Beck. Singles by Piazza, Karros, and Mondesi loaded the bases with no outs. Candlestick went from agony to ecstasy as Zeile struck out looking and pinch-hitter Eddie Murray grounded into a second-to-home-to-first double play.

The 52,188 fans were drained after watching Beck's great escape, but at least they got a chance to catch their breath as both teams went down quietly over the next 12 outs. The crowd could be forgiven if it didn't have visions of immediate dramatics in the last half of the 12th as Johnson led off the frame against Mark Guthrie. One good omen for the Giants: Johnson was swinging the bat well this day, having gone two for four as he stepped into the batter's box. One bad omen for the Dodgers: While Guthrie enjoyed the best season in his nine-year career in 1996 with a 2.22 ERA in 66 appearances, he was not at the top of his game now. The left-hander took the mound having allowed 11 runs in his last 13⅔ innings.

The crowd rose at contact as Johnson drove Guthrie's pitch over the left-field fence for a 6–5 win. Johnson not only earned employee of the month honors, but placed himself among rivalry legends with the most electrifying Giants homer against the Dodgers since Bobby Thomson's "shot heard 'round the world."

—∿∿—

The Dodgers stumbled immediately after their heartbreaking defeat, losing three straight to Colorado, while the Giants took three out of four from San Diego. The Giants had suddenly taken a 2½ game lead, and on September 27, they defeated San Diego 6–1 to clinch the West.

The Giants' first postseason appearance since 1989 ended quickly as they fell in three straight games to Florida. The Dodgers went home after the season puzzled at how they let the Giants pass them. Los Angeles out-hit the Giants by 10 points (.268 to .258), and out-pitched them (3.62 ERA to 4.39), yet still finished two games behind.

The results of the 1997 season would leave the frustrated Dodgers with an incentive to overtake the Giants in 1998, while the revitalized San

Francisco club would be hungrier after getting a taste of postseason play. But the two teams instead were heading for a quiet finish to the 1990s: the Giants wouldn't get another postseason shot until they moved into their new ballpark, and the Dodgers would have to go through two ownership changes before they would legitimately contend again.

O'MALLEYS HAND OVER KEYS (1998)

Since the clubs moved west, the Dodgers always seemed to be the more stable franchise. The Dodgers built the better ballpark, consistently dwarfed the Giants at the gate, had two managers for the first 38 years on the West Coast while the Giants had 14, had 13 first-place finishes to the Giants five, won five World Series championships to the Giants none, and were 20 games better than the Giants in head-to-head play since 1958. The Giants were the subject of constant rumors over the years that the team would leave San Francisco, coming close at least twice, while the Dodgers were cemented in Los Angeles.

The Giants were now under their third San Francisco ownership, while the Dodgers had been run by the O'Malleys since 1950. But the Dodgers' stability was about to be shaken up, both off and on the field, while the Giants would suddenly find themselves as the less volatile of the two organizations.

The change began on March 19, 1998, as Rupert Murdoch's Fox Group purchased the Dodgers. The new owners took little time to make an impact as they faced their first big challenge in trying to re-sign all-star catcher Mike Piazza to a long-term deal. Piazza was seeking a new contract for a reported seven years and $100 million. Bob Graziano, the new Dodgers president, said as the new owners took over, "We want to sign Mike Piazza. Mike is a very important player for the Dodgers, and we're going to move forward at the appropriate time." Less than two months later, with neither side able to agree on a contract, the new owners made a multiplayer deal in May that sent Piazza and Todd Zeile to the Florida Marlins for catcher Charles Johnson, outfielders Gary Sheffield and Jim Eisenreich, third baseman Bobby Bonilla, and rookie pitcher Manuel Barrios.

The Giants ownership, following several significant roster shake-ups since taking over in 1993, pulled off two surprises by signing former Dodgers ace Orel Hershiser to a free agent contract for the 1998 season. The 39-year-old Hershiser had 179 career wins and the Giants hoped he still had a few more victories in the tank. The Giants, taking advantage of a salary purge in Florida after the Marlins' World Series championship, gave up three players of no consequence for Robb Nen, one of the game's best relievers. Nen would take over for Rod Beck, who signed with the Chicago Cubs.

The wheeling and dealing by the ownerships were a reflection of how the game, and the rivalry, had evolved. In the 1960s, the rivalry was played out mostly by the players on the field. In that pre-free agency period, the same players returned year after year to the same team. The here-today, gone-tomorrow parade of players in this new era put more pressure on the owners to constantly fill gaps before and during the season. The Giants and Dodgers players would still battle over individual games, but in many ways, the rivalry had shifted from the field to the front office.

The 1997 season marked the first time since 1982 that the Dodgers and Giants were embroiled in a head-to-head race. Over that 16-year span, the Dodgers finished first five times and the Giants three, but the clubs couldn't match their competitive years. Both teams entered 1998 with indications that a second straight down-to-the-wire battle might be in store.

—⁓—

The Dodgers' roster was in a war of attrition as the clubs finally hooked up for a July 3–5 series, and it was losing the war. The combination of the multiplayer Piazza trade and injuries that put seven players on the disabled list left the Dodgers with only 15 players remaining from their opening day roster. The Dodgers were in third place, 11½ games behind San Diego. Tommy Lasorda, named general manager June 22, made news with his first trade, sending Paul Konerko and Denny Reyes to Cincinnati for closer Jeff Shaw.

The Giants were 50–36, but still trailed the strong Padres by 4½ games on July 3. The Giants took two out of three from the Dodgers, but by the time the teams next convened for three games in Los Angeles July 13–15, it was becoming evident that San Francisco's best road to the postseason was through the wild-card route. The Giants entered the series seven games behind San Diego, but were 1½ games in front of Chicago in the wild-card race. The Dodgers trailed by 13½ games.

—⁓—

The Dodgers only remaining incentive was to slow the Giants' wild-card quest as the clubs would meet six times in September. San Diego's command of the NL West with an impressive 90–50 record meant that the Giants would have to edge out Chicago and New York to earn the wild-card spot. The Giants hoped to get off to a good start in their September 4–6 series against the Dodgers with the help of Shawn Estes, who was making his first start in two months since coming off the disabled list with a strained muscle in his throwing shoulder. Estes, whose last win came on July 5 against the Dodgers, was easy prey upon his return. The Dodgers scored three in the second and three more in the third on the way to an 8–5 win. Bonds went four for four with a walk, tying a National League record by reaching base in 15 consecutive at-bats. During the remarkable stretch, Bonds had five singles, two doubles, two home runs, and six walks to get to within one of the major league record set by Ted Williams in 1957.

On the next day, the Dodgers beat up Hershiser, who had been 2–0 against his old team this year to push the Giants four games down in the wild-card race. Hershiser was knocked out in the third, surrendering six runs in the Dodgers' 6–3 victory. Los Angeles also put a stop to Bonds's record bid, as Chan Ho Park struck him out in his first at-bat.

The Giants avoided a sweep with a win in game three, and then won the first two games of their next series with Los Angeles on September 18–20. The series closer was a heartbreaker for the Giants, who couldn't afford a loss. Trenidad Hubbard homered in the first inning and pitcher

Carlos Perez made it stand up. The loss dropped the Giants four behind Chicago and New York with seven to play.

The Giants battled back, and as the final day of the season dawned, the Giants and Chicago were tied for first in the wild-card chase while New York was a game behind. The Giants were on the verge of making the postseason for the second straight year, leading Colorado 7–0 after 4½ innings while Chicago and New York were losing. But in one of the most painful defeats in San Francisco Giants history, the Rockies stormed back to win it 9–8. The Giants and Chicago finished tied, necessitating a one-game playoff the next day. San Francisco's season came to a quiet end at Wrigley Field as the Cubs advanced to the postseason with a 5–3 victory.

POLAR GROUNDS (1999)

The Giants bid farewell to their cozy Seals Stadium in a September 20, 1959, loss to the Dodgers. A part of San Francisco baseball history was about to disappear as Seals Stadium faced the wrecking ball. The opening of the $1 million field, built for the minor league San Francisco Seals, came on April 7, 1931, highlighted by pregame festivities in which Mayor Angelo Rossi threw out the first ball to Ty Cobb, serving as the ceremonial first batter. The baseball legend, now retired, took a look at the stadium and called it the finest park in America.

They were saying the same thing about Candlestick Park in 1959. But in 1960, when the gates opened and the wind blew, opinions would begin to change.

"Graceful." "Show place." "Dramatic in concept." "A dream come true." Those were the words used to describe Candlestick Park in the 1960 Giants yearbook. An article referred to "a wind baffle atop the stands for protection from the prevailing Pacific Ocean breezes," and boasted that the stadium provided "unexcelled comfort and convenience" for the fans. "Radiant heating … circulating hot water … would be carried through wrought-iron steel pipes in the concrete slab under the seats from a central boiler plant," maintaining a floor level temperature of 85 degrees, the article said.

Candlestick Park quickly became an easy target for detractors. The baffles didn't stop the chilling breezes, the heating system didn't work, and the gusty winds swatted down balls driven to left field.

A San Francisco sportswriter in 1958 solicited ideas from readers as to what the as-yet unnamed park should be called. A Berkeley man, apparently acquainted with San Francisco weather patterns as well as Giants' history, suggested it be called the Polar Grounds.

It didn't take the Giants long to realize that the wind would be a factor in their new home. During batting practice the day before the 1960 home opener, Willie Mays blasted a drive to deep left center field amid gusts of 25 mph which knocked the ball down short of the warning track. A flabbergasted Mays, shocked that his shot didn't clear the fence, blurted out: "I hit the cork out of that ball!"

The Giants had difficulty getting acclimated to their new ballpark and its gusty, chilly climate. Home run totals dropped: The powerful club hit just 130 out at Candlestick after producing 167 the previous year. Don Blasingame believed the team could turn the park into an advantage, saying, "We're not this bad. We'll adjust to the park, the same as Los Angeles did (in 1959). The first year in the Coliseum, the Dodgers griped. The next year, they won the pennant and the World Series."

The fans were in for a shock that had nothing to do with the weather. The stadium concessionaire, citing growing labor costs, announced the bad news: Prices were going up. A beer was now rising from 35 cents to 40 cents, and a hot dog jumped a nickel more to 30 cents.

—◦◦◦—

The abuse directed at Candlestick Park went on for 40 years. But on September 30, 1999, all appeared to be forgotten. The Giants, ready to move into their new downtown park for the 2000 season, would be playing their final game at Candlestick. A crowd of 61,389, the largest total for a regular season game ever at the park, was there not to toss a last brickbat at the old yard, but to rejoice in the memories the stadium held and to commemorate the passing of an era of baseball in San Francisco. Appropriately, the Dodgers would be the opponents. The Dodgers were among the strongest critics of the ballpark since their first game there on April 19, 1960. Dodgers outfielder Rick Monday once suggested that the stadium be blown up. Possibly the loudest lambasting of Candlestick came from Tommy Lasorda, who rarely passed up the opportunity to rip the park's unruly fans. But even Lasorda softened up for the closing three-game series. Before the first game, he reenacted the long walk from the clubhouse to the dugout he made every game, blowing kisses as the fans good naturedly reenacted their barrage of boos. Later, a more serious Lasorda reflected on the park he loved to hate, saying, "It's going to be gone, but there are so many memories there."

The final game at Candlestick was all about nostalgia as both teams were being overwhelmed by Arizona's 100-victory season. The Giants would finish in second, but were 14 games behind the Diamondbacks. The Dodgers would finish third, 23 games out, ending a franchise streak of playing in a World Series in every decade since the 1940s.

In the Candlestick farewell game, the Dodgers put together two three-run innings for a 9–4 victory. Marvin Benard hit the Giants' last homer at the stadium in the first inning for a 1–0 lead. The score was tied 2–2 after three, but the Dodgers scored three in the fourth with the help of two bases-loaded walks and three in the sixth on Raul Mondesi's three-run homer. Benard grounded out to first baseman Eric Karros for the final out, triggering a memorable postgame celebration highlighted by the return of some former Giants and the flying of home plate by helicopter from Candlestick to Pacific Bell Park, the club's new home for 2000. The Dodgers hit the final home run, scored the final run, and got the final victory at Candlestick. Lasorda, remaining True Blue during the emotional farewell, couldn't help but rub it in. "It's always good to beat the Giants. Now they won't be able to say they won the last game here," he said.

LONG BALL: 2000–2009

It was the decade of the dinger. A time to touch 'em all, over and over again. You didn't even have to be naturally big to hit a Big Fly. The suspicions about an outbreak of four-baggers began in the late 1990s and continued through the decade of 2000–2009. The Giants and Dodgers found themselves in the middle of the long ball furor as the controversy enveloped both teams and their star players.

PARTY CRASHER (2000)

While Giants owners spent the offseason getting ready for the 2000 opening of their new downtown park, Dodgers owners were opening their wallets to pull off a shocking deal for the third straight year.

In May 1998, the Dodgers traded All-Star catcher Mike Piazza to the Florida Marlins in a seven-player deal. Prior to the 1999 season, the Dodgers signed free agent Kevin Brown to a seven-year, $105 million contract, making him the highest paid pitcher in history. The Dodgers made headlines again leading up to the 2000 season when they sent discontented Raul Mondesi to the Toronto Blue Jays for Shawn Green in a deal of sluggers with staggering dollars. Green was given a six-year contract worth $84 million.

As significant as those mega-deals were, there was a small-print acquisition that would provide a quicker, more satisfying dividend for the Dodgers. Shortstop Kevin Elster had a mostly mediocre career, with the exception of a 24-homer season with the Texas Rangers in 1996. Elster, 35, stayed home in Las Vegas in 1999, saying he was taking a mental break as well as a physical break to get over lingering injuries. Dodgers manager Davey Johnson, who was Elster's skipper in 1986 with the New York Mets, talked him into signing with Los Angeles for the 2000 season.

———

Just like that, baseball had a new life in San Francisco in 2000. Splash hits. McCovey Cove. Knothole Gangs. A full house every night. Better weather. Intimate seating that brought fans close to the field. Spectacular views of the bay and beyond from the upper deck. A massive Coke bottle in left field. A right-field wall with more carom possibilities than a pool table. These were among the endearing features of Pacific Bell Park, the stunning jewel which the Giants were about to unveil.

Crews were still putting the finishing touches on the park as the clubs began spring training, hurrying to have things in shape for April 11, when the Dodgers would help the Giants open their new home. Questions flowed. Would the 307-foot distance down the right-field line be a place for cheap home runs by left-handed pull hitters, or would the 24-foot-high wall serve as an equalizer? Would the 420-foot gap in right-center field turn into a triples alley, or would long, high drives that outfielders might run down turn it into a death valley for frustrated sluggers? Would the new location of the stadium and its setting cut down on the wind and cold that iced Candlestick Park, since even the talented designers of PacBell couldn't change San Francisco's cool evening climate?

Only time would answer such questions, but one point was mutually agreed upon: the Giants and the visiting teams would feel the invigoration of playing daily before packed crowds. Attendance at Candlestick Park had picked up in the final three years, bolstered by the division-winning

1997 season. In 1999, the Giants drew just over two million, only the third time they had reached that mark in San Francisco. But with the expected sold-out new park, the Giants were heading toward their first ever three-million attendance season. Such crowds were nothing new to the Dodgers, who had exceeded the three-million figure 14 times in the last 22 years.

The Giants and Dodgers began their seasons on the road, the Giants going 3–4 and the Dodgers 3–3. But for the Giants, and in some ways the Dodgers, too, the real opening of the season was to come when the clubs would play the first game at Pacific Bell Park. Anyone from the talented rosters could emerge to put their own imprint on that historic day, but the likely list of suspects would have to include someone like Barry Bonds, Jeff Kent, or J.T. Snow from the Giants, or Green, Eric Karros, or Gary Sheffield from the Dodgers. It is safe to say that no one put the name Kevin Elster on their list.

The Giants dubbed their new ballpark "The Miracle on Third Street," and it wasn't a stretch. The park fulfilled expectations and the weather was perfect for the inaugural game. The teams both hoped to use the occasion to jump-start their season, while the Arizona Diamondbacks were already going full-throttle to lead the Dodgers by 2½ and the Giants by three.

Bonds brought in the first run at the park with a double in the first, but the rest of the day belonged to Elster. Elster tied it with a solo homer in the third. Bonds answered with a solo blast in the bottom half of the inning to give the Giants a 2–1 lead. The Dodgers broke out for three in the fifth off Kirk Rueter on Green's RBI single and Elster's two-run homer. The Giants got to within one in the sixth when Kent scored on a wild pitch. The teams traded runs in the seventh, the Dodgers scoring on Geronimo Berroa's RBI single, and the Giants on Doug Mirabelli's home run. Elster slugged his third home run of the game in the eighth for a 6–4 lead. Snow's homer in the ninth off Jeff Shaw closed the gap, but the Dodgers held on for a 6–5 victory.

The Dodgers were not only rude guests for the big party, they continued to hang around and ransack the Giants' house. Los Angeles swept the
opening series, and then won its fourth straight in San Francisco when
the club returned June 30. In that game, Dodgers catcher Todd Hundley
stroked a home run over the right-field stands into McCovey Cove,
becoming the first player other than Bonds to have a so-called PacBell
Park splash hit. The Giants finally got their first home victory over the
Dodgers the next day.

—⁓—

The Giants would overcome the Dodgers' start in 2000, and reach the
postseason with a remarkable second half and a final 97–65 record. Only
their slow start had prevented them from making a mockery of the division
race. The Giants lost their first six games at PacBell Park, but then went
55–20 the rest of the way at their new home. On September 28 against the
Dodgers, the Giants set a franchise record for home runs as Felipe Crespo
hit one out in the eighth inning. Crespo's blast was the Giants' 222nd home
run, breaking the record held by the 1947 New York team. Among that
team's sluggers was 23-year-old outfielder Bobby Thomson, who hit 29.

The Giants entered the division series against the New York Mets
confident in their pitching and powerful offense. Their expectations were
met in the opener of the five-game series as they banged out 10 hits and
got a strong performance from starter Livan Hernandez and relievers Felix
Rodriquez and Robb Nen. But the Mets won two straight extra-inning
games, and then Bobby Jones fired a one-hit, 4–0 shutout to derail the
Giants' hopes.

It was a frustrating year for the Dodgers, who seemed to have a solid
statistical season, but fell short too often. The club was fourth in the league
in homers with 211, and the staff's ERA of 4.10 was the second best, but
it only resulted in an 86–76 record.

In the end, the Dodgers would have to console themselves with having
crashed the Giants' opening day party. The Dodgers satisfaction at marring

what had been a day of glory for the Giants franchise was summed up by catcher Hundley, who said, "It was nice to upset a bunch of fans."

GAME CHANGER

One of the questions Dusty Baker was asked most frequently during spring training in 2001 was how the Giants would replace the bat of Ellis Burks. The slugging outfielder, who hit .344 with 24 home runs and 96 RBIs in 2000, had signed with the Cleveland Indians. The Giants manager seemed to reach a point of frustration responding to the question about whether his remaining players could make up for the offensive loss when he said, "How much more can they do? A man can only do what a man can do. ... I can't ask Jeff (Kent) to hit 52 homers and drive in 172 runs, or ask Barry (Bonds) to hit 68 home runs and drive in 175 runs."

Baker, as it turned out, had underestimated what Bonds was capable of doing, as the year of 2001 would see a home run season like no other in the history of the game.

Among those to witness the Bonds show were the Dodgers, who were reluctant participants in his conquests of pitchers and his drive toward coronation as the Home Run King.

—⁓—

Bonds was already on the way to greatness when the Giants signed him in 1993 after his first seven years with Pittsburgh that featured two MVP awards, three division titles, 176 homers, 556 RBIs, and a .275 batting average. But what made the signing even more intriguing was that Bonds was arriving just as his career appeared to be taking off. In the last three years in Pittsburgh, he had 92 homers and 333 RBIs. His offensive force made him a game-changer, and his potential seemed limitless. Peter Magowan, the leader of the investment group that purchased the club in 1993, said of his prized acquisition, "It's a lot of money, but there's only one Barry Bonds."

Dodgers manager Tom Lasorda, whose club didn't appear to have a chance to match the Giants firepower now, could only express surprise at the Bonds deal. "I'm shocked. That would be the last place I'd think he'd go."

Bonds did not let the Giants down, hitting 46 home runs and driving in 123 in 1993.

By the end of 1998, Bonds had become the only player in history with 400 home runs and 400 stolen bases. Bonds had another solid year in 1998 (37 HR, 122 RBIs, .303), and appeared on an unstoppable march to a Hall of Fame career. But despite his consistent power numbers, other sluggers were leaving him behind. Until 1996, when Mark McGwire hit 52, the only players to reach the 50-homer mark since George Foster in 1977 were Albert Belle (50) in 1995 and Cecil Fielder (51) in 1990. But suddenly, balls were flying out of the parks. McGwire hit 58 in 1997 while playing with Oakland and St. Louis, while Ken Griffey had 56. In 1998, McGwire belted 70 and Sammy Sosa 66 in their classic home-run derby that some say revived baseball after the fan disgust from the 1994 strike. McGwire hit 65 in 1999 and Sosa had 63. During the post-strike period, Bonds hadn't won any home run crowns, missing out by one to Sosa's 50 in 2000. In 2001, everybody would get into the long-ball act. Alex Rodriquez would lead the American League with 52. In the National League, Luis Gonzalez would knock out 57 and Sosa would have 64.

Bonds had taken a back seat to the game's star sluggers in the past four years, but in 2001, he would thrust himself into the home run record books like no other who had ever played the game.

GOING DEEP (2001)

The 2001 season began with Barry Bonds's future with the Giants unsettled. Bonds was looking to sign an extension of his contract—due to expire in the fall—during the season. The club wished to wait until the end of the year so it would have a better outlook about its financial situation. The contract talk provided some spring training speculation, even trade rumors, though the Giants promised they would not deal Bonds.

The Giants entered spring training in 2001 still aching from their failure in the division series against the New York Mets in 2000. Lost in that disappointment was an achievement that seemed unlikely during the more than 30 years of Dodgers command. While the Giants wouldn't be popping open bottles of champagne over it, 2000 marked the fourth straight season that the Giants had a better record than the Dodgers. San Francisco began the season with the offense and pitching to make them a serious postseason threat. The Giants scored 925 runs, the most in franchise history since the 959 compiled by the 1930 squad that batted .319, and included stars such as Bill Terry (.401 in 1930), Fred Lindstrom (.379), and Mel Ott (.349).

Among offensive standouts returning to the Giants lineup were 2000 MVP Jeff Kent, J.T. Snow, and Rich Aurilia. The Giants bolstered their attack two weeks before the season with the signing of catcher Benito Santiago, a four-time all-star. The Giants would make two key transactions during the season, acquiring first baseman Andres Galarraga and pitcher Jason Schmidt.

The Giants boasted a pitching staff they hoped could be one of the best in baseball. The five starters won in double figures in 2000. The rotation consisted of Livan Hernandez, Russ Ortiz, Shawn Estes, Kirk Rueter, and Mark Gardner. The bullpen was led by closer Robb Nen (41 saves).

The Dodgers, in contrast, were in disarray. An unhappy Gary Sheffield, their top hitter, threatened to be a disruptive force in spring training as he demanded a big contract extension or a trade, and criticized deals given to other players. Chairman Bob Daly, who said he expected better results in 2000, fired manager Davey Johnson at the end of the season. Jim Tracy, a Dodgers bench coach with no big league managerial experience, was hired to turn it all around.

On offense, the Dodgers would have to start the season with only three of their Big Four in Sheffield, Eric Karros, and Shawn Green, while Adrian Beltre recovered from abdominal surgery. Kevin Brown was starting the season on the disabled list with a sprained Achilles tendon, leaving Chan Ho Park to take over the role as ace at least until he returned.

The home-run era was still going strong early in the 2001 season, at least from the Dodgers' perspective, as they hit 10 out in the clubs' first two meetings April 6–7 at Los Angeles. Mark Grudzielanek hit three and Karros had two as the Dodgers won 10–1 and 10–4. The Giants turned the tables in the third game of the series, as Aurilia, Russ Davis, and Santiago slugged two-run homers in an 8–3 victory to avoid a sweep. The homer fever seemed to strike everyone but Bonds, who went 0-for-13 in the series.

When the clubs next met on April 17 at PacBell Park, the stage was set for some history and hard feelings. The first-place Giants led the Dodgers by a half-game, giving the series some meaning even though it was early, and Bonds was one swing away from reaching 500 home runs. The Dodgers took a 2–1 lead into the bottom of the eighth. With Aurilia at third, and no outs, Bonds turned on a 2–0 pitch from Terry Adams and drove it into McCovey Cove. The Giants stopped the game to celebrate while the Dodgers cooled their heels on the diamond. The nine-minute ceremony featured a word from Bonds, and the appearance on the field of Willie Mays, Willie McCovey, and Bonds's family. Adams, irked that he had to stand on the mound for the party, said later when asked about the homer, "I could care less about Barry Bonds's achievements. All I worry about is winning and losing a game." Adams and the Dodgers lost 3–2.

Bonds followed the milestone clout the next day with a homer that broke a 4–4 tie in the seventh in a 5–4 Giants win. It was his sixth home run in six games, the 501st of his career, and already speculation began about whether the 36-year-old could reach 600.

Kent beat out Barry Bonds for the MVP award in 2000, but he and the rest of the Giants were taking a back seat to Bonds this year. As the Giants and Dodgers met for a three-game series June 25–27, Bonds already had slugged 39 home runs with more than half the season remaining. Kent, however, flashed his MVP credentials in a one-man beating of the Dodgers in the series opener. Kent went four for four, driving in three with a homer and double in the Giants' 5–2 win. The Bonds home run assault was drawing much of the attention, but Arizona was quietly taking charge in the division, leading the Giants by 6 and the Dodgers by 7½ entering the series.

The Dodgers came back to win the next two games, 14–8 and 7–3. In the series finale, Adams got some consolation from Bonds's midgame celebration of No. 500 as he held down Bonds and picked up his first win as a starter. Bonds doubled in a run in the first, but ended up going one for five and popped out with the bases loaded and two outs in the fourth.

The Dodgers took three out of four a week later in San Francisco. Los Angeles, propelled by a nine-game winning streak, had passed San Francisco in the pursuit of Arizona. On July 5, the Diamondbacks led the Dodgers by 4½ and the Giants by 6½. Bonds had now gone 10 games without a homer, remaining at 39.

<hr />

The baseball world was focused on the Giants and Dodgers as they next met for a three-game series September 24–26 in Los Angeles. It wasn't because of the division race, though there was a good one. Arizona led the Giants by two games and the Dodgers by four with 12 games to play. The Giants also were just two games down in the wild-card standings. The story line was focused instead on Bonds's pursuit of Mark McGwire's single season home run total of 70. Bonds stood at 66 at the start of play, and could conceivably tie or pass McGwire in this series. If he did, the Dodgers made it clear that they weren't going to put up with another on-the-field celebration. Derrick Hall, the Dodgers' senior vice president, even rejected a postgame ceremony, saying, "We would not recognize one of their players during the stretch run. We don't believe our fans want to sit through a ceremony for the Giants in Dodger Stadium." However, Hall couldn't protect Dodgers fans from having to witness more heroics by Bonds in this game. Doubles by Kent and Aurilia in the third gave the Giants a 1–0 lead. In the seventh, with two outs, Bonds launched home run No. 67 off James

Baldwin for a 2–0 lead. Beltre's solo shot in the seventh made it 2–1, but the bullpen blanked the Dodgers over the last two innings.

The teams split the next two games. The Dodgers won game two 9–5 triggered by a seven-run sixth inning. The Giants followed with a 6–4 win that drew them to within 1½ games of Arizona. Bonds was walked five times in the two games, going one for five, and remained at 67 homers.

———ᴡ———

Would the Dodgers pitch to Bonds and would Los Angeles be able to end its rival's postseason hopes? That was the plot as the clubs met for the final series of the season October 5–7 at PacBell Park. The Dodgers were eliminated on October 2, but the Giants were still alive. San Francisco trailed first-place Arizona and wild-card leading Houston by two games, necessitating a sweep if the Giants had any chance to at least force a playoff. Meanwhile, Bonds hit his 70th homer the night before against Houston, giving him three games to set the record. Bonds wasted no time, driving his record-breaking 71st homer off Park in the first inning over the wall in right-center field. Two innings later, Bonds drilled No. 72 off Park to center field. The Dodgers made some noise with their bats, too, compiling 15 hits while Sheffield drove in four and Marquis Grissom three. The Dodgers held a 9–8 lead after four innings. The Giants' tied it at 10–10 after six innings, but the Dodgers got one more and made it stand up for an 11–10 victory in a four-hour, 27-minute marathon. The Giants loss eliminated them from the division and wild-card races, a point of satisfaction made by Green, who noted that his club would not want to let the Giants get into the postseason by beating them. "The Dodgers are the one team that would least like to see this happen," Green said, "mainly because of the rivalry. That's the way it is."

With the season over for both clubs, the only remaining suspense in the final two games was whether Bonds could pad his record. Bonds got No. 73 on the last day of the season with a right-field shot in the first off Dennis Springer.

ENCORE (2002)

Did that just happen?

Baseball historians had to be asking the question all offseason. The once unreachable 60 of Babe Ruth fell after 34 years to Roger Maris. The 61 of Maris had given way 37 years later to McGwire's 70. And now McGwire's 70 was obliterated three seasons later. Bonds was well on his way to 600, and if he stayed healthy, Ruth's 714 and Hank Aaron's 755 could be in jeopardy. But amid the homer barrage, Bonds insisted that all he really wanted was a World Series ring. The chance was about to come, as the Giants headed for 2002 to resume their quest for a World Series crown that had eluded them for 44 years in San Francisco.

The Giants and Dodgers played well enough at times in 2001 to indicate they had legitimate shots at the postseason, but both were victimized by tough stretches that doomed their chances. The Giants won eight of the last 10 games before the final Dodgers series, but had stumbled before that run, losing 16 of 28. The Dodgers were 65–49 on August 8, but then went 16–25, putting them on the verge of elimination.

The Dodgers topped the Giants in the new 19-game format in 2001, making it the third straight year they won the series. The Dodgers had not lost a season series to the Giants since 1992. The Giants, however, could boast of topping the Dodgers in a category that at one time seemed impossible. For the second straight year, San Francisco outdrew Los Angeles at home, thanks to the excitement over PacBell Park. The Giants drew 3,318,800 to the Dodgers 2,880,242 in 2000, and 3,311,000 to 3,017,143 in 2001. Until 2000, the Giants had never beaten the Dodgers in attendance since the teams came to the West Coast.

Only four games separated the Giants and Dodgers in 2001, but it really was a tale of two seasons. Even though the Giants fell two games short, their year was among the best of times with the excitement generated by a division race and the spectacle of Barry Bonds's electrifying home run pace. The Dodgers' year may not have been the worst of times, finishing just six games out of first, but it did extend the frustration the ownership was experiencing. In the three years before the Fox Group took over, the Dodgers made the postseason twice and missed out on a division title by two games in 1997. Since the sale in 1998, the club went four years without making the postseason. The Dodgers, after successive 86–76 records the last two seasons, appeared stuck.

The Giants had appeared to put together a strong supporting cast around Bonds. Steady third baseman David Bell came over in a trade with the Seattle Mariners, and free agent Reggie Sanders, who put up impressive numbers with Atlanta in 2001, was signed on to take over right field. The remainder of the lineup consisted of shortstop Rich Aurilia, coming off a spectacular 37 home-run season, Jeff Kent, J.T. Snow, and Benito Santiago. A July 28 trade would bring in veteran outfielder Kenny Lofton to help the team down the stretch.

Giants players were often quoted as noting that this was more than a one-man team, that it took everyone on the roster to be successful. While the logic of that position was hard to argue with, it was difficult not to be overwhelmed by Bonds. His 2001 statistics were unfathomable even beyond the 73 homers, such as the .863 slugging percentage and the 177 walks. If they pitched to him, he might have hit 80. Giants owners left no doubt that they were impressed. On January 14, they announced that Bonds was given a five-year, $90 million contract. The 37-year-old Bonds would start the year with 567 home runs. Within his reach this year: Harmon Killebrew (573), Mark McGwire (583), and Frank Robinson (586).

As the 2003 season dawned, there were questions. Would the Giants live up to their high expectations and not only reach the postseason, but advance much deeper than they did in 2000? Would this be the year that the Dodgers and their relatively new owners break out of the doldrums? And what would Bonds do for an encore after his out-of-this-world 2001 season? The answer to the latter question came quickly, as Bonds would open with an offensive flurry against the Dodgers.

The Dodgers did not shy away from pitching to Bonds as the clubs met on opening day April 2 in Los Angeles. Bonds came out swinging, smacking two homers as the Giants mauled the Dodgers 9–2. Bonds went three for four, scored two runs, and drove in five. His three-run blast in the second highlighted a five-run inning against Kevin Brown, who entered the game with an 8–1 record and 1.86 ERA against the Giants.

Bonds was making it look too easy, as he keyed a second straight bombardment of Dodgers pitching the next day in a 12–0 Giants romp. In a near repeat performance, Bonds went two for two, scored three runs, drove in four, and drilled two more home runs. A newspaper noted that Bonds was on a pace to hit 324 home runs. The long balls were contagious, as Santiago contributed a three-run homer while pitcher Russ Ortiz joined in with a two-run shot. Hideo Nomo survived only three innings, giving up four runs and six hits. The back-to-back drubbings left the Dodgers in a bad mood, as they refused a Giants' request to move up the start of the final game of the series so the team could get back to San Francisco earlier in preparation for its home opener the following day.

The Dodgers' mission in the series wrap-up—stop Bonds and get their offense started—failed on both counts. Three Giants pitchers combined to extend the Dodgers' scoreless string to 24 innings, and Bonds continued to be a pest, though in a less dramatic way. Ryan Jensen went seven innings, allowing just three hits. Felix Rodriquez and Robb Nen preserved the 3–0 shutout and series sweep. Bonds was 1-for-2, with a double, walk, and hit by pitch.

A lively division race was well under way as the clubs prepared to meet six times in 10 days starting July 19 in Los Angeles. Arizona led the Dodgers by 1½ games despite Los Angeles having lost eight of its last nine. The Giants were two games back. Bonds was removed in the first game with a hamstring injury that would keep him sidelined for the remaining five July contests, but the Dodgers were unable to take advantage of his absence.

The six-game stretch came down to a July 28 matchup in San Francisco, significant in that it marked the last time the clubs would meet until September 9.

Kent hit a two-run homer, Jason Schmidt gave a strong 10-strikeout performance, and the bullpen closed it out for a 3–1 victory. First-place Arizona showed no signs of any cracks, leading the Dodgers by five games and the Giants by six. Three other teams were within four games of the Dodgers and Giants.

⎯⎯⎯

It was becoming clear that the wild card was the only postseason option for the teams as they squared off in a four-game series in Los Angeles September 16–19. The Giants went into the series trailing Arizona by seven while the Dodgers were eight back.

September 16 (Dodgers 7, Giants 6): Marquis Grissom stunned the Giants with a ninth-inning sensational catch, and Eric Gagne finished them off as the Dodgers pulled even with San Francisco in the wild-card race. The Dodgers entered the game frustrated after dropping three of four to Colorado, and the Giants arrived in a fighting mood a day after manager Dusty Baker, pitching coach Dave Righetti, and catcher Santiago were ejected during a tough loss to San Diego. The clubs went into the top of the ninth with the Dodgers leading 7–6. Aurilia appeared to have tied it up with a long drive to center field off Gagne, but Grissom jumped up to snare the ball above the fence. Gagne struck out Kent, walked Bonds intentionally, and then struck out Santiago to end the game.

September 17 (Giants 6, Dodgers 4): Bonds and Santiago gave the Giants a strong start, and five relievers combined to provide a strong finish as San Francisco moved back into the wild-card lead. The Giants knocked out Omar Daal in the second inning while getting out to a 5–1 lead, spurred by run-scoring singles by Santiago and Aurilia, and a two-run double by Bonds. Kirk Rueter got the win while allowing four runs in five innings, but had the bullpen to thank, as it shut down the Dodgers on two hits.

September 18 (Giants 7, Dodgers 4): Starter Ortiz helped his own cause with his bat as the Giants took a two-game lead in the wild-card race. Ortiz gave up three runs in six innings to get the win. His sacrifice fly in the second helped the Giants take an early lead, and his home run in the sixth broke a 3–3 tie.

September 19 (Dodgers 6, Giants 3): The Dodgers exploded for six runs in the third off Livan Hernandez on a three-run double by Brian Jordan, a two-run single by Dave Roberts, and an RBI single by Eric Karros. Odalis Perez tossed a complete game, allowing seven hits while striking out seven. The Giants now held a one-game advantage in the wild card with just a little over a week to go.

The Giants won their next eight games. The pitching was phenomenal, as the Giants allowed only nine runs and recorded two shutouts in the eight games. The Giants clinched the wild-card berth on September 28 with a 5–2 victory over Houston. The Dodgers didn't fold, winning six of their last nine, but were eliminated on September 28 despite shellacking San Diego 14–2.

In the best-of-five division series against the Atlanta Braves, the Giants won the opener, but dropped the next two to put themselves on the verge of elimination. The Giants took the fourth game 8–3 behind the pitching of Hernandez, and took the series with a 3–1 victory as Ortiz and three relievers held down the Braves. The Giants began their five-game championship series against the Cardinals with two straight wins in St. Louis. The clubs split the next two. On October 15, the Giants recorded one of their most thrilling moments in San Francisco history, as Lofton singled in Bell in the ninth for a pennant-winning 2–1 victory.

After losing two of the first three in the World Series against the Anaheim Angels, the Giants roared back for two wins, including a 16–4 rout in Game Five. Leading 5–0 in Game Six, and just eight outs away from a victory, it appeared the Giants were about to win their first World

Series title on the West Coast. The Angels rallied for three runs in the seventh and three more in the eighth to deliver the heartbreaking loss. The shell-shocked Giants tried to act as if the crushing defeat wouldn't affect them in Game Seven, but after the Angels scored a quick four runs off starter Hernandez, San Francisco went down quietly.

Bonds's wish for a ring didn't come true, but he put up golden numbers again. The Giants would make some surprising changes before the 2003 season, but as long as Bonds could even come close to his 2002 output (46 HR, 110 RBIs, .370 average), the Giants felt more postseason drama was ahead.

THE BETTER TEAM (2003)

The Giants won 95 games in 2002. The Dodgers won 92. But both teams had contrasting interpretations of the year. The Dodgers were frustrated at missing out on the postseason for the sixth straight year, but they didn't see the need for an overhaul in 2003 despite the frustration, reasoning they stayed in the wild-card hunt until the last week despite having their Number One starter Kevin Brown (3–4 in 10 starts) limited by injury. The Giants, on the other hand, slightly rewrote the old adage to say "if it ain't broke, blow it up, and start all over again."

The Giants of 2002 had the third highest number of victories the club had compiled since 1965. They came within eight outs of winning the World Series. Their skipper was a three-time National League manager of the year. The team's 3.54 ERA was the second best in the league. Only one other club hit more home runs. An outside observer might suggest that all the Giants needed to do in the offseason was to make sure everybody knew the reporting dates for spring training and then get ready to make another run with the same crew. But the economic realities of baseball in this era and front office discontent with some of the club's big names called for radical change.

The changes began at the top, as manager Dusty Baker was replaced by former Giant Felipe Alou. Alou, 67, began his 17-season playing career with the Giants, and led the pennant-winning club of 1962 with a .316

average. He compiled a 691–717 record from 1992–2001 as manager of the Montreal Expos.

The departure of slugging second baseman Jeff Kent appeared to make Alou's task even more challenging. Kent had been a dynamic offensive presence since coming to San Francisco in 1997. He hit at least 22 home runs and drove in more than 100 runs in all six seasons, providing a second explosive bat in the lineup so that opposing pitchers couldn't only worry about Barry Bonds. But the end of Kent's time with the Giants wasn't surprising, following his criticism of the way the club was reshaping the roster, a conflict with management over a dugout fight with Bonds, his handling of an off-the-field spring training injury, and the lack of progress on a new contract.

By the time the 2003 season would roll around, the Giants would part ways with starting pitchers Livan Hernandez and Russ Ortiz; outfielders Reggie Sanders, Kenny Lofton, Tsuyoshi Shinjo, and Tom Goodwin; and infielders Kent, David Bell, and Bill Mueller. The Giants entered the season uncertain about the health of closer Robb Nen, who underwent shoulder surgery.

The Dodgers did make two headline-grabbing moves in the offseason, trading away first baseman Eric Karros and signing his replacement, Fred McGriff. Karros took over at first base in 1992 after Eddie Murray handled the job for three years to give the Dodgers their first long-term stability at the position since Steve Garvey left after the 1982 season. McGriff, 39, who had 478 career homers, still appeared to be an offensive threat, slugging 30 homers and driving in 103 last year with the Cubs.

X-ray charts seemed more appropriate than pitching charts in evaluating the Dodgers' rotation. Three of the spots were set in Hideo Nomo, Odalis Perez, and Kazuhisa Ishii. But the Dodgers were also banking on injury-plagued Kevin Brown and Darren Dreifort. Brown had been on the disabled list six times in the past three years. He was limited to 19 starts in 2001 and 10 in 2002 after starting at least 32 games from 1996–2000. Dreifort had been out since mid-2001 with elbow and knee surgery. There were no questions in the bullpen, which was led by Paul

Quantrill (2.70 ERA in 86 appearances) and closer Eric Gagne (1.97 ERA, 52 SV).

As the 2003 season neared, much of the discussion centered on whether elder statesman Alou would have the communication skills necessary to relate to the players. Such talk made for good baseball chatter, but it seemed that as long as a Giants manager could write down Barry Bonds's name in the lineup on most days, success would follow.

The 2002 season marked a notable development in the rivalry: For the first time since 1992, the Giants won the season series from the Dodgers. Los Angeles won the head-to-head series seven times with three ties during that period. But in 2002, the Giants went 11–8. It was not a fluke, as San Francisco would demonstrate in 2003 when the Giants would enjoy their most dominant season over the Dodgers in 20 years.

Los Angeles fans had hoped that the strong record of last season was a sign that the Dodgers might finally get back to postseason. However, the season unfolded with some uncertainty, as News Corp. looked to sell the franchise.

The Giants swept San Diego and Milwaukee to open the year, and won two out of three in a second series against San Diego before meeting the Dodgers on April 10. The Dodgers had no better luck as they would lose their first five meetings with the Giants. Things were going so well for the Giants that even their minuses turned into pluses. In an April 13 game, the teams were tied 4–4 in the 12th inning. Paul Lo Duca singled to right with one out and Todd Hundley at first. Right-fielder Marvin Benard fired the ball back to the infield, aiming for the cutoff man. His errant throw was so high that it came directly to third, where Hundley was tagged out. The Giants took advantage of the apparent divine intervention in the bottom of the inning, as Benard brought Marquis Grissom home with the winning run on a drive off the right-field wall. The Dodgers finally broke through for a win on April 20, but the 15–3 Giants led them by 7½ games, with Colorado 3½ behind.

The apparent Giants' runaway season hit a roadblock over the next two months, setting the stage for a summer stretch in which the clubs would play six times in nine days. The Dodgers had roared back to get within two games of the Giants, while Colorado fell 8½ games out.

The Dodgers kept their foot on the accelerator, winning the first two games of a June 17–19 series behind solid pitching performances by Brown and Ishii to tie the Giants for first place. The Giants came back the next day on Jason Schmidt's three-hit, 11-strikeout performance in a 2–0 win to retake the lead. The Dodgers' revival had revved up their fans as the three-game series drew nearly 150,000. The teams got back together four days later in San Francisco, where the Giants took two out of three to stay in front by a game. Benito Santiago drove in Bonds with a single off Gagne in the 11th inning for a 3–2 win in the first game. Grissom drilled a two-run homer and Schmidt limited the Dodgers to four hits in a 2–1 victory the next day. The Dodgers avoided a sweep behind the pitching of Nomo and Wilson Alvarez for a 6–0 win in game three. Fans were already marking their calendars for the clubs' next meeting in three months, when the Giants and Dodgers would meet six times in September.

—⁓—

The division race that once seemed promising had dissolved. The Giants clinched the division on September 17, but there was still some suspense left. The team needed to win seven of the remaining 10 games to finish with 100 victories; home field advantage for the playoffs was still undecided; and Bonds was only four shy of 660 home runs, which would tie him with Willie Mays for third on the all-time list. The Dodgers still had a mathematical shot at the wild card, but their collapse had dropped them to fourth in that race. The Giants further damaged the Dodgers' wild-card hopes in this series opener with a 6–4 win as Bonds launched his 657th homer.

The Dodgers' desperate bid for the wild-card spot came to an end September 25 with a 6–1 loss to San Diego, narrowing interest in the clubs' final four-game series September 26–28 to Bonds's pursuit of Mays, and the Giants' pursuit of 100 wins. The series included a doubleheader to make up for a rainout. Bonds reached No. 658 in the first game of the series and the Giants took three out of four to reach No. 100 on September 28. Edgardo Alfonzo had a two-run homer and Pedro Feliz had a triple and homer to lead the Giants to the 12–3 milestone win.

———*m*———

The Giants, having won 100 games for the third time since coming to San Francisco and finishing strong with 11 victories in their last 15 games, believed they had a club that could return to the World Series. A 2–0 victory in the opener of the five-game division series against Florida behind the dominating pitching of Schmidt reinforced that view. But the Giants struggled the rest of the way, as Florida sent them home with three straight wins.

There were no easy answers for the Giants' disappointing showing against Florida, although the fact that the Marlins went on to win the World Series suggested that San Francisco had simply run into baseball's hottest team.

The Dodgers tried to shake up their slumping squad in mid-2003 with the acquisitions of Jeromy Burnitz, Rob Ventura, and 44-year-old Rickey Henderson. The moves fizzled as Burnitz hit .204, Ventura .220, and Henderson .208. The club's batting average of .243 was the second lowest in the major leagues, barely ahead of the .240 mark by the 119-loss Detroit Tigers. New owners would take over before opening day of 2004, and make their mark in midseason with deals that would lead to the Dodgers' first postseason win since 1988. But as the 2003 season closed, the Dodgers' outlook was cloudy. Manager Jim Tracy, whose club lost 13 of 19 games to the Giants, recognized that his team faced a challenge. Referring to the Giants, Tracy said, "Their team is clearly better than we are right now. Sometimes, it's painful to say that. We know we have some work to do."

SLAMMING THE DOOR (2004)

Sixty years later, Bobby Thomson's historic clout remains the gold standard for home runs in the Giants-Dodgers rivalry. For a home run to qualify for this standard, it should be a combination of either capturing a title or catapulting a team toward one, while providing a gut-wrenching knockout blow to the victim. Brian Johnson's dramatic homer against the Dodgers that propelled the Giants to the flag in 1997 fit the qualifications well enough to rank at the time as the biggest since the 1951 shot. But on October 2, 2004, the Dodgers' Steve Finley would challenge it for the No. 2 spot behind Thomson in one of the West Coast's hottest seasons.

On October 20, 1988, Orel Hershiser pitched the Dodgers to a 5–2 victory over the Oakland A's in Game Five to lock up a World Series championship. But over time, the moment that marked one of the great triumphs for the club had turned into a symbol of great frustration. In the 15 years since, the Dodgers failed to win a postseason game. They reached the playoffs in 1995 and 1996, but were swept both times. When new owner Frank McCourt took over on January 29, 2004, the first promise he made was to end the winless playoff drought, as he boldly told the fans, "Welcome to a new era of Dodger baseball."

McCourt inherited a franchise that had lost its winning edge. The club failed to reach the playoffs for seven straight years. It was the longest period of time without qualifying for the postseason since the team suffered through a seven-year lapse from 1967–1973.

The picture was much brighter in San Francisco as the 2004 season shaped up. In the last seven years, the Giants finished first three times, second four times, reached the postseason four times and played in a World Series. The club won at least 90 games in the last four years, the first time that happened since 1964–67. Winning had become not just a tradition, but an expectation. The Giants, however, had some postseason frustration of their own. They were knocked out of the playoffs in the first round three times and let the World Series championship slip away in the disastrous Game Six loss to the Anaheim Angels in 2002. The Giants had even gotten a rare upper hand on the Dodgers, going 24–14 over the last two years against them. It was the Giants' best two-year record against their rivals since the clubs arrived in California.

While the Dodgers' new owners had only been on the job for a couple of months, their demands were high. McCourt's wife, Jamie, who was the club's vice chairman, created a stir when she said the Dodgers should be drawing four million fans. She added: "This should be a team that's in the playoffs every year. To not be in the playoffs is crazy." The owners looked at their new 31-year-old general manager, Paul DePodesta, as among the best and the brightest. The small window of time between DePodesta's hiring in mid-February and opening day didn't allow much time for roster moves.

Brian Sabean, DePodesta's counterpart with the Giants, had turned into a master of filling the gaps to consistently keep the club in the postseason hunt. Although he made no splash signings, the Giants figured they were still okay as long as Barry Bonds was unloading splash hits into McCovey Cove.

As the teams prepared to meet for a four-game series June 21–24, the Dodgers were in first, but the Giants had moved to within 1½ games.

Cody Ransom singled home the winning run in the ninth to give the Giants a 3–2 win in the first game. Edgardo Alfonzo drove in six runs to lead the Giants to an 11–5 win in game two to put the club in first place. The Giants completed the job the next two days, gaining a four-game sweep with 3–2 and 9–3 victories. The tension of the high-stakes matchup intensified on June 23. The Giants' Michael Tucker made contact with Dodgers pitcher Jeff Weaver while trying to beat out a drag bunt. Weaver took exception and shoved Tucker, causing the dugouts to empty, but order was restored before any other confrontations could break out. The next day, Eric Gagne threw a high, inside fastball to Tucker in the eighth inning.

Tucker objected, and in the ensuing stare down, Gagne and Tucker were ejected. While no one scored a knockout during the confrontations, the Giants won all the rounds during play as they now held a 2½ game lead.

On July 30 and 31, the Dodgers shook up their roster and their fans with deals involving four teams and 14 players. Among prominent players traded away by the Dodgers were catcher Paul Lo Duca, outfielders Dave Roberts and Juan Encarnacion, and set-up man Guillermo Mota. Key players joining the Dodgers were first baseman Hee Sop Choi, pitcher Brad Penny, catcher Brent Mayne, and outfielder Steve Finley. The initial reviews were not good. Lo Duca was called the heart and the soul of the Dodgers, and critics believed the club would suffer from the loss of his bat and his leadership. The club management countered that while Lo Duca had performed well, the Dodgers had other leaders in the clubhouse that they could rely on. One of those the Dodgers felt could fulfill that role was the veteran, 39-year-old Finley.

As the clubs met September 24 for the first of six games in the season's final week and a half, the division title and wild-card spot were up for grabs. The Dodgers led the division by 1½ games over the Giants. Chicago led the wild card, a half-game in front of the Giants and 2½ ahead of Houston. The Dodgers barely survived for a 3–2 win in the series opener as Gagne retired Yorvit Torrealba on a line out to left field in the ninth after loading the bases on three walks. Pedro Feliz broke a 5–5 tie in the eighth the next day with a grand slam in a 9–5 Giants win. Home runs by Jayson Werth and Joey Cora sparked the Dodgers to a 7–4 win to take the series and increase their lead over the Giants to 2½ games.

One more critical series remained.

———ᴧᴧ———

It was do-or-die for the Giants as far as the division title was concerned, but they remained alive as well in the wild-card race as they met the Dodgers in Los Angeles in the season's final weekend October 1–3. The Dodgers had won three of four from Colorado, while the Giants were taking two of three from San Diego. That left the Dodgers with a three-game division lead with three to go. The Giants were tied with Houston for the wild-card lead, with Chicago one game back.

San Francisco stayed in the division race in the first game by beating the Dodgers 4–1 on Friday behind the pitching of Kirk Rueter. The left-hander allowed just two runs and three hits over seven innings, and Jim Brower and Dustin Hermanson each pitched one scoreless inning in relief. Marquis Grissom doubled home two runs in the second against Weaver. Tucker singled in a run in the top of the seventh, and J.T. Snow homered in the eighth to provide some insurance.

The stage was set for a white-knuckle Saturday. After eight innings, the Giants led 3–0. Three more outs, and the division race would go down to the 162nd game. A Giants win on Sunday would put the clubs in a one-game division championship contest on Monday. But then came the ninth inning. Reliever Hermanson gave up a single to Shawn Green and walked Robin Ventura. Cora struck out, but Jose Hernandez drew a walk to load the bases. Choi walked to force in the first run. Jason Christiansen came in to pitch to Cesar Izturis, who reached base when shortstop Ransom made an error on his ground ball to make it 3–2. With the bases still loaded and Matt Herges now on the mound, Werth singled in the tying run. The Giants brought in their fourth reliever of the inning, Wayne Franklin, to face Finley.

Finley's record justified any fears Giants fans had as they followed the ninth-inning drama on television or radio. In his 15 major league seasons with four clubs prior to 2004, Finley batted .276 with 249 homers and 977 RBIs. Franklin, who began the season with a 5.29 ERA in 76 games, was no match. Finley unleashed his powerful, smooth swing and launched Franklin's serving over the right-field fence for a 7–3 victory to give the Dodgers their first division crown since 1995 and their first spot in postseason since 1996. The grand slam was a one-two punch to the Giants. It not only finished off their division title quest, but combined with Houston's win over Colorado, put them one behind in the wild-card chase with one to play.

On Sunday, Houston defeated Colorado to clinch the wild-card race, making the Giants' 10–0 win meaningless. When the Dodger Stadium message board announced the Astros' result, Los Angeles fans rubbed it in with some taunting applause in recognition that San Francisco's season was over.

—⁓—

The Dodgers' quest for their first postseason victory since 1988 got off to a rocky start. The St. Louis Cardinals hit five home runs in the first game of the best-of-five playoff to win 8–3. The Cardinals put together two three-run innings in the second game while limiting the Dodgers to six hits for another 8–3 victory. Finally, in game three, the Dodgers broke through. Before 55,992, Jose Lima hurled a shutout, Green hit two home runs and Finley drove in two runs with a double for a 4–0 Los Angeles win. The Cardinals came back to win 6–2 in game four to take the series.

While the quick elimination was disappointing for the Dodgers, the division title and the breaking of the postseason losing spell was a triumph for the new owners and their new general manager. They had accomplished in their first year what no other Dodgers team had done in 15 seasons.

Finley, meanwhile, had placed himself among the Big Three in Giants-Dodgers home runs, joining Thomson and Johnson on the list of the best back-breaking clouts in the rivalry. Footnote: Finley would become a Giant for a year in 2006, and Johnson would play his final game as a Dodger in 2001.

THE MILD WEST (2005)

You win some, you lose some. While not an enthusiastic plan for success, a club following that pattern day-in and day-out in the NL West in 2005 might find that an 81–81 record would make it a contender.

As spring training closed, the questionable status of the clubs' two superstars, Giants slugger Barry Bonds and Dodgers closer Eric Gagne, created apprehension for both teams. But it wasn't enough to make the clubs believe that they wouldn't be in another pennant race. Momentum was on their side. The Giants had reeled off eight consecutive winning seasons. The Dodgers were coming off five consecutive winning seasons.

Despite the uncertainty over Bonds and Gagne, and questions about the Giants' age and the Dodgers' offseason lineup changes, the clubs appeared destined for another lively September. One reason was that the division appeared to offer little competition. San Diego won a respectable 87 games in 2004, but didn't appear to be any better. Colorado only won 68 and Arizona 51 in 2004, and neither was ready to contend.

The high hopes had given way to a degree of desperation by the All-Star break in July. A combination of injuries and sub-par performances left the Dodgers 7½ games out while the Bonds-less Giants had fallen 10½ behind. The Dodgers' biggest blow came when Gagne was lost for the season with an ailing elbow. Meanwhile, the Giants were still awaiting the return of Bonds, who was still trying to get over the effects of three knee operations.

Another year in the Mild West allowed the Giants to make one desperate charge in September, getting to within 5½ games after winning three out of four against the Dodgers. The last-minute rush was boosted by the return of Bonds, who hit his 704th and 705th homers in the series. As bad as the division was, an under-.500 record would not be enough. The Giants eventually got within three, but lost three of four to San Diego to drop out of the race. The Padres won the division with a lowly 82-80 mark, adding to the frustration of the Giants (75–87) and Dodgers (71–91).

The Dodgers' plunge, coming at a time when players, coaches, and management thought they were building perennial competing teams, left the organization stunned. The frustration showed during the season among players. Pitcher Odalis Perez lashed out at a teammate and said he had been targeted for criticism at a players-only meeting. Milton Bradley accused Jeff Kent of having trouble getting along with black players after Kent criticized him for not scoring from first base on his double. The Dodgers, coming off a first-place finish in 2004, won 12 of their first 14 games, but then went on a season-long dive, posting a 59–89 mark the rest of the way. An outbreak of injuries wasn't enough of an excuse for the Dodgers owners. The club's record was the worst since 1992 (63–99), and the second worst mark since the team moved to Los Angeles. The dissatisfaction didn't take long to play itself out: Within a month after the final game of the season, manager Jim Tracy and General Manager Paul DePodesta were gone. A search was on for new leadership on the field and in the suites, as the Dodgers sought an immediate fix to their club.

The Giants had become consistent contenders since moving to their new downtown ballpark in 2000 until their step backwards in 2005. Giants management, committed to reload each season rather than build for the future, took heat for choosing an aging squad instead of going with youth. The centerpiece of the strategy was Bonds. As long as Bonds was a force in the lineup, whether by his slugging or as a mere disruption to the opposition, the strategy had a good shot at winning. This became painfully clear in 2005, when Bonds was sidelined almost the entire year with knee problems. While the Giants suffered through injuries and disappointment with the pitching staff, it was hard to argue that the absence of Bonds was not the main reason for a season of mediocrity.

RIVAL STRATEGIES (2006)

The Giants and Dodgers had contrasting reactions to the wreckage of their 2005 seasons. The Giants slightly changed the roster and prayed for the full recovery of Barry Bonds. The Dodgers replaced their manager and general manager, and made dramatic changes to the lineup. Both strategies appeared valid, mainly because the NL West was again unlikely to produce a dominant team.

The Dodgers' shake-up began one day after the 2005 season ended when manager Jim Tracy stepped down under pressure. On October 29, general manager Paul DePodesta was fired. The changes came amid internal warfare. Tracy was critical of the front office and its allowing of some key players to go; DePodesta, who inherited a division-winning team in 2004 and then dismantled it, was unhappy with Tracy's criticism; and owner Frank McCourt, displeased about the dismal season and still trying to establish a new management culture, wasn't convinced that the 32-year-old DePodesta was the right fit to achieve his goals.

McCourt's search for a successor to DePodesta had an unlikely stop. Giants assistant general manager Ned Colletti, a key figure in San Francisco personnel moves, was tapped as DePodesta's replacement on November 16. Three weeks later, Colletti's managerial choice, Grady Little, was unveiled. The former Boston Red Sox skipper was no stranger to the volatility of big league management. Little compiled a 188–136 record in two years at Boston, but almost was run out of town for his handling of game seven of the AL Championship Series. Little's choices in a postseason game meant little for now. The Dodgers would be satisfied if Little's experience at least put them back into the postseason.

Colletti made an immediate impact, reshaping three-fourths of the infield with free agents. Nomar Garciaparra, limited by injuries in 2005, was brought in to play first. Shortstop Rafael Furcal was signed to provide speed in the leadoff spot and Bill Mueller was enlisted to give the club a fixture at third. The infield, rounded out by Jeff Kent, gave the Dodgers a reliable group of run-producers.

The rotation held promise. While the one-through-four starters had losing records in 2005, the reasons had at least something to do with lack of offensive support. At the top of the staff were Derek Lowe and Brad Penny. Closer Eric Gagne hoped to come back from elbow surgery, but his effectiveness remained the biggest spring training question for the club.

The Giants appeared unfazed about the criticism of 2005 that the team had too many aging players, as the lineup featured mostly the same names, now a year older. First baseman Lance Niekro, at 27, was the only projected regular under the age of 30. The Giants could on some days have an all 40-something outfield once Moises Alou turned 40 in the summer. He would be the youngster in that alignment with 41-year-olds Barry Bonds and new pickup Steve Finley.

While the Dodgers would open the 2006 season under new field management, Felipe Alou would be returning for his fourth year. Alou's first two seasons (100–61 and 91–71) kept critics of his style at bay, but last season's collapse opened the floodgates. The 70-year-old Alou came under increasing scrutiny in 2005, with some questioning whether he overused and exhausted his bullpen, and others wondering whether his detached relationship with his players hurt team communication and unity.

For the Giants, however, issues such as Alou and the team's age were a sideshow to Bonds. The near-mythical and often-maligned slugger appeared in just 14 games in 2005 (.286, 5 HR, 10 RBIs), but still got more attention than anyone on the field. In the short-term, the focus on Bonds as the season got under way would be on his pursuit of Babe Ruth's home run total. Bonds had 708, putting him six away from catching one of the most magical numbers—714—in sports. Hank Aaron subsequently passed Ruth and finished with 755, but Bonds's chances of catching that mark seemed in jeopardy because of his recent health problems.

Bonds entered the season while a federal grand jury continued to look at whether he committed perjury when he testified about steroids. While Bonds could look forward to another summer of love at his home ballpark, the road promised to be a bitter place. It wouldn't take long for Bonds to get a preview of what he faced as a fan tossed a fake plastic syringe at him in the Giants' opening series at San Diego. When he would arrive for the Giants first visit of the year to Los Angeles, he received extra security by the Dodgers. Nothing would be thrown, but the taunts would go on.

The Dodgers-Giants showdown in 2006 would come down to two questions: Would Bonds pass Ruth against the Dodgers, and would the Giants prevent the Dodgers from clinching a postseason spot on their field?

Bonds was still at 708 home runs when the teams hooked up in the second week of the season, as he slumped with a .188 batting average in the first seven games. Dodgers fans, given few reasons to make noise except for Kent's game-tying homer in the sixth, got their vocal chords in early season form by heaping verbal abuse on Bonds in a 2–1 loss April 14. Tensions rose two days later when Kent suffered a mild concussion when he was hit in the head by Giants pitcher Brad Hennessey. The Dodgers' Tim Hamulack responded the next inning by hitting Bonds above the right elbow. Hamulack was ejected, but Bonds showed little reaction to the pitch.

The Babe Ruth watch was in full operation when the clubs next met May 12–14 as Bonds had reached the 713 home-run mark. The Dodgers took two out of three, but what might have been even more meaningful was their success in preserving Ruth's No. 2 place on the home run list for now. Bonds was 0-for-8 for three games with four walks, one intentional.

It was becoming evident that mediocrity might qualify for the NL West crown again as the clubs met for a four-game series July 6–9 before the All-Star break. The Dodgers, Padres, and Rockies were in a three-way tie for first at 44–40, with the Giants 1½ back at 43–42. Bonds had passed Ruth since the clubs last met, with Hank Aaron now the new target. The teams split the series. The Dodgers had 31 hits combined in games two and three, but won only one of them.

The teams would meet six times in 10 days starting August 11 at Los Angeles. The Dodgers swept their home series—the 15th win in their last 16 games—with three one-run victories culminating with a classic pitching gem August 13. Greg Maddux matched scoreless innings with Jason Schmidt through eight. Maddux, acquired in a three-team trade on July 31, allowed just two hits, and retired 22 straight after giving up two hits in the first. Brett Tomko and Takishi Saito completed the 1-0 shutout. Russell Martin won it in the 10th with a leadoff home run to left field off Vinnie Chulk. The Dodgers were now in front of San Diego by 1½ games. The Giants had fallen 7½ behind.

The Giants rallied following the sweep by the Dodgers to win four straight against San Diego, but still trailed the Dodgers by six games. The Giants took the opener of an August 18–20 San Francisco series, but the Dodgers came back to win the next two. The Dodgers now led Arizona and San Diego by four, while the Giants were tied for last with Colorado, seven games back.

The Dodgers were moving in for the kill as the clubs met for three games in the season's curtain closer September 29-October 1 in San Francisco. Los Angeles was poised to clinch a postseason berth and the already eliminated Giants were faced with the consolation prize of trying to prevent the Dodgers from rejoicing on their field. Dodgers pitcher Tomko, who never became a crowd favorite in his stint with the Giants, was looking forward to the celebration, saying, "I'm sure there's nothing more they want to do than knock us out of the playoffs, and there's nothing more we want to do than clinch on their field."

September 29 (Dodgers 4, Giants 3): The series began with San Diego in first in the division race, with the Dodgers one game behind. In the wild-card race, the Dodgers led Philadelphia by two games. The Giants, behind Noah Lowry's seven strong innings, led 3–2 after eight. In the ninth, the Dodgers' Olmedo Saenz drove in the tying run with a single, and the go-ahead run came home on a wild pitch by Mike Stanton. The 4–3 victory clinched a tie for a postseason berth for the Dodgers.

September 30 (Dodgers 4, Giants 2): The Dodgers clinched a playoff spot as the Giants went down with a whimper. The final 18 San Francisco hitters were retired as Maddux got the win with seven strong innings, and Jonathan Broxton and Saito pitched the final two. J.D. Drew and Julio Lugo drove in two runs each, and Kenny Lofton had three hits and scored two. The Dodgers and Padres were now tied for first with one game to play. If the clubs tied, the Padres would win the title and the Dodgers would take the wild card because San Diego won their season series. After the game, Dodgers owner Frank McCourt got into the rivalry spirit, saying of the clincher, "To do it here in enemy territory and take it to them is a nice feeling."

October 1 (Dodgers 4, Giants 3): The Dodgers rested their regulars for the postseason, but still had enough to sweep the series with a 4–3 win. The Padres defeated Arizona to give them the division title, while putting the Dodgers in as the wild card.

The Dodgers, who had won only one game in their last three postseason appearances, had their confidence of advancing in this postseason boosted because of their fast finish. The club won its last seven and nine of its last 10 heading into the best-of-five division series against the New York Mets. But the story would have a familiar ending, as the Dodgers were swept.

Despite the quick exit, the Dodgers appeared to turn a corner in 2006. The Dodgers developed into a sturdy mix of veterans and rookies in the closing months. Colletti further lifted hopes through his successful first-year moves that the Dodgers could find whatever pieces of the roster puzzle that might be missing. The Dodgers could truly look ahead to 2007 not only as a team that could contend to get in the playoffs, but as a club that could be a force once it got there.

The outlook was far less rosy in San Francisco. The club had just endured its first successive losing seasons since 1995–96, and the game plan for recovery was fuzzy. There were uncertainties about the closer, the starting pitching and the lack of sufficient punch in the lineup. One certainty was that Felipe Alou would no longer be at the helm. The end of Alou's contract allowed the Giants to look for a change in managerial philosophy and style.

Bruce Bochy was coming off two successive division titles as manager of the San Diego Padres. The former catcher had guided the club for 12 years, and had four titles overall, including an NL pennant in 1998. A streak of five dismal losing seasons from 1999 to 2003 pushed his career record with the Padres below .500, but his reputation as a knowledgeable baseball man who was a players' manager and communicator was just what the Giants were looking for.

Not surprisingly, the offseason would be dominated by the question of whether the Giants would re-sign Bonds. Bonds had respectable numbers in his comeback from three knee operations that all but sidelined him in 2005. But they weren't the Bonds numbers that led the Giants to build a team around him. Some felt the Giants would be better off ending their relationship with Bonds, and use his salary to either bring in younger players with potential, or find a new offensive threat to anchor the lineup.

Of course, the home-run chase made the decision far more complicated. Bonds was 22 home runs away from passing Aaron. Bonds's pursuit of 755 would keep the excitement stirring at the Giants ballpark, even if the team struggled. Whatever the decision, it seemed clear that the Giants would put their money on offense in the offseason. But even that expectation would be shattered when the Giants decided to dig deep into their pockets to pursue a free-agent left-hander.

As the 50th year of Giants-Dodgers West Coast baseball dawned, the Dodgers appeared to have the edge in looking ahead to 2007. But the recent history of the NL West had shown that no one had been able to break away from the pack. The other teams in the division were expected to make moves that could keep them in the battle. If the Giants could settle the Bonds matter, add some clout to the lineup and bolster their pitching, there was hope that perhaps the 50th year could conclude with one more memorable Giants-Dodgers race.

CIRCUS IS IN TOWN (2007)

The atmosphere around sluggers such as Barry Bonds had changed since baseball embraced the tidal wave of record-shattering homers of the 1998–2001 period as a way to win back strike-demoralized fans. Since that time, suspicions about the link between performance-enhancing drugs and the home-run boom had grown. It was an issue Bonds faced when asked during a news conference in the first week of the 2002 season whether a substance such as steroids had anything to do with his offensive explosion. An irritated Bonds replied, "You can test me and solve it real quick. The media just stirs up stuff sometimes to talk about it. In baseball, you've got to hit the ball, no matter what. You still have to have hand-eye coordination."

It is left to the legal system, published reports, public opinion, and baseball itself to determine who played fair or foul, but if nothing else, it did seem like someone had slipped some rocket fuel into Bonds's coffee.

Bonds's extraordinary outburst in 2001 put him on a pursuit of milestone home runs. He hit No. 600 on August 9, 2002. He passed Willie

Mays with No. 661 on April 13, 2004. No. 700 came on September 17, 2004. Bonds tied Babe Ruth with No. 714 on May 20, 2006, and passed him eight days later. On July 28, 2007, Bonds hit No. 754, putting him one behind Hank Aaron's all-time mark. Three days later, Bonds would still be sitting on No. 754 as the Giants traveled to Los Angeles for a three-game series. Once again, similar to 2001, Bonds would be gunning for home-run supremacy with the Dodgers as possible victims.

After the 2006 season, following two straight sub-.500 years, some felt the Giants would be better off ending their relationship with Bonds. Of course, the home-run chase made the decision far more complicated. Bonds's pursuit of 755 would keep the excitement brewing at the Giants ballpark, even if the team was flat.

A strong hint that the Giants were prepared to part ways with Bonds after the home-run record was achieved came on December 28, 2006, with the shocking $126 million signing of pitcher Barry Zito. The acquisition of the veteran Oakland A's ace and former Cy Young award winner signaled that the Giants were ready for a new face of the franchise.

———

The Giants-Dodgers contrast remained the same in 2007: the Dodgers were focused on trying to reach the postseason and the Giants were distracted by Bonds's pursuit of Aaron's No. 755. As the clubs prepared to meet for a three-game series July 31–August 2 in Los Angeles, the Dodgers were tied for first with Arizona, the Giants were in last place, and Bonds was at 754.

The opener of the series at Dodger Stadium was a spectacle. A sellout crowd showed up, security was tightened, hecklers were in full force by batting practice, the right-field stands were filled with glove-wearing fans hoping to catch a piece of potentially profitable history, anti-Bonds T-shirts were sold outside the stadium and cameras flashed with every swing. Los Angeles sportswriters, after surveying the scene, wrote that the circus was in town.

Bonds got only one hit in 12 plate appearances in the series, and walked five times, three intentionally. The quest for the record would have to wait as the circus would pack up and quietly leave town, on its way to the next venue in San Diego.

Bonds hit No. 755 on August 4, 2007, and passed Aaron three days later against the Washington Nationals. Bonds would have limited playing time when the Giants and Dodgers next met September 7–9, though San Francisco damaged the Dodgers' postseason hopes by winning two out of three. By the time the teams met again, on September 28 for a season-closing series, the Dodgers had been eliminated and the Giants were 19 games behind Arizona. The Giants had finally announced that Bonds wouldn't be back in 2008. Bonds, nursing a sprained big toe, would sit out all three final games. For 15 years, Bonds was a fixture in the rivalry—idolized in San Francisco, an irritant in Los Angeles. But love him or hate him, most would have to agree that in the rich history of the rivalry, few could dominate and shape a game like Barry Bonds.

SLUGGERS WITH SWAGGER

Barry Bonds was Willie Mays with an attitude. Both players possessed power and speed, made big plays in the field, and had a flair for delivering at dramatic moments. The difference: Mays did it with joy; Bonds did it with a scowl. Dodgers fans would watch Mays tear through them with his bat, arm and legs, and yet react with admiration and appreciation of his skills. Bonds would hammer the Dodgers with his offensive and defensive exploits, and fans would react with taunts and outrage. The departure of Bonds appeared to mean that the rivalry for a time would have to go on without any colorful, central character who could ignite a crowd just by taking his position in left field.

That is, until the Dodgers found Manny Ramirez. Now it was the Dodgers turn to discover, as the Giants had with Bonds, that there was a risk to signing sluggers with swagger:

"Starting this coming homestand, fans will have the opportunity to sit in 'Mannywood,' an area named to honor left fielder Manny

Ramirez. Field Level seats, fair of the foul pole in left field, will be sold in pairs with exclusive Mannywood T-Shirts for $99. Ramirez wears Number 99. The seats, the closest to the Dodgers left fielder, are in sections 51 and 53. Fans can order online at dodgers.com. The limited edition Mannywood T-shirts are only available through the promotion. On May 5, in celebration of Cinco de Mayo, a limited edition 'I was in Mannywood' T-shirt will be given to fans who purchase tickets in Mannywood." — From dodgers.com April 27, 2009.

"(Manny) Ramirez, the All-Star outfielder who revitalized a once-proud franchise, mired in mediocrity and coined the term 'Mannywood,' had become the most famous player to be suspended under the drug policy implemented by baseball in 2004."— From latimes.com May 8, 2009

"Within minutes of Ramirez's suspension, the 'Mannywood' ticket promotion was removed from the Dodgers' Web site and the team announced that it would be discontinued until further notice and the 3,100 promotion tickets that were sold for games while Ramirez is on suspension would be refunded—if fans chose to ask for a refund. Those that will still go to the games will receive a Dodgers T-shirt unless they specifically ask for a Mannywood T-shirt."—From SI.com May 8, 2009

Those who bought into Mannywood were devastated, but said they would support their fallible hero when he returned. Sure he got caught doing a bad thing, but if he returned with his bat blazing, they might also buy into his special rationale.

It was just Manny being Manny.

Giants fans watched the Ramirez-Dodgers fiasco with a certain satisfaction. They, too, had a powerful Hall of Fame-type slugger who marched to his own drummer, became a defensive liability, didn't always run out ground balls, and got linked to the performance-enhancing-drug controversy, but who thrilled them with his offensive exploits. Dodgers fans, sitting in the future Mannywood section, heaped scorn and verbal abuse at the Giants' superstar, only to later overlook the similar traits of their left fielder. Giants fans taunted Ramirez with similar chants in San Francisco, but easily overlooked the eccentricities of their left fielder. They too had a rationale that dismissed any negative.

It was just Barry being Barry.

ONE-MAN WRECKING CREW (2008)

Manny Ramirez and Barry Bonds were not on the radar of the Dodgers or Giants as the clubs prepared for the 2008 season. Ramirez was coming off his lowest offensive output (20 HR, 88 RBIs) in his seven years with Boston, but experts expected him to rebound and help the world champion Red Sox return to the postseason. The Giants seemed relieved to have the Bonds distraction out of the way, as they shifted focus on how to become competitive again after a three-year plunge.

The Dodgers' disappointing fourth-place finish in 2007 was blamed in part on a clubhouse divided between young players and veterans. Jeff Kent brought the rift to the forefront near the end of the season with comments about the newer players not having respect for the older ones.

Los Angeles appeared to have some promising young talent in catcher Russell Martin, first baseman James Loney, outfielders Andre Ethier and Matt Kemp, and pitcher Chad Billingsley. The trick was how to get that group of potentially rising stars to mesh with old hands such as infielders Kent, Rafael Furcal, and Nomar Garciaparra, outfielders Andrew Jones and Juan Pierre, and pitcher Brad Penny.

General manager Ned Colletti found the magician they thought could pull it off shortly after New York Yankees manager Joe Torre walked away from a one-year contract offer at the end of the 2007 season. Within days, Torre had agreed to a three-year deal to skipper the Dodgers. Torre's mandate would be similar to the one he operated under in pressure-cooker New York as the McCourts looked to the 67-year-old respected baseball man to fulfill their promise to bring the first world championship to Los Angeles since 1988.

The Dodgers also saw another possible benefit to their new manager. Torre was an All-Star and a Gold-Glove winner with a career batting average of .297 and 252 home runs. He had four World Series titles and 12 consecutive years in the playoffs as a manager. His credentials, and his proven ability to manage big-name personalities in New York made him a lure to draw top players to Los Angeles. The Dodgers had lacked top-gun offensive players who could command the No. 3 and 4 spots in the order. The offense misfired too much in 2007 as the club finished 10th in runs scored and 15th in home runs. Torre's hiring triggered rumors that the Dodgers might have a shot at signing the Yankees' Alex Rodriquez or at least be in a better position to bring a big hitter to Los Angeles.

—⁓—

Matt Cain's 7–16 record in 2007 was not a match for his solid 200 innings, a 3.65 ERA, and 163 strikeouts, as he was victimized by lack of run support. Tim Lincecum's dominant minor league performance forced the Giants to bring him up in 2007. The small but powerful right-hander struck out 150 in 146 innings with a 4.00 ERA, enough to keep him in the rotation for 2008. The Giants saw enough promise in reliever Brian Wilson that they planned to give him a shot at closer. If the three pitchers clicked, the Giants might be amending a baseball cliché to read Lincecum and Cain (with Wilson in the ninth) and three days of rain. It wasn't clear what else the Giants had to offer to hold the attention of the home crowd drained from three straight disastrous years and no more Bonds at-bats.

The three days off for rain might actually serve as a welcome break for the Giants aging lineup, as the club's win-with-Barry philosophy had prevented enough focus in the farm system to provide some home-grown offensive talent. The Giants were 15th in runs scored, and 14th in batting average and home runs in 2007's 91-loss season. The projected starting lineup included infielders Ray Durham, 36, Rich Aurilia, 36, and Omar Vizquel, 40; outfielders Dave Roberts and Randy Winn, 33; and catcher Bengie Molina, 33.

The jury was still out on the impact of the Giants' two mega-signings. The Giants expected more from Barry Zito, and could only hope his lack of consistency wasn't a sign of a career on the downslide. Expectations were high this year for hard-nosed Aaron Rowand, signed for $60 million, as the Giants hoped his 27-homer season in cozy Citizens Bank Park in Philadelphia would translate in the wide open spaces of AT&T Park.

—◆◆◆—

The Dodgers and Giants got their first chance to compare notes on how the preseason questions and issues might play out as they opened 2008 with a three-game series in Los Angeles.

Penny made it a mismatch of opening day pitchers, blanking the Giants for 6⅔ innings on four hits before three relievers kept the shutout in a 5–0 Dodgers win. Zito, struggling with a drop in velocity, got in a hole quickly as Kemp knocked in a run with a single and Kent followed with a two-run homer for a three-run first inning. It took the offensively challenged Giants 16 innings to score a run in the new season, as Derek Lowe kept them scoreless through six innings in game two on the way to a 3–2 Dodgers victory. Cain continued to be haunted by lack of support as he shut down the Dodgers into the sixth. The Giants avoided a sweep in game three as five pitchers stymied the Dodgers in a 2–1 win, although San Francisco's hitting woes showed no sign of ending.

The clubs would have a three-month gap before meeting again, as the schedule-makers had them playing 15 of their 18 encounters in the last three months. Meanwhile, the Dodgers and Arizona were demonstrating that .500 ball might be sufficient to win the NL West. Going into a series with the Giants July 28–30, the Dodgers were only 52–52, yet trailed the first-place Diamondbacks by just one game. The Giants, at 43–61, could not even get in the contention conversation despite the lack of any team taking charge in the division. San Francisco's bats came to life to build a 7–0 lead after four innings in a victorious opener, but went back into hibernation as the Giants failed to score for the remaining 23 innings of the series. Jason Johnson blanked the Giants over six innings in the second game followed by three shutout innings by the bullpen, and Billingsley went the distance in a 4–0 win in game three.

The back-to-back shutouts of their rivals were a satisfying pitching achievement for the Dodgers, but they knew they would need more hitting for their best shot at winning the apparent two-team race with Arizona.

The relationship between Manny Ramirez and the Red Sox had been deteriorating, and the cute "Manny being Manny" excuse for his antics was turning ugly enough that Boston was ready to cut the ties. On July 31, the Dodgers took their chance on one of the game's most dangerous offensive threats when they acquired Ramirez in a three-team deal that also involved Pittsburgh. Ramirez, with 515 career home runs, was amid another productive season on the field with 20 homers, 68 RBIs and a .299 average. Ramirez's arrival for the two-month stretch drive of August and September was not about contending—it was about titles, as the Dodgers owner emphasized. "We're focused on winning the division and going as deep as we can into October," Frank McCourt said. "We want to win right here and right now, and that's why we made this trade."

The Ramirez deal came five days after a less sensational but significant move when the Dodgers bolstered their offense with the acquisition of third baseman Casey Blake from Cleveland. The Dodgers weren't through jolting their roster, as they would sign four-time Cy Young Award winner Greg Maddux on August 19. Maddux, now 42, helped the Dodgers to the wild card in his 2006 stint with the club.

Ramirez was on an early tear when the Giants got their first look at him in Dodger blue, having gone 13-for-23 with four homers in his first six games. The Giants stopped him with an 0-for-5 day on August 8 in the opener of a three-game series, but the Dodgers won 6–2. The Giants came back the next two games as they scored winning runs in the last inning both days.

The Dodgers were closing in on a division title, 3½ games ahead of Arizona, when the teams next met September 19, leaving the Giants an opportunity to at least slow their momentum. San Francisco did just that with two strong pitching performances. Zito limited the Dodgers to a run in 7⅔ innings in a 7–1 win in the opener, and Cain threw six shutout innings while the bullpen added five scoreless frames in a 1–0, 11-inning win in the third game. The two losses trimmed the Dodgers' lead to 2½ games.

Any chances the Giants had to slow or even derail the Dodgers' title quest in the clubs' season-closing series September 26–28 ended when Los Angeles clinched the NL West on September 25 as Arizona fell to St. Louis.

The Dodgers swept the Cubs 3–0 in the divisional series, but were knocked out in five games in the championship series by eventual World Series winner Philadelphia. Any questions about whether the steady stewardship of Torre would match well with the unpredictable Ramirez appeared to be put to rest. Ramirez exceeded hopes, becoming a one-man wrecking crew with a .396 average, 17 homers, and 53 RBIs in 53 games for the Dodgers.

The Giants' biggest story of 2008 happened off the field as general partner Bill Neukom succeeded Peter Magowan as managing partner in August, putting him in charge of the club.

Critics like to accuse Magowan of looking the other way regarding performance-enhancing drugs, though more evidence since then has revealed that many baseball officials for many teams could face the same allegations. Fans, on the other hand, harbor little if any resentment of Magowan, and view him more as savior than sinner. Magowan, with the help of other high-powered, civic-minded leaders, saved the Giants for San Francisco in 1993, brought the crowd-thrilling Bonds on board and oversaw the construction of one of baseball's best ballparks. Fans at AT&T Park are smart enough to know that if it wasn't for Magowan, they might today be munching on their garlic fries from some Bay Area tavern while watching the Giants on TV conduct business in faraway Florida or some other distant venue. And even Magowan's much-maligned signing of pitcher Barry Zito would eventually turn around, as the left-hander would become a savior himself in the Giants' 2012 postseason comeback.

Among new owner Neukom's biggest tasks were to invigorate the team's farm system in the post-Bonds years, and bring some firepower to the offense after four consecutive noncompetitive seasons. Any list of potentially available big bats had to include free agent Ramirez, who would be entering discussions with the Dodgers about returning in 2009. The Giants, growing desperate for run-producers, would not rule Ramirez out if he couldn't come to terms with Los Angeles. The Giants got a good look at Ramirez in 2008, as he went 11 for 27 with seven RBIs and two homers in eight games against them.

The outcome of Ramirez's talks with the Dodgers was a story through-out the offseason. Ramirez's two-month blitz had brought a new excite-ment to Dodger Stadium, and his return to Los Angeles would seem to guarantee a full year of big offense, big crowds, and perhaps another run at that elusive World Series.

DISTRACTION (2009)

The season-closing Giants-Dodgers game September 28, 2008, was mean-ingless in the standings. The Dodgers were about to begin the postseason, and the Giants were completing their worst four-year run since coming to San Francisco. The Giants could have turned that game into an exhibition-like contest, but instead decided to start Tim Lincecum, giving Cy Young Award voters one more look at their young phenom. Lincecum dazzled the Dodgers, allowing one run and four hits in seven innings while striking out 13 in a 3–1 victory to boost his record to 18–5.

Lincecum was becoming the centerpiece of a pitching staff that the Giants thought might bring dramatic improvement to the club, especially if the offense could find a way to push in a few more runs. Matt Cain's 8–14 record again belied his quality year, as his 3.76 ERA and 186 strikeouts weren't enough to overcome the anemic offensive support. Barry Zito failed to live up to the contract in his first two years, but his credentials still had the Giants hoping he could serve as an innings-eater in the No. 4 or 5 spot. Jonathan Sanchez showed promise, striking out 157 in 2008. Brian Wilson appeared to have arrived as a closer with 41 saves in 47 opportunities.

The Giants, uncertain about what young pitcher in their system might fill out the rotation, decided to stretch the age qualification by signing 45-year-old free agent Randy Johnson. The five-time Cy Young Award winner arrived after a presentable 11–10 record and 3.91 ERA for Arizona in 2008. Johnson wasn't brought in as a museum piece just to attract curious fans—the Giants reasoned that his motivation at being five wins away from his career 300th win would make him a key contributor to the staff.

As promising as the pitching appeared, the offense promised to bring more frustration. The Giants were 15th in runs scored for the second straight year and last in home runs. The Giants hoped that newly acquired veteran Edgar Renteria would provide some timely hitting, Aaron Rowand would put up his Phillies numbers, and that the colorful youngster Pablo Sandoval would demonstrate that his .345 average and 24 RBIs in 41 games in 2008 could be repeated over a full season.

The Dodgers nearly made a clean sweep of veterans as a youth movement took hold. Among those not returning were Jeff Kent, Derek Lowe, Brad Penny, Greg Maddux, and Nomar Garciaparra. The pitching staff, which had the lowest ERA in the league in 2008, appeared solid with a rotation highlighted by Chad Billingsley, Hiroki Kuroda, and Randy Woolf, and a deep bullpen anchored by closer Jonathan Broxton.

Compared to the Giants' Misdemeanor Row of hitters, the heart of the Dodgers' order looked like Murderer's Row. The club entered spring training with a lineup filled with potent bats. Rafael Furcal, limited by injury in 2008, provided speed at the top and there were no easy outs in the following procession of Andre Ethier, Matt Kemp, Russell Martin, James Loney, and Casey Blake. There was one significant, lingering question remaining: Would the offense include Manny Ramirez?

—◆◆◆—

The Ramirez contract soap opera ended on March 4 as the Dodgers signed him to a two-year, $45 million deal. The Giants were rumored to be interested in Ramirez, but the club shrugged off news of the signing. "We're always looking for ways to improve our club and we always will be," said managing general partner Bill Neukom. "The question is, how much he could have improved the club and at what cost?"

The hyped-up signing of Ramirez and the less dramatic addition of second baseman Orlando Hudson gave manager Joe Torre even more power and speed as he reconfigured his lineup. The Ramirez buzz was already in high pitch for Dodgers fans as the club prepared for its home opener April 13 against the Giants. It would be an early test for San Francisco to see if the team was finally ready to rebound from four years of gloom.

—◆◆◆—

One game does not make a winning season, but if it did, the Dodgers home opener might be the template. The Dodgers got superb pitching, as Billingsley allowed just one run and struck out 11 in seven innings. They got an offensive eruption of 11 runs and 15 hits, led by Ethier's two home runs. They mauled Johnson, the Giants' prized acquisition, for seven runs in 3⅔ innings. The Giants put up a fight in game two, but lost in the ninth 5–4 on a bases loaded walk to Loney. The Dodgers got to Zito for six runs in game three for a 7–2 win and a sweep.

The Giants got back a little respectability when the clubs met in San Francisco April 27–29, winning two out of three. The clubs split the first two, but the Giants took over game three as Bengie Molina's two-run triple and solo homer helped build a 7–0 lead after seven. The Dodgers broke through against Lincecum in the eighth for three runs, but the Giants held on for a 9–4 win.

The Dodgers returned home after the series and launched the "Mannywood" section in the left field stands, a special value promotion dedicated to Ramirez's fans. By May 7, Manny-mania was in full swing, the first-place Dodgers had a remarkable 13–0 home record, and the depth and talent of the Los Angeles roster seemed strong enough to survive any adversity a baseball season might dish out.

Dodgers Nation was stunned.

> "When I heard the news on the radio this morning, I had a large pit in my stomach, like I had just lost a good friend. When he came here, it was like watching the Dodgers of the '70s and '80s when they were champions. I'm just so disappointed. Everyone here in this section came here to see him and he let us down. We'll support him when he comes back, but we're still in shock right now."

That was the reaction of a "Mannywood" seat holder, still wearing his Manny T-shirt, after news broke May 7 that Ramirez was suspended for 50 games for testing positive for a drug that is used by steroid users to restore testosterone production to normal levels. The Dodgers brass vowed to support Ramirez, too, keeping an upbeat face on the sudden turmoil coming as the team was rolling. The Dodgers had to keep the crisis into perspective. Ramirez would return to the lineup in early July, giving him at least 2½ months of playing time. The Dodgers likely would not need Ramirez to duplicate his late-season tear of 2008 because this year's club appeared stronger.

The Giants arrived in town May 8, the day after the suspension was announced, giving them a chance to take advantage of Ramirez's absence and the distraction it caused the Dodgers. If the Dodgers were distracted in the first game of the three-game series as Zito delivered a decent six-inning performance in a 3–1 Giants win, they got over it quickly. Eric Stults blanked the Giants on four hits the next day in an 8–0 Los Angeles victory. The Giants took their second consecutive series against the Dodgers with a 13-inning win in game three. The Manny-less Dodgers may have taken an emotional detour after the shocking news, but they were still in the driver's seat with a 4½-game lead.

The relentless Dodgers were continuing to set the pace as the clubs next met on August 10, with Los Angeles now 5½ games in front of the Giants and Colorado. Ramirez already had achieved one milestone and neared another upon his return. He passed Mickey Mantle for career homers with 537 on July 20, and hit his 21st grand slam July 22, second behind Lou Gehrig. The latter blast came on Manny Ramirez Bobblehead Night. The Mannywood section had long been discontinued, but the Manny statuettes survived.

The Giants would get a crack at disrupting the Dodgers' title quest as the teams would meet six times in September. Instead, San Francisco quickly learned that the Dodgers' prescription for success in 2009—a dose of strong pitching and hitting—was not about to run out. The Dodgers opened the September 11–13 series with a 13-hit attack featuring a two-run homer by Blake and eight solid innings from Kuroda in a 10–3 win. They followed that up with a 9-1 victory highlighted by a three-run homer by Martin and a two-run shot by Loney, along with six smooth innings by Vicente Padilla. The Giants finally snapped out of it with a 15-hit outburst in a 7–2 win to avoid a sweep, but with just three weeks left in the season, the Dodgers remained in first by three games while the Giants sat in third, 7½ games back.

The Dodgers built their lead to five games over Colorado with 15 to play as the clubs met again in a series September 18–20. The Giants trumped a Ramirez home run in the opener with a three-run blast by Sandoval, and solo shots by Eugenio Velez and Rowand for an 8–4 win. The Dodgers roared back, giving Giants starters Brad Penny, a late August acquisition, and Lincecum early showers on their way to 12–1 and 6–2 victories the next two days. Los Angeles finished its head-to-head competition against the Giants with an 11–7 mark. The Dodgers were now 43–30 against the Giants in the past four years, as the Giants had not taken a series from their rivals since 2005.

The Dodgers clinched a postseason berth the next weekend with an 8–4 win at Pittsburgh, but Torre put the champagne celebration on ice. Torre decided to postpone the party until the club could clinch its second straight NL West title. That achievement came on October 3 as the Dodgers topped Colorado 5–0. The clincher marked a remarkable season for the Dodgers. They moved into a tie for first on April 15 against the Giants, took sole possession of the top spot on April 19, and stayed there through game 162.

Los Angeles swept St. Louis 3–0 in the division series, but couldn't handle Philadelphia in the NLCS, falling in five games. The Dodgers' quick demise to the Phillies was surprising given the strength of this year's team, whose 95 wins was the most for the club since 1985. The Dodgers had the league's best ERA and the offense had the best batting average even with Ramirez's 50-game absence.

The Giants finished seven games out in third place with an 88–74 record, a 16-game improvement from 2008, and the first winning season since 2004. San Francisco's offense scored the fifth fewest runs in the league, but was bailed out often by a pitching staff with the league's second best ERA.

The Dodgers felt they had built a team of powerful arms and armament that could again mow down the National League. Perhaps more significantly, the young team showed maturity under Torre's guidance to overcome the Ramirez distraction. The Giants believed they could make some noise by either finding a long-ball threat or tweaking their roster enough to raise the run production for their impressive starters and bullpen. The realistic hopes of both teams for 2010 were a contrast. The Dodgers, who had not been to a World Series since 1988, would be satisfied with nothing less. The Giants, who had not won a World Series since the New York squad took the title in 1954, would surely be content if they could just get into a playoff series where they could find out just how far pitching might take a club in the postseason.

Part Five

NEW ERA
2010–2016

9

CHAMPIONSHIPS: 2010–2016

*If the season doesn't end with a big parade, what's the point of having
a season? That appeared to be where the rivalry evolved by the end of
2016. The Giants had three massive city celebrations in five years, and the
Dodgers were banking on the premise that a big payroll means a big year-
end party. For both clubs, and their fans, anything short of
a championship suddenly seemed unacceptable.*

A GIANT SEASON (2010)

The Dodgers were flying high and the Giants were just hoping to become relevant again as the start of the season neared. That was the scenario as the teams got ready for action in 1954. The Dodgers bounced back from the bruising playoff loss in 1951 to win back-to-back pennants in 1952 and 1953, although they fell in the World Series both years to the Yankees. The Giants, edged out by Brooklyn in the 1952 pennant race, collapsed in 1953. They finished 70–84 in fifth place, 35 games behind the Dodgers. The Giants had one good excuse for their 1953 nosedive: Willie Mays missed the entire season because of military service.

The return of Mays and his 41-homer, 110-RBI year, and a trade that ignited the pitching staff spurred the Giants to a 27-better win performance as they outlasted Brooklyn by five games to capture the National League

1954 flag. During the offseason, they picked up starter Johnny Antonelli in a six-player trade that sent 1951 hero Bobby Thomson to the Milwaukee Braves. Antonelli led the way in a stellar, about-face pitching performance which saw the staff give up 197 fewer runs in 1954 while leading the league with the lowest ERA.

Despite the Giants' impressive comeback year in 1954, few gave them a chance to win their first World Series since 1933. Their opponent would be the Cleveland Indians, whose overpowering 111-win season ended the 103-victory Yankees' stretch of five straight pennants. The experts who gave the Giants little chance against the Indians didn't figure on the ability of the New York staff to rise to the occasion. Mays's legendary catch of a 450-foot drive by Vic Wertz lives on as the biggest moment of the Series, but it was pitching that limited the Indians to nine runs and a batting average of .190 that keyed the stunning four-game sweep.

—⁓—

Fifty-six years later, the outlook of the Dodgers and Giants as they entered the 2010 season had some similarities. The Dodgers were coming off back-to-back NL West titles, and had been in the postseason three of the last four years. The offensive firepower that helped produce five straight 90-plus win seasons for the Giants from 2000 to 2004 had long been extinguished. The Giants went the next four years without winning at least 80 games. The club broke the losing spell in 2009 with an 88–74 record, but that was only good enough for a third-place finish.

The Dodgers had taken charge of the rivalry. The Giants had not won a season series against the Dodgers since 2005. Los Angeles held a 43–30 record over the Giants since 2006. The Dodgers entered 2010 with a young core of offensive threats. Matt Kemp, with 26 homers and 101 RBIs in 2009, and Andre Ethier, with 31 homers and 106 RBIs, were expected to get even better. Manny Ramirez dropped off after returning from a 50-game steroids suspension, but the Dodgers expected him to bounce back. Chad Billingsley and Clayton Kershaw gave the Dodgers a strong 1–2 punch in the rotation, and the bullpen was solid, led by closer Jonathan Broxton.

The Giants hoped that Pablo Sandoval would repeat or even improve his numbers of .330, 25 HR, and 90 RBIs, and that highly touted catcher Buster Posey would live up to the press clippings once he was promoted to the major league roster. The lack of offense might have prevented the Giants from making a legitimate run at the Dodgers in 2009. The Giants were 13th in runs scored, 11th in batting average, and 15th in home runs for that season. San Francisco fans could only dream of what might be possible if the offense provided a little more support for the rotation of two-time Cy Young Award winner Tim Lincecum, Matt Cain, Jonathan Sanchez, Barry Zito, and promising 20-year-old rookie Madison Bumgarner.

The Dodgers showed no respect for manager Bruce Bochy's 55th birthday in the first meeting of 2010 between the clubs April 16, as they opened all the presents and ate all the cake. Kemp and Ethier's back-to-back homers in the first, and Ethier's grand slam in the second gave the Dodgers a 7–0 lead. In the fifth inning, the Giants lost outfielder Aaron Rowand when a pitch by Vicente Padilla slammed into his face, causing two small fractures in his left cheekbone. The Giants, trailing 10–3 in the ninth, made the score respectable with a five-run frame highlighted by Eugenio Velez's three-run homer. The Giants came back the next day for a 9–0 victory behind Lincecum, who threw six shutout innings. The Dodgers took the series with a 2–1 win when Ramirez slugged a two-run homer off reliever Sergio Romo in the eighth.

By the time the clubs next faced off for a three-game series June 28–30 in San Francisco, San Diego was establishing itself as the team to beat. The Padres, at 45–30, held a 4½ game lead over the Giants with the Dodgers five back. The series turned into a disaster for the Giants as the Dodgers took advantage of mistakes for a sweep. Base-running gaffes by Sandoval in the first two games were costly, prompting boos from the home crowd

in back-to-back 4–2 Dodgers victories. Los Angeles knocked around
Sanchez in game three and went on to an 8–2 win. The Giants scored only
six runs in the three games as rookie Posey was hitting just .143 in his last
14 games after a hot start. In the first game, the slumping Giants hit into
five double plays, giving them 81 in 75 games. The beating was made even
worse because of a passive attempt to retaliate against Padilla for beaning
Rowand. Giants pitcher Santiago Casilla threw a ball behind Padilla in the
seventh, but it was far from the menacing type of payback that had marked
the rivalry over the years. Umpire Tom Hallion warned both benches, and
the matter appeared to be over with Padilla escaping untouched.

—⁘—

The clubs' next meeting would produce one of the oddest moments in the
rivalry, involving rules requiring when a pitcher must be removed from
a game. Some said they had never seen anything like what happened on
July 20, 2010, at Dodger Stadium, but a look back at the rivalry recalls two
other fierce arguments in circumstances with at least some similarities.

On May 10, 1963, Don Drysdale was on his way to a complete game
performance as the Dodgers led the Giants 2–1 in the ninth. With no
outs, and Willie Mays at third after reaching base on an error and Willie
McCovey at first following a single, Dodgers manager Walter Alston came
onto the field to warn catcher John Roseboro about a possible double steal.
When Alston came out for a second time, this one to go to the mound,
an infuriated Giants manager Alvin Dark argued that the trip constitut-
ed a second visit, which by rule would require him to remove Drysdale.
The umpires, however, said the first visit to Roseboro didn't apply, leading
Dark to play the game under protest. Drysdale, not distracted by the delay,
retired the next three batters for the victory. The protest was denied.

On May 19, 1978, the teams slugged it out figuratively through six
innings, with the score tied at 7–7, and then almost slugged it out literally.
The Giants announced they were playing the game under protest when the
Dodgers brought in Mike Garman to pitch in the seventh even though it

had been made known that he was being traded to Montreal. The Dodgers argued that the trade would not be official until the next day, making Garman eligible to pitch. The Dodgers' Reggie Smith, upset at the protest, shouted at Giants third base coach Jim Davenport, prompting umpire Nick Colosi to step between them before the confrontation could get physical. The Giants went on to a 10–7 victory, so the protest became moot.

As the clubs prepared for the three-game series July 19–21, the Padres continued to set the pace, leading Colorado by four, the third-place Giants by 4½ and the fifth-place Dodgers by 5½. The Giants jumped out to a 4–0 lead after four innings in the first game, and won it 5–2.

Game two turned into a Dodgers-Giants classic.

The Dodgers took a 5–1 lead after three with Ethier's two-run homer the big blow. In the fifth, Lincecum sent Kemp ducking from one pitch before plunking him with another, possibly as a more substantial answer to the Rowand incident. Kemp stepped toward the mound, but rerouted himself to first base. The Giants scored three in the sixth to narrow the lead to 5–4. Giants reliever Denny Bautista responded in the last half of the sixth by nearly hitting Dodgers catcher Russell Martin. Los Angeles bench coach Bob Schaeffer was tossed out when he argued that Bautista should be ejected. In the seventh, Kershaw and manager Joe Torre were automatically ejected when Rowand was hit with a pitch again. With the bench coach and Torre dismissed, hitting coach Don Mattingly was left in charge. The Giants loaded the bases in the ninth, and Mattingly went out to talk to reliever Broxton. Mattingly had just left the mound, but turned and went back to it when first baseman James Loney asked a question. After Bruce Bochy came out to make the argument, the umpires concurred that Mattingly's move was an official second visit and ordered Broxton removed from the game. The Dodgers were further penalized when reliever George Sherrill was limited to eight warm-up pitches.

When play finally resumed, Andres Torres doubled home two runs and Posey singled home another for an eventual 7–5 Giants win. The umpires' ruling on Broxton's removal and Sherrill's restricted pitches was subsequently questioned by major league officials, but the second guessing came too late to help the Dodgers avert a devastating defeat. The Dodgers failed to file a protest during the game, so the controversial rulings on the field stood.

The Dodgers avoided a series sweep as Billingsley tossed a five-hit shutout for a 2–0 win in the third game, but the Giants had made a statement.

By the time the teams met nine days later, the Dodgers were reeling and the Giants were rolling. San Francisco poured it on with a sweep of the three-game series. As August began, the Giants were within 1½ games of the Padres, while the Dodgers had dropped eight back.

The Dodgers' surprising tumble took another twist at the end of August when the club allowed Ramirez to go to the Chicago White Sox on a waiver claim. Ramirez had gone from boon to bust. Right leg injuries put him on the disabled list three times in 2010, his defense was limited and he had been relegated to a backup role. His Dodgers career ended when he got tossed out for arguing a strike call while pinch-hitting with the bases loaded. The club had seen enough, and decided to cut their ties without getting anything in return.

The Dodgers, who would finish the year 80–82 in fourth place, were now reduced to the spoiler role. They were unsuccessful in that venture also as the Giants won four of the six games between the clubs in September. The Giants, with a huge assist from a 10-game Padres losing streak, suddenly found themselves in a race to the wire.

The Giants-Padres battle went down to the final day of the season. San Francisco's 3–0 win put them into postseason and eliminated San Diego. The Giants' business model for winning in 2010—extraordinary pitching and timely hitting—carried them to victories over Atlanta in the division matchup, Philadelphia in the NL championship, and Texas in the World Series. The Giants of 2010, like the Giants of 1954, had defied the experts.

Fifty-six years after Johnny Antonelli recorded the final out for a sweep of Cleveland, the Giants were back on top of the baseball world.

RIVALRY ROCKED (2011)

"Laughing" Larry Doyle had every reason to be happy. The second baseman won a batting title, played on three consecutive pennant winners, and won an MVP award. His minor league contract was purchased by the big league club for a then-record amount. He had batting averages of .320, .330, and .310. It was no wonder that the standout New York Giant told writer Damon Runyan in a 1911 interview that "it was great to be young and a Giant."

One hundred years later, it was still great to be a Giant—made especially so by the 2010 World Series championship. The baseball experts weren't rushing to declare the club a dynasty in the making as the 2011 season approached, with legitimate questions about the offense. Third baseman Pablo Sandoval's output dropped dramatically to a .268 average, 13 home runs, and 68 RBIs in 2010. The Giants benefited from outstanding clutch contributions from several players who had inconsistent careers, raising speculation whether they could repeat those performances. Much of the offensive load was expected to be carried by rookie of the year catcher Buster Posey, who had most observers believing that he would match or exceed his offensive performance. No one doubted the Giants rich pitching staff. Starters Tim Lincecum, Matt Cain, Jonathan Sanchez, and midseason addition Madison Bumgarner were complemented by a reliable group of middle relievers and set-up men, and topped off by closer Brian Wilson. The Giants appeared comfortable enough with the World Series-year formula of lights-out pitching and a "different-offensive-hero-everyday" offense that they again shunned the quest for the elusive "big bat."

While it was the Giants' Larry Doyle who delivered the famous quote, many members of the Brooklyn and Los Angeles teams throughout the years would probably declare it was also great to be "young and a Dodger." It took the Giants 53 years to win a world championship in San Francisco. The Dodgers did it in their second season out west. Still, all that mattered now was how the Dodgers might rebound from a sub. 500 season in 2010. While the bullpen had questions after faltering in 2010, the rotation gave hope led by the one-two tandem of Clayton Kershaw and Chad Billingsley. The Dodgers big bats all carried question marks: Would Andre Ethier stay healthy? Would James Loney avoid a second-half stumble? Would the talented Matt Kemp turn the corner after an unsettling year which brought public criticism from a coach and general manager Ned Colletti?

While those questions could be answered on the field, a more significant question simmered in the executive suites. The publicly messy divorce of Dodgers owner Frank McCourt and his wife Jamie, the former chief executive officer, and the financial complications, had created an uncertainty about the future of one of the most prominent franchises in sports history. The conflicts left confusion over how the club would conduct baseball business, including roster moves and pursuit of free agents. The prized organization was at a crossroads, and it didn't seem as if things could get any worse. But they did, on opening night of 2011 in Los Angeles, as the rivalry became ensnarled in the ownership fiasco when fan violence took its mostly ugly turn.

———

Lincecum vs. Kershaw.

With the exception of Marichal vs. Koufax, there had been no other more exciting, anticipated pitching duel in a Dodgers-Giants game on the West Coast. Lincecum picked up two Cy Young awards and a World Series ring in his first three full years. Kershaw, at 23, was already seen as a lock for stardom, and his 2.91 ERA with 212 strikeouts in 204 innings in 2010 gave validity to such predictions. A Dodgers-Giants season opener didn't need such a gun-slinging showdown to spice up the game, but that is what was in store for the 56,000 fans at the March 31 meeting at Dodger Stadium.

The Lincecum-Kershaw duel lived up to expectations, with the game scoreless in the bottom of the sixth. Then defense, an almost overlooked reason why the Giants won it all in 2010, betrayed Lincecum. After Kemp walked, an apparent double play groundball to Miguel Tejada turned into disaster, as the shortstop threw the ball into right field. After Juan Uribe was hit by a pitch, Lincecum bounced a pitch to Rod Barajas. When Posey tried to gun down Kemp as he retreated to third, the ball got past Sandoval, allowing Kemp to score. Loney doubled in a run in the eighth, and Pat Burrell homered in the ninth as the Dodgers took the opener 2–1.

The traditional audience participation symbolic of most Dodgers-Giants games began early during the opener as Los Angeles fans shouted "Giants suck," while Giants supporters got even by sending a plane over the stadium with a banner reading DODGERS STILL SUCK. While the language was not original or creative, it was the norm of what one would hear or see at either of the Dodgers or Giants home venues over the years. Such nonviolent taunts would have been long forgotten if not for a horrific postgame incident in which Giants fan Bryan Stow, a 42-year-old paramedic from Santa Cruz, was viciously beaten in the parking lot after the game. The legal process has had to sort out exactly what happened that night, and whether security was lacking, but the sickening incident became part of the ongoing turmoil over the Dodgers ownership. The series of problems came to a head for major league baseball on April 20, when Commissioner Bud Selig announced the league was taking over operation of the team.

It was Mayday in Los Angeles. The organization was in distress, complicated by a bitter divorce and uncertainty about management of the team, and the outlook for 2011 and beyond was complex and chaotic. For the first time since the Dodgers' inception in the late 1800s, one could seriously ask: "Is it really great to be young and a Dodger?"

———

The Dodgers went on to win three out of four in the opening series in Los Angeles. Poor defense again haunted the Giants in a 4–3 loss in game two, and their bullpen faltered in a 7–5 loss in game four. The Giants only win came in a 10–0 rout in game three as Cain and a trio of relievers blanked the Dodgers.

When the teams met eight days later for a three-game series April 11–13 in San Francisco, the normally revved-up mood for a Dodgers-Giants game was dulled by the tragic event at opening night in Los Angeles. Security was increased, and before the game players from both sides came onto the field, where a representative from both clubs pleaded with fans to enjoy the competition but to avoid the violence that had marred the rivalry. In a goodwill peace gesture by the Giants, Uribe was presented his World Series ring in an on-field ceremony. One of the integral parts of the Giants' championship was now a Dodger. While the initial plan was to give Uribe the ring in private, it seemed in keeping with the spirit of the night to allow him to receive his well-deserved honor as appreciative fans applauded and teammates stepped forward with congratulatory hugs.

The teams split the first two contests, as the Dodgers got a strong performance from Kershaw in a 6–1 win in the first game, while Giants closer Wilson, who had been sidelined with an oblique muscle injury, struck out the side in a 5–4 San Francisco victory the next day. While the stands were peaceful during the series, Dodgers pitcher Ted Lilly stirred up emotions on the field in the third game when he hit Posey in consecutive at-bats, both with two outs and the bases empty. Posey flipped the bat after being hit for the second time, and umpires warned the benches, but there were no further incidents. The Giants retaliated with offense, as Sandoval and Mike Fontenot hit solo homers in the sixth off Lilly for the 4–3 win.

Security continued to be tight when the clubs met again May 18–19 in Los Angeles about five weeks later. The Giants swept the two-game series, highlighted by the offense finally roughing up Kershaw in an 8–5 win in the opener. The Giants got to the Dodgers ace for four runs in five innings, and Cody Ross capped the day with a three-run homer in the ninth that broke a 5–5 tie. A 3–1 victory in game two behind strong pitching by Bumgarner left the Giants in first place, while the Dodgers were five games back in fourth place.

The Dodgers continued to lose ground, and by the time the teams met again for a three-game series July 18–20 in San Francisco, they were at 42–53, 12½ games behind the first-place Giants. Injuries had hit just about all positions, leaving the Dodgers to rely on the arm of Kershaw and the bat of Kemp. But the loss of players and the failures of others to step up had the organization asking the agonizing question of whether they were buyers or sellers in the trade market.

Meanwhile, a lack of hitting and a devastating injury kept the Giants feeling uneasy despite a 55–41 record that had them in first place. On May 25, Posey suffered a fractured fibula and three torn ankle ligaments when Florida's Scott Cousins slammed into him while scoring the tie-breaking run on a sacrifice fly in the 12th inning. The Giants also had lost second baseman Freddy Sanchez to a dislocated right shoulder. The loss of the two potent bats at a time when much of the rest of the offense was struggling had the Giants wondering how long their superior pitching could keep the club on course.

The teams' six matchups in September had little suspense. A blistering hot Arizona had taken control of the NL West, the Giants had fallen under the weight of the punchless offense, and while the Dodgers had shown improvement, their efforts came too late to become a factor in the division. The Dodgers did provide some damage to the Giants' postseason hopes, winning five of the season's last seven games between the clubs. The Diamondbacks took over first place for good August 10. They closed out the season with a 25–9 run. The Giants finished 86–76 in second. They were at 61–44 and held a four-game lead July 28, but Arizona's surge and a Giants' 14–26 record from July 29 to September 10 doomed their quest for a repeat. It also meant that once again the offseason would involve pursuing more offense, and discussions of how to keep the prized starting pitching staff together.

———————

Victor Alvin Lombardi didn't look like a Giant slayer. But in just his second major league season in 1946, the Brooklyn Dodgers' 5-foot-7, 158-pound left-hander starter took ownership of the New York Giants. Lombardi went 5–0 against the Giants, with four complete games. He won the fifth by turning in seven strong innings, as Ralph Branca got the save with two scoreless innings. In the five games, Lombardi threw 42 innings, allowed 12 runs, and struck out 14.

Lombardi's five-win season against the Giants stood until Kershaw matched it in 2011. Kershaw's might have been more impressive since it came against the defending world champions, while Lombardi was facing a Giants team that went 61–93 and finished 36 games out in eighth place. Then again, Kershaw's domination came against the worst run-producing team in the National League.

A final argument in favor of Kershaw was his total pitching line against the Giants, and the fact that four of his victories came against Lincecum. Kershaw also threw 42 innings against the Giants, giving up just 6 runs and striking out 49. Kershaw's matchups against Lincecum in 2011 are classics:

	Kershaw					Lincecum				
Date	IP	R	H	SO	BB	IP	R	H	SO	BB
March 31:	7	0	4	9	1	7	1	5	5	3
July 20:	8	0	3	12	1	7	1	5	7	4
Sept. 9:	8	1	3	9	1	8	1	6	6	2
Sept. 20:	7.1	1	6	6	2	7	2	8	5	3

Kershaw's September 20 victory against the Giants made him the Dodger's first 20-game winner since Ramon Martinez went 20–6 in 1990, a performance that earned Kershaw the Cy Young Award. Kershaw's outstanding season was matched on offense by Kemp, who finished the year with 39 homers and 126 RBIs. Kemp came up short in his bid for the Triple Crown, but left the Giants pitchers bruised in trying for the rare feat. Kemp slugged his 35th homer against the Giants on September 21, and went four for five with a homer and three doubles in the final game between the teams September 22.

The year 2011 proved to be a challenging one for the rivalry. Another season passed without the clubs involved in a head-to-head race, leaving the drought at seven years. Some pondered whether the cloud over the Dodgers ownership would hinder the renewal of intense Giants-Dodgers competition, as attendance and interest dropped in Los Angeles. While the events of 2011 rocked the rivalry, those reaching for the panic button might find comfort from the past. During the 50-plus years on the West Coast, the Giants organization excelled at operating under a cloud. The Giants ownership started packing its bags for a rivalry-killing move of the franchise in 1976, 1984, and 1992. Somehow, those moments of crisis were quickly trumped. The Giants roared back as a contender in 1978, featuring a pennant race with the Dodgers that included one of the rivalry's most dramatic games before a record-breaking Candlestick crowd. The Giants turned around the rumored move of 1984 with a front-office overhaul that led to a bounce-back 1986 and a division title in 1987. The seemingly all-but-certain franchise move in 1992 turned into a footnote with a new ownership, new manager, and the signing of Barry Bonds.

The Giants franchise would enter the 2012 season with an unexpected change. Managing general partner Bill Neukom was retiring, and veteran Giants executive Larry Baer was stepping into the top post as CEO. Baer's accomplishments included playing a major role in getting the Giants' downtown park financed and built. The Dodgers also were facing a change in leadership, but their transition promised not to be as smooth and quiet. As 2012 was shaping up, prominent potential ownership groups were lining up to buy the Dodgers. Baseball hoped new owners could invigorate the traditions that made the Dodgers a jewel of a franchise, update aging Dodger Stadium, and restore the fan-friendly atmosphere. Such steps could immediately remind fans of the great Dodgers-Giants on-field traditions, as Kershaw duels Lincecum, and Kemp faces Cain. It would be fitting that 50 years after the glorious pennant race of 1962, another classic race for the flag would develop where members of both clubs could say it's great to be young and a part of the rivalry.

DO YOU BELIEVE IN MAGIC? (2012)

A baseball fan survives winter by keeping in mind those three special words: "Pitchers, catchers report." Starting around mid-February, there are a couple of weeks of drills, and then the games begin. They don't count, but baseball is being played under mostly sunny skies in Arizona and Florida, and that's good enough. As the exhibition schedule finally closes, fans and the sports pundits analyze and debate about what the new season will bring. Which teams will reach the postseason, who will be the stars? And they also might ask, what will be that one iconic moment that will define a club's season, for better or worse?

The Giants and Dodgers each had their moment in 2012. After all the games and all the up-and-down drama of a baseball season, two scenes are frozen in time.

The schedule-makers seemed insistent on making sure the Giants and Dodgers would go head-to-head multiple times in the second half of the season to determine if they would reach the postseason. The teams weren't scheduled to meet until a May 7 three-game series, with three more in late June. But between July 27 and the end of the season, the clubs would meet 12 times. The grand finale, marked down early on the calendar of the clubs and fans, was a season-ending three-game series in Los Angeles.

The highly anticipated series of October 1–3 lost some of its steam, because the Giants had already surprisingly clinched the division title by then with a scorching run in September. The series still retained some attention because the Dodgers, while coping with a disappointing year, weren't dead yet. The Dodgers entered the series with a slim hope for the second wild-card slot over the St. Louis Cardinals, whose magic number to clinch the spot was two. Giants center fielder Angel Pagan, in his first year of the rivalry, didn't take long to catch on to the history of the feud. Said Pagan, "That's what we want to do, to knock them out of the playoffs." The Dodgers kept their hopes alive in the opener of the series, defeating the Giants 3–2 on Elian Herrera's bases-loaded single in the ninth inning. Meanwhile, a Cardinals victory meant the Dodgers were a defeat away from elimination.

The next day, the Giants were poised to end the Dodgers' slim hopes by taking a 4–1 lead into the seventh. A. J. Ellis cut the lead to 4–3 in the seventh with a two-run homer. Mark Ellis was thrown out at third when he tried to stretch a double, but Shane Victorino gave the Dodgers new life with a triple. The season now rested on the shoulders of Matt Kemp. With many in the crowd of 42,473 sensing that the year had come down to this one at-bat, Kemp struck out on a slider from reliever George Kontos, and threw down his bat in disgust. The Dodgers would go down scoreless in the eighth and ninth to be eliminated, but it was the image of Kemp's reaction that many would remember as summing up a season of frustration.

The Giants signed infielder Ryan Theriot in January 2012 as a safeguard should second baseman Freddy Sanchez not be able to bounce back from injury. Theriot was a career .282 hitter with 17 home runs. On July 27, the Giants traded a prospect to the Colorado Rockies for infielder Marco Scutaro. The Giants hoped to benefit by the experience of Scutaro, 36, a career .270 hitter with 72 home runs.

The Giants' march through the postseason came to a head in the top of the 10th inning in Game Four of the World Series against the Detroit Tigers. Theriot led off with a single and advanced to second on a sacrifice bunt. After a second out, Scutaro hit a soft liner that fell in front of the center fielder. Theriot, running all out all the way, slid hard across the plate and jumped to his feet triumphantly with what would be the World Series winning run. He took an Incredible Hulk–like pose, something you might see from a defensive lineman after a sack. The image, shown on national television, is forever burned into the hearts and minds of Giants fans.

The two iconic images, one capturing the grim ending of the Dodgers for 2012, and the other capturing the glory of the Giants' season, live on as enduring snapshots at what might be one of the most pivotal years in the history of the West Coast rivalry.

While the Giants would have the big finish in 2012, it was the Dodgers who had the big start both on and off the field. Frank McCourt filed for Chapter 11 bankruptcy protection in June 2011 when the then-Dodgers owner couldn't meet financial obligations to pay players or cover other bills. The once model franchise was in turmoil, its ability to assemble a competitive team was in question and the rivalry with the Giants appeared to be a victim.

With less than two weeks to go before the beginning of the 2012 season, the Dodgers-Giants earth shifted.

"The Dodgers appear to be bigger, wealthier threat to S.F." said a *San Francisco Chronicle* headline. "When you have a team like the Dodgers that has renewed spirit and the energy of a Magic Johnson, I don't think it can hurt the rivalry. It will make the Dodgers-Giants rivalry more compelling," said Giants President Larry Baer.

Those were among the reactions to the news that Guggenheim Baseball Management had purchased the team and Dodger Stadium from McCourt for a record $2 billion. The principals would be controlling partner Mark Walter, CEO of Guggenheim Partners; president and CEO Stan Kasten, a veteran sports executive; and Magic Johnson, basketball great and businessman who provided a public face to the franchise.

Walter, in announcing the deal, said, "We look forward to building upon the legacy of the Dodgers and providing long-term stability to one of the most revered franchises in baseball."

Walter's quote was certainly an appropriate one for the top man, but more significantly, the big issue was what the lost and forgotten Dodgers fans would say about the new ownership. Many fans had either stopped going or cut back on the number of games they attended. Fans said they felt like pawns under McCourt, their ticket money being used as a personal ATM for the owner rather than to improve the roster. They grew impatient waiting for renovations and updates to their once perfect ballpark, and some said the stadium had become dangerous because of a mix of unruly fans and insufficient security. What was most upsetting was that the Dodgers had not been to the World Series since 1988, while all the teams in their division had made it to the series since then. The toughest blow came in 2010 when the Giants took the championship.

Those frustrations were why the words of fans were more significant than those uttered by Walter. A lifelong Dodgers supporter, who gave up his season tickets amid the ownership chaos, was quoted as saying, "I decided to wait until I knew who the owner was to go ahead and buy tickets. I love the Dodgers. And it was heartbreaking to stop buying season tickets. Hopefully now it's all for the better."

—–///—–

The sale would not officially close for a month, but the Dodgers came out of the gates on opening day in full stride. The Dodgers liked their chances with the star-power duo of outfielder Kemp and pitcher Clayton Kershaw. Kemp was coming off a dazzling 2011 in which he led the league in homers (39) and RBIs (126), batted .324, stole 40 bases, and won a Gold Glove award. Cy Young Award winner Kershaw established himself as the leader of the rotation with 21 wins, a 2.28 ERA, and 248 strikeouts in 2011. Holdover pitchers Chad Billingsley and Ted Lilly would be joined by newly acquired Chris Capuano and Aaron Harang to give the Dodgers a solid staff of starters. The Dodgers won nine of their first ten games, and built a four-game lead over the Giants by the time the two clubs met in Los Angeles for the first time in the season.

The injury prone, scoring-challenged Giants stumbled immediately, being swept by Arizona in their opening series. The Giants came into the Dodgers series with closer Brian Wilson lost for the year after undergoing Tommy John surgery, third baseman Pablo Sandoval sidelined with a hamate bone fracture, doubts about whether second baseman Sanchez would ever return, and club officials watching nervously as catcher Buster Posey tried for a comeback after his devastating injuries in 2011. Still, a rotation that included Matt Cain, Tim Lincecum, Madison Bumgarner, and Ryan Vogelsong, and a bullpen with quality arms gave the Giants some hope if only they could improve on their run production of 570, the worst in the league in 2011.

The Dodgers padded their lead over the Giants to five by taking two of three in the opening series between the clubs May 7–9. Los Angeles took advantage of poor Giants fielding for a 9–1 win in the first game and jumped on a struggling Lincecum for a 6–2 win in the final game. The Giants achieved some unusual success in the second game as Brett Pill's two-run homer defeated Kershaw, who was 5–0 against them in 2011. The opener of the series marked the official first home game under the new ownership, and Dodgers pitcher Lilly claimed he felt it. "I definitely thought the stadium had quite a lot of energy," he said. The night was indeed special. In a moving pregame celebration, Magic Johnson escorted Rachel Robinson, the widow of Jackie Robinson, and Dodgers legend Don Newcombe to the mound for the throwing out of the ceremonial first pitch.

The Dodgers kept rolling, and by May 27, had extended their lead over the Giants to 7½ games. The Giants went on a 15–10 run at that point to cut the Dodgers lead to three as the teams met for a June 25–27 series in San Francisco. Manager Bruce Bochy's call to arms was answered with overwhelming firepower, as the Giants pitchers threw three consecutive shutouts—8–0, 2–0, and 3–0—for a sweep. Barry Zito, Vogelsong, and Lincecum all blanked the Dodgers for seven innings, and the cavalry from the bullpen finished off Los Angeles. Asked what got into the Giants pitchers, Vogelsong replied, "When you've got 42,000 people screaming 'Beat L.A.', you don't want to let them down."

Seventy-six games into the season, the clubs were tied for first at 43–33.

—⁓—

A lively pennant race seemed likely. Neither the Giants or Dodgers appeared to be a powerhouse, but they did appear superior to their division opponents. The new extra wild-card berth also gave every contender additional hope. The clubs seemed evenly matched for a competitive stretch run, but there was one unanswered question that could upend the race.

Would the Dodgers owners, smelling a shot at postseason, start writing checks in a go-for-broke bid for a championship?

Dodgers Chairman Walter addressed the matter point blank prior to the July 31 trading deadline: "I think if we make a few moves, we can (win the World Series)." Walter said there would be no financial limits to acquire the necessary personnel. The first shot over the Giants bow came July 25, when the Dodgers acquired three-time all-star infielder Hanley Ramirez in a trade with the Florida Marlins. The Dodgers agreed to pick up a nearly $40 million obligation to Ramirez. The deal came prior to a three-game series in San Francisco with the Giants now holding a three-game edge. Dodgers accountants had to smile at the quick return on their investment as Ramirez launched the Dodgers to a game one 5–3 victory in what would be a three-game sweep with a tie-breaking, two-run homer in the 10th inning. Ramirez's new slugging mate Kemp took over the next night going four for five with four RBIs in a 10–0 win, and Kershaw finished the Giants off with a 4–0 shutout in the finale. Six days later, the Dodgers picked up two-time All-Star center fielder Shane Victorino in a trade with the Philadelphia Phillies. The night before, they acquired former All-Star reliever Brandon League from the Seattle Mariners.

San Francisco countered with two nice signings, but it still appeared the free-spending Dodgers could keep throwing knockout punches all day while the Giants were just hoping to land some jabs. The Giants first signed Scutaro, and then four days later acquired outfielder Hunter Pence from Philadelphia. Pence brought power and a high-energy mentality to the game. The Giants felt they were poised to make a good run for postseason with the signings. What they didn't know was that they were only about two weeks away from suffering a potentially season-shattering jolt.

———

In just over four months of the 2012 season, outfielder Melky Cabrera had become one of the most popular Giants. The club, in desperate need of offense, acquired Cabrera from the Kansas City Royals on November

7, 2011, parting with talented but inconsistent starter Jonathan Sanchez. Cabrera hardly would have seemed like the answer to a team's hitting woes two years ago, as he batted just .255 with four home runs for the Atlanta Braves in 2010. His value was further diminished because reports of poor training habits followed him. Cabrera claimed he refocused himself to be better prepared for the rigors of a baseball season, and cited that for his impressive numbers in Kansas City in 2011. Cabrera hit .305 with 18 home runs and 87 RBIs for the Royals. He had 201 hits, 44 doubles, and stole 20 bases. The new Giants left fielder picked up right where he left off. He was challenging for the batting title with an average above .340, became a fixture in the third spot in the batting order, and was one of the main reasons the Giants were in a race for the division lead. His MVP performance in the All-Star game added to what appeared to be one of the best Giants stories in years. The Cabrera feel-good vibe took off for fans as the Giants milked the "Melkman" nickname. Men and women dressed as Melk Men and Melk Maids roamed the stands as Cabrera delivered key hit after key hit.

It was too good to be true.

On August 15, major league baseball suspended Cabrera 50 games for use of a performance-enhancing drug. The laughter, the feel-good buzz and the joy of watching the Melkman's offensive exploits had soured. The club lost a significant threat, and the clubhouse was shaken. While the Dodgers were adding bats, the Giants were subtracting a big one. A season that seemed so promising was now in jeopardy.

—⁓—

The 2012 season was beginning to feel like that glorious period in the 1960s when every Dodgers-Giants game was the biggest one yet. The clubs had not gone head-to-head down the stretch with postseason at stake for both teams since 2004, making a three-game series in Los Angeles on August 20–22 perhaps the most significant one in eight years.

The Dodgers entered the series with a half-game lead on the Giants, and intent on taking advantage of the momentum from the July sweep in

San Francisco. But three days later, the Giants pitchers had turned a show-down series into a shutdown series.

Bumgarner blanked the Dodgers for eight innings and struck out 10 in a 2–1 win in the first game, defeating Kershaw. Sandoval drove in both Giants runs with a sacrifice fly and a single. Ramirez homered in the ninth off Sergio Romo, but it wasn't enough. Lincecum limited the Dodgers to one run in 5⅔ innings, and the bullpen shut them out the rest of the way in a 4–1 victory in the second game. Cain allowed just one run as the Giants took an 8–1 lead after seven innings in the final game and reserve Joaquin Arias knocked in five runs. The Dodgers rallied late, but the Giants finished off the sweep with an 8–4 win. The Giants were now 2½ games in front.

The three-game collapse caused the Dodgers ownership to huddle one more time. The previous deals had not done enough damage—it was now time for a direct hit.

Writing that the Baseball World was shocked about anything might be an overstatement after so much has happened in the game, but the seis-mic needle had to move at least a bit when news came that the Dodgers had unleashed multimillions at their quest to overtake the Giants. On August 25, a trade with the Boston Red Sox brought the Dodgers slugging first baseman Adrian Gonzalez, starting pitcher Josh Beckett, utility man Nick Punto, and injured outfielder Carl Crawford, who wouldn't be able to play until next season. The price tag for the four totaled more than $250 million. Gonzalez was the centerpiece in the deal. The four-time All-Star hit 203 home runs over the last seven years, and gave the Dodgers one of the best offensive quartets in baseball along with Kemp, Andre Ethier, and Ramirez.

The mega-deal went beyond moneyball. No sabermetrics here. This was a dash with cash. "We fully expect to make the postseason," said Dodgers CEO Kasten. The Giants couldn't pretend to compete with the monopoly money being tossed around by their rivals. The Dodgers were buying up Boardwalk and Park Place, while the Giants were looking for a one-bedroom apartment on Baltic Avenue. For the Giants, the upcoming stretch run wasn't about high finance, it was about banking on a team concept that they hoped would pay off in the end.

—⁓—

The spending spree was not working. The Dodgers were still alive when the clubs met for three games in San Francisco September 7–9, but Los Angeles entered the series 4½ games behind the Giants. The wild card was starting to seem a more realistic goal, with the Dodgers just 1½ games out in that race.

Scutaro's two-run, broken bat single with the bases loaded in the seventh inning off Beckett broke a 2–2 tie and led the Giants to a 5–2 win in the opener. Lincecum contained the Dodgers by allowing just two runs in 6⅓ innings. The Dodgers came back the next day for a 3–2 victory, scoring the winning run in the ninth when Gonzalez tripled, and Ramirez drove him home with a double. The Giants took the series with a 4–0 win behind Zito, who came up big against the Dodgers again with 6⅓ innings of shutout ball. Five relievers combined to finish off the shutout. Pence drove in two runs with a double, Scutaro got another home with a sacrifice fly, and Posey homered. The Giants caught a break when injuries limited Kemp to playing just one of the games, and caused Kershaw to miss a start. What was more painful to the Dodgers was that their big bats—Kemp, Ramirez, Gonzalez, and Ethier—were just a combined 5-for-39 with two RBIs for the three games.

The Giants now had the reins to the division title firmly in their grip, and went on a full gallop to leave the Dodgers in the dust. The Giants went on a streak of 10 wins in 11 games, which led to a division-clinching 8–4 victory over San Diego on September 22.

Main Street had toppled Wall Street.

The Scutaro-Pence signings vs. the Dodgers blockbusters had turned into a mismatch. After the Scutaro deal, the Giants were 39–24. After the Red Sox trade, the Dodgers went 18–18. Scutaro became the regular second baseman, batted .362, and had 44 RBIs. Giants players mocked the Dodgers' big deals by nicknaming Scutaro "Blockbuster."

———

The Giants memorable regular season of 2012 was about to turn into a postseason to forget. The Cincinnati Reds followed up their 5–2 win in the first game of the best-of-five National League Division Series with a 9–0 thrashing of the Giants. Bronson Arroyo baffled the Giants in game two, shutting them out on one hit in seven innings, and the Reds lineup bashed around the San Francisco pitching staff for 13 hits. The Giants now had three obstacles to overcome to avoid elimination: the Reds pitchers, the Reds batters, and history. The history part might be the most challenging since no team ever came back to win three consecutive road games in a five-game series after trailing 2–0. The pundits said they were dead, but the Rev. Pence decided reports of the Giants' demise were premature.

Hunter Pence plays the game like he's double-parked. He never seems relaxed, he's always on the move and it's amazing that he doesn't injure himself with his violent practice swings. The Giants signed him for his power, but on October 9, it was his power of positive thinking that was on display. Manager Bruce Bochy gave what turned out to be the warm-up speech before game three at the Great American Ball Park, hoping to inspire his troops. Pence then took over, and by the time the wild-eyed preacher was through with his excited, passionate, and moving address, he had 24 converts who bought into the teamwork message and still believed they could win.

The newly inspired Giants came out swinging, but unfortunately for them few connected. Reds starter Homer Bailey and three relievers struck out 16 and allowed just three hits in the 10-inning game. Maybe it was the uplifting sermon, or perhaps just pure luck, but the Giants squeaked out a 2–1 victory as veteran infielder Scott Rolen bobbled a ground ball to bring home the winning run. Lincecum, in relief, saved the club the next day in game four with a strong 4⅓ inning appearance, and the Giants bats finally erupted in an 8–3 victory.

It was now down to game five.

———ᴡᴡ———

Mat Latos was born to be a Dodger. At 6-foot-6 and weighing 235 pounds, the hard-throwing right-hander was Don Drysdale–like with his intimidating presence on the mound. Another similarity Latos had with the legendary Dodgers hurler was a dislike for the Giants. During the 2010 pennant race between Latos's Padres and the Giants, Latos lashed out at the Giants for their late-season acquisitions. While common for all teams—including San Diego—to make such signings, Latos insinuated that the Giants were more or less trying to buy the pennant instead of going with their players who had been there all year. In case anyone missed that criticism, Latos came back with another high-and-tight rip while signing autographs for charity in early 2011. Latos added to his signature, "I hate the Giants." Latos had reason to be sore, since the Giants defeated him on the final day of the 2010 season to win the division.

Baseball gods may be supreme beings who preside over the game with spiritual awakening. Or, perhaps, they're a bunch of wise guys. The latter might have been true at least for game five in Cincinnati on October 11 because when the Giants looked out on the mound, there stood No. 55, Mat Latos.

Latos mowed down the Giants through four, and Cain matched him so the teams went into the fifth inning at 0–0. The Giants finally got to Latos when Gregor Blanco singled and Brandon Crawford brought him home with a triple. After one was out, shortstop Zack Cozart couldn't handle Pagan's chopper and Crawford scored. Scutaro walked, Sandoval singled and the bases were loaded for Posey. With the count at 2–2, Posey gave Latos one more reason to keep the Giants off his Christmas card list. Posey's grand slam crashed off the second-deck facing in left field, and the Giants had a 6–0 lead. The strong Reds team had come too far to go out passively, and got the margin down to 6–4 with two on and one out in the ninth. Romo and the Reds' Jay Bruce squared off in an epic 12-pitch at-bat that ended with a soft fly out to left. Rolen struck out, and the Giants had come back from the brink to earn a spot in the National League Championship Series. The fired-up team's "never quit" attitude had worked, but in order to get to the World Series, it would be tested one more time.

———

Team chemistry.

It's probably an overused phrase in sports and its value can be debated. No one talked about the great Yankees teams of the 1950s and early 1960s as winning because they had great chemistry. Manager Casey Stengel wrote out lineup cards featuring such names as Maris, Mantle, Berra, Skowron, Kubek, Richardson, and Howard, and gave the ball to Whitey Ford every fourth day, and that simple formula was good enough to dominate the American League. They called Stengel the "mad perfessor," not the mad scientist.

Yet, when the lab work was done examining the Giants and Dodgers seasons in 2012, the conclusion was that at least part of the difference was team chemistry. The results: The Giants had it and the Dodgers didn't. The Giants who stormed to the finish in 2012 were a band of brothers. The Dodgers who quietly faded away were a band of distant relatives. The Dodgers dug deep into their pocketbooks to hire big talent, but couldn't buy enough victories. The Giants dug deep into their souls to overcome adversity, and turned that spiritual lift into wins. Following the clubhouse revival meeting, the Giants would gather in the dugout before every game for an enthusiastic bonding ritual that was reminiscent of an NFL team's pre-kickoff hoot-and-holler session. The theme: "Playing for 25 guys together; playing for the guy next to you."

Cynics might downgrade the benefits of rah-rah clubhouse camaraderie, but even Dodgers manager Don Mattingly acknowledged there might be something to this chemistry thing. Speaking amid the Dodgers' troubles after the dramatic turnover of their roster, Mattingly said, "It's important that a group of people is working toward a common goal. That's hard to get 25 guys working in the same direction. And I think that's the fight that we have now, getting to know each other while we're trying to do that."

—·····—

The St. Louis Cardinals arrived in San Francisco for the first two of the seven-game National League Championship Series without a yell leader or a motivational pregame ceremony. Yet, there was no doubt about their heart and ability to play together. The Cardinals proved that on the field in 2011 when they finished 23–9 to make up a 10½-game deficit to Atlanta to earn the wild card berth. They came back from deficits in the ninth and 10th innings of Game Six of the World Series against Texas, and went on to win the championship. In 2012, they had to win the new do-or-die wild card game against Atlanta to move forward in the postseason. The Cardinals were anchored by catcher Yadier Molina, who was surrounded by a strong offensive cast that included Matt Holliday, Carlos Beltran, David Freese and Allen Craig.

St. Louis also had a bullpen of powerful arms, putting pressure on the opposition not to get too far behind early. The Giants learned that the hard way in game one. St. Louis hammered Madison Bumgarner to take a 6–0 lead after 3½ innings. The Giants got to Cardinals starter Lance Lynn in their half of the fourth to make it 6–4, but six St. Louis relievers shut them down the rest of the way with 5⅓ innings of two-hit scoreless ball. The Giants seemed like the last team to need any more inspiration, but they got it in game two when Holliday crashed into Scutaro in the first inning while trying to break up a double play at second base. While the debate started on whether the slide was legal or even downright foul play, the Giants' biggest concern was the health of their second baseman. The wounded Scutaro stayed in the game, and three innings later, made the Cardinals wince. The Giants had scored once in the fourth to break a 1–1 tie, and went on to load the bases with two outs. Scutaro got instant revenge with a single to left off Chris Carpenter that scored two runs. A third came home when the Giants fans' new enemy, Holliday, fumbled the ball. The Giants got their payback and a 7–1 victory, as the clubs headed to St. Louis. Cardinals starter Kyle Lohse, assisted by another shutdown performance by the corps of relievers, dealt the Giants a 3–1 loss in game three. It even got messier for the Giants in game four as St. Louis rolled to an easy 8–3 victory with a 12-hit attack to go up 3–1 in the series.

Once again, the Giants were on the brink.

Maybe it was Pence's pulpit. Maybe it was Scutaro's toughness. Maybe it was team unity. It might have been all those things that helped the Giants come back from the dead again to beat the Cardinals three straight to advance to the World Series. Or more simply, it might have been these game totals: game five: 0 runs, 7 hits, 8 strikeouts; game six: 1 run, 5 hits, 11 strikeouts; game seven: 0 runs, 7 hits, 8 strikeouts. Those were the Cardinals' numbers for the final three games of the series as the Giants ran off victories of 5–0, 6–1 and 9–0 to win the National League pennant. Zito, who didn't even make the team in the 2010 postseason, started it off with a remarkable 7⅔ inning, 115-pitch outing. Vogelsong followed it up with a seven-inning, 102-pitch gem. Cain helped close the door with an effective 5⅔-inning, 102-pitch performance, assisted by a 3⅓-inning shutout mop-up by the bullpen.

In the ninth inning of game seven, with the outcome no longer in doubt and a party just outs away, the rain came. Even a few drops at a ballgame often send spectators scurrying for the overhang or the concourse. But nobody at AT&T Park was moving. As the rain grew more intense, the crowd got louder and wetter. The field was becoming a quagmire, and it was at or near unplayable condition. At second base, a beaming Scutaro looked skyward, his arms spread as the rain pounded down on him. Fittingly, Holliday was at the plate and lifted a popup to the right side. Scutaro looked to the heavens once more, this time his eyes on the baseball as it came down and settled into his glove. The Giants had won six straight elimination games in the two series, and were heading to the World Series and a first-game appointment with one of baseball's greatest pitchers.

In seven full seasons, Detroit Tigers Game One starter Justin Verlander compiled a 124–65 record with a 3.40 ERA. His records the last four years were 19–9, 18–9, 24–5 and 17–8. His ERA in 2011 was a remarkable 2.40. He tossed no-hitters in 2007 and 2011. He won the MVP and Cy Young Award in 2011. Even if Verlander slipped a bit against the Giants in the World Series opener at AT&T Park, it was likely that 2012 Triple Crown winner Miguel Cabrera and power-hitting Prince Fielder would make up the difference. Cabrera and Fielder combined for 74 homers in 2012. The Giants hit 103. The Giants' struggle against St. Louis left them with little option but to start Zito. While he had delivered in game five of the NLCS, Zito had provided enough inconsistency in his time with the Giants to give doubters something to worry about. Despite the mismatch on paper, major league baseball decided to go ahead with the game.

Pablo Sandoval was little more than a spectator in the 2010 postseason, limited to a part-time role because of physical conditioning issues and a big drop-off from his offensive output of 2009. This postseason was far different, as Sandoval already was making a case for himself as Mr. October. In the two series against the Reds and Cardinals, Sandoval was hitting .320 with four doubles, three home runs, and a .320 average. Sandoval's hot bat would not cool down, even when facing heat from Verlander. Sandoval homered in the first and third off Verlander, and added a record-tying third homer in the fifth off reliever Al Alburquerque that put him in the books with Albert Pujols, Reggie Jackson, and Babe Ruth. Zito was solid again in the 8–3 triumph while allowing just one run in 5⅔ innings, and Lincecum followed him with 2⅓ innings of shutout relief.

It was only one win, but the significance was huge for the Giants as they beat the best. Verlander lasted just four innings, was knocked around for five runs, and ended up with an 11.25 ERA in the World Series. At least it was an improvement from the All-Star Game, where Sandoval's bases-loaded triple off Verlander highlighted a five-run inning for the National League. Verlander's ERA in that game: 45.00.

The Giants pitchers would see to it that there would be no need for any more dramatic comebacks. Strong starting performances by Bumgarner in

Game Two and Vogelsong in Game Three, supported by an unyielding bullpen, put the Giants a game away from the championship with successive 2–0 victories. A sturdy outing by Cain in Game Four, along with shutout relief, put Scutaro and Theriot in position to break up the 3–3 tie in the 10th inning to propel the Giants to a sweep. The title meant that Bochy, who brilliantly overcame the twists and turns of the season to keep the Giants on an even track, now shared a revered place with John McGraw as the franchise's only managers to win at least two World Series titles. And as if the Giants needed any extra satisfaction, the championship season was their seventh in franchise history, one more than the Dodgers.

While the Giants celebrated with a grand victory parade, one Dodger decided to rain on the festivities. Reliever League, one day after signing a contract to stay with the Dodgers, said, "The Giants had a great year. They won the games they needed to win. I think in 2013 the Los Angeles Dodgers are going to be the team everyone wants to beat, or tries to beat. We're going to have a target on our backs next year and we welcome it."

The 2012 season always will be known as the year of the Giants. In a year in which the Giants were outspent by their rivals, and outgunned on paper offensively by postseason opponents Cincinnati, St. Louis, and Detroit, they still found a way to win their second World Series in three years. MVP Posey set the tone in 2012 with the most inspirational comeback by a Giant since pitcher Dave Dravecky in 1989. Sandoval's three-homer barrage set the tone in the 2012 Series opener, and Zito's postseason gems earned him redemption. Two-time Cy Young award winner Lincecum got lit up often in a struggling season as a starter, but was lights-out as a reliever in postseason. In a year of team glory, Cain stood out on a June night in San Francisco with a perfect game. In a city with an abundance of nightlife and hot social spots, AT&T Park had turned into the biggest ongoing party of them all with passionate fans and sellouts every game.

Despite the Giants' big year, 2012 also might become known as the one when the rivalry landscape took a dramatic change for the better. The Dodgers opened spring training as an organization in chaos, but ended with a new ownership pledging to revitalize the club and proving it was willing to spend whatever it takes. The club's late season downfall almost hid the fact that the Dodgers were a contender for much of the year. The Dodgers took over first place on April 11, built a 7½ game lead on May 26, and stayed in the lead until June 28. They were in and out of first from then until August 19. The team fell hard after that, but it can reasonably point to a number of injuries as at least one of the obstacles of 2012.

The position the two franchises have put themselves in for the coming seasons might mark the most significant moment in the history of the clubs since they moved west. The rivalry has had many seasons when it has been the undercard, with other teams and even other rivalries in the main event. Now, the Dodgers-Giants rivalry is Ali-Frazier. For baseball fans in general, or for those passionate about either team, it's a rivalry for a new generation that still promises to contain some of the sizzle of the '60s. Maybe the Giants will keep winning with their magic, with a never-say-die attitude, and sticking with a strategy of stellar pitching and defense. Maybe it will be the Dodgers' turn to shine, with Magic Johnson's all-in commitment to the spending spree for top talent, exclaiming, "We want to win now!"

The rivalry is poised to thrive in the coming years, but as for which club will have most success, it might all come down to not whether you believe in magic, but what kind of magic you believe in.

POOL PARTY (2013)

Just 101 days after the Giants participated in their second World Series championship parade in three years, they were back on center stage again. The occasion was Giants FanFest, the unofficial opening of the new season at AT&T Park where the faithful could stand on the field, get autographs, and buy tickets. Despite the crush of fans, it is a low-key event. The mostly blue jeans–clad players, still in an offseason relax-mode before spring training opens in a couple weeks, are interviewed on stage by local media as the crowd listens. The FanFest interviews are a lovefest, players ribbing each other and telling the adoring spectators that they are the best fans in baseball. There is so little real news that comes out of the event that it is a surprise that one of the police officers on hand to provide security doesn't say, "Move along folks, nothing happening here."

Apparently, Brandon Belt didn't get the memo.

The Giants' first baseman got a good look at Giants vs. Dodgers in his first full-time big league season in 2012, and was now ready to place his name in rivalry lore. Asked during his interview whether the Giants were worried about the Dodgers' bankroll, Belt responded, "All I can say is, you can't buy chemistry." The crowd went wild.

The quote swept through Los Angeles as if it was caught up in the Santa Ana winds. A pro-Dodgers website, Think Blue LA, noted Belt was 1 for 13 with seven strikeouts in the 2012 World Series, and said he was "preaching to the choir of frenzied and probably stoned Giants fans." A reporter placed Belt's quote on a tee for Dodgers outfielder Matt Kemp, and he took his hacks. "If I was a World Series champ, I wouldn't be saying anything about anybody's team. . . . I don't have to say anything. I'm a World Series champ. We have chemistry here that's really going to be good. . . . We really don't care about what people say or how they feel. We have a great team."

—⁂—

It's not known whether Giants management cringed or chuckled when it heard Belt's broadside, but in truth, his comments appeared to reflect the San Francisco company line. The Giants looked over the NL West for 2013 and didn't see any powerhouse. There was no good argument to make that Arizona, Colorado, or San Diego would be anything special. The Giants didn't believe money could make the Dodgers mesh. The Dodgers of 2012 couldn't capitalize on the cash, playing unimpressive .500 ball after the blockbuster $250 million August trade with Boston. The Giants, as a result, built their offseason strategy on the premise that the NL West would again be the *Mild* West like in the 2005 season when the Padres won the division with an 82–80 record. The Giants like to reward loyalty, but the main justification for bringing back basically the same club that won the 2012 title was the belief that superior pitching would be enough despite a meager offense to outlast the mediocre competition.

Giants Chief Executive Officer Larry Baer addressed the Dodgers' willingness to spend during an interview on *Yahoo! SportsTalk Live* on the Giants' flagship television station. Asked if the Giants have to stay up with the Dodgers to be competitive in the West, Baer said, "I think it's dangerous business to say, 'OK, we make this move, what's the Dodgers' counter move? ...I think we've got to keep our eye on the ball on where we want to be coming into spring training. Where do we want to be as we go through the season, and maybe add during the season, and not be focused on what the Dodgers do or don't because we can't control it."

It is understandable that Baer would shape his answer that way, but the fact is the new Dodgers ownership has ratcheted up the rivalry so there's a lot of ego and competitiveness not just on the field but in the front offices for both teams. AT&T Park is sold out every night, Giants merchandise is hot, and fans are vocal about what moves the club should make to stay on top. Baer, general manager Brian Sabean, manager Bruce Bochy, and the ownership are being driven by the need to Beat L.A. because it doesn't seem that the Dodgers are going to let up in trying to build a consistent winner. But at this point prior to the 2013 season, it is the Giants who have the winning formula. They beat teams in the 2010 and 2012 postseason who thought they could slug their way to the championship. The Giants changed the game by proving that dominant pitching was the magic bullet. Dodgers fans are taking notice.

The key pieces of "Bochy Ball" were coming back for another championship run in 2013. Catcher Buster Posey, the 2012 MVP (.336, 24 HR, 103 RBIs), was returning with a new $167 million contract. Outfielder Hunter Pence got national publicity for his preaching, but Giants fans who watched him grind away from the spotlight knew it was his bat that did the talking. Pence hit seven homers and drove in 45 runs in his 59 games in 2012 with the Giants following the trade from Philadelphia and had 97 homers and 343 RBIs from 2008 to 2011. Others included postseason marvel Pablo Sandoval, Belt, and Angel Pagan, whose glove and bat (.288, 38 doubles, 15 triples and eight HRs) sparked the team in 2012. Still, no one expected the Giants lineup to draw fear from opposing pitchers as they finished sixth in runs scored and 16th in homers. Starters Matt Cain (16–5, 2.79 ERA), Madison Bumgarner (16–11, 3.37) and Ryan Vogelsong (14–9, 3.37) lead the rotation. The secret weapon of Bochy Ball was the bullpen Core Four of Sergio Romo (1.79 ERA), Santiago Casilla (2.84), Javier Lopez (2.50) and Jeremy Affeldt (2.70), who could be counted on to lock down leads.

It should not have been a surprise that Las Vegas was swayed more by cash than chemistry. The oddsmakers put their money on the Dodgers' payroll in making the club a 5–1 favorite to win the 2013 World Series. The Giants were well back on the list at 22–1. Oddsmakers undoubtedly were influenced by the signing of pitcher Zack Greinke to a six-year $147 million contract to join Clayton Kershaw as a one-two starting combination of Cy Young Award winners. The Dodgers also had high hopes that Korean star Hyun-Jin Ryu would bolster the rotation in his major league rookie season. The team also had formidable bats in Adrian Gonzalez, Matt Kemp, and Andre Ethier, though the offense suffered a significant blow when slugging shortstop Hanley Ramirez was lost for the start of the season after being injured during the World Baseball Classic. The Dodgers could easily dismiss the chemistry issue by reasoning that the shake-up of the roster late in 2012 didn't allow the club enough time to gel, and that having the players from spring training on in 2013 should help build a team concept.

Sandy Koufax tossed a six-hitter in a 4–0 win over the St. Louis Cardinals on opening day at Dodger Stadium on April 14, 1964. It marked the first opening day shutout at the Dodgers' new ballpark, which opened in 1962. Don Drysdale, one of the best hitting pitchers in baseball history, drilled a two-run homer on opening day in 1965 against the Mets' Al Jackson and pitched the Dodgers to a 6–1 win. He was the last Dodger pitcher to hit a homer in an opener. Kershaw would channel both of the Dodgers greats as the Giants and Dodgers opened the season April 1 in Los Angeles.

The Giants watched as the Dodgers linked their glory years of the 1960s to today's team with a pregame ceremony in which co-owner Magic Johnson took a place on the mound. Manager Don Mattingly came out for a visit in the orchestrated scenario and waved in Koufax for relief. Johnson stepped aside as Koufax delivered the ceremonial pitch to former ace Orel Hershiser, a hero of the Dodgers' last World Series championship in 1988. Kershaw was Koufax-like through eight innings, but Giants pitchers were just as stubborn. Cain blanked the Dodgers over six innings and reliever George Kontos continued the shutout through seven. Kontos was likely looking ahead to the Dodgers' top of the order heading into the eighth as he tried to get the first pitch of the inning over to Kershaw, who was a career .146 hitter with no home runs entering the game. Kershaw sent the crowd of 53,000 into a frenzy as he smashed the Kontos serving over the center-field fence. The Dodgers added three more in the inning for a 4–0 lead, but they wouldn't need them. Kershaw finished off the Giants in the ninth to complete a 94-pitch, seven-strikeout gem.

The optimism and excitement of the opening day win for Dodgers fans didn't last long, as the Giants won the next two to take the series. Bumgarner pitched eight scoreless innings while giving up just two hits as the Giants got the best of Ryu in his big league debut for a 3–0 victory. The defense let Ryu down as a throwing error by shortstop Justin Sellers led to two of the runs. Sandoval and Pence homered in game three to help the Giants to a 5–3 win. Tim Lincecum walked seven in five innings but didn't allow any earned runs. In the three games, the Dodgers failed to score an earned run against Giants starters.

The Giants ran their winning streak against the Dodgers to five with a sweep of a three-game series May 3–5 in San Francisco. The Dodgers, who entered the series 3½ games out with a disappointing 13–14 record, were stung by walk-off homers in the first two games. Kershaw continued his mastery over the Giants in the opener, taking a no-hitter into the sixth when Marco Scutaro tripled and Posey followed with a run-scoring double for a 1–1 tie. Posey ended it in the ninth with a leadoff homer on a 3–2 count off Ronald Belisario. The Dodgers overcame a 6–1 deficit the next day with a seven-run fifth, but the teams were knotted at 9–9 after nine. Giants backup catcher Guillermo Quiroz stroked a line drive over the left-field wall off Brandon League to end it in the tenth. The Giants finished off the sweep as Pence drove in all the runs in a 4–3 victory.

The 1906 Chicago Cubs were so good that a poem was written about their infielders. Franklin Pierce Adams turned the Tinker-to-Evers-to-Chance double play combination into a baseball legend with his 1910 verse, "Baseball's Sad Lexicon." The club also included one of the most colorful names in baseball: Mordecai "Three Finger" Brown. Brown lost parts of two fingers on his right throwing hand in a farm accident in his youth. Brown compensated for it with a grip that produced a dominating curveball, which helped him to a 26–6 record with a 1.75 ERA. The Cubs won the National League pennant with a 116–36 mark, but what made their brilliant year stand out even more was a 45–5 streak. Going into the 2013 season, it still stood as the best 50-game streak in baseball. A few teams have come close: The Christy Mathewson-led New York Giants had a 43–7 run in 1912; the New York Yankees of 1941, spurred by Joe DiMaggio's 56-game hitting streak, achieved a 42–8 tear; and the 1942 St. Louis Cardinals, boosted by Stan Musial in his first full season, matched the Yankees' mark.

As of June 21, 2013, the Dodgers looked more like a team poised to go on an 8–42 slide. Dodgers owners, still waiting for dividends from the multi-millions they quickly invested in talent, had to wince if they were listening to *Dodger Talk* on AM570 in Los Angeles when a frustrated caller said it hurt to say so as a lifetime Dodgers fan, but that maybe it was time for the club to adopt the Giants' Bochy Ball brand of baseball. With the Dodgers at 0–8 in May, other callers said it even more directly: "Fire Mattingly!"

The Dodgers recovered slightly, finishing May with a 10–17 record, so there was some reason for hope. Kershaw remained effective, rookie Ryu showed he could pitch in the big leagues, and Greinke had returned to the rotation after breaking his collarbone during a brawl with Arizona in April. But the team still needed a spark.

The Dodgers made headlines in 2012 when they signed Cuban defector Yasiel Puig to a seven-year, $42 million contract. The 22-year-old outfielder surpassed the expectations when he batted .526 in the Cactus League in 2013. The Dodgers decided against putting him on the opening day roster, sending him to their Double-A affiliate in Chattanooga, Tenn. Puig continued to perform there, hitting .313 with eight homers and 37 RBIs.

By the start of June, the Dodgers couldn't wait any longer. In his major league debut June 3, Puig went 2-for-4 and doubled off a runner at first from right field to end the game. He hit four home runs in his first five games. Puig had 31 hits in his first 19 games, and was batting .425 on June 24, as the Dodgers began a three-game home series against the Giants. Despite Puig's meteoric start, the Dodgers were still unable to get their season off the ground. The Dodgers were just 9–12 in June, and entered the Giants' series in fifth place, 8½ games behind with a 32–42 record.

The Giants were in a free fall themselves, as a solid start had been ruined by a disappointing skid. Ironically, the slump was linked to what had been the most exciting moment of the season for the Giants. Leadoff hitter Pagan, an early season spark, drilled a pitch from Colorado's Rafael Betancourt off the wall in deep right-center field on May 25 at AT&T Park in the ninth inning with the Giants trailing 5–4. Brandon Crawford scored easily from second and Pagan never stopped running, beating the relay to the plate with a headlong slide for a game-winning inside-the-park homer. The drama came with a price, however, as a hamstring injury suffered by Pagan during his dash shelved him for nearly the remainder of the season.

Maybe the Giants should have seen it coming. Exactly two years earlier, on May 25, 2011, Posey's season ended with severe leg injuries caused by a home-plate collision. The Giants of 2011 never recovered from that blow, and the Giants of 2013 were now experiencing a similar nosedive.

On May 26, the Giants were tied for first with Colorado. The club was just 10–15 since then, and had fallen 3½ games out of first from the charging Arizona Diamondbacks. While both teams' struggles had dulled the anticipation of the mid-summer matchup, the debut of the exciting Puig in the rivalry created an extra buzz.

Puig did not disappoint in his first game against the Giants. He drilled a home run to right field off Bumgarner in the first inning, and contributed an RBI single in the eighth to help the Dodgers to a 3–1 win. A two-run homer by Ramirez and a game-saving catch by center fielder Kemp in the ninth with two on helped the Dodgers to a 6–5 victory the next day. Kershaw limited the Giants to a two-run Posey homer in the series finale while lasting into the eighth inning as Los Angeles got the sweep with a 4–2 win.

By the time the clubs met nine days later in San Francisco, the Dodgers had passed the Giants, and were now in third place, 3½ games behind Arizona. The Giants, coming off a 1–8 road trip, had fallen to fifth, 4½ games behind. Former Giant Juan Uribe propelled the Dodgers to a 10–2 romp in the opener July 5 with a double, triple, homer, and seven RBIs. Bumgarner held the Dodgers to two runs in seven innings in game two and struck out Puig three times for a 4–2 victory. A.J. Ellis stroked a three-run double in the ninth in the third game against Romo to give the Dodgers a 4–1 win. An incident in game two demonstrated the contrast between the charging Dodgers and the vulnerable Giants. Mattingly seemed destined to live in Bochy's shadow, as pundits constantly gave the Giants the edge in skipper know-how. Posey doubled home a run in the first inning of the second game of the series, but Mattingly successfully protested the score, noting the Giants batted out of order. While it didn't change the game's outcome, Mattingly's rare moment of one-upping Bochy was a sign that this could be a Dodgers year.

The streak ran from June 22 through August 17. During that 50-game stretch, the Dodgers went 42-8. They were 9½ games out on June 22 and 8½ games in first place on August 17. The club had eight shutouts and allowed just one run in 12 of the games and two runs in 10 of the games. The Dodgers finished off the historic run with a 10-game winning streak. The dominant performance featured phenomenal pitching and clutch hitting. Kershaw was 4–1 with a 1.34 ERA in July. Greinke was 5–0 with a 1.23 ERA in August. The club won a franchise-best 14 consecutive road games. They took over first place July 22 with a 14–5 win over Toronto and never relinquished the lead.

While the Dodgers were streaking, the Giants were plummeting, trailing by 19½ games as the teams met for a four-game series September 12–15. Yet, the series still had significance because the Dodgers could clinch the NL West title depending on how second-place Arizona fared. A split of the first two games meant the Dodgers would have to hold off on a celebration until they visited the Diamondbacks in their next series. The Giants unleashed a yearlong frustration in the third game with a 19–3 rout. Pence had a grand slam and seven RBIs, and Belt had five hits and a home run as the Giants collected 22 hits. The runs were the most ever scored by a team at Dodger Stadium. The Dodgers took the final game, reducing their magic number for winning the NL West to two.

The Dodgers arrived in Phoenix for a four-game series against the Diamondbacks ready to party. The Diamondbacks proved stubborn, however, winning two of the first three and battling the Dodgers in the finale. But aided by two Ramirez homers and a game-deciding blast by A.J. Ellis in the eighth, Los Angeles won 7–6. The win marked the club's first division crown since 2009, so there was reason to celebrate. Yet it seemed that a more subdued celebration might be more fitting for a team that was on a "World Series or Bust" mission under the new owners. The players instead reacted as if the mission was already accomplished as they climbed the right-field wall and jumped into the Chase Field swimming pool. The Diamondbacks weren't pleased. "They won the division; congratulations to them, but I would expect them to act with a little more class than they did," Arizona infielder Willie Bloomquist was quoted at the time.

———

The final series of the season between the clubs was meaningless, but two incidents unrelated to the actual games made it bizarre and deadly.

Brian Wilson was a good Giant. The colorful reliever pitched for the club for seven years. He appeared in 315 games and threw 320 innings. He had an ERA of 3.21, with 170 saves and 340 strikeouts. He recorded the last out of the 2010 World Series. It was the first franchise World Series title since 1954. He had a big role in raising the championship flag at opening day 2011. When Wilson entered the game in search of a save at AT&T Park, the ballpark sound system would crank up his "Jump Around" entrance song, and were there any Giants fans who didn't get up and jump around?

The September 24–26 series would mark Wilson's first visit to AT&T Park as a Dodger. To his credit, he had said the right things to Giants fans. A tweet following his signing with the Dodgers on July 30 said, "It was an honor to pitch in front of you all these years." And in fairness to Wilson, it wasn't like he abandoned the Giants for Dodgers' riches. It became pretty clear that Giants management was through with Wilson, possibly weary of his flamboyant personality. The Dodgers were willing to take a chance on the Tommy John–repaired pitcher, and who could blame Wilson for that?

After the final game of the series, Wilson charged from the dugout to an area behind home plate, where Giants CEO Baer was sitting, in a public tantrum to complain that the Giants hadn't given him his 2012 World Series ring. The Giants later said they had been trying to arrange the presentation for months without success. Baer ended the flap by giving the ring to Dodgers staff members so they could deliver it to Wilson. The development was strange, but it was also sad that the final memories of Wilson in San Francisco will be a clash between The Beard and The Baer.

On July 12, 1938, a Dodgers fan walked into a Brooklyn bar following a Giants-Dodgers game. After some Giants fans who were there began taunting him, the man left the bar for a few minutes. He returned with a gun and in the ensuing barrage of bullets, one of the Giants fans was killed and the bartender was wounded.

On September 25, 2013, following a Giants-Dodgers game at AT&T Park, two groups got into some type of confrontation a few blocks from the ballpark. A member of one group wore a Dodgers jacket; a person in the other group reportedly wore a Giants cap. Events of that night were unclear, but when it was over, one of the Dodgers fans had been stabbed to death.

Two incidents, 75 years apart, and other similar moments involving fans in between, demonstrate that amid the baseball thrills there remains a dark side of the rivalry.

The Dodgers arrived in Atlanta for their best-of-five division series against the Braves with a more businesslike approach than was shown at the pool party. Kershaw struck out 12 in the opener and came back on short rest for six solid innings as the Dodgers took the series in four games. The Dodgers outscored the Braves 26–14 and outhit them 46–28. Now it seemed the Dodgers players were on a mission as they prepared to meet the St. Louis Cardinals in the NL Championship Series.

The biggest play of the NLCS might have come in Game One when Cardinals pitcher Joe Kelly drilled the hot-hitting Ramirez in the ribs, limiting him as a factor for the rest of the series. There was no indication that Kelly hit him on purpose, but the lack of retaliation raised the question of whether this Dodgers team was prepared to play hardball against a tough competitor. The Cardinals displayed their go-for-the-throat attitude in postseason against the Giants in the 2012 NLCS when the 250-pound

Matt Holliday took out 185-pound second baseman Scutaro with a devastating slide that might have been a felony if it happened on the street. The Cardinals jumped out to a two-game lead, but the Dodgers battled back to force a Game Six with St. Louis holding a 3–2 edge. The Dodgers had high hopes with Kershaw on the mound, but their ace was knocked out in the fifth after allowing seven earned runs and 10 hits. The Cardinals took the series with a 9-0 win as the Dodgers managed just two hits.

Would the Giants have jumped into the pool?

That was a relevant question in analyzing why the very talented Dodgers continued their World Series drought while their rivals won two titles in four years. Both Giants' championships were marked by no-nonsense gritty play, highlighted by a bulldog-type rotation, a lights-out bullpen, and clutch hitting. Maybe the biggest contrast between San Francisco going all the way and Los Angeles coming up short was that the Giants played humble while the Dodgers played Hollywood. It doesn't seem likely that Bochy's championship teams would have jumped into the Diamondbacks' pool. After a Game-Five victory in the 2013 NLCS, Mattingly was so overtaken by the moment that he said, "I think if you look at it now we've kind of become America's team, because everyone wants to see a seventh game." America might have been wondering why Mattingly took out his slugger Gonzalez for a pinch-runner in a tight Game One, meaning the Dodgers had to play without one of their biggest offensive threats when the game went into extra innings.

Mattingly's bewildering comment was only part of how the Dodgers lost their way in the NLCS. Gonzalez, who seems to play the game pretty straight, even got caught up in the Hollywood hype. His hand-jive motions following a double in Game Three were interpreted by Cardinals pitcher Adam Wainwright as "Mickey Mouse stuff." After Gonzalez homered in Game Five, he responded by making a wagging ears Mickey Mouse gesture. Ironically, the Dodgers had been hoping some veterans would help the unpredictable Puig to mature as a ballplayer. Gonzalez seemed to be the type who could fill that role, until he let himself become a cartoon figure.

In the fourth inning of Game Three of the NLCS, Puig launched a drive to deep right, flipped his bat, and went into his home run trot—until the ball hit at the base of the wall. Realizing his gaffe, Puig suddenly began dashing to second like an Olympic sprinter. After arriving at third, he stood on the bag as if he had just conquered it and extended his arms to the sky. This was Puig on the big stage, though his act was becoming a bit worn. He had irritated his team and fans at other times by showing up late on a game day, missing cutoff men, getting carelessly picked off, and displaying almost out-of-control anger over umpires' calls.

Still, Puig's raw talent couldn't be ignored. He batted .319 with 19 homers and 42 RBIs in 104 regular season games and was a driving force in the Dodgers' streak. Puig was probably the hottest rookie in the rivalry since the Giants' Willie McCovey's debut in 1959. In 52 games, McCovey was 68 for 192 with 38 RBIs, nine doubles, five triples, and 13 home runs. McCovey's numbers weren't enough to carry the Giants that year. He debuted while the Giants were in second place, a half-game behind the Dodgers. The Giants went just 28–26 the rest of the way, and finished third. In 2013, the Dodgers were 8½ games out and in fifth place when Puig played his first game. The club went 69–38 after that to win the division.

McCovey was a unanimous selection as rookie of the year. If Puig had debuted that same season, would he have beaten McCovey out of that honor? Would voters have been influenced negatively by Puig's three-bagger swagger after he initially jogged out of the batter's box? Failure to hustle was not part of McCovey's makeup. In a night game at Candlestick Park in 1960, McCovey launched a high but routine fly to Dodgers outfielder Duke Snider, who lost it in the thick San Francisco fog. McCovey was running hard from the outset and ended up at third. It would be interesting to see if Puig would have gotten that far.

The Giants' streak of four consecutive winning seasons came to a resound-ing end in 2013. A good part of the blame could be attributed to a rotation that had a 4.37 ERA, with only Bumgarner able to display consistency. The club was 10th in the league in runs scored, and its 107 errors tied for third most in the NL. Yet even Bay Area talk-show callers who like to blister the team when it stumbles were strangely subdued during 2013's struggles because of the two championships in four years. The Dodgers didn't have that buffer from the critics, however, as the disappointing departure from the postseason fueled questions about how the new ownership was assem-bling the team.

NEW SHERIFF IN TOWN (2014)

It must have been quite a surprise to Giants fans to discover that the club had moved out of San Francisco during the thrilling 2014 postseason. Story after story kept referring to the Resilient Giants. The natives who thought they knew California had to be puzzled about where this mys-tery town of "Resilient" was located. After much research, it was found that Resilient was in Dogged County, south of Steadfast and just east of Determined.

The writers began to invoke the name after the Giants won the NL Division Series against the Washington Nationals in four games, despite scoring just nine runs in 44 innings. A Nobel Prize mathematics genius couldn't make those numbers work out to three victories in four games. Pitcher Jake Peavy set the tone with a gritty five-plus innings start in a Game One 3–2 Giants' victory. Game Two lasted so long that the Nats' bearded Jayson Werth could have started out clean-shaven and still looked like a caveman when it ended. Most teams would have lost it 1–0 in regulation, but the Giants rose from the dead with a ninth-inning score, and then won nine innings later 2–1 with a Brandon Belt solo homer. Two mistakes on one play—Madison Bumgarner's unwise and off-target throw to third on a bunt—doomed the Giants in a Game Three 4–1 defeat and had the entire populace of Resilient wondering how their punchless-at-the plate boys were going to stop the Nationals now.

Some call it small ball, the art of manufacturing runs without the big blast. But what happened in Game Four might be better described as "mall ball." The Giants just sort of hung around most of the day, browsing the storefronts for some bargain runs. They found great deals, as two runs scored on wild pitches and another on a weak ground ball for a series 3–2 clincher. Chicks dig the long ball, but in Resilient, the gals can't get enough of those wild pitches.

The Giants continued to live up to the name of their proud new home in the NL Championship Series against the Cardinals. In Game Three, with the series tied 1–1, the Giants blew a 4–0 lead but won it in the 10th. The Cardinals built an early 4–1 lead in Game Four, but the Giants rallied for a 6–4 victory. The Giants were six outs away from a Game Five loss when Michael Morse tied it with a homer and Travis Ishikawa won it in the ninth with a Thomson-like three-run shot. The dramatic win not only propelled the Giants into the World Series but was a triumph over the overused phrase "The Cardinal Way," meant to describe how the St. Louis organization develops players through its farm system and teaches winning ways and winning attitudes. Do an Internet search for "The Cardinal Way," and you are still getting references to the club's philosophy 20 pages later. Search for "The Giant Way," and the first three listings are the Giant's Causeway, a Northern Ireland tourist attraction of basalt columns formed by an ancient volcano; Andre the Giant; and the New York football Giants.

This raises the question: What happened to "The Dodger Way"?

The Dodgers' bubble machine used for dugout celebrations was put into storage for the long winter after the Cardinals burst their bubble in the 2014 NLDS. This was not the plan back when the new ownership promised an instant world championship. Injuries to the pitching staff were a challenge to the Dodgers this year, but under "Millionaire Ball," it was always thought that the club would use its cash to fill any need that developed. It was unfortunate for baseball historians that the Dodgers were eliminated in the NLDS. A Giants-Dodgers matchup with a World

Series berth at stake would have been riveting. Game Six of the NLCS was scheduled for October 18, which marked the 125th anniversary of the first-ever official game between the franchises. The series would not only have been a fierce competition but also would have served as a glorious celebration of the rivalry. Of course, the Giants would have probably been the underdog to the Dodgers, just as they were to the Cardinals. But the Giants and their fans never seemed to be bothered by such slights. That's just the way the good folks roll in Resilient, California, where they were already planning for a victory parade right down Never Say Die Boulevard.

As teams from both leagues began arriving for spring training camps for the 2014 season, probably no other individual in the game had more pressure on him to win a championship than Don Mattingly. The Dodgers manager was handed a three-year contract, ending the uncertainty about the club's commitment to him. At the same time, the Dodgers' payroll was projected to reach $235 million, replacing the Yankees as baseball's biggest spenders. The preseason buzz favored the Dodgers to win the West. An MLB.com article listing the top 10 teams in the game for 2014 ranked the Dodgers fourth and omitted the Giants. San Francisco's disappointing 76–86 record in 2013 made their recent two championships seem like ancient history to the pundits, who appeared to have forgotten that they had the same manager and some of the same players who pulled off those titles. The Giants can flash some well-earned fancy jewelry, but the baseball world has never viewed the team as the gold standard for success.

Both teams came up with new slogans for 2014. The Dodgers: "Live, Breathe, Blue." The Giants: "All Together—Stronger Together." One wonders if the Dodgers really thought their slogan out, since it might be interpreted as "Live, breathe the Southern California air, turn blue." The Giants didn't knock one out of the park with their slogan either. It's been used in similar forms for promotions by Hyundai Motors, nationwide food co-ops, and Greece ("All together, building a stronger future for Greece.").

A more practical slogan for the wealthy Dodgers might have been "there's an app for that," because the club has the money to order up whatever is needed to upgrade as the season goes on. Facing holes in the fourth and fifth spots in the rotation because of uncertainty over injury comebacks by Chad Billingsley and Josh Beckett, and the departure of Ricky Nolasco, the team added veteran starters Dan Haren and Paul Maholm. The Dodgers needed a regular, reliable second baseman, so they gave promising but untested Cuban defector Alexander Guerrero $28 million over four years.

The letdown by the Giants' starting rotation last year, with the exception of Bumgarner, gave Giants fans a reason to take the exhibition games more seriously. Normally, if a starter gets lit up in a spring training outing or two, the team writes it off that the pitcher was just getting loose and will be ready for the bell when the season starts. Fans weren't buying that this year. They wanted to see Matt Cain (2013 ERA 4.00) regain his top pitching form, Tim Lincecum prove that he is relearning the art of pitching to offset the decline of his heat, and Ryan Vogelsong and newly signed Tim Hudson give signs that their injuries of 2013 are behind them. Beyond the pitching, the Giants' MIP (most important player) for 2014 might be first baseman Belt, who had an impressive second-half surge in 2013. A true breakout season by Belt could be the offensive game changer for the Giants.

Unlike the Giants, the Dodgers didn't have key players who needed to show their talents during the spring games. Their biggest goal was to break camp for the regular season in good health. Slugger Matt Kemp is unlikely to be ready following ankle surgery, but the Dodgers are counting on outfielder Carl Crawford and shortstop Hanley Ramirez, who both missed significant time in 2013, to play a good share of games this season. In fact, the Dodgers' roster is sound enough that their MIP might be new bench coach Tim Wallach. The Dodgers got a bit out of hand last season, with Yasiel Puig's unpredictability, the normally restrained Adrian Gonzalez making goofy Mickey Mouse ears at the Cardinals in the NLCS, and the bizarre jump into the pool after clinching at the Diamondbacks' ballpark. Mattingly could use the veteran presence of Wallach to help him keep the Dodgers steady and focused. The Giants blamed some of their 2013 troubles on the shorter offseason because of postseason play and longer training camps necessitated by the World Baseball Classic, so it would be interesting to see if a similar scenario bothers their rival. The Dodgers, who played in October, had their offseason cut even shorter because they had to report to camp a week earlier to get ready to open the regular season March 22–23 against the Diamondbacks in Australia. If nothing else, the flight, time change, and trip back to camp before heading to Los Angeles seems like a rough way to prepare for April. The Giants, who play the Dodgers six times in the first three weeks, might have considered sending a thank-you text to Commissioner Bud Selig for upsetting their competition's schedule.

<hr />

The ceremonial opening battery for the Los Angeles home opener and the first Giants-Dodgers series of the season April 4–6 featured two legends of the rivalry: broadcast icon Vin Scully made the ceremonial first pitch to Dodgers pitching great Sandy Koufax. The feel-good moment for the packed L.A. crowd didn't last long as the Giants jumped on Hyun-Jin Ryu for six runs in the first inning, the most runs in the initial frame in a rivalry opener between the teams since they moved west. Mattingly had to start Ryu in the opener because Clayton Kershaw was sidelined with inflammation in his upper back. Morse and pitcher Vogelsong had two-run singles, and Belt and Angel Pagan drove in the other two with base hits as the Giants went on to an 8–4 win. Despite having an 8–0 lead heading into the fourth, Vogelsong couldn't survive the fifth inning and was removed as he allowed four runs on 94 pitches. More significant to the Dodgers than the loss was that Puig arrived late for the opener, claiming he had the wrong starting time, which prompted Mattingly to bench him for the game. If the frustrated Mattingly was in need of some silver lining after the disastrous opener, he could look to his bullpen as four relievers no-hit the Giants over the last seven innings while striking out 10.

A three-run homer by Pablo Sandoval and solo clouts by Morse and Buster Posey led the Giants to a 7–2 victory in the second game of the series. Bumgarner got the win, allowing two runs and striking out 10 in 6⅓ innings. The Dodgers avoided a sweep the next day as Kemp and Ramirez each homered twice in a 6–2 win. The Dodgers' bullpen was impressive again, blanking the Giants over the final three innings while striking out six. The first-place Giants, at 5–2, now led the Dodgers by a half-game. The clubs played grind-it-out baseball in their next meeting, a three-game series April 15–17 in San Francisco. The cumulative score of the series was Giants 6, Dodgers 5, with the Giants coming out on top two games to one. The opener lasted just six minutes short of five hours, as the Giants prevailed 3–2 in 12 innings. Hector Sanchez drove in the winning run with a single off Brandon League. Starters Vogelsong and Maholm battled to a 1–1 tie after six in Game Two, but the Giants' bullpen was a bit better as it shut down the Dodgers the rest of the way. Sandoval's RBI single off J.P. Howell in the seventh broke the deadlock and led to a 2–1 victory. Ryu shut out the Giants on four hits in Game Three in a 2–1 Dodgers' win, as Bumgarner lasted only 4⅓ innings after throwing 99 pitches. The clubs stood tied for first at 10–6.

The race remained close when the teams met three weeks later for four games May 8–11 in Los Angeles, but the Giants were about to break away. The series began with Colorado percentage points ahead of the Giants for first place, with the Dodgers 2½ back. Strong starts by Vogelsong, Bumgarner and Hudson were the keys to the Giants taking three of four. Vogelsong allowed one run in 7⅓ innings in a 3–1 win in the opener. The Giants broke open a 1–1 tie with two in the 10th, loading the bases on three walks, and scoring on a sacrifice fly by Sanchez and an RBI single by Belt. Bumgarner went eight innings in Game Two while giving up one run and striking out eight in a 3–1 victory. Brandon Crawford's two-run homer in the fifth off Maholm was the decisive blow. Hudson kept the Giants in the game in the series wrap-up, allowing two runs in six innings in a 7–4

Giants win. The Giants again triumphed in overtime, scoring three in the 10th on a two-run single by Sanchez and an RBI single by Sandoval to break a 4–4 deadlock. The Dodgers' lone victory came in Game Three, as Zack Greinke held the Giants to two runs over seven innings, and Dee Gordon scored two runs, had two hits, and stole three bases. The Giants, at 24–14, now led the third-place Dodgers by 4½ games.

"Basically, we're *bleep*."

Those were the words of motivational speaker Mattingly on June 4, faced with the challenge of trying to get his club to make up an 8½ game deficit in the NL West standings. Mattingly buzzed his squad with a high inside shot about the importance of team play. "I think that's the one thing we're missing at this point, a collective group fighting and pulling in one direction trying to win a game," he said.

It would get worse for the Dodgers over the next few days, as they dropped 10 games behind June 8. Still, history indicated the Dodgers shouldn't panic. They were down 9½ games on June 22 in 2013 and had clearly appeared chemistry-less until they went on their remarkable 42–8 run. That didn't happen because of team unity but because of a torrid offense, clutch hitting, and drop-dead pitching. Some pundits, the same ones who coronated the Dodgers this March, were now conceding the division to the Giants. The uphill climb is made even steeper for the Dodgers because they only play the Giants three times until mid-September, when they meet six times in the closing weeks of the season. So far this season, the Giants have won seven of ten in head-to-head play.

There were still 98 games to play, so the Dodgers had plenty of time to respond to their skipper's scolding. But would they? Early indications hinted that Mattingly's message might not have gotten through yet. In one game, Kemp smacked a pitch and assumed it was gone, and even slowed down for a congratulatory handshake from first base coach Davey Lopes. Minor problem: the ball stayed in the park and Kemp had to break into a full sprint to reach second. He was called safe, but in a replay challenge, it was ruled that he had been tagged out when he overslid the bag.

If the Dodgers were "*bleep*" on June 4, one can only wonder what word Giants manager Bruce Bochy would use to describe the collapse of his team. The Giants lost 18 of 23 games during one stretch, while the Dodgers won 18 of 26. Incredibly, by July 4, the Giants had blown the entire lead, and the Dodgers were now in first place by a game. Heading into the All-Star break on July 13, Los Angeles held a half-game lead. The Dodgers battled back from injuries and a power outage from Puig, whose long-ball threat had seemed to dry up. The rotation continued to be Mattingly's savior, as the starters pitched the "bleep" out of the ball for him, recording a 3.04 ERA at the break. Injuries to Pagan and Marco Scutaro had robbed the Giants of their expected one-two combination at the top of the order, and the rotation was leaking oil. It had been a volatile season for both clubs, but the dramatic ups and downs were irrelevant as the clubs prepared to face off in a high-stakes weekend series July 25–27 in San Francisco.

It was also Hall of Fame weekend in Cooperstown where three managers—Tony LaRussa, Joe Torre, and Bobby Cox were inducted. That raised speculation locally whether Giants manager Bruce Bochy would someday deserve the honor. Bochy's two championships and total wins had already made him a lock to the Hall of Fame to many, and few could argue against him. But Bochy did nothing in that weekend's crucial series to win any votes.

Bochy curiously began the series in retreat, playing down its importance. In that, he might have been the first manager in the 125 years that the Giants and Dodgers have been playing not to view a late July meeting between the historic rivals in the middle of a pennant race as having any more meaning than a three-game weekday series against the Rockies. Said Bochy prior to the series: "I don't know what's not a big game." Apparently, the Giants' front office didn't get the word as it jacked up prices for the games. The cheapest ticket for the series was $51.50 Friday, $68.75 Saturday, and $51.50 Sunday, and these were not particularly great seats.

Bochy's counterpart saw it differently. Mattingly explained that with the new format, where two wild-card teams played a loser-goes-home game to determine who gets a berth in the playoffs, winning the division took on new meaning. That meant that this series with the Giants had extra strategic importance. Mattingly made the point when he lined up his rotation following the All-Star break so that the "Big Three" of Kershaw, Greinke, and Ryu would face the Giants. Mattingly understood far more than Bochy that this was a statement series. Bochy still had a good argument in his corner: while Bumgarner would not throw in this series, he had two starts since the break and won them both. The Giants went 5–2 in this period leading up to the series, while the Dodgers went 2–4. As a result, the Giants entered the series with a 1½ game lead over the Dodgers. The answer to what approach to the series was the best would have to come on the field.

The first thing that stood out when one surveyed the 40,000-plus gathered at AT&T Park for one of the biggest Giants-Dodgers series of recent times was that there was a lot of blue mixed in with the black and orange in the stands. The best theory about the large contingent of Dodgers fans was that Giants' season ticket holders who were not affected by the jacked-up admission price for the series had been prompted to make a quick profit by putting tickets for sale online. Dodgers fans got their money's worth in the opener thanks to Puig, who gave an electrifying performance displaying the raw talent that often got lost in his many distracting adventures on and off the diamond. Puig had three triples, tying a modern-day record, and added a double to lead the Dodgers to an 8–1 win in the July 25 opener. The Dodgers had five triples in all, the other two coming from Dee Gordon and Kemp. Lincecum was the victim of the Dodgers' onslaught, as he was pounded for six runs and nine hits in 4⅓ innings. Greinke blanked the Giants on four hits and struck out 10 in seven innings.

It got no better for the Giants in Game Two as Kershaw tossed a two-hit shutout in a 5–0 victory to put the Dodgers in first by a half-game. The Dodgers got to Giants starter Vogelsong for four runs in six innings, with Juan Uribe leading the way with two run-scoring singles. On the same day, it was announced that the Giants acquired starter Peavy from the Boston Red Sox to try to give the inconsistent rotation a shot in the arm. Peavy was just 1–9 with a 4.72 ERA, but the Giants looked for him to be an instant success in avoiding a crushing sweep. Things went well for the new Giant through Game Four as San Francisco led 2–1. The fifth inning became a turning point of the regular season with a combination of Peavy's wildness and a Giants defensive lapse. The Giants' horror show began when Gordon struck out swinging on a wild pitch, allowing him to reach first. After Puig walked, another wild pitch put runners at second and third. Gonzalez struck out on a pitch that bounced away from Posey. The Giants catcher threw to first to retire Gonzalez, but the alert Gordon outsmarted Posey and sped home for the score. Ramirez singled home a run and Crawford drove in another with a triple, putting the Dodgers ahead to stay for a 4–3 win and a series sweep. Greinke, Kershaw, and Ryu held the Giants to three runs in 22 innings, and the Dodgers now led the Giants by 1½ games. Two full months remained, but for this series, Mattingly's special focus and his fired-up team had trumped Bochy's laid-back philosophy.

———

The Giants and Dodgers had gone 46 days since they last met. Now, they would play six times in 13 days in September. At stake: the NL West, with the second-place team likely relegated to the wild-card game. Neither team had been able to create separation since that July series as they gathered September 12–14 in San Francisco. The Dodgers had gone 24–16 and the Giants 24–17, leaving Los Angeles two games ahead. Mattingly again had the rotation set up so Ryu, Greinke, and Kershaw would pitch. This time, Bochy arrived at the fight with his main weapon on the mound in the opener. Bumgarner threw seven shutout innings, giving up just three hits and striking out nine. The Giants, who had won 12 of the last 15, came out swinging against Ryu. Joe Panik and Posey got it started with back-to-back doubles, and Hunter Pence, Joaquin Arias, and Crawford drove in runs with hits for a 4–0 first-inning lead. Crawford added a two-run homer, and Ishikawa finished it off with a three-run homer for a 9–0 rout. If Game Two was a heavyweight fight, they would have stopped it during batting practice. At least one has to believe that the Dodgers were making sound contact in their pregame swings. It was 4–0 after one; 8–0 after two. When the carnage was complete, the Dodgers had a 17–0 victory. They had 24 hits, with Ramirez getting four and Puig and Kemp three. Twelve Dodgers had hits. Greinke had two hits, including a home run, and contributed six shutout innings. Hudson gave up six runs and eight hits, and was gone in the second inning. Lincecum in relief was tagged for five runs and seven hits in three innings. Mike Kickham was knocked around for four runs and six hits in 1⅔ innings.

The shell-shocked Giants were easy pickings for Kershaw the next day as he breezed through eight innings, allowing two runs and striking out nine on the way to a 4–2 victory. Kershaw wasn't the only problem for the Giants. On the big stage, the Giants forgot their lines and knocked over the scenery. They made two errors on one play, which led to two Dodgers runs. The first came when right fielder Pence threw off-line while trying to nail Ramirez at third. Giants pitcher Yusmeiro Petit retrieved the ball, but his throw to home to try to get Ramirez was wild. Petit had only himself to blame for the debacle, because he failed to get to the right angle in backing up third. Petit also hurt his own cause when he failed to advance a runner in a bunt attempt. Later, in the sixth, center fielder Pagan misplayed a Gonzalez shot which turned into a double, and Kemp followed that with a home run. The Dodgers now led by three games with 13 to play. A Giants-Pirates wild-card game was becoming more of a likelihood, and with those clubs tied at 84–71, San Francisco was playing not only for a hope at catching the Dodgers but for the all-important wild-card home game.

In the NFL, there would have been a 15-yard penalty for taunting. In the NBA, such a flagrant foul would have resulted in possible ejection. The

NHL would have sent the perpetrator to the penalty box. The unwritten rules of baseball have at least a full chapter devoted to things that you shouldn't do to show up your opponent. The guilty party in this case: Dodgers skipper Mattingly, for his in-your-face move in the ninth inning of the final Dodgers-Giants game of the season.

The Dodgers, now leading the Giants by 4½ games, entered the September 22–24 home series looking to clinch the division title. The Giants needed a sweep to give them any shot at catching the Dodgers, but their realistic goal was to edge out the Pirates for home-field advantage in the wild-card game. The Giants, also trying to prevent a Dodgers NL West celebration while they were in town, scratched out a 5–2 win in 13 innings in the opener. The Dodgers clinched a tie for the division crown the next night and prevented the Giants from locking up a playoff spot with a 4–2 victory. Bumgarner supplied all the offense for the Giants with a two-run homer in the third off Greinke, but first-inning homers by Justin Turner and Kemp had given the Dodgers a 3–0 lead. The game marked a rematch of the Bumgarner-Puig feud. The pair had a previous dustup May 9 when Puig homered against Bumgarner at AT&T Park. It was a two-fer for Puig as he flipped his bat and then did one of those "Chariots of Fire" impersonations as he ran the bases in slow motion. A steaming Bumgarner met him near home plate to voice his displeasure at the display. The fireworks occurred when Bumgarner struck Puig in the lower leg, sparking an exchange of words that brought both teams onto the field for the obligatory "hold me back" scrum. Kershaw was masterful in Game Three, allowing just one run and striking out 11 in eight innings. The Dodgers scored four in the sixth and eighth innings, and went into the ninth with a 9–1 lead, needing just three outs to win the West. Mattingly had plenty of choices for pitchers. He could have stayed with Kershaw or given the job as a reward to his closer Kenley Jansen. He could have used a mop-up reliever or a September call-up to record the clinching outs. Instead, he went with Brian Wilson. The once-revered Giant had burned his bridges and incinerated much of the good will from his San Francisco times when he berated Giants Chief Executive Officer Larry Baer in the postgame, on-the-field tantrum in 2013 over his World Series ring. Wilson closed out the Giants on one hit in 14 pitches to trigger a Dodgers' party as the Giants watched. The Dodgers' skipper gets little respect against the Giants, as he is often rated as a second-tier manager to the Giants' Bochy. But on this night, Mattingly got the last laugh, at least for now.

It had been 52 years since the Giants and Dodgers last played one another in a postseason series with a World Series berth at stake. The Giants did their part in the 2014 postseason, defeating the Pirates in the wild-card game, and downing the Nationals in the NL Division series. However, the Dodgers fell in four games to the St. Louis Cardinals. The quick disappearance of the Dodgers was surprising, but the fact that Kershaw was defeated twice to run his postseason losing streak to four was shocking. Kershaw's 2014 regular season numbers were dominant: 21–3, 1.77 ERA, 239 strikeouts. Yet, in the series against the Cardinals, he couldn't hold a 6–1 lead in Game One, and surrendered a back-breaking three-run homer in the deciding Game Four loss. Kershaw's postseason record was now 1–5 as he allowed 29 runs in 51 innings. During the regular season, Kershaw was the gunslinger who sent grown men scattering as he walked through the saloon doors. But baseball was about to discover that there was one steely-eyed stud who didn't flinch, cool and content to order another round from his table in the corner despite the impending danger. He was an imposing figure at 6–5, 235 pounds, and in the high-noon tension of postseason play in 2014, he stared down all challengers. This postseason was supposed to be Kershaw territory, but the menfolk and womenfolk of San Francisco knew there had been a change out west: There was a new sheriff in town, and his name was Madison Bumgarner.

———

It's bad enough for people in Kansas City that Game Seven of the 2014 World Series was followed by Halloween. Royals fans are likely to wake up in the middle of the night screaming, haunted by the dominance of Bumgarner, who carried the Giants on his broad shoulders in a 3–2 win in

Game Seven for their third championship in five years. But there is another reason for those who proudly wear the Royals colors to have nightmares: the realization that the Royals passed up on the chance to select Bumgarner in the 2007 MLB draft where they had the second pick. The Royals instead chose Mike Moustakas. The "Moose," as he is affectionately called in Kansas City, did well overall in this postseason, slugging five home runs. But he did not become a World Series legend and instead quietly went 0-for-3 in Game Seven. It's not like the Royals didn't know about Bumgarner before the draft. A scouting report on him at the time said: "He certainly looks the part with the body type and fastball of a professional pitcher. Lefties from the high school ranks with plus velocity like that don't come around very often."

Bumgarner opened the World Series with seven strong three-hit innings in a 7–1 Giants victory. The clubs went into Game Five even at 2–2, where Bumgarner got the best of "Big Game" James Shields in a four-hit shutout and a 5–0 Giants win. The Royals tied it up in Game Six with a no-nonsense 10–0 thrashing of the Giants. There was speculation among Giants fans and writers whether Bumgarner had enough left in the tank to maybe throw an inning in relief or at least face a couple batters if needed in Game Seven. As it turned out, it was the Royals bats that were running on empty as Bumgarner came out of the bullpen to throw five shutout innings on two days' rest to preserve the lead and wrap up the title. Bumgarner raised his remarkable World Series record to 4–0, allowing one run in 36 innings for an 0.25 ERA with 31 strikeouts.

Meanwhile, the Dodgers' World Series drought had now reached 26 years: one more year than the 25-year-old Bumgarner has been on the planet.

DODGERS VS. DYNASTY (2015)

In a five-year period, the Giants had spent more time at the White House with President Barack Obama than the Republican leadership had. Obama was dealing with a debt-ceiling crisis during the first visit in 2011, so the nation's "Sports Fan in Chief" found the visit of the 2010 champions to be a welcome distraction. He saluted Willie Mays, and in recalling a flight with him to the 2009 All-Star Game in St. Louis, the president joked, "Very rarely on Air Force One am I the second-most-important guy on the plane." When the club returned for a visit in July 2013, Obama and the 2012 champion Giants had something in common, as Obama had recorded a repeat victory himself with his reelection that past November. The Orange and Black would make yet another trip to the White House in 2015 to celebrate their 2014 title. Obama did everything but have the White House band play "Hail to the Skipper" as he referred to three-time champion Bruce Bochy as "a manager who seems to be making his own course for Cooperstown."

The Dodgers had to look at the Giants' D.C. visits with envy and frustration. From 2010 to 2014, the Giants compiled a regular season record of 436–374. During the same period, the Dodgers were 434–375. Both teams had two division titles. The first-place 2014 Dodgers finished six games ahead of the Giants and won the head-to-head season series 10–9. It was as if the Dodgers had tied the Giants in the popular vote but lost the Electoral College.

So the Dodgers did what any candidate who kept coming up short in the big election would do—they brought on a new campaign staff. Baseball was changing both off the field in the way clubs assessed talent and on the field in how game decisions were made. Analytics was the new strategy, using technology and precise research to inform baseball decisions. Some teams were slow to accept any of the new thinking, and other clubs, such as the Giants, studied the new concepts without becoming fanatical about them. The Dodgers, however, were now all in.

A front-office shake-up brought in analytics true believers Andrew Friedman as president of baseball operations, Farhan Zaidi as general manager, and Josh Byrnes as vice president of player personnel. The trio accepted the reality that the massive spending of the last couple of years wasn't going to bring the franchise its first world championship since 1988 without a new master plan. This approach focused on improving the defense, adding flexibility to the roster, building depth, and finding hitters who were consistent run-producers. But even in an analytics-driven system that could measure such needs, the new front office couldn't completely ignore the positive impact that old-school clubhouse chemistry might have in building a champion. Friedman and Co. couldn't move fast enough, lighting up the offseason and winter meetings with a staggering roster reshuffling. The Dodgers cut ties with outfielder Matt Kemp and shortstop Hanley Ramirez, believing their combined 2014 production of 38 homers and 160 RBIs could be replaced by more positive players that fit into their new team concept. Dee Gordon showed signs that he could become the next Maury Wills with a .289 average, 64 stolen bases, and a team-high 92 runs and 176 hits. But Gordon's play at second base didn't fit the new emphasis on defense, so he was traded to Florida. Veterans Jimmy Rollins (shortstop) and Howie Kendrick (second base) were brought in, and Triple-A standout Joc Pederson was placed in center field to solidify a strong up-the-middle defense. The experienced Rollins and Kendrick were viewed as a pair who might find a way to help mature the gifted but still unpredictable Yasiel Puig. Old-fashioned statistics from 2014, not analytics, were all you needed to know that Clayton Kershaw (21–3, 1.77 ERA) and Zack Greinke (17–8, 2.71) gave the Dodgers the best one-two punch of any rotation in the game.

During one 24-hour period of the winter meetings, the Dodgers made six deals with four teams involving 19 players and a free agent. The contrast between the hectic offseason activities of the Dodgers and the Giants' quiet offseason signings of third baseman Casey McGehee and outfielder Nori Aoki was clear. The Dodgers stood in a long line with three loaded carts in their shopping spree, while the Giants quickly went through the express line with their bargain purchases.

—ᴡᴡ—

The absence of any significant signings or trades wouldn't normally be a concern for a team that had won three of the last five titles and was returning much of its 2014 championship roster for the 2015 season. But none of the Giants' title teams ever resembled a powerhouse, at least in the regular season. Newspaper headlines called them a dynasty in a clever marketing tool to sell special sections. But was that designation justified?

The last National League team to win three championships in five years was the St. Louis Cardinals in 1942–44–46. That club, led by Hall of Famer Stan Musial, isn't on anyone's dynasty list. In six seasons, from 1941 through 1946, the Cardinals won four pennants and twice finished second. They went to the World Series four times in that period, dropping the 1943 Series to the Yankees. They won 106 games in 1942 and 105 games each in 1943 and 1944.

In the six-year stretch from 2009 to 2014, the Giants twice finished in first, second, and third. They got to the postseason in 2014 as the wild card. The Cardinals won 606 regular season games in those six years, while the Giants won 524. If there had been a wild card in the 1940s, the Cardinals would have gone to the postseason all six years. If the Cardinals of that time haven't earned dynasty status, the Giants don't qualify either.

Merriam-Webster defines a dynasty as "a family, team, etc. that is very powerful or successful for a long period of time." The Imperial House of Japan is used as an example of a dynasty because it has existed since 660 BC. The Roman Empire, which lasted for more than 500 years, gets a mention as well. The Giants are going to need to build a far deeper farm system if they expect to be mentioned in the same breath as those two behemoths.

So how high is the bar to reach the sports dynasty status? The Yankees of 1949–1964 won 14 pennants and nine World Series championships in 15 years. The Yankees of 1996–2003 reached the postseason all eight years, winning seven division titles, six pennants and four World Series crowns. The A's get dynasty consideration because they won three consecutive World Series, while winning their division during the five-year stretch from 1971–1975. The Boston Celtics established themselves as a dynasty by winning 11 NBA championships in 13 years from 1957 to 1969. The Los Angeles Lakers won five championships in a 12-year-run from 1979–1991, which included nine conference titles and 12 winning seasons. The

Chicago Bulls won six titles in eight years from 1993 to 1998. The Green Bay Packers won five titles in seven years in the 1960s, including the first two Super Bowls. The 49ers captured five Super Bowls and 11 division titles from 1981–94, and the Steelers won four Super Bowls in six years in the 1970s. The UCLA basketball team from 1964–1975 is arguably the top all-time sports dynasty with 10 national championships in 12 seasons, including seven straight from 1967–1973, four undefeated seasons, and a stretch of 88 consecutive wins.

But so much for the numbers.

Dynasties are usually feared and favored. For example, in their heyday, the Celtics, the 49ers, and the Roman Empire were all expected to push around the opposition in every battle. The 2015 Giants, however, couldn't even sway *Sports Illustrated* with their three rings, as the magazine forecast them for second place behind the Dodgers. The *Sports Illustrated* ranking couldn't be dismissed as merely a lack of respect. Madison Bumgarner's 270-inning 2014 workload and his postseason stamina as a starter and reliever raised questions about whether he could come back firing at the same level in 2015. The question marks about the rest of the rotation were far more worrisome. Matt Cain was coming back after two surgeries, and no one could make a very good case that Jake Peavy, Tim Hudson, Ryan Vogelsong, and Tim Lincecum would be able to make enough consistent starts so as not to drain the bullpen. The Giants' spring began badly, when slugger and team leader Hunter Pence's left arm was broken in the first exhibition game. But the up-the-middle contingent of catcher Buster Posey, second baseman Joe Panik, shortstop Brandon Crawford, and center fielder Angel Pagan (if he stayed healthy) was one of the best in the game. Still, there were holes, such as how the Giants would replace the power of the departing Pablo Sandoval and Michael Morse (32 homers, 134 RBIs combined).

Giants fans, who now considered victory parades every other year as routine, scoffed at the Dodgers' makeover on the field and in the front office. Dynasty or not, in the three recent title years, the Giants' postseason record was 34–14, while the Dodgers were 6–8. Times had changed in the way fans of each franchise looked at their clubs. Giants GM Brian Sabean, once the target of harsh criticism on sports talk radio in the frustrating post-Bonds era, mostly escaped any heat for the Giants' quiet winter. It was now a case of "In Sabes We Trust," as fans believed the general manager would find a way to address the needs. Not so in Dodgerville. An article on MLB.com about how the Dodgers' new front office wanted to use analytics to change the organization's culture was met with a resounding thud in the fan comments section that followed.

—⁓—

As the 2015 season began, the State of the Giants Union was looking good in San Francisco as they prepared to raise another championship flag at the home opener, while the State of the Dodgers Union remained uncertain after all the changes. The only thing that seemed to be working against the Giants was this even-odd thing: dynasty-like in 2010, 2012, and 2014, and disappointing in 2011 and 2013. The odds were not in the Giants' favor, perhaps leaving an opening for the Dodgers in 2015.

The Giants were faced with playing at least the first month of the season without the injured Pence. The club was batting just .233, and there was already talk about the Giants considering trades to beef up the roster as they prepared to host the Dodgers in the first series between the teams April 21–23. San Francisco was on an eight-game losing streak with a 4–10 record, trailing first-place Los Angeles by six games. The Dodgers, who were on a seven-game winning streak, had the chance to create serious separation.

The Giants combined small ball with strong pitching and defense to end both teams' streaks with a 6–2 win in the opener. The Giants built a 4–0 lead, scoring on an RBI single by Posey, an RBI bunt single by Crawford, an Aoki infield roller, and a Dodger error. Lincecum allowed just one run in six innings, and the Giants pulled off four double plays, including a highlight-reel Crawford flip to Panik. Justin Maxwell finished off the Dodgers with a brilliant sliding catch in the top of the eighth with two runners on, followed by a two-run homer in the bottom of the inning.

A duel between World Series MVP Bumgarner and league MVP Kershaw received much publicity the next day, but pitch counts have lessened the drama of such matchups from the days where prized starters would battle deep into the game. Bumgarner was gone after giving up two runs in 6⅓ innings on 109 pitches, and Kershaw was removed after allowing two runs in six innings on 93 pitches. Their departures turned the game into a bullpen matchup, and the Giants got the best of that showdown as Panik's sacrifice fly in the ninth gave the Giants a 3–2 victory.

The Dodgers, now trying to salvage one win after having lost a chance to bury the Giants in the early season, held a 2–0 lead after five innings in Game Three. The Giants battled back, tying the game on Brandon Belt's RBI single in the sixth and Crawford's RBI triple in the ninth, and winning it 3–2 on Maxwell's run-scoring single to left in the 10th. The key to the sweep was the Giants' bullpen, which allowed just one run in 9⅔ innings.

The Dodgers bounced back as the teams hooked up four days later, April 27–29, winning two of three in Los Angeles. Game Two featured another matchup of aces, with Bumgarner getting the best of Kershaw in a 2–1 win. Bumgarner gave up one run and struck out nine in eight innings, while Kershaw allowed two runs in seven innings.

It wouldn't seem that the Dodgers needed a wake-up call. They were the owners of repeat division titles and as May 19 dawned, were an impressive 24–13, leading the second-place Giants by 4½ games. They certainly couldn't take the Giants and their trio of recent championships lightly. The Giants' horrible start to 2015 was already a faded memory, more attributable to parade and postseason hangovers than a sudden disappearance of talent. The Giants had gone 16–8 since April 21. But what happened in San Francisco during a three-game series May 19–21 surely had to shake the most loyal Dodgers rooter.

The Dodgers arrived at AT&T Park having scored two runs in their last two games against Colorado, a 7–1 loss and a 1–0 victory. Hudson continued to keep the Dodgers' bats silent in the opening game of the series, throwing scoreless ball in 6⅓ innings. The bullpen did the rest as the Giants took a 2–0 win. Posey singled in what would be the game winner in the third off Carlos Frias, and Belt, who reached base on an error in the eighth, ended up scoring on a wild pitch. Lincecum delivered for the Giants the next night, blanking the Dodgers on three hits over seven innings on 106 pitches. Posey's two-run homer in the eighth off Yimi Garcia was the big blow, and the bullpen again tossed zeroes as the Giants triumphed 4–0. Bumgarner added the exclamation point in game three, smashing the first pitch he saw from Kershaw over the left-field fence for his seventh career home run. Bumgarner got the best of the matchup on the mound also, keeping the Dodgers from scoring over 6⅓ innings while striking out seven. Pence added two RBI singles, and Crawford drove in another with a base hit as Kershaw surrendered all the runs in a 4–0 Giants win, giving them a sweep and three consecutive shutouts. The Dodgers tied a franchise record for the lowest-scoring five-game period, and their scoreless streak would reach a Los Angeles Dodger record of 35 innings before finally ending the next game against San Diego. Meanwhile, the Giants had a major league–high eight shutouts—an accomplishment attributable to a stingy bullpen. Pence had returned to the lineup with his bat in fine form, and the defense was delivering.

The Giants still weren't through with their sudden dominance of the Dodgers, going on to win the first two games of their next series June 19–21 against Los Angeles to move within a half-game. The Dodgers allowed two four-run innings in a 9–5 loss in the opener, highlighted by Posey's grand slam to deep left off Mike Bolsinger in the third. They finally ended their 32-inning scoring drought against the Giants with Yasmani Grandal's RBI single in the second. Two-run homers by Belt and Maxwell and an effective six innings by Hudson led the Giants to a 6–2 win the next day to bring them within a half-game of the Dodgers. Los Angeles, almost as if to say "that's enough," rocked the Giants 10–2 with a 16-hit outburst to maintain the club's division lead. Lincecum lasted a career-short 1⅓ innings, allowing five runs and seven hits, and Yusmeiro Petit was battered for five more runs in 3⅔ innings. The Dodgers pounded four homers, including two by Grandal and one each by Adrian Gonzalez and Justin Turner.

Los Angeles soon rebounded from its troubles with the Giants, going 12–8 in the next three weeks leading up to the All-Star break for a 51–39 record. The Giants were 8–10 during the same period and entered the break at 46–43, 4½ games behind the first-place Dodgers.

Clayton Kershaw not in the All-Star Game? It would be like having the Inaugural Ball and not inviting the president. It would be like going to the Vatican to watch the pope celebrate High Mass on Christmas only to learn the pontiff had been replaced by a parish priest. The players who had been flailing away at Kershaw's electric repertoire of pitches for the last four dominating years didn't find him worthy for one of their selections for the 2015 All-Star Game. Giants manager Bruce Bochy could have righted this wrong by selecting him with one of the three pitching openings he had. But Bochy delivered a broadside to Dodger Blue, making the blow even more severe by choosing instead his own Madison Bumgarner. Kershaw wasn't having a dominant first half (6–6, 2.85 ERA), but he swept the MLB's pitching Oscars last year with the MVP and Cy Young awards. Kershaw, who eventually made the game when a spot opened up, showed class in not complaining about the snub.

Both teams looked to shore up their rotations at the July 31 deadline. The Dodgers added 24-year-old Alex Wood and veteran Mat Latos, and the Giants acquired Mike Leake. The teams would meet a month later for a three-game series August 31–September 2 at Los Angeles with the division title still up for grabs. The Giants had gone 23–18 since the All-Star break while the Dodgers were 21–18, narrowing the lead to 3½ games. The rivalry was at its best in a 14-inning, five-hour and 29-minute opener eventually won by the Dodgers 5–4. The clubs used a total of 42 players, as the Giants went with nine pitchers while the Dodgers used seven.

Gonzalez won it with a line drive to deep left with the bases loaded that went down as an RBI single for a 2–1 win. Greinke would get the best of Bumgarner the next night, allowing only one run in 7⅓ innings on 114 pitches. Bumgarner, by contrast, surrendered two runs in seven innings on 108 pitches. Pederson's solo homer in the seventh proved to be the game winner. Kershaw took over from there, allowing just one run while striking out 15 in a 132-pitch complete game. Newly acquired Chase Utley's solo homer in the sixth gave the Dodgers the lead for good in another 2–1 victory and a series sweep. After scoring three runs in the third inning in the opening game of the series, the Giants only managed three runs in the next 29 innings. The Dodgers had made a statement when it counted, building their lead over the Giants to 6½ and looking like they might be ready to pull away.

The Giants left Los Angeles with one goal: chip away at the Dodgers' lead over the next three weeks enough to be in contention when they hosted Los Angeles for a four-game home series September 28–October 1. San Francisco posted a respectable 12–10 record during the three-week span, but it wasn't enough. The Dodgers went 12–11 and would have eliminated the Giants prior to the four-game matchup if they had not been swept by Colorado September 25–27. That left the Giants, who were out of the wild-card picture, needing to sweep the Dodgers to keep their post-season hopes alive and prevent their rivals from celebrating an NL West title on their home turf. The Giants took the opener in a gritty playoff-like atmosphere, winning 3–2 in the 12th inning on a sacrifice fly by Alejandro De Aza.

The Dodgers were still in command, but the defending champions apparently weren't going to go down easy, setting the stage the next night for another Kershaw-Bumgarner showdown. Bumgarner, then with 18 wins, had his eye on reaching 20 if he could beat the Dodgers and get a victory in his scheduled start on the last day of the season against the Rockies. Visions of that milestone began disappearing as quickly as some of the Bumgarner pitches hit by the Dodgers. Kike Hernandez unloaded a 430-foot blast in the third, and Justin Ruggiano and A.J. Ellis delivered solo homers in the sixth to end the season for the Giants and their ace. The Dodgers added four more in the eighth, which only served to delay their champagne celebration as they won their third straight NL West title with an 8–0 rout.

The key moment came in the top of the fifth when Kershaw forced Bumgarner to throw him 13 pitches, fouling off eight before grounding out. The 31-pitch inning took some steam out of Bumgarner, who then surrendered the two homers in the sixth. Kershaw allowed only one hit, a third-inning single to Kevin Frandsen. He struck out 13 and walked one in the complete-game masterpiece, throwing just 104 pitches. In his two September starts against the Giants, Kershaw tossed two complete games, allowing one run and seven hits in 18 innings while striking out 28. He would finish the season 16–7 with a 2.13 ERA. It was a performance worth that of an All-Star.

As the Dodgers celebrated on the field, the Giants placed a message on the scoreboard: "Congratulations L.A. Dodgers! #Respecttherivalry." The message was a reminder to fans of both teams to avoid the tragic altercations of recent years. To the credit of the Dodgers, there were no shenanigans in the vein of the Arizona pool party—they acknowledged their cheering fans in the stands and took the celebration inside to the locker room. Yet, to longtime followers of the rivalry, the high-profile congratulations in the home park had to be something they thought they'd never see.

The Giants tried to put a spin on a mediocre 2015 by saying they were still alive in the division race until the final week, but that was more of a case of the Dodgers not being able to nail down the crown than it was a sign of any serious San Francisco surge. The Giants pointed to a series of injuries that damaged their chances to reach the postseason, but that also exposed the club's lack of depth. The one exception was Pence, who was sidelined for all but 52 games, with injuries. Pence had played in 383 consecutive games so the Giants couldn't be blamed for not having a reserve ready for this big loss. The club's failure to assemble a reliable rotation raised questions as to why the team hadn't landed a significant No. 2 starter either before or during the season. None of this soured the fan base, who filled AT&T Park every night and cheered just as loudly after the team was eliminated as they did when the club was in contention. The fans had a good reason for their good mood. An even year was ahead—and that's when they hold parades.

The Kershaw-Greinke combination in a five-game postseason series gave the Dodgers confidence that they would surely advance into the next round. Kershaw's solid season was even topped by Greinke's 19–3, 1.86 ERA. But high hopes were dashed as the Dodgers fell in five games to the New York Mets.

Once again, the Dodgers were left looking for answers as to why their championship drought continued. Explaining why one team has won three championship rings in six years and another has none, despite winning three consecutive division titles, would take deep and lengthy analysis. However, a breakdown of the Giants' postseason success and the Dodgers' postseason frustration can be summed up with a look at two plays.

The first play was the stealth steal of third base by the Mets' Daniel Murphy during the fourth inning of the NL Division–deciding fifth game against the Dodgers. Murphy was on first base with left-handed-hitting Lucas Duda at the plate facing Greinke, and the Dodgers leading 2–1. The Dodgers applied the shift defense, leaving only shortstop Corey Seager on the left side of the infield. When Duda walked, Murphy trotted to second. The alert Murphy saw that the non-attentive Dodgers hadn't shifted back to have someone cover third, so he breezed into the bag without a throw. He then scored the key tying run on a sacrifice fly to right by Travis d'Arnaud.

The Mets went on to a 3–2 win to advance to the NL Championship Series, and the absentminded Dodgers ended up looking like part of an Abbott and Costello skit (who's on third?). The once-rare shifts have become common defensive strategy, but it is a risk moving players out of their familiar positions. In this case, as soon as Duda walked, there should have been an automatic re-shift where Seager would break to third base. This wasn't on the rookie Seager. Manager Don Mattingly should have had this already drilled into his team so the positioning was natural. The Dodgers' deadly blunder might create a new sabermetric category, RAWS (Runs Allowed While Sleeping).

In Game Two of the 2012 World Series between the Tigers and Giants, Detroit's Prince Fielder was on first base in a scoreless game in the second inning when Delmon Young slashed a line drive off Bumgarner down the left-field line. While left fielder Gregor Blanco tried to track down the ball as it careened around in the corner, third base coach Gene Lamont waved Fielder around third. Blanco's throw sailed over the head of shortstop Crawford, who was the cutoff man. At that moment it appeared the Tigers would take a 1–0 lead. However, second baseman Marco Scutaro had hustled all the way over to the third base line just in case, and he was in position to grab the errant throw, wheel, and fire the ball to catcher Posey as the 275-pound Fielder neared home. Posey made a classic catch and sweeping tag in one motion and Fielder was out. It was Detroit's only scoring threat, and the Giants won 2–0 on their way to a sweep.

While there are obviously other factors that affect postseason success and failure, those two plays speak a lot about focus, preparation, and a baseball sense to react to sudden developments on the field.

With the 2015 season in the books, the Giants and Dodgers turned their attention to 2016. Both were expected to compete vigorously for needed starting pitchers, and the pressure was particularly on the Dodgers, who were in danger of losing Greinke to free agency. Beyond speculation about changes in the rosters, there was also talk about the fate of Mattingly. The skipper always seemed to be on the hot seat with the new owners, despite having now won three successive division crowns. That clearly wasn't good enough for the "win it all now" philosophy demonstrated on day one of their takeover. The Giants' incredible success added to that frustration, and now the Dodgers wondered whether new field leadership would be needed to finally nail down the big prize.

DODGER SHAKE-UP (2016)

The Dodgers' eight-year experiment to see if former Yankee star power could take them to the promised land ended on November 23, 2015, when the club hired a former Giant as manager. Joe Torre won four World Series titles in 12 years as the Yankees' skipper but was unable to achieve another as manager of the Dodgers from 2008–2010. Don Mattingly was a Yankees legend with brilliant offensive and defensive skills, including six All-Star appearances, an MVP, and nine Gold Glove awards. Mattingly succeeded Torre in Los Angeles but also came up short in the quest to win the team's first championship since 1988. Mattingly's five-year reign ended October 22, though Dodger management stumbled around like an outfielder trying to track down a high fly on a windy day in explaining why. The official party line adopted by management and Mattingly was the old tried and true "mutual parting of ways." But President of Baseball Operations Andrew Friedman and General Manager Farhan Zaidi took the explanation to a new level. "As we got into the back-and-forth, organically it just crystalized," Friedman said at the goodbye press conference. In a separate interview, Zaidi said, "It organically evolved that maybe it's a good time for a change."

On November 23, Dodgers management apparently found organic harmony with the signing of Dave Roberts as the new manager. Roberts did not possess the baseball stature and experience of Torre and Mattingly, which might explain why management went with him. Mattingly appeared to be more of a traditionalist, where the manager made the baseball decisions on the field. The Dodgers front office saw success as more of a collaborative approach from everything from the players they signed to how to position the fielders in a shift. Roberts, who had no managerial experience, no sign of an ego, and no resistance to management's love for analytics, was a perfect fit. Friedman called Roberts "a baseball man and a people person." Roberts explained his philosophy, saying, "When I see people who don't buy into the team, it frustrates me." The Dodgers won a lot of games under Mattingly, but they never built the team concept that management now sought. There might have been a time when talk about team unity was dismissed as overrated, but the team to the north had changed all that. No one knew that any better than Roberts, who had learned some of his baseball smarts as a player under the tutelage of Padres then-manager Bruce Bochy during his days in San Diego in 2005 and 2006. Now Roberts— who played three years with the Dodgers and two with the Giants in his 10-year career—would get an instant test as he prepared to match wits with the Giants' Bochy in what many predicted would be a battle for the 2016 NL West crown.

Neither the Los Angeles Dodgers, the San Francisco Giants, the Baseball World, nor A.J. Schugel could believe it. The Zack Greinke "sweepstakes" had kept the rivalry on the front burner during the hot-stove league, as the Dodgers and Giants tried courting the 32-year-old ace right-hander. Greinke opted out in the third year of a six-year contract with the Dodgers, figuring his 19–3 record and 1.66 ERA in 2015 would put him in position for a break-the-bank deal from either Los Angeles or some other suitor. All the experts said the signing came down to two clubs: the Dodgers and Giants. Dodgers partner Magic Johnson called signing Greinke "our No. 1 priority in the offseason," as the club wished to keep him teamed with Clayton Kershaw. The Giants saw a win-win-win situation in pulling off the deal. They would break up the dominating one-two punch Greinke formed with Kershaw in the Dodgers' rotation. They would avoid any more games against Greinke, who was 7–0 with a 2.19 ERA in 10 career starts against the Giants. And they would have Greinke pitching half his games at pitcher-friendly AT&T Park, where he had an ERA of 1.78 in four outings. The Giants' inability to sign any top free-agent pitchers and a lack of any minor-league arms ready to join the rotation as a force were starting to put the Giants in desperation mode.

It seemed like a slam dunk that either Magic Johnson or the Giants would get their man, but on December 4, 2015, Greinke deserted them for the desert. The Arizona Diamondbacks nabbed Greinke with a six-year, $206.5 million contract. The surprised baseball world likely had a good chuckle over the Dodgers and Giants losing out in the sweepstakes, but it is certain A.J. Schugel wasn't finding any humor in the deal. The 27-year-old right-hander was dropped from the 40-man Arizona roster to make room for Greinke and was designated for assignment.

The loss of Greinke didn't appear to faze the well-to-do club, which had millions in cash available to shop for alternative free-agent pitchers. A couple of years ago, that sentence would clearly refer to the Dodgers, but in a turnabout in the rivalry, it was the Giants who had the checkbooks out. The day after the Great Arizona Greinke Heist, the Giants signed starting pitcher Jeff Samardzija, a durable innings eater. Other clubs had shied away from Samardzija after he led the American League in 2015 in homers, hits, and earned runs, but the Giants were attracted by his 200-plus innings pitched the last three years. The Giants followed that up about 10 days later with the signing of the colorful Johnny Cueto, slotting him behind Madison Bumgarner to give the Giants a one-two rotation threat. Cueto had experienced an inconsistent year in 2015, yet showed enough signs of brilliance in the postseason for Kansas City to convince the Giants he was worth the price. He pitched eight strong innings in the Royals 7–2 win in Game Five of the American League Division Series against Houston. After getting roughed up in Game Three of the league championship series against Toronto, Cueto bounced back with a stellar, two-hit complete-game 7–1 victory over the Mets in Game Two of the World Series. The Giants had hopes that they were getting the consistent Cueto of 2014 when he went 20–9 with a 2.25 ERA. Despite their $220 million commitment to the additions, the Giants still weren't through, and on January 7 they added free agent Denard Span to fill needs in center field and for a leadoff hitter. Span was limited by injuries in 2015 but had a strong 2014 with 184 hits, a .302 average, and 31 steals.

The Dodgers countered the loss of Greinke with the signing of free-agent starting pitchers Kenta Maeda and Scott Kazmir. The 6-foot, 154-pound, right-handed Maeda, a star in Japan where he pitched the last eight years, was coming off a season in which he went 15–8 with a 2.39 ERA. Maeda, 28, signed an eight-year deal with a potential payout of $106 million with the Dodgers, who didn't seem bothered by an exam that found "irregularities" in his right elbow. Kazmir, 32 and signed to a $48 million contract, was coming off a season in which he made 31 starts for Oakland and Houston and posted a 7–11 record with a 3.10 ERA. These two signings, along with Kershaw and Alex Wood, gave the club a set staff of four starters, with the fifth spot still uncertain. The club would open the season with starters Hyun-Jin Ryu, Brett Anderson, Brandon McCarthy, and Mike Bolsinger on the disabled list. Waiting in the wings to possibly join the rotation was 19-year-old left-hander Julio Urias, though the Dodgers didn't want to rush him to the majors.

The Dodgers hoped that shortstop Corey Seager, 21, a rookie of the year candidate, and second-year center fielder Joc Pederson, 23, would provide a youthful combination of offense and defense. The club was counting on Pederson's mysterious second-half collapse in 2015, during which he hit just .178, as being an aberration. The club would have no such worries about first baseman Adrian Gonzalez, who remained one of the most consistent offensive threats in the game. On the opposite side of consistency was Yasiel Puig, who would enter the season with questions lingering about his health and his approach to the game. Puig hit a disappointing .255 in 2015 while playing just 79 games because of injuries to both hamstrings. Mattingly never seemed to be able to reach the undisciplined Puig, and it was hoped that the personal touch of Roberts could get through to the potential five-tool right fielder. Roberts also could face a challenge in the bullpen, which was 11th in ERA in the league in 2015. However, his job late in games should be made easier with Kenley Jansen, one of the best closers in the game, and a strong bench that includes Chase Utley, Scott Van Slyke and Kike Hernandez.

Beyond the issues about player performances and injuries, the biggest question for the Dodgers was whether rookie manager Roberts was ready to step into the big shoes of predecessors Torre and Mattingly. At least Roberts had a little experience with that kind of pressure. Barry Bonds played his last season with the Giants in 2007. On opening day 2008, the Giants starting left fielder was Dave Roberts.

The Giants entered 2016 watching one "Core Four" begin to break up while another geared up for a long run. The relief pitching Core Four of Santiago Casilla, Sergio Romo, Javier Lopez, and Jeremy Affeldt was reduced to three with Affeldt's retirement. All four had been keys to the Giants' three championships, but the club had reason to believe that the powerful stuff of Hunter Strickland and Josh Osich could strengthen the bullpen even further. The new Core Four consisted of home-grown infielders Brandon Belt, Joe Panik, Brandon Crawford, and Matt Duffy. The unit possessed offensive and defensive skills as both run-producers and run-stoppers, and they had some wondering whether the group would turn into the Giants' version of the legendary Dodger infield of Garvey-Lopes-Russell-Cey. Buster Posey was on his way to establishing himself as the best overall catcher in the game with his bat (.318, 19 HR, 95 RBIs in 2015), defense, and game command. There were no real holes in the Giants lineup, as long as one-time ironman Hunter Pence could come back full time after being limited to 52 games in 2015 because of injuries.

The experts again predicted that the Giants and Dodgers would be in the race for the NL West title or at least a wild-card slot, but the Greinke signing put Arizona in play as well. The Giants and Dodgers wouldn't need the experts to advise them about the makeup of either squad, as the clubs would meet seven times in the first two weeks.

KERSHAW-BUMGARNER (2016)

The St. Louis Cardinals began the 1963 season with an untouchable pitching performance. The Cardinals blanked the New York Mets 7–0 and 4–0 and the Philadelphia Phillies 7–0. The scoreless streak extended into the sixth inning of the club's fourth game, finally ending when the Phillies' Wes Covington doubled off Cardinals' starter Ernie Broglio to score Tony Gonzalez. The 32 scoreless innings were the longest of any team to start a season. The Dodgers of 2016, who opened the season with a pitching staff that was still unsettled, wouldn't have been anyone's choice to chase that Cardinals record. Yet the Dodgers not only chased the mark but put themselves into position to tie and break it as they met the Giants in the teams' first series of the year.

Kershaw began the Dodgers' opening game in a three-game series against San Diego with a one-hit, seven-inning gem in a 15–0 win. Kazmir followed with six scoreless innings in a 3–0 victory. Maeda threw six shutout innings the next day as the Dodgers extended the scoreless streak to 27 innings. Dodgers starter Wood continued to throw zeroes in the Giants home opener, the first of a four-game series April 7–10, as the streak reached 31 innings with Los Angeles leading 4–0 after four innings. The Giants avoided being the foil for their rivals by breaking through for a run in the fifth on a groundout to second base by Span that scored Crawford. The breakthrough run got the Giants' bats going as Panik's RBI triple and Posey's RBI double narrowed the Dodgers' lead to 4–3 after five. The Giants scored four more in the sixth to go up 7–4, as Angel Pagan drove in two with a single, and base hits by Panik and Posey tallied two more. Pederson pulled the Dodgers within one in the eighth with a two-run homer. Reliever J.P. Howell surrendered four consecutive singles in the Giants' eighth, and Pence capped off the day with a grand slam off Pedro Baez for a 12–6 win.

While there was plenty of the usual buzz about the opener, the most anticipated game of the series was the third one because it featured Kershaw against Bumgarner. As a result, game two—wedged between the San Francisco home opener and the classic pitching matchup—seemed more like a breather until the series would return to high gear. The Dodgers sent Ross Stripling, who was coming off Tommy John surgery two years earlier and who had never pitched above Double-A ball, to the mound for his first major league start. The Dodgers broke up a 0–0 tie in the fifth against Matt Cain as A.J. Ellis and Seager drove in runs with singles. Meanwhile, Stripling, 26, was doing an impressive Kershaw-Bumgarner imitation, keeping the Giants hitless through seven innings. The eighth inning provided Roberts with his first big decision. Stripling retired the first batter, but walked Pagan as he reached the 100-pitch mark. Roberts, concerned about Stripling's medical history, removed him from the game with the no-hitter intact, and brought in Chris Hatcher to face Trevor Brown. The Giants catcher greeted Hatcher with a game-tying two-run homer. The score remained at 2–2 until the bottom of the 10th, when Crawford led off the inning with a walk-off homer off Joe Blanton. Roberts, whose frustration showed when he was ejected during the eighth for arguing balls and strikes, maintained the decision to pull Stripling was a "no brainer" because of the health issues.

The Kershaw-Bumgarner duel provided the expected low-scoring contest, but turned into a heartbreaker for the Giants when the failure to turn an apparent game-ending double play led to a 3–2, 10-inning Dodgers victory. Bumgarner put the Giants up 1–0 with a home run off Kershaw in the second. Bumgarner gave the run back in the third when he hit Van Slyke with the bases loaded. Giants utility man Ehire Adrianza surprised the crowd with a solo shot in the fifth to give the Giants a 2–1 lead, putting him just 10 behind Bumgarner in career homers. Bumgarner's 102-pitch count ended his day after six innings, and Kershaw left after eight. The Dodgers loaded the bases with one out in the ninth off Casilla, but Gonzalez's bouncer to reserve second baseman Kelby Tomlinson had the Giants poised to celebrate. However, Tomlinson bobbled the ball, and although he was able to throw out Gonzalez at first, the failure to turn two allowed Utley to score the tying run. The Dodgers seized the momentum and the game, as back-to-back doubles by Seager and former Giant Charlie Culberson off George Kontos scored the go-ahead run in the 10th, which stood up for the victory.

The Dodgers, who were on the verge of losing three straight to the Giants before the Tomlinson misplay, suddenly looked like they were on the way to evening the series as they scored five times in a marathon first inning in their first meeting against Cueto in his Giants uniform. The damage came on five singles, a walk, hit by pitch, and a sacrifice fly. The lead didn't last long. The Giants answered for two runs in the bottom half against Kazmir on RBI singles by Belt and Duffy and tied it at 5–5 in the third on a solo homer by Posey and two-run shot by Belt. The teams traded runs in the fourth, and the Giants broke up the 6–6 tie in the sixth with a three-run outburst on a two-run double by Panik and sacrifice fly by Pence.

Cueto overcame the disastrous first, surviving seven innings for a 9–6 win as the Giants took three out of four.

The Dodgers wouldn't have to wait long to get another shot at the Giants as the clubs got together just five days later for a three-game series in Los Angeles April 15–17 with the teams tied for first with 6–4 records. Another Kershaw-Bumgarner matchup grabbed the pregame headlines, but it was bench player Hernandez who made the front-page news as he unloaded on the Giants for two homers and a double, drove in four runs, and saved two runs with a diving catch in left field in a 7–3 Dodgers win. Hernandez homered on Bumgarner's first pitch, and the Giants ace never recovered, allowing seven runs in five innings. Kershaw got the win with a solid seven-inning outing. The defense betrayed Bumgarner as Panik and Tomlinson botched double play opportunities in a four-run Dodgers fourth. Cueto bounced back from the five-run first in the previous weekend in San Francisco as he retired the first 13 batters and took a shutout into the seventh the next day as the Giants held on for a 4–3 victory. The Giants again roughed up Kazmir, building up a 4–0 lead after four innings. Seager gave the Dodgers hope with a two-run homer in the eighth that narrowed the lead to 4–3, but Casilla retired pinch-hitter Puig on a fly ball in the ninth with the tying run on third. The Dodgers came back to take the final game of the series through the mastery of Maeda. The Dodgers starter pitched six shutout innings in his first two major league games, and gave up just one earned run—a Panik home run—in seven innings for a 3–1 victory. Pederson's two-run homer off Samardzija provided the only runs needed by Maeda, whose ERA was now at 0.47. The series win put the Dodgers atop the West, a game over the Giants and Colorado.

Move over, Madison Bumgarner? While no one was disputing the fact that the all-business Bumgarner was still the king of the hill in San Francisco, the colorful Johnny Cueto was shaking and shimmying his way into the hearts of Giants fans. Out on the mound, Bumgarner looks grim while Cueto is likely to grin. Bumgarner throws the ball to the plate with seemingly no effort. Cueto, dreadlocks flying, spins around like he's about to perform a triple axel before delivering the pitch. The season was still early as the Giants and Dodgers prepared for a series June 10 in San Francisco, and for the first time since Tim Lincecum dropped out of the picture, there was electricity about a pitching matchup between the clubs that didn't involve Bumgarner. Kershaw, 8–1, was going against Cueto, 9–1.

The Giants had gone 29–19 since their last meeting with the Dodgers, who played just .500 ball during that period at 24–24 to take a four-game lead. The Dodgers had established a 2½ game lead over Colorado on April 24, with the Giants 3½ back. Los Angeles then lost six straight and by April 30 was tied for first with the Giants with 12–13 records. The Giants ruled May with a 21–8 mark, including a stretch where they won 13 of 14. Those 13 wins included two shutouts, and five games where the opposition scored just one run. The Dodgers had a decent May at 16–12, but lost significant ground when they dropped six of seven during one period. The Giants finished May at 33–21, holding a 4½ game lead over the second-place Dodgers, who were 28–25. The Giants entered the June 10 series having lost three of their last four, but the Dodgers could not take advantage of the mini-swoon, and trailed by four games.

Cueto's duel with Kershaw got off to a shaky start, as he plunked lead-off batter Utley, allowed a swinging bunt single to Seager, and advanced the runners on a wild pitch. The home plate umpire then decided that there was too much razzle in Cueto's razzle-dazzle delivery and called a balk to score a run as the Giants lost the argument that the hesitation move was part of the pitcher's normal delivery. Gonzalez followed with a run-scoring single for a quick 2–0 lead. Duffy made it 2–1 in the bottom half with a homer, and then the expected pitching duel broke out. Posey's RBI double in the sixth tied it at 2–2. Kershaw and Cueto battled for eight innings. Kershaw gave up just five hits and struck out 13. Cueto allowed three hits, fanned eight, and retired 23 of the last 24 batters he faced. The win went to Kershaw, however, as Justin Turner opened the ninth with a home run off Casilla, and Jansen closed the Giants out for a 3–2 victory.

The next day added a new twist to the rivalry, and it didn't even involve baseball. The Giants-Dodgers series was being played as the Golden State

Warriors were playing Cleveland in the NBA championship series. The Warriors' Klay Thompson, beloved in the Bay Area for his spectacular three-point shooting, tossed an air ball as he showed up at AT&T Park wearing a Dodgers cap to watch his brother Trayce, a Los Angeles outfielder. When Thompson and his blue cap were shown on the scoreboard, the crowd saw it as flagrant rivalry foul and unleashed a chorus of boos. Shortly after, peace was restored as the fans roared when Warriors coach Steve Kerr, also in attendance, was shown without any Dodgers garb.

Klay Thompson and Kerr might have thought they were experiencing the baseball equivalent of triple overtime as the clubs battled for 10 innings over four hours, the Dodgers using 16 players and the Giants 20, including nine pitchers. The Giants led 3–2 after six, but the Dodgers tied it in the seventh when Cory Gearrin walked in a run with the bases loaded. Gearrin was one of five pitchers used in the inning as Bochy tried to keep the lead. With the Giants' bullpen just about barren, Bochy had to go with Chris Stratton as the 3–3 game went into the 10th. Stratton, who had made his major league debut less than two weeks previously, saw his second pitch to Gonzalez hammered to left field for a home run. The Giants were down to their last two outs in the bottom of the 10th against Jansen when Span provided hope with a double. Panik tied it with a single and Belt moved him to second with a blooper that fell for a base hit. Posey drilled one up the middle to score Panik with the winning run to bail out Stratton and give him his first big league victory.

The ballpark DJ might have used "When I'm Sixty-Four" as Peavy's walkup song as the well-worn 35-year-old veteran with an aching neck went up against teenager Urias in the final game of the series. Yet, it was Peavy who got the best of the 19-year-old, although he needed a little help from his friends in the bullpen. The game was scoreless until Belt followed Panik's single in the sixth by planting a slider into the arcade in right field for a 2–0 lead. Peavy had to retreat to his recliner after aggravating the sore neck with a tumble. Bochy trotted out six relievers to get the final six outs, interrupted only by a Pederson solo homer for a 2–1 victory. The Giants, 38–26, now led the Dodgers, 33–31, by five games.

HOT TO COLD (2016)

No matter how hard one team would serve, the other would return it. Such was the competitiveness of the Giants and Dodgers over the next four weeks leading up to the All-Star break. The clubs wouldn't go head-to-head again until late August, but they were both surely engaged in scoreboard-watching to see if their rivals would blink. Neither would. The Giants went 19–7 from June 13 to the break, while the Dodgers were 18–9, allowing San Francisco to bump up its lead to 6½. San Francisco's 57–33 record was the best in baseball at the break. The Dodgers completed their roll up to the break with a phenomenal show by the bullpen. The club won eight of its last 11 games, as the relievers allowed only eight runs in 49 innings. In seven of the games, the bullpen didn't permit any runs in 27 innings. In a 14-inning loss to Baltimore, six relievers held the Orioles scoreless on three hits during one seven-inning stretch. Both clubs went into the break with pitching gems. Bumgarner took a no-hitter into the eighth against Arizona and settled for a complete game one-hitter with 14 strikeouts in a 4–0 victory. Maeda retired the first 14 of 15 Padres batters, and allowed just one run and two hits while striking out 13 in a 13–1 romp.

How players bounced back from injuries appeared to be a key storyline for both teams when play resumed. The Dodgers got a shocker when Kershaw had to be placed on the 15-day disabled list (DL) June 27 with a sore lower back. Kershaw was 11–2 with a 1.79 ERA. Starting pitchers McCarthy and Ryu finally got back into action before the break. McCarthy, who had not started a game since April 2015, had two winning five-inning stints. Ryu, who hadn't started since September 2014, had a rougher time in his one outing, allowing six runs and eight hits in 4⅔ innings. Their ability to come back was made more urgent because of Wood's placement on the 60-day DL with elbow problems. Pederson joined Kershaw on the DL after injuring his shoulder when he crashed into the center-field wall while making a catch at Milwaukee. The shaky state of the Dodgers' rotation was steadied by Jansen, who posted a 1.16 ERA and passed Eric Gagne as the Dodgers' all-time saves leader; and a surprising Adam Liberatore, who allowed just two earned runs in 29 innings in relief for an 0.61 ERA.

Seager was everybody's choice as one of the can't-miss prospects going into the season, and he didn't let them down, leading the club in average (.297) and home runs (17) and finishing just two behind Gonzalez and Turner with 42 RBIs. The rivalry suddenly had the best two shortstops in the league in Seager and Crawford (.281, 9 homers, 61 RBIs), though Crawford couldn't join Seager in the All-Star Game because Chicago Cub voters rallied to place their entire infield, including shortstop Addison Russell, on the squad.

The Giants got significant help from reinforcements from the bench and the minors to help offset the loss of injured starters Pence, Panik, and Duffy, though their return seemed vital to the club's success in the final months. The Giants lost setup man Romo to injury for almost the entire first half, which contributed to some instability in the bullpen, including a league-high 17 blown saves. The bullpen was helped greatly by the work-load of the rotation, as Bumgarner (10–4, 1.94 ERA), Cueto (13–1, 2.47) and Samardzija (9–5, 3.91) pitched an impressive total of 377 innings. Besides Crawford, the Giants got consistent offense from Belt (.302), Posey (.292), and Pagan (.287), although the latter missed six weeks with a leg injury.

The Giants and Dodgers would meet in just one three-game series between the resumption of play after the break July 15 and September 18. If the clubs were close by then, a tense final two weeks would be looming as they met for three in Los Angeles September 19–21 and then wrapped up the regular season with three in San Francisco.

The hottest team in baseball suddenly was the coldest team in baseball. The pushover Padres, who lost their first nine meetings with the Giants in 2016, pushed around San Francisco's top starting trio on the way to a three-game sweep in San Diego as post–All-Star play resumed. No other team began the so-called second half with three straight losses. Bumgarner (6 innings, 4 runs), Samardzija (5, 4), and Cueto (5, 4) each allowed two home runs against a club that entered the series 38–51. While it would be easy to brush off the beatdown as a fluke, an ensuing five-game road trip to play the Boston Red Sox and New York Yankees made it likely the Giants would have to right the ship in rocky waters.

History was not on the side of the Giants in the two games at Boston. On June 3, 1915, the New York Giants banged out 16 hits in a 10–3 rout over the Boston Braves at Fenway Park, where that team played some of its games. Giants ace Rube Marquard scattered 13 hits in the complete game performance and Fred Merkle drove in four runs in the tidy one-hour, fifty-three-minute game before a crowd of 1,500. It was the last time the Giants had won a game at Fenway.

The Giants didn't play at the park again until 2007 under interleague play, where they were swept 10–2, 1–0, and 9–5. The Red Sox kept the Giants' Fenway jinx alive with 4–0 and 11–7 victories July 19–20, as spiraling San Francisco was now 0–5 since the break. Giants starters continued the long-ball trend, as Peavy allowed two and Cain three. The losing streak extended to six in a 3–2 loss in the opener of a three-game series July 22–24 against the Yankees as defensive wizard Crawford made three errors. The bullpen provided the Giants their first post-break victory the next day with six scoreless innings in the 2–1, 12-inning contest. Everything one needed to know about the Giants' 5–2 loss in the series wrap-up could be found on one line in the box score: LOB—Giants 10, New York 2, as San Francisco continued to struggle to deliver with runners in scoring position.

The Dodgers only went 5–4 while the Giants were going 1–7, but it was good enough to chop the deficit down to three games. Los Angeles stumbled out of the post-break gate themselves, dropping two out of three to lowly Arizona July 15–17, but came back to win two of three from formidable Washington and St. Louis. The Dodgers went where no team had gone before in the Washington series, as they handed Stephen Strasburg his first defeat of the season after a 13–0 start. Turner did almost all the damage in the 6–3 win with a three-run homer and two-run homer off Strasburg. Los Angeles lost the opener of a July 22–24 series 4–3 in 16 innings against the Cardinals after Jansen blew the save in the ninth. The Dodgers pounded veteran Mike Leake and rookie Mike Mayers the next two games to take the series.

The Giants and Dodgers both had two series to play before the August 1 trading deadline, as rumors about deals competed with action on the field. Injuries were expected to influence what the clubs might do. The Giants, at least, were in a more positive position as sidelined starters Pence, Duffy, and Panik were expected to return soon. The Dodgers could not be as optimistic.

Dodgers announcer Vin Scully has led the league in eloquence throughout his legendary career, so he is the last one who would have to steal the line of another broadcaster to describe any phase of the game. Yet, it would have been understandable if Scully had surveyed the injury-riddled Dodgers and borrowed the trademark phrase of fellow legend Red Barber to state, "Oh Doctor!"

Roberts dropped the bombshell on July 20 when he said surgery for the ailing Kershaw "is more of a possibility." Kershaw, with mild disk herniation, felt discomfort while throwing four days earlier. Though Roberts didn't get his information from a doctor, he was making a practical assessment, as Kershaw's back soreness was not letting up. Stunningly, the Dodgers cut the Giants' lead from eight games to three from the day Kershaw went out with the injury, but the Giants' post-break plunge had more to do with that. Meanwhile, injuries to other pitchers continued to mount. Wood, trying to return from an elbow ailment, faced a new medical procedure that would keep him out another eight weeks. Ryu was out of action again with elbow tendinitis after a brief return to the mound. Starter Anderson continued to rehabilitate from his March back surgery. Reliever Hatcher was shelved with side pain, making him the 22nd Dodgers player to go on the disabled list in 2016.

While Roberts didn't need a medical degree to diagnose Kershaw's obvious physical setback, armchair managers didn't need to have played the game to know that the Dodgers needed to make a deal for pitching. Dodgers management and fans would surely keep one eye on the field and one on the trade deadline over the next week.

The Dodgers split a two-game series with Tampa Bay July 26–27, but it was good enough to shrink the Giants' lead to 2½ games. The Giants hoped that Cincinnati, tied for the third-worst record in baseball, would be the cure for their 1–7 post-break record. But the Reds took two out of three in the July 25–27 matchup, as the Giants wasted an eight-inning, one earned-run performance by Bumgarner in a 2–1 loss in the final game of the series. The frustration of the Giants in their recent slide rose to a new level in the second of a four-game home series July 28–31 against Washington when a potential bases-loaded rally in the eighth inning was wiped out by a line drive that turned into a triple play. The Giants split the series, while the Dodgers took two of three from Arizona. The August 1 trading deadline began with the Giants (61–44) hanging on to a two-game lead over the Dodgers (59–46). The players and coaches had set the stage on the field for a 57-game race for the NL West crown. Now, at least for this one day, the rivalry shifted directly to the clubs' front offices, whose decisions could have a significant impact on the outcome.

A rivalry doesn't necessarily need villains, but they sure help. Don Drysdale, Steve Garvey, and Manny Ramirez could get the blood of Giants fans boiling just by walking onto the field. Juan Marichal, John Montefusco, and Barry Bonds needed to only have their names announced during starting lineups to spark an unkind reaction from Dodgers fans. The Giants' Bumgarner is starting to move into villain territory with a trigger temper that surfaces whenever a batter breaks baseball etiquette rules. He has not reached the level of infamy among Dodgers fans as the above-mentioned Giants trio, but he's working at it. Giants fans will boo anything blue, but the needle on the emotion meter especially starts jumping whenever Puig comes into the picture. It's not just his dustups with Bumgarner that rile them, but his whole body of work, which Giants fans interpret as not respecting the game and overall showboating. Some Dodgers fans might have the same take, but nothing turns a hometown crowd around more than a sensational catch or a clutch hit, which Puig has demonstrated he can deliver. Whatever his flaws, Puig's explosive personality and potential to be a showstopper on the MLB stage make him a perfect fit for the rivalry. Thus, followers of the rivalry were filled with deep concern when they learned that the Dodgers were considering dumping Puig if they could find the right deal at the August 1 trade deadline. Puig, hampered by bad hamstrings, and with minimal production (.260, 7 HR, 34 RBIs in 81 games) and behavioral baggage, was wearing out the patience of the brass. The Dodgers were unable to move Puig to another major league team, so they instead ticketed him for a demotion to the minors, and traded for Oakland slugging right fielder Josh Reddick to be his replacement.

Dodgers management didn't need a reminder that they should probably add to the rotation, but they got one anyway in the game before the trading deadline when recently acquired starting pitcher Bud Norris had to leave the game with a side injury after retiring one batter. Yet, the Dodgers made a deal that sounded like it was concocted by a late-night comedian—they traded for a starter who was injured. The A's Rich Hill, 36, who had Tommy John surgery in 2011, was 9–3 with a 2.25 ERA in 14 starts for the year but was out of action for the time being with a blister. The Dodgers added to their bullpen by acquiring Jesse Chavez, who has the durability to be a long reliever when needed.

Tom Hanks would have a tough time persuading Giants fans that there's no crying in baseball after they learned that the club had sent popular third baseman Duffy to Tampa Bay along with two well-regarded prospects for left-handed starting pitcher Matt Moore. Fans who followed the club closely might have seen it coming when the Giants acquired versatile infielder Eduardo Nunez from Minnesota several days earlier. Nunez brought decent offensive skills with him (.296, 12 HR, 27 stolen bases), but that didn't soften the blow. Duffy helped the championship team in 2014 in a utility role, finished second in NL Rookie of the Year voting in 2015, and won the annual team most-inspirational award, named after Willie McCovey. Duffy got off to a slow start in 2016, and a strained Achilles tendon put him on the disabled list, making him more vulnerable for the right deal. Hanks's character in *A League of Their Own* might as well have added "it's a business, not a game" as far as Giants fans were concerned as they bid a fond farewell.

The Giants hoped Moore, 27, would help dry fans' tears by bolstering the rotation. He allowed just one earned run in 6⅔ innings five days earlier against the Dodgers in his 10th consecutive start going at least six innings. San Francisco also added depth to the bullpen by acquiring left-hander Will Smith from Milwaukee. In another surprise move the next day, the Giants announced that starter Peavy would be sent to the bullpen, leaving a rotation of Bumgarner, Cueto, Samardzija, Moore, and Cain. The Dodgers, beset by all the injuries, did not have the luxury of setting out a fixed rotation. Just when the Dodgers might conclude that at least the injury situation couldn't get any worse, they had to add relievers Liberatore (left elbow) and Louis Coleman (shoulder) to the disabled list on August 3. The Dodgers gave up three good prospects to acquire Reddick and Hill, and the Giants raided their farm system for their top prospect in 21-year-old right-hander Phil Bickford to get Smith. But for Giants and Dodgers management— and the fans as well—the future was all about the next two months with the NL West title as the prize.

LEAD VANISHES (2016)

"Can't anybody here play this game?" Mets manager Casey Stengel asked the famous question during the inaugural 1962 season of his expansion New York Mets on the way to a 120-loss season. No one overheard Bochy or Roberts saying the same thing about their clubs, but both had to be frustrated as their stumbling teams posted matching 1–3 records following the trade deadline. The Giants, hoping the additions and the roster shake-up they necessitated might stop their slide, couldn't put together a winning streak of two. The Dodgers, seeing that the Giants were on the ropes, were wasting a chance to deliver the blows that would allow them to catch and pass the Giants.

As the teams began play August 9, the Giants had been in sole possession of first place for 85 days and were clinging to a one-game lead. The Giants, playing in Miami, fell behind 2–0 in the first inning as new acquisition Moore allowed a broken-bat, line-drive RBI double to Giancarlo Stanton and a run-scoring groundout by Marcell Ozuna. Moore kept the Marlins quiet through six innings, but the offensive-challenged Giants fell 2–0 to starter Tom Koehler and the Miami bullpen. The Giants game ended just as Maeda was taking the hill in Los Angeles against Philadelphia. Maeda wasn't sharp, but the Dodgers lineup stuck a dagger into the Phillies pitching early, scoring four in the second, and two each in the third and fourth on their way to a 13-hit, 9–3 victory. Back in Miami, any Giants following the game now knew that the solo lead they had held since May 15 was gone as the clubs sat together atop the NL West at 64–49. Since the All-Star break, the Dodgers were 13–9 and the Giants 7–16. The offensive numbers told the story of that stretch: The Dodgers scored 122 runs and hit 32 homers in 22 games; the Giants scored 80 runs and hit 19 homers in 23 games. Adding to the Giants' frustration was that they lost the lead while the injured Kershaw was on the sidelines. The adventures of the Giants' three top starters also helped explain the plunge. Bumgarner had been winless since the break despite three strong outings as the Giants continue to fail to give him any support. Cueto also had been winless, with an ERA of 5.02 in five starts since the break. Samardzija, after getting off to a decent year, had now lost six of his last seven starts and given up 21 homers. Giants pitchers had allowed a league-leading 35 homers since the All-Star break.

The next 11 games on the clubs' schedules seemed more like a version of *How the West Was Lost* than *How the West Was Won* as the Dodgers struggled to a 5–6 record, while the Giants continued their fall with a 4–7 mark. The Dodgers' rotation chaos hit bottom in back-to-back games August 13–14, as the two starters recorded a cumulative eight outs and eight runs, requiring Roberts to use six relievers on successive days to cover 15⅓ innings requiring 318 pitches. McCarthy lasted 1⅔ innings before leaving with right hip tightness, and Anderson was removed because of a sprained wrist after one inning. Yet, the Dodgers demonstrated the kind of fortitude that had kept them in the hunt despite the pitching turmoil as they won the August 13 game with a one-run bullpen performance and a 17-hit attack that produced an 8–4 victory over Pittsburgh. The Dodgers lost two of three to the Pirates, but took two of three from Philadelphia August 16–18, while the Giants were dropping two of three to Baltimore August 12–14 and getting swept by Pittsburgh August 15–17. On August

16, Utley celebrated his return to Philadelphia with a grand slam and solo homer as the Dodgers rolled to a 15–5 rout that put them alone in first place. The Dodgers split a four-game series against Cincinnati, winning the last two. The Giants split a series against the New York Mets, losing the last two. The results left the Dodgers with a one-game lead as the teams got ready to meet for three-game set August 23–25 in Los Angeles.

A baseball cliché says that momentum only goes as far as the next day's starting pitchers, so the Giants could brush aside the last two games knowing that Bumgarner would open against the Dodgers' Maeda. Still, it was hard to ignore the fact that the Dodgers were coming off a 21-hit outburst in an 18–9 win over the Reds, while the Giants were coming off a shutout against the Mets in which they produced only three hits. The Dodgers slugged seven home runs off the Reds, four coming in one inning. The Giants had five home runs in their last seven games, including one by Bumgarner. While the series would be significant because of the fight for first, there was a secondary competition that could eventually be the key to deciding who wins the West. A tie for first at the end of the regular season would force a one-game playoff to be hosted by the team with the best record in head-to-head games. With nine games remaining between the clubs, it was advantage Giants, as they held a 6–4 edge over the Dodgers so far in 2016. Still, while it was a big series, it wasn't a do-or-die series. In fact, if the season ended now, both teams would be in postseason play. The Giants, like in 2014, would again have the greater challenge in having to survive the wild-card game, but they would at least have a shot. As the clubs entered the series, the Giants held a 1½ game lead over St. Louis and a three-game lead over Miami in the wild-card race. The series was probably more important psychologically as well as practically for the Giants, who needed to end their post–All-Star break slide, which was now at 11–23.

Suppose Bobby Thomson's historic three-run blast landed in the glove of left fielder Andy Pafko at the wall instead of in the grandstands at the Polo Grounds in the 1951 playoff? It was a moment of clearly less significance, but a bid for a dramatic three-run homer against the Dodgers by the Giants' Crawford showed how a few feet could make the difference between glory and gloom.

The three-game series in Los Angeles began with the Dodgers' middle of the order roughing up Bumgarner, as Seager, Turner, and Gonzalez went seven for seven with a walk and a sacrifice fly against him. Even worse, Bumgarner served up a solo home run to rookie Rob Segedin in the second and eventually allowed five runs and nine hits in five innings while losing his fourth straight decision to the Dodgers. The Giants kept themselves in the game against Dodgers starter Maeda despite the shelling of their ace and trailed by just 5–4 going into the last of the fifth. It was now a game of bullpens, and it was all Dodgers. The Dodgers jumped on reliever Gearrin for two quick runs in the fifth for a 7–4 lead, and rookie Andrew Toles drilled a two-run homer off Lopez in the eighth. Meanwhile, three Dodgers relievers held the Giants to a ninth-inning meaningless solo homer by Span for a 9–5 win. The Giants had to view this series as a way to reignite the fire of their first half, but a play in the fourth doused those hopes. Panik, who was on first, and Nunez, who was on second with one out, were running with the pitch while Bumgarner was batting. The apparent hit-and-run play turned into a disaster as Bumgarner didn't swing and Nunez was gunned down at third by catcher Yasmani Grandal. Bumgarner never got the sign, and Bochy labeled the fiasco as "miscommunication."

Game two marked the Dodger debut of trade acquisition Hill, and the club was desperate for him to deliver after adding their 26th and 27th names to the disabled list the previous day in starters Kazmir and Anderson. Cueto and Hill matched zeroes early, until Turner got the first Dodgers hit with a 387-foot shot into the left-field seats in the fourth for a 1–0 lead. It was the only run allowed by Cueto in his 94-pitch, six-inning performance. Hill, apparently recovered from his blister problems, also went six while throwing 81 pitches. He baffled the Giants hitters with a curve that might have looked like a Dodger Stadium beach ball when it left his hand, only to turn into a diving super ball by the time it reached the plate. The Giants got their one chance in the eighth against reliever Blanton as a walk to Pagan and single by Pence put runners on first and third with two outs. Roberts stuck with Blanton instead of bringing in another southpaw to face the left-handed Crawford, and the decision almost blew up. Crawford drove a pitch off the bat that had Giants fans in the stands and players in the Giants' dugout believing the ball would clear the wall, but right fielder Reddick pulled it down at the warning track. The Dodgers made the Turner homer stand up for a 1–0 win, and the Giants now faced the prospects of a sweep as well as being pushed four games down.

"The Hoosier Thunderbolt" was the first Giants pitcher to throw a no-hitter against their rivals from Brooklyn, coming at a time when the pitching distance to home plate was just 50 feet. The right-handed, 6-foot-1, 200-pound Amos Rusie, named to the Hall of Fame by the Veteran's Committee in 1977, possessed a fastball that was one of the most powerful and feared of the era, reportedly reaching into the upper 90s. He further terrified batters because he was one of the wildest pitchers in the game and was partly responsible for baseball officials extending the pitching distance in 1893 to its present 60 feet 6 inches to improve safety. Rusie threw his 6–0 no-hitter July 31, 1891, against the then-Bridegrooms, just 53 days after Tom Lovett beat him 4–1 while tossing the first-ever Brooklyn no-hitter over the Giants. Rusie's gem shouldn't have been unexpected. In 1891, he went 33–20 with a 2.55 ERA and struck out 337 while throwing 500 innings and 52 complete games. The Bridegrooms also were a vulnerable team, posting just a 61–76 record that year.

The Giants weren't looking for trading deadline pickup Matt Moore to do an Amos Rusie impression—six solid innings would probably work, and hopefully the bullpen could make one of today's "quality starts" stand up. Moore's new teammates gave him something to work with, as RBI singles by Belt and Span and a two-run homer by Panik put the Giants in front 4–0 against Stripling after six innings while the Dodgers searched for their first hit. Moore kept rolling, and standout catches by center fielder Span in the second and on a leadoff liner in the ninth had helped keep the no-hitter alive with just two outs left. Howie Kendrick grounded out to third, putting only Seager between Moore and Giants-Dodgers history.

The Dodgers rookie hit a weak blooper to short right field, but right-fielder Gorkys Hernandez never had a chance as the ball fell in front of him for the first hit. Moore, after 133 pitches, was replaced by Casilla, who wrapped up the 4–0 victory on a one-pitch out as Turner popped out. The Dodgers should have been able to walk away from the ballpark satisfied that they had at least won the series and extended the lead over the Giants to two games. But a front office decision to deal away clubhouse leader A.J. Ellis for another catcher, Philadelphia's Carlos Ruiz, stunned the players. Ellis had been Kershaw's personal catcher, and the Dodgers ace admitted he shed tears when he heard the news. The trade was all about offense, as the management wanted more output than the .194, one-homer, 13-RBI numbers they were getting from Ellis. Ruiz was batting .261 with three homers and 12 RBIs in 48 games and was hitting .340 since the All-Star break. Still, it was a curious move in that the chemistry concerns that had plagued the Dodgers in recent seasons had seemed to ease. Now, at least for moment, the club had to face another clubhouse sideshow with 35 games to go.

DODGERS IN CHARGE (2016)

Was this race for the NL West crown suddenly turning into a runaway? In just two weeks, the Dodgers had extended their lead by five games, and Giants fans found themselves starting to follow the wild-card standings as a means for their club to reach the postseason. The contests played by the Giants and Dodgers against the Chicago Cubs during this 12-game stretch from August 26 to September 7 provided some significant insight into the status of the teams. The Cubs were considered the best team in baseball by just about everyone, and the road to the World Series appeared likely to run through Wrigley Field, making the Chicago club a barometer for opponents to measure themselves against. The Dodgers eked out two one-run victories, 3–2 and 1–0, as the bullpen allowed just one run in seven innings to help the team win two of three against the Cubs. The Giants dropped three out of four to Chicago, while managing just 10 runs and 14 hits. The Cubs bullpen gave up just three hits and no runs in 16 innings during the four games, while Casilla recorded his seventh blown save of the year in a shattering Giants defeat. The Giants played the Cubs tough as all four games were decided by one run, but in the end, the Dodgers gained a game-and-a-half over the Giants in the clubs' respective series against Chicago.

Los Angeles closed out the 12-game period with five consecutive wins. The Dodgers' chaotic, injury-battered rotation seemed to have put them at a disadvantage over the mostly steady Giants starting staff, but that was not the case during this time. The Dodgers used seven different starters who allowed 24 runs in 63 innings, to the Giants' five different starters who gave up 30 runs in 65 innings. The Giants' starters went seven innings four times but lasted fewer than five innings four times. The Dodgers' rotation had a longest start of 6⅓ innings, but only one starter didn't go at least five innings.

The period produced the most stirring Dodgers' win of the year when they scored eight runs in the last two innings against Colorado, winning it in the ninth 10–8 on a walk-off grand slam by Toles. It also featured a five home-run barrage against Arizona's Greinke in a 10–2 rout and the return of Puig from the minor leagues. Puig helped the Dodgers to wins September 4 against San Diego with a three-run homer and September 7 against Arizona with a homer and two RBIs. But the biggest story in Los Angeles, even more so than the five-game lead, was the scheduled return of Kershaw, who was slotted to pitch September 9 against Miami.

A healthy Kershaw to help protect the Dodgers' lead was another reason for the Giants fans' interest in the wild-card route, as the club held a half-game lead over St. Louis and New York on September 7. The Giants had hoped that the club would magically click into a September pennant-drive mode, but Bochy's flying carpet remained grounded. The Giants were 2–5 in September, and their post–All-Star break record was now at 17–32. How bad is that? The Giants of 1985 lost 100 games. In that club's 49 games after the break, they were 21–28. The Giants once had such a comfortable lead that the major story at the time in San Francisco was a frivolous one—whether the powerful Bumgarner should be allowed to participate in the All-Star Game home-run derby. The frivolity was now long gone, as the club had only 23 games left to chase down the Dodgers or at the least cling to survival by grabbing a wild-card spot.

It was now a 10-game countdown to the long-anticipated September 19–21 matchup of the clubs in Los Angeles. The Giants got off to a roaring start by sweeping the Diamondbacks September 9–11 in Arizona. The long dormant Giants offense came to life as they produced 23 runs and 39 hits. Pence, who needed a breakout September if the Giants were to reach the postseason, went 8 for 11, with a homer, three doubles, four walks, eight runs, and a highlight reel–worthy diving catch in a 7–6 win in the opener of the series. Meanwhile, the Marlins required the Dodgers to be near perfect just to win one game as they took two out of three in Miami. The opener featured the return of Kershaw, who left trailing 2–0 after throwing 66 pitches in three innings. Miami went on to win that game 4–1 and took the series with a 3–0 victory in game three. Hill threw seven perfect innings in game two, and though his pitch count was at only 89, Roberts pulled him out because of concern about further blister problems. The Marlins broke up the perfect game in the eighth, but the Dodgers got the 5–0 win. The two series put the Giants within three games of the Dodgers, but San Francisco's sudden hopes of closing the gap even more turned to frustration. The Giants were swept in a three-game series September 12–14 in San Diego in which they scored just five runs and batted .216 (21 for 97). The Giants jumped on St. Louis for victories in the first two of a September 15–18 four-game series in San Francisco, and were on the verge of sending the wild-card contenders four games behind them when the bullpen imploded in the 9th as Romo and Casilla turned a 2–1 lead into a 3–2 defeat. The revitalized Cardinals, having ended a seven-game losing streak, shut down the Giants the next day 3–0. Meanwhile, the Dodgers took two out of three against the Yankees September 12–14 in New York. Kershaw demonstrated not only his pitching skills but his toughness and leadership in a 2–0 victory in game three as he sat through two rain delays to pitch five shutout innings. The Dodgers split a four-game series September 15–18 at Arizona, and on the eve of the Giants-Dodgers series, Los Angeles still held on to the five-game lead.

The frustration was building at the usually happy Giants ballpark, and in a rare break in fan loyalty, struggling closer Casilla was loudly booed when he failed in the ninth-inning loss to St. Louis. Fans had hoped that the club would propel itself into a neck and neck race with the Dodgers during the 10-day countdown, but as the clubs prepared to meet, the Giants still sat at the launch pad wondering why they still couldn't get lift-off in the second half of the season. Even one of the two wild-card berths was now in jeopardy. The Mets (80–69) led the Giants (79–70) by a game, with the Cardinals (78–71) right on their heels.

Robert De Niro, in his role as the desperate, unbalanced Travis Bickle in the 1976 movie *Taxi Driver*, performed one of film history's most memorable scenes when he stared into a mirror while repeating three times, "You talkin' to me?" and adding, "Then who the hell else are you talkin' to?" A sequel to the scene played itself out when Bumgarner became engaged in yet another stare-down with Puig in the opener of the September 19–21 series against the Dodgers.

The Giants took a 1–0 lead in the third on a Nunez one-man highlight show, beginning with an infield single against Kershaw. Nunez then dove into second for a stolen base, dove into third after a bad throw by catcher Grandal and dove into home to score on a wild pitch. The Bumgarner-Kershaw duel continued through six, when Roberts pulled his starter in the interest of easing his injury comeback. Bumgarner continued on and appeared in control in the seventh, when he suddenly lost all control. Puig, whose second-inning double was the only Dodgers hit, bounced a chopper to the right side. Bumgarner dashed over to make the pickup and toss the ball to Belt for the out. The eyes of Puig and Bumgarner locked on to each other, and Bumgarner warned "Don't look at me," while Puig demanded "What are you going to do to me?" The dugouts and bullpens emptied again, and while no punches were thrown, the intensity and jostling of bodies in the mass meeting at first base created the potential for actual battle. Bumgarner had thrown seven innings of one-hit ball with 10 strikeouts, but now his night was over. Bochy never made it clear why he removed Bumgarner after the fracas, since the pitch count of 97 wasn't enough to pull his ace in the club's biggest game of the season. Bumgarner's departure left the outcome up to an inconsistent Giants bullpen, and the result was a disaster for San Francisco. Pinch-hitter Toles singled off Derek Law, Seager singled off Lopez, and Turner singled off Strickland to tie it at 1–1. Gonzalez then followed with a drive to deep right for a game-ending double as the Giants recorded their 30th blown save of the season.

Cueto blanked the Dodgers for 5⅓ innings the next night before having to leave with a strained left groin, but three relievers kept the shutout intact in a 2–0 victory. Solo homers by Nunez and Belt accounted for the Giants' runs, but the injury to Cueto and a dislocated left pinkie suffered by Crawford offset any Giants celebration.

Game three was over in a hurry. Puig rocked Moore for a three-run homer in the first, and the Dodgers built an 8–2 lead after three, a seemingly insurmountable obstacle for the Giants' quiet offense to overcome. The eventual 9–3 victory put the Dodgers six games up on the Giants and reduced their magic number to clinch the division to five. The Giants arrived in Los Angeles with hopes of a sweep and a run for the NL West crown. That seemed like a possibility until Bumgarner's game-changing Travis Bickle moment. The team was still in the wild-card hunt, but the division was now little more than a dream. The Dodgers had not only stared the Giants down but mocked them and their ace as well by wearing T-shirts that said, "Don't Look at Me."

MR. SCULLY (2016)

Is there a "Big Dodger" in the sky? Tommy Lasorda thinks so, and that may be all the proof Los Angeles fans require. Lasorda made the revelation with his famous quote, "I bleed Dodger blue, and when I die, I'm going to the Big Dodger in the Sky." If there were any baseball atheists holding out for more concrete evidence that such a deity existed, their moment was about to come.

Vin Scully, 88, would be broadcasting his final Dodgers home game on Sunday, September 25, ending his 67-year career as the voice of the club. The Dodgers would celebrate Scully during the four-game September 22–25 series against Colorado, with giveaways, fireworks, and a pregame ceremony Friday. The Dodgers, playing with confidence after dispatching the Giants, roared to wins of 7–4, 5–2, and 14–1 in the first three games against the Rockies. Kershaw continued his comeback with a seven-inning scoreless performance on 91 pitches in the 14–1 rout. The Giants, playing a concurrent four-game series at San Diego, won two of their first three games, but the Dodgers' magic number to clinch the West had fallen to one heading into Sunday. Dodgers players continued the salute to Scully, as each batter in the starting lineup tipped his cap toward the broadcast booth. An old-fashioned movie script that might have been written before the game would have Scully calling a Dodgers-clinching victory, but that appeared unlikely as Colorado led 3–2 in the ninth. The youngster Seager is far from old-fashioned, yet he grabbed the sentimental role with gusto with a solo home run off Adam Ottavino to tie it at 3–3. Utility man Culberson, an understudy in the drama, then unleashed a game-winning homer in the 10th off Boone Logan. The blast came just moments before the Giants fell to San Diego, allowing the Dodgers to win the West with a victory rather than a Giants loss. The celebrating Dodgers players recognized the historic significance of the moment and turned to pay a final Dodger Stadium salute to Scully, whose last call at home was a division-clinching home run. There could be no other interpretation: the Big Dodger in the sky had pulled up a chair in the heavens above Chavez Ravine, and made believers of everyone.

The struggling Giants remained in the wild-card hunt, a game behind the Mets and a half-game behind the Cardinals, but nothing that happened during the weekend split against the Padres gave San Francisco fans much hope. After scoring three runs in the third in the Sunday loss, the Giants went down quietly in the last six innings in contrast to the stadium-rocking events down South. The Giants (82–74) were now 25–41 since the All-Star break and barring a sudden turnaround, seemed to almost certainly need the Cardinals or Mets to stumble in the final week.

San Francisco performed like it did in those good old pre–All-Star days in the opener of a September 27–29 series against Colorado. The offense featured 19 hits and homers by Posey, Pence, and Conor Gillaspie, and Moore struck out 11 while allowing just one run in 7⅔ innings in a 12–3 romp. Game Two mirrored the second-half frustration as the Giants wasted a strong effort by Samardzija (6 innings, 2 runs) and the bullpen, collecting only five singles in a 2–0 loss. Cueto came to the rescue in the final game of the series, holding the Rockies to two runs in seven innings while striking out 11 for a 7–2 win. The two wins against Colorado were enough to keep the Giants (84–75) second in the wild-card standings, with the Mets (85–74) on top and the Cardinals (83–76) in third. The Mets would play the Phillies and the Cardinals would play the Pirates on the final weekend. For the Giants, the road to the wild card would have to go through the NL West champs.

So far, so good for Dave Roberts. The Dodgers skipper was already being suggested for manager-of-the-year honors. He became the first Dodgers rookie manager to win a division title since Lasorda. His club had survived the placement of 32 players on the disabled list and an injury-racked rotation that had been unsettled all season. The Giants' collapse had helped the Dodgers get back into the race, but Roberts deserved credit for guiding them in the comeback. Roberts's was a feel-good story, but Dodgers management and fans weren't really going to feel good until the club's World Series championship drought was over. The Dodgers still had six games to go in the regular season, and the first postseason game—against Washington—was still 11 days away, but Roberts knew that the postseason had already started for him. The Dodgers still had a chance to catch the Nationals for home-field advantage in the division series, but Roberts also had to balance that quest with getting his pitching in line, juggling the need to keep regulars rested and sharp, and not allowing the team to lose its winning edge. Those challengers were evident as the Dodgers dropped two out of three to San Diego September 27–29, leaving the club two games behind the Nationals with three to play. Adding to the pressure was that the final three games were against the desperate Giants, who might not be able to afford even one weekend loss. Roberts did not back off, going with his big three starters in Hill, Kershaw, and Maeda. The spoiler role had been a big part of the rivalry over the years, but neither Roberts nor his stars had publicly announced that their mission this weekend was to eliminate the Giants from the postseason. Still, there was something quite valid to a strategy that would focus on knocking the rivals out now rather than possibly have to contend with them in a championship series.

The Giants arrived fired up for the September 30–October 2 series, which was unfortunate for both the Dodgers and two spectators in blue shirts who ran onto the field in the fourth inning. One of the trespassers got too close to Giants left fielder Pagan, who body slammed him and then held his victim down until security took over. Two innings later, the Giants scored a team knockout of the Dodgers with a seven-run sixth in a 9–3 win. The normally reserved Gillaspie and the temperamental Bumgarner gestured triumphantly when they reached second base with two-run doubles in the inning, but their gyrations were more of an expression of emotion after the frustrating second-half than attempts to show up their rivals. Belt capped the frame with a three-run homer. Bumgarner appeared to be on his best behavior as he limited the Dodgers to three runs in 7 ⅓ innings without making eye contact.

Bochy played a hunch in Saturday's game by starting rookie Ty Blach, comforted with the fact that the bullpen was well rested should he falter early. As it turned out, the bullpen, save for a ninth-inning appearance by Romo, could have spent the afternoon hanging out on the AT&T Park arcade checking out the boats in McCovey Cove. Blach blanked the Dodgers over eight innings, allowing three hits while throwing 99 pitches. He lowered his ERA to 1.06 and raised his batting average to .500 by delivering two base hits off Kershaw. Pagan's homer gave Blach a 1–0 lead in the fifth, and a throwing error by third baseman Turner helped the Giants build a three-run cushion in the seventh, which stood for a 3–0 victory. The win assured the Giants of a possible tiebreaker game, while ending the Dodgers' bid for home-field advantage. The Giants kept the pedal to the metal the next day, jumping on Maeda for a 5–0 lead after two innings on the way to a 7–1 victory, a series sweep and a wild-card date with the Mets on October 5. Moore continued the streak of solid outings by starters, holding the Dodgers to one run in eight innings.

The Giants joined in the farewell to Scully with a classy tribute in the seventh, serenading him with "Take Me Out to the Ballgame," while fans waved "Thanks Vin" signs. For a touching moment, Giants vs. Dodgers took a back seat to an expression of admiration and appreciation for a broadcast legend whose work will live on as a soundtrack to the rivalry.

CURSED BY THE CUBS (2016)

In the end, the Dodgers and Giants were no match for the Cubs. Chicago finished the season in first with a 98–56 record. The Dodgers (87–67) set-tled for third place, 11 games behind, and the Giants (78–74) were fifth, trailing the Cubs by 19 games. The Cubs dominated the Dodgers in head-to-head play, winning 14 of 22 contests between the clubs. The Giants split with the Cubs at 11–11, but Chicago won 11 of the teams' last 17 meet-ings. Such was the story of the Chicago, Brooklyn, and New York clubs in the 1945 National League season.

The Cubs put themselves into a position that year to win their first World Series since 1908 as they took a 2–1 game lead over the Detroit Tigers. That's where the story gets a little complicated. Billy Sianis, owner of the Billy Goat Tavern, wanted to take his pet goat to Game Four at Wrigley Field, and they say he even bought a ticket for his companion. But the goat's odor was deemed too overwhelming, so the Cubs denied it admission. Sianis was so upset that he vowed the Cubs would never win a World Series. Detroit went on to win three of the next four games to capture the World Series, outscoring suddenly struggling Chicago by 29–17. Entering the 2016 season, the Cubs hadn't won a pennant since then. Poor management and poor performance on the field might have had something to do with the non-title drought, but Cub fans could never ignore the possibility that the team was indeed doomed by the Curse of the Billy Goat.

Reaching the World Series had become far more taxing since 1945. Then, you beat out seven other teams in the regular 154-game season and you were in the World Series, which would conclude by mid-October. Today, it's possible for a wild-card team to cap the 162-game schedule by playing three teams and up to 13 games to reach the Series, which doesn't play its seventh game until early November. That has made the postseason a grinding test of endurance and put much emphasis on depth and reliability in the rotation and the bullpen.

The Giants pretty much had the rotation part in their favor, as Bumgarner did what most thought he would do, blanking the New York Mets 3–0 in the wild-card game. Utility man Gillaspie, who was starting only because regular third baseman Nunez was injured, provided the offense with a three-run homer off Mets closer Jeurys Familia. The victory meant the Giants would play the Cubs in the NL division series while the Dodgers would play the Washington Nationals. The Giants and Dodgers were just a series win away from a date in the NLCS with the World Series berth at stake.

Such a scenario was building at AT&T Park on October 11. The Dodgers tied their series with the Nationals earlier at 2–2. The Giants, trailing 2–1 in their series, took what appeared to be a comfortable 5–2 lead into the ninth. Moore had contained the Cubs through eight innings and 120 pitches, leaving the Giants bullpen with the task of getting three outs and sending the series to Chicago for a deciding game. That would make October 13 one of the most dramatic days in rivalry history, as the clubs would play back-to-back with victories sending them to a championship series showdown. But five Giants relievers couldn't stop the ninth-inning Cubs offensive onslaught, and San Francisco's season ended in a stunning 6–5 defeat. The Dodgers, meanwhile, advanced to the NLCS against Chicago with a 4–3 win in Game Five against Washington.

Roger Kahn wrote a beautiful book, *The Boys of Summer*, about the Brooklyn Dodgers, which tracked the lives of the players from that era leading up to their 1955 World Series championship. It is doubtful that any writer will try a sequel, *The Boys of October*. Once again, the Dodgers were tripped up in the postseason—and in some ways tripped themselves up—as they fell to the Cubs in six games. The Dodgers showed life, blanking the Cubs in Games Two and Three for a 2–1 lead as Kershaw threw seven shutout innings and Hill followed with six. The Cubs then outscored the Dodgers 23–6 to win the next three games for their first pennant since 1945. The Dodgers' October baseball has been more tragic than magic for the team's fans, and this year the warts showed up again. The club made four errors and had two base runners thrown out in Game Four. Game Four and Five starters Urias and Maeda couldn't make it out of the fourth inning, and the bullpen allowed 13 runs in the two contests. The Dodgers tallied only two hits in their 5–0 loss in Chicago's Game Six clincher. Base runners were rare for the Dodgers against the spectacular Kyle Hendricks, but even when a Cubs error put Reddick on first, he promptly got picked off. A dropped fly ball in the first inning by left fielder Toles made things even worse for an ineffective Kershaw, who allowed five runs in five innings. The loss extended Kershaw's postseason frustration, but it is difficult to pin the team's elimination entirely on him since the Dodgers' bats gave him no support. In the NLDS, Kershaw started Game One and came back on three days' rest to start Game Four, with the Dodgers winning both. He got the save two days later as the Dodgers wrapped up the series.

The Giants and Dodgers of 2016 were flawed teams, but they weren't pushovers. Baseball experts could point to the Giants' major league–high 30 blown saves and lack of timely hitting and to the Dodgers injury-depleted rotation as contributing to both clubs' eliminations by the Cubs. On the other hand, experts of the supernatural could surmise that it was the desire to overcome the curse that motivated the Cubs and made them such a tough and determined team. Maybe the only way the Giants and Dodgers would have had a chance against the Cubs was if those ticket takers had just let that darn goat into Wrigley 71 years ago. Giants and Dodgers fans still looking for solace could also accept the fact that after watching Chicago's dramatic seven-game World Series victory over the Cleveland

Indians, this much was clear—their clubs had simply been beaten by the champs.

—✕✕—

The 2017 and 2018 seasons will be milestone years for the Dodgers-Giants rivalry. The year 2017 marks the 60th anniversary of the final seasons in New York and Brooklyn, and the following year will bring celebrations of the 60th year of the clubs playing on the West Coast. The New York Giants led their head-to-head matchups against Brooklyn 722 to 671 from 1890 to 1957. The Dodgers have led the Giants since the move west by 529–510. That gives the Giants a 1,232 to 1,200 advantage for a 32-game all-time lead. That might sound like a comfortable margin for the Giants, but as is often said at some point during every season, there's still plenty of baseball to play. For fans of this great rivalry, that's good news.

Part Six

RIVALRY NOTEBOOK

10

CHANGING SIDES

*Maybe there should be a law: Once you wear Dodger Blue, you could not
wear Black and Orange, and vice-versa. It often seemed awkward or
downright wrong when players ended up as both a Dodger and Giant
at some point in their career. Yet, the changing of sides has been part of
the history of the rivalry. West Coast fans got their first taste of it with a
transaction involving infielder Daryl Spencer.*

SWITCH HITTER

Daryl Spencer was the first player in the California version of
the rivalry to change sides. Spencer started at shortstop for the
Giants in the 1958 opener where he hit the first West Coast
homer, and went on to have a solid season with 17 homers and 74 RBIs.
He had big roles for the Giants in two early routs of the Dodgers. He hit
two homers and drove in six runs in a 16–9 win May 13, 1958, and went
four for four with three RBIs in a 9–3 victory May 8, 1959. Spencer was
traded to the St. Louis Cardinals on December 15, 1959, but he wasn't
through with the rivalry. The Dodgers acquired Spencer on May 30, 1961,
and four days later, he beat his old team. Spencer broke a 3–3 tie with a
game-winning home run in the ninth off Juan Marichal at the Coliseum.

CORNFIELDS

The Dodgers celebrated the 50th anniversary of West Coast baseball on opening day of March 31, 2008, with a moving ceremony before their game with the Giants. As a medley from the Field of Dreams was played, 40 former Dodgers, many in uniform, walked out and took the positions where they once ruled. There was Koufax, Newcombe, Erskine, and Wills from the early years. There was Russell, Karros, Valenzuela, and Finley from the modern era. But it was how the ceremony started that brought the biggest lump to the throats of Dodgers fans. As 56,000 looked on, old No. 4, wearing a Brooklyn jersey, suddenly appeared as if he had just walked out of a cornfield from the movie and took his old position in center field. Applause broke out for one of the legendary Boys of Summer, Duke Snider.

For connoisseurs of the rivalry, order had now been restored. Snider belonged only in Dodger blue, whether it was the Brooklyn or Los Angeles version. On April 1, 1963, Los Angeles sold Snider to the expansion New York Mets. As disturbing as that was, a year later, Snider was wearing a San Francisco Giants uniform. Snider, a seven-time all-star with the Dodgers, compiling 389 home runs and 1,271 RBIs, spent his final year in baseball competing for the team he battled so hard to beat in his 16-year Dodgers career. Snider still had something left. On May 2, 1964, Snider drilled a two-run homer in the ninth inning to tie the score, and the Giants went on to win it in the 12th. The opponent: the Los Angeles Dodgers.

BREWHAHA

Reggie Smith could make the Giants miserable. He ruined the Giants home opener on April 15, 1977, blasting two-run homers in the first and third innings to pace a 7–1 victory. He had a domineering series against the Giants during the pennant race of 1978, going 10-for-19 with four homers and eight RBIs. He also could draw the worst out of Candlestick Park fans. A series against the first-place Giants in late May 1978 turned particularly ugly as 43,646 fans set a San Francisco night game attendance record. The confines were anything but friendly to the Dodgers, as the series was marred by confrontations between unruly fans and Los

Angeles players. Objects were thrown at Dodgers outfielders, prompting an announcement that the Giants would have to forfeit the game if the misbehavior continued. Smith, reacting to a fan who threw a beer can near him, tried to climb into the stands at the end of the game before security and teammates pushed him into the clubhouse entrance. Smith, responding the next day to questions about the ruckus, returned the fire. "Obviously, they can't handle a winner," he said of the fans, "but I don't think they're going to have to worry about that much longer."

In the third inning of a game on August 5, 1978, Smith was nearly struck with beer thrown from the stands while chasing a drive down the right field line, drawing an argument from Smith and manager Tommy Lasorda, who wanted fan interference called. In the winning clubhouse, Smith tried to find some humor in the incident. "At least the guy could have handed it down and I would have taken a drink. This is a vicious crowd here."

Smith's duels with the fans finally exploded on September 24, 1981, in San Francisco. In the sixth inning, Smith got into a shouting match with a heckler that escalated when the fan threw a batting helmet at him. Smith climbed into the stands, and police and security guards jumped into the fray, hauling away the offenders, while the umpires tossed out Smith. Dodgers coach Danny Ozark shrugged off the incident, saying, "Aren't these things kind of normal when the Giants and Dodgers play?"

Normal or not, the Giants blurred the rivalry in the offseason by signing Smith, who had become a free agent. The Giants, in the end, were desperate for sluggers, and hoped forgiving fans would shower the new Giant with applause instead of beer. Smith remained outspoken even in his new uniform. Asked about the differences in the teams over the recent years, Smith said, "Whenever the Dodgers play the Giants, we would say, 'We can beat these guys,' and we believed it. Fortunately, they did, too."

DIDN'T LEAVE HEART IN S.F.

The Giants got an early indication of Orel Hershiser's pitching skills on September 30, 1984, his first year in the rotation. Hershiser delivered a complete game, 7–2 victory, the first of many good performances against the Giants. Hershiser became a target of Candlestick Park hecklers during his 12 years with the Dodgers. While he had a couple of incidents involving inside pitches, the fans' behavior appeared to be based more on their frustration with his success than on any specific confrontation. The Dodgers and Hershiser cut ties after the 1994 season, with the pitcher heading to Cleveland. Giants fans were shocked in 1998 when it was announced that Hershiser was joining the club. The 39-year-old Hershiser, aware of his low approval ratings in San Francisco, tried making peace by saying of his desire to retire as a Giant, "That's my dream."

Hershiser won over some fans as he relied on the motivation of facing his former team to pitch the Giants to a 6–3 victory July 3. A crowd of 56,788, lured to the park for a postgame fireworks show as well as for the first Giants-Dodgers clash of the season, showed their appreciation with applause. Hershiser later acknowledged that the game had extra meaning, saying, "It was fun to win and the fact that it was the Dodgers made it a little more special."

The warm, fuzzy moment was short-lived. Hershiser became a free agent after the 1998 season and his dream quickly ended. Hershiser's heart was now with the New York Mets.

BOOS FOR BUTLER

The Giants' hopes for the 1988 season got a boost with the free-agent signing of center fielder Brett Butler, not only because he would fill the leadoff void in the lineup, but because he would arrive with a chip on his shoulder about the Dodgers. Butler, disappointed that the Dodgers and manager Tommy Lasorda didn't show enough interest in signing him, could hardly wait for opening day against Los Angeles. "I want to let Tommy know he made a mistake," Butler said. "I'll be pumped up."

Butler fulfilled expectations in the leadoff spot, hitting .287 with 43 stolen bases in 1988, .283 with 31 stolen bases in 1989, and .309 with 51 stolen bases in 1990. Butler's solid play and hustle made him a fan favorite. The relationship soured after the 1990 season as Butler got into a contract dispute with the Giants. Butler said he wanted to remain a Giant and insisted his contract demands were fair, but when the Giants didn't meet his numbers, he complained that he felt unwanted. This time, the Dodgers moved swiftly, and Butler would join Los Angeles.

A crowd of 55,883 jammed into Candlestick Park for the Giants 1991 home opener, and a good portion of them took the opportunity to bombard friend-turned-instant-enemy Brett Butler with boos. Afterward, Butler considered the rough reception from his former fans: "I might've been naïve enough to think I'd get a few cheers, but I should have known better wearing this uniform."

WASTED POTENTIAL

The Dodgers had high hopes when they landed free agent slugger Darryl Strawberry for the 1991 season, coming off a 37-homer, 108-RBI year with the New York Mets. Strawberry posted good numbers in 1991, but an ailing back limited his playing time to just 75 games in 1992 and 1993. The frustration over Strawberry's health peaked in early 1994, when he failed to report for an exhibition game on April 3, angering manager Tommy Lasorda and the Dodgers organization. The next day, Strawberry was placed on the disabled list for substance abuse and announced he would enter a drug rehabilitation program. Giants fans, who enjoyed serenading Strawberry with mocking chants of "Darryl," could barely hide their enjoyment at watching the Dodgers' high-profile free agent crash and burn. But Strawberry had not played his last Dodgers-Giants game. On July 25, Strawberry would be suited up in black and orange when the clubs met in San Francisco. Lasorda had ripped Strawberry for his absence at the exhibition game, and Strawberry said an incentive to joining the Giants was to give him a chance to beat the Dodgers. However, the hard feelings were put aside, as Lasorda hugged Strawberry before the game and expressed hope that his problems were behind him.

Even for his detractors, the Strawberry story would end more with sadness than satisfaction. Strawberry was suspended for 60 days by major league baseball for violating the drug policy and terms of his aftercare program, prompting the Giants to release him in February 1995. Strawberry, a one-time feared slugger with unlimited potential, would depart the Giants and the rivalry after only 92 at-bats, four homers, and a .239 average.

DUSTY

The Dodgers, looking for more production from their outfield, pulled off a five-player trade after the 1975 season to bring Dusty Baker to Los Angeles. Baker made his presence felt immediately, homering in his first at-bat in his Dodgers debut during opening day against the Giants at Candlestick Park. Baker was an offensive force, joining slugging teammates Steve Garvey, Reggie Smith, and Ron Cey to give the Dodgers one of their most powerful lineups.

In 1984, with the Giants facing a leadership gap after the loss of veterans Joe Morgan and Reggie Smith, they acquired Al Oliver, 37, Manny Trillo, 33, and the 34-year-old Baker. His departure from the Dodgers was bitter. Baker, a main cog in the Dodgers lineup for eight years, still felt he could contribute. The Dodgers, saying they wanted a younger outfield, tried to deal Baker to Oakland, but he used a contract clause to block the trade. The Dodgers put him on waivers in February, and the Giants signed him two days before the season. When the clubs met for the first time in 1984, it marked his first visit to Los Angeles since the team let him go. Baker was reluctant to be honored, but the fans greeted him warmly with chants of "Dusty, Dusty."

After one year with the Giants, Baker played two years with Oakland. He came back to the Giants as a coach from 1988 to 1992. In a surprising trio of moves in 1993, an ownership group was found that would keep the team in San Francisco, Barry Bonds was signed, and manager Roger Craig was replaced by Baker. While he had no managerial experience, the Giants banked on Baker's 19-year productive career as a hard-nosed competitor, his baseball know-how, and his reputation as a coach who worked well with players. Some thought the latter was the most significant attribute, since one of his first tasks would be to make sure that the strong egos of new teammates Will Clark and Bonds didn't clash. Baker dismissed the concerns, saying, "There's some envy and jealousy on all teams, especially great ones. People are anticipating something bad to happen even before it comes to pass."

Baker's final year with the Giants concluded with a World Series appearance in 2002, but the Giants didn't take much time to enjoy their accomplishments. One of the reasons was the uneasy relationship between club president Peter Magowan and Baker. Magowan said in spring training that the club was the best since the new ownership took over, which Baker appeared to interpret as putting him in a win-or-else pressure cooker. On November 6, 2002, the inevitable parting became official. Baker bowed out after 10 years at the helm with a record of 840–715 and three postseason appearances. He had the second most wins of Giants managers, topped only by the 2,583 victories of the legendary John McGraw. A week later, it was announced that a former Giant, Felipe Alou, would replace the former Dodger.

Despite the fallouts at the end of his time with each club, Dusty Baker had become a rarity in the rivalry—a great Dodger and a great Giant.

SOLITARY MAN

Giants management, in particular new general manager Brian Sabean, faced months of criticism for the November 13, 1996, trade that sent popular third baseman Matt Williams to the Cleveland Indians for second baseman Jeff Kent, shortstop Jose Vizcaino, and pitcher Julian Tavarez. Over the next six years, Kent would make Sabean look like a genius. Kent hit 175 homers, drove in 689 runs, and batted .297 from 1997 through 2002. He was the NL MVP in 2000. His offensive threat provided a second explosive bat in the lineup so opponents couldn't just worry about Barry Bonds. Most significantly, the Kent years included six straight winning seasons with four of them involving at least 90 wins, two division titles, and a World Series appearance.

The Giants spring training in their World Series year of 2002 got off to a disruptive start when Kent broke a bone in his wrist on March 1. The uncertainty over whether he would be ready for opening day was overtaken by Kent's initial explanation that he suffered the injury while washing his truck. Subsequent information that he actually hurt himself while riding his motorcycle appeared to hurt his relationship with management. Kent would demonstrate toughness in being ready to play in the first week of the season, but the incident would set the stage for Kent's eventual departure from the club.

By the end of the 2002 season, Kent's conflict with management over an altercation with Bonds and the lack of progress on a new contract signaled the end of his time in San Francisco. Kent signed with the Houston Astros on December 18, 2002. Kent made the Astros management look like geniuses, too, as he produced 49 homers and 200 RBIs with a .293 average in two years with Houston.

The Dodgers gave the rivalry a charge on December 15, 2004, when they signed Kent as a free agent. Kent's hard edge and his evaluation that the Giants were going in the wrong direction in 2005 turned many Giants fans against him. That was evident on opening day on April 5, 2005, as San Francisco fans greeted their former star with a boisterous round of boos before and during the game. In contrast, the love was still burning bright for Kent's former sparring partner. Bonds, sidelined indefinitely with knee problems, received a long, thunderous ovation when he came onto the field before the game to receive his 2004 MVP award.

Kent's four years with the Dodgers featured 75 homers, 311 RBIs, and a .291 average, but personal conflicts continued to follow him. He got into a verbal scrap with volatile teammate Milton Bradley in 2005 after Kent criticized him for lack of hustle. In 2007, Kent questioned the Dodgers' reliance on younger players, and manager Grady Little had to admit there was a problem with clubhouse cohesion.

Kent's comments since retiring have given the impression that his hyper-tense approach was part of a game-face strategy so he could focus on the job. He chose to play the game as a solitary man, priding himself on not having a lot of baseball friends. But a softer side showed when the Giants decided to honor him by placing his name on the revered Wall of

Fame at the Giants' ballpark on August 29, 2009. Kent was gracious and humble, and said if he made it to the Hall of Fame, he would enter as a Giant.

DODGERS PICK UP TAB

A lively division race was well under way on July 19, 2002, as the clubs met for a three-game series in Los Angeles. Arizona led the Dodgers by 1½ games, and the Giants were two out. San Francisco won two out of three, and had the Dodgers to thank for it. The teams entered the 12th inning of the opener tied 2–2, with Barry Bonds shelved in the 11th with a hamstring injury. With two outs and two on in the 12th, Bonds's replacement, Tom Goodwin, singled in the go-ahead run. The Dodgers won the second game, but the Giants came back to take the series on Goodwin's two-run game-deciding homer in the ninth. Goodwin's clutch contributions were especially sweet to the Giants because the Dodgers were still paying most of his $3.25 million salary since releasing him at the start of the season.

THIS BEER'S FOR YOU

Outfielder Marquis Grissom got a taste of the rivalry, literally, compliment of a Giants fan. Grissom had key moments in his time with both clubs. His homer April 10, 2003, helped the Giants to a 2–1 win in the clubs' first meeting of the season. Grissom stunned the Giants in a crucial game the previous September as a Dodger when he made an electrifying catch in deep center field to save a 7–6 Los Angeles win. Earlier in the 2002 season, as Grissom caught a drive by Jeff Kent at the center field wall, a fan showered him with a beer. The anti-Dodgers action, more reminiscent of spectators from the Giants' old rowdy ballpark than the more sedate PacBell crowd, was taken in stride by the smooth Grissom, who said, "It's a great rivalry when fans enjoy throwing beer at you."

THE OFFBEAT

While the West Coast rivalry is filled with headline-grabbing plays and games, there also are offbeat moments that have added to the color of Giants-Dodgers baseball.

TRICKERY

The hidden-ball trick appears to have become a lost art, but the Giants and Dodgers have both experimented with it at one another's expense. The Dodgers pulled one off May 8, 1994, though the Giants scored twice in the ninth for a 5–4 win to ease the embarrassment. The Dodgers got the rare out after a single by pitcher Salomon Torres. First baseman Eric Karros visited Orel Hershiser on the mound, and came back to the bag with the ball tucked away. When Torres took his lead, Karros tagged him out. The Giants got revenge seven weeks later. The Dodgers outlasted the Giants 7–4 on June 28 in a game featuring six home runs, but it was San Francisco payback that drew the attention. After Dodgers rookie Rafael Bournigal tripled, Giants third baseman Matt Williams went to the mound and pretended to give the ball to pitcher Dave Burba. Williams returned to third and tagged out Bournigal when he stepped off the base. The hidden-ball caper resurfaced on June 26, 1999. Todd Hundley's three-run homer in the ninth gave the Dodgers a 7–6 win, but the Giants fooled them again. In the fourth inning, Giants first baseman J. T. Snow kept the ball after Carlos Perez singled, and tagged out the Dodgers pitcher when he stepped off the base.

CLIMATE CHANGE

A meteorologist could not have illustrated the contrast in Candlestick Park-Southern California climate any better than what occurred at events at the two regions on July 15, 1960. In San Francisco, Willie McCovey hit a fly ball to Duke Snider in the second inning, and ended up safely at third base with a triple when the Dodgers outfielder lost the ball in the fog. Umpire Frank Dascoli, declaring the conditions unplayable, waived the teams off the field for what turned out to be a 24-minute delay before the fog cleared enough to play. Giants infielder Ed Bressoud, frustrated with the wintry weather, said later, "This is a joke. This is the worst park I ever played in." But while the Giants and Dodgers were trying to fend off frostbite, things weren't necessarily any better 400 miles away in scorching Los Angeles. About 100 people were overcome with heat while watching John F. Kennedy speak at the Coliseum after he won the Democratic presidential nomination in front of 50,000 supporters who sweltered in near-90 degree temperatures. Eventually, the Dodgers saw their way to a 5–3 victory.

HIS WAY

Baseball has always been a stage to Tommy Lasorda, so it was no surprise that he share it with the best when he made his managerial debut on opening day against the Giants in Los Angeles on April 7, 1977. Lasorda showed the crowd of 51,022 that his Dodgers would be entertaining, starting with the national anthem, as he enticed pal Frank Sinatra to perform. Ol' Blue Eyes was back, but of more concern to the Giants was that Don Sutton was back, as he picked up where he left off in 1976 with an opening day pitching gem in a 5–1 Dodgers win. The Giants had star power of their own for the home opener a week later against the Dodgers. The 40,008 fans gave a huge welcome-back ovation to Willie McCovey, who returned after a three-year absence. The applause was on par with that given to Sinatra, who showed no favorites by coming to San Francisco to toss out the ceremonial first pitch. The real celebrities of the day, however, would be Doug Rau, who limited the Giants to one run in seven innings in the 7–1 win, and Reggie Smith, who smacked two home runs and drove in four as the Dodgers did it Lasorda's way.

PERFECT MATCHUP

It took six years and a change of cities, but the Dodgers finally got a shot at paying back World Series perfect game pitcher Don Larsen in a 1962 contest that marked the first Giants' visit to Los Angeles's new park. Sandy Koufax struck out 10 while allowing just five hits in an 8–1 victory. The Giants saw things get out of hand in the eighth inning when Los Angeles sent 12 batters to the plate and scored five runs off Larsen. It was the former Yankee's first meeting with the Dodgers since he threw his masterpiece against Brooklyn in Game Five of the 1956 World Series. Larsen showed he still had enough left to frustrate the Dodgers, as he helped the Giants to a 5–4 win September 8, 1963, while Los Angeles was in the heat of a pennant race. Larsen pitched the final three innings for the win, giving up a solo homer to Wally Moon, but preserving the lead.

COSTLY FREE PASS

A Candlestick Park crowd of 41,051 enjoyed seeing a rare bit of strategy backfire on the Dodgers on September 21, 1969, as both teams battled for the flag. In the 10th inning, with the score tied 3–3, and two outs and none on, Dodgers manager Walter Alston ordered Willie McCovey walked intentionally. Reliever Pete Mikkelsen then unintentionally walked Bobby Bonds and Ken Henderson to load the bases, and Jim Davenport's grounder went between shortstop Maury Wills's legs for a game-ending error. Alston later explained his walking of McCovey, who had already gone four for four and was on his way to a 45-homer, 126-RBI season: "With a low-ball pitcher, a low-ball hitter, and the wind blowing to right field, I'm not going to get beat by one swing of the bat."

WALKMAN

After Barry Bonds belted 164 home runs in three years, the Dodgers should have had enough evidence entering the 2004 season that throwing him strikes was not a good business plan.

Yet, the Dodgers stuck to their stubborn strategy as they played their first series against the Giants April 16–18 in San Francisco. The Dodgers swept the series, but learned a lesson. Bonds homered in the first two games, and in the third game, he went four for four with five RBIs and two more home runs. Even in a losing effort, it was a dominating performance that would affect how manager Jim Tracy pitched to Bonds in key situations throughout the year.

When the clubs next met on April 23, Bonds was hitting .500 with nine homers and 20 RBIs. The Dodgers responded by walking him intentionally four times, and it paid off in a 5–4 Los Angeles victory in 12 innings. On June 29, the Dodgers walked Bonds four times, two intentionally in a 2–1 victory. The Dodgers momentarily slipped back to old habits when they pitched to Bonds in the opener of a late September series with the division and wild card up for grabs. Bonds made them pay with a homer to help the Giants take an early lead, though the Dodgers rallied for a win. The next day, Bonds walked five times. In the third game of the series, the Dodgers pitched to Bonds after walking him seven straight times. Bonds answered with a homer.

The Giants fell short of postseason play in 2004 because they lacked another powerful bat to at least make the opposition consider pitching to Bonds in certain situations. The Dodgers exposed that weakness in the crucial games down the stretch when they in effect removed Bonds from the game. In the last six games between the clubs, Bonds had only 10 official bats, three hits, and two RBIs, and he was walked 14 times.

BOOSTERS CLUBBED

The Dodgers entered the last month of the 1968 season hoping to avoid a 10th-place finish. The Dodgers were 27 games out of first. The New York Mets were 25 games back and Houston was down 23 games. If ever a club needed its boosters, this was it. But that wasn't going to happen at Candlestick Park. The Dodgers Booster Club claimed mistreatment from the Giants at a September 1 game between the teams, saying that Candlestick Park security harassed them by not letting the group unfurl its banner, and by ordering them not to stand during the visitor's seventh-inning stretch.

PILLOW FIGHTS

The clubs had seat cushions available for the comfort of the fans, never expecting that they would be used as weapons.

A Candlestick Park crowd got out of control after a disputed call during a 4–3 Giants victory over the Dodgers on June 26, 1964. Jim Ray Hart was called out at second on a close force play to end the eighth inning, following another controversial ruling favorable to the Dodgers in the top of the eighth. Fans responded by tossing cushions onto the field and one spectator jumped out of the stands, delaying the start of the ninth inning by five minutes.

Some Dodgers fans might have arrived in a foul mood for a May 25, 1971, game against the Giants because their club was already trailing San Francisco by nine games. The crowd's displeasure was temporarily put aside as the Dodgers honored the 20th anniversary of Willie Mays's major league debut. Mays received a warm ovation, but the good will disintegrated by the end of the game. A wine bottle was thrown near Bobby Bonds, a smoke bomb was tossed into center field, a fan rushed onto the field and, of course, spectators threw cushions. Adding to the fan frustration: Juan Marichal, bombarded with boos throughout the game, responded with a seven-hitter and slugged a three-run homer.

ORIGINAL MILKMAN

A June 11, 1966, matchup between the teams at Candlestick Park wasn't billed as a doubleheader, though there were two distinct competitions. The Giants appeared in control as Bob Bolin took a 2–0 lead into the seventh, only to see the Dodgers tie it with a pair and then win it in the ninth with the help of Lou Johnson's squeeze bunt. The Giants did earn somewhat of a split as Jim Davenport squeezed his way past Jim Brewer in the pregame cow-milking contest behind home plate to celebrate the dairy industry. Davenport's triumph made him the original Giants milkman. Melky Cabrera would be granted that title with much fanfare and publicity during his short stay with the Giants in 2012, as most apparently forgot how Davenport delivered against the Dodgers 46 years earlier.

INSIDE JOB

Johnnie LeMaster, a 21-year-old Giants infielder just up from the minors, had one of the most remarkable debuts in the rivalry on September 2, 1975. LeMaster, in his first major league at-bat, lined a pitch to center field that bounced over John Hale's head and rolled to the fence. LeMaster sped around the bases for an inside the park home run as the Giants went on to a 7–3 win.

PITCH AROUND HIM

They walked the wrong guy. The Giants and Dodgers matched up in an old-timers game before the clubs met in Los Angeles on June 23, 1974. Participants included Don Newcombe, Pee Wee Reese, Carl Erskine, Hank Sauer, Sal Maglie, Don Drysdale, and Willie Mays. Drysdale drew boos from the 52,563 Dodger Stadium crowd when he walked Mays on five pitches. The Dodgers apparently just never learned. The guy they should have walked was Bobby Thomson, who sparked the old-time Giants to a 3–0 victory with a double to right field off Ralph Branca to score Mays.

JUAN'S BAD DAY

Juan Marichal has enjoyed some of his best times against the Dodgers, but on June 24, 1967, he set a baseball standard for having a bad day in a game at Los Angeles. Marichal accidentally struck and killed a low-flying sparrow while he was warming up, committed a throwing error which led to a run, grounded out with the bases loaded to end a threat, and lost to the Dodgers 2–0. Bill Singer countered with one of his best days, recording his first major league shutout and first complete game while striking out 10, including Willie Mays three times.

FRONT-OFFICE FEUD

The Giants were in fifth place and the Dodgers in eighth in the summer of 1967, leaving little chance for any sparks in the rivalry to flare up on the field. However, the poor seasons made the front offices cranky enough to ignite their own dust-up. Giants Vice President Chub Feeney was quoted as saying that the Dodgers were rebuilding and could not win the pennant this year, prompting a headline, "The Dodgers are dead." Responded Dodgers Vice President Buzzie Bavasi, "If that is his considered opinion, we might as well end the season right now." That might have been a wise choice as the Giants finished the season 10½ games out while the Dodgers ended up 28½ games behind.

GAYLORD SHINES

Gaylord Perry was winless in his last seven starts and pitching in the heat of a pennant race July 10, 1971, but he was most concerned about having to expose his shiny head on a day when Bobby Bonds helped the Giants to a 3–1 late-inning victory over the Dodgers. In the ninth, Bonds, who went four for five, drove in Tito Fuentes and Willie Mays with a double for the winning runs. In the fifth, with Maury Wills batting, the Dodgers questioned whether Perry was using a foreign substance on the baseball. Umpire Ed Sudol went to the mound to search Perry, who cooperated although he was reluctant about removing his cap. Perry explained, "With all those people in the stands, I wasn't too happy about taking my hat off. I'm getting kind of thin and gray on top."

EARTHQUAKE

Baseball was the last thing on anyone's mind on October 1, 1987, as a 6.1 earthquake rocked Southern California at 7:42 A.M., resulting in several deaths, damaged structures, and some closed freeways. The season-ending night game between the Dodgers and Giants, which had now become even more insignificant, went on anyway after a check found no structural damage at Dodger Stadium. Bob Welch dominated the contest, firing a one-hitter, and driving in the first three runs with a bases-loaded single in the 7–0 Dodgers victory.

GUTTING THE RIVALRY

The Giants and Dodgers played 22 regularly scheduled games against each other from 1958 through 1961. The frequency of matchups helped get the rivalry humming in the early West Coast years. Expansion in 1962 cut their matchups to a still meaty 18 games. Major league baseball diluted the rivalry in 1993, with the teams going head-to-head only 12 or 13 times through 2000. The cutback meant that in the eight-year stretch, the clubs didn't meet during April for six of the seasons. In 1997 and 1999, the clubs didn't see each other until June. The all-time bonehead schedule came in 1998, when the clubs, fresh off one of their most dramatic seasons, would not play each other until July 3, just three days before the All-Star break. Some sanity was restored in 2001 when the teams started meeting 19 times. The clubs were scheduled for 18 games from 2007 through 2012, and the matchups were increased to 19 for 2013.

BLEEDING ORANGE AND BLACK

The year 1992 was a frustrating season for the Giants, though only in part because of their dreary performance on the field. They couldn't even promise to wait 'til' next year with any conviction because of the pending sale of the team by owner Bob Lurie and the possibility that the franchise would be moved to Florida. One report in August 1992 had Vince Piazza, Tommy Lasorda's childhood friend, named as a principal investor in a group trying to buy the Giants in the Florida deal, triggering speculation that the Dodgers manager could become general manager or skipper for the Tampa Bay team. These wouldn't be the San Francisco Giants. They might not even be called the Tampa Bay Giants. But it would sure seem like Lasorda would be taking over the helm of his archenemy. Fortunately, Lasorda, in his normally candid reaction, put everyone at ease that he wouldn't suddenly start bleeding black and orange. Lasorda made it clear he had no plans to leave Los Angeles, but he added a dig at those weeping over the Giants' apparent pending departure. "I will not miss that ballpark, nor will I miss those fans. They are the worst fans in the league. They're so far out in front, there's nobody close. Those people throw things at players, and you want to call that civilized?"

PHONE BILL

The stakes were high as the Giants and Dodgers squared off June 23 in San Francisco during the pennant race of 2003. The Giants took a 2–0 lead into the ninth, but the Dodgers tied it with the help of a Giants throwing error. In the 11th, Barry Bonds singled off closer Eric Gagne and stole second. Benito Santiago's single brought Bonds home with the winning run, setting off a celebration in the stands and a tantrum in the dugout. Gagne was so infuriated that he ripped out the phone to the bullpen, prompting the Giants to bill him $500 for the repairs. When *San Francisco Chronicle* columnist Scott Ostler informed Giants Executive Vice President Larry Baer that one can find a basic phone for a much cheaper price, Ostler said Baer replied, "For the Dodgers, there's a markup."

12

MERCY RULE

The wildest slugfest on the West Coast went to the Giants 14–13 on July 17, 1969, in San Francisco. Maury Wills hit the first pitch for a home run. The Dodgers had 16 hits and the Giants had 15. The Giants were in front 11–6 after six. The Dodgers took the lead with a seven-run seventh. A Bob Burda three-run homer in the seventh won it. While that explosive game was up for grabs until the end, the teams have engaged in other offensive shows on the West Coast that were one-sided enough they would have triggered a mercy rule if one existed in major league rules.

AMONG THE BIGGEST ROUTS:

Giants 19, Dodgers 8 (April 16, 1962): This was the only other game in which the teams combined for 27 runs. The Giants built a 12–3 lead, and that was even before they had their big inning. The Dodgers outhit the Giants 15 to 12, but hurt themselves by allowing 10 walks and committing three errors. Billy O'Dell benefited from the offensive output, completing the game and getting the victory despite giving up eight runs, 15 hits, and four walks. The Giants poured it on with seven runs in the seventh off Dodgers rookie Willard Hunter, who surrendered 10 runs in two innings. The rout would have been bigger as the Giants led 19–3 in the ninth, when the Dodgers gained some respectability with a five-run rally highlighted by Tommy Davis's two-run homer and Doug Camilli's two-run double.

Dodgers 17, Giants 0 (September 13, 2014): Fortunately there is a lot to do in downtown San Francisco, because it's likely that some Giants fans might have gone looking for the exits at AT&T Park three innings into the game. The largest shutout in West Coast history featured 24 hits by the Dodgers, including four by Hanley Ramirez. It was a team effort as 12 Dodgers got hits and nine had RBIs. Giants starter Tim Hudson gave up six runs in the first and the Dodgers led 9-0 after three.

Dodgers 19, Giants 3 (May 26, 1970): Despite losing by 16 runs, the Giants picked up a half-game over first-place Cincinnati. The oddity, made possible by the Reds losing a doubleheader, provided little comfort to the Giants as the opposing pitcher led the onslaught. Claude Osteen starred on the mound and at the plate, holding the Giants to three runs while surrendering 12 hits, and going four for five with a double, home run and four RBIs. Ex-Giant Tom Haller went four for five, Jim Lefebvre drove in four runs, and Bill Grabarkewitz had three hits and scored five runs. The Dodgers went through five Giants pitchers, with Rich Robertson (six runs in 3⅓ innings) and Mike McCormick (six runs in 3⅓ innings) the main victims.

Giants 19-3 (September 14, 2013): The Giants finally avenged the 1970 19-3 drubbing by clobbering the Dodgers by the same score 43 years later. Hunter Pence drove in seven runs and Brandon Belt six as the Giants exploded at Dodger Stadium for 22 hits. A 12-6 lead after six wasn't enough for the Giants, who piled on seven more runs in the final three innings.

Giants 18, Dodgers 4 (September 19, 1998): Jeff Kent and Bill Mueller hit grand slams to highlight a 19-hit spree. Doug Mirabelli and Brian Johnson also homered. The Giants had an early knockout, scoring seven in the third against Ismael Valdes and six in the fourth against Mike Judd to take a 13–0 lead.

Giants 16, Dodgers 2 (July 29, 1987): The Giants matched their run total with 16 hits, and displayed efficient production in three bases-loaded situations. With the bases filled, Will Clark had a two-run single, Chili

Davis a two-run double, and Mike Aldrete a two-run single that resulted in a third run crossing the plate when Pedro Guerrero had trouble handling the ball. Davis, finishing with five RBIs, also had a three-run homer. The Giants battered four Dodgers pitchers, building a 12–1 lead after four innings. Mike Krukow threw a complete game while allowing just six hits.

Dodgers 15, Giants 1 (July 26, 1993): The Dodgers launched a 17-hit attack, which included nine extra-base hits and three home runs. Orel Hershiser was the beneficiary of the Dodgers bats, giving up just five hits and getting two of his own. Eric Karros, Mike Piazza, and Henry Rodriquez homered.

Giants 15, Dodgers 1 (August 4, 1995): The last-place Giants, having lost five of their last six meetings with the Dodgers, exploded for 16 hits. John Patterson, Royce Clayton, Glenallen Hill, and pitcher William Van Landingham homered for the Giants, and Mark Carreon drove in five runs. Van Landingham gave up one run and seven hits in seven innings. Tom Candiotti was roughed up for 10 runs and 10 hits in four innings.

Dodgers 16, Giants 3 (September 21, 1990): The Dodgers amassed 20 hits off four Giants pitchers. Giants starter Don Robinson was knocked out in the fourth, allowing eight runs and nine hits. The Dodgers scored five in the first and five in the fourth to build an 11–2 lead. Kal Daniels went four for four, Eddie Murray three for three, and Lenny Harris three for four. Hubie Brooks drove in four runs. Mike Morgan went eight innings for the win.

Dodgers 15, Giants 2 (October 2, 1982): The Dodgers kept their title hopes alive while mathematically eliminating the Giants with a 17-hit attack. The Dodgers scored 12 before the Giants finally could break through with a pair in the seventh. The Dodgers jumped on starter Renie Martin and reliever Al Holland for six in the second inning. Bill Russell drove in two with a bases-loaded single, Steve Sax knocked in another with a base hit, and Ken Landreaux drilled a three-run homer. Ron Cey homered in the third for a 7–0 lead, and Mike Sciosia had a three-run blast in the fifth. Bob Welch won his 16th game with five innings of shutout ball.

Dodgers 16, Giants 4 (April 20, 2003): The Dodgers spotted the Giants four runs, keyed by home runs from Barry Bonds and Andres Galarraga. The Dodgers roared back with three runs in the fourth, four in the fourth, eight in the seventh and one more in the eighth as they compiled 18 hits. Fred McGriff went four for five with four RBIs and two doubles. Shawn Green went four for five with two RBIs and a double.

Dodgers 15, Giants 3 (May 13, 1973): The Dodgers, having dropped four of their first six meetings with the Giants this season, got their frustrations out with a 20-hit barrage that featured a nine-run fourth inning. The Dodgers sent 13 men to the plate in the fourth, compiling the runs on two homers, two doubles, and five singles. Ron Cey had four singles and five RBIs. Willie Davis went four for five with two doubles and two RBIs. Joe Ferguson had a homer and four RBIs and Davey Lopes hit a homer and drove in three. Andy Messersmith went the distance. Giants starter Jim Barr was battered for seven runs and nine hits in 3⅓ innings. With the game out of hand, Giants infielder Dave Kingman came in to pitch the last two innings, giving up two runs and two hits.

13

SKIPPERS

The managers at times have been as much a part of the rivalry as the players. Some of the skippers got their posts because of their skills as players. Others became skippers solely on their baseball acumen. The West Coast has had a variety of men take the helm for either the Dodgers or Giants.

One of the greatest contrasts in how the clubs operated on the West Coast was how they handled their skippers. From 1954 to 1996, managing the Dodgers was the most secure job in America. During that time, only Walter Alston and Tommy Lasorda held the post. From 1954 to 1985, managing the Giants required the incumbent to keep their resume updated. During that stretch, it was Durocher, Rigney, Sheehan, Dark, Franks, King, Fox, Westrum, Rigney (again), Altobelli, Bristol, Robinson, Ozark, and Davenport.

Alston's clubs went 2,040–1,613 in his 23 years at the helm. He guided the Dodgers to seven pennants and four World Series titles. After Alston announced on September 27, 1976, that he was stepping down, first baseman Steve Garvey said, "Players come and go, but he's the person most responsible for the most popular team in baseball. This is really the end of an era."

Two days later, the Dodgers named Tommy Lasorda as his replacement, and a new era was under way. Lasorda, who spent 28 years in the organization as a pitcher, scout, minor league manager and coach, was a contrast to the low-key, businesslike Alston. Lasorda would provide years of entertainment with his bubbling enthusiasm for the Dodgers, fiery outbursts, and successful teams. Lasorda, the Dodgers third base coach the last four seasons, gushed after he got the top job, saying, "It only proves to me that loyalty is a two-way street, that after all the love I've shown to the Dodgers over the years, the Dodgers love me a little, too."

The Giants' approach to managers was more like love 'em and leave 'em. Only two managers—Alvin Dark and Herman Franks—held the job for at least four full seasons during the Giants first 28 years in San Francisco. Dark, while not a demonstrative personality, was the quirkiest. As the Giants searched for a new manager for the 1961 season, rumors produced a list of potential candidates, including Leo Durocher, Casey Stengel, Yogi Berra, Red Schoendienst, Bobby Bragan, Fred Haney, and Dark, a former New York Giants infielder.

The Giants had dissolved into a team of factions and dissension toward the end of the 1960 season, and Dark was given the immediate task of bringing a new attitude to the club.

One of Dark's oddest moves was his no-bullpen experiment, triggered by his frustration with his top three starting pitchers failing to go the distance. After Jack Sanford completed just two of 18 starts, and Mike McCormick seven of 20, Dark said they and Juan Marichal would have to pitch without a bullpen. In the several days of the experiment, Sanford and McCormick won their starts, and Marichal, pitching with a sore finger and bruised foot, won two in a row, both on shutouts. Dark let that experiment fade away, but he wasn't through with his tricks. When the Giants were stumbling out of contention in September, he inserted himself as the third base coach against the Dodgers to try to change the club's fortunes.

The Dodgers won 5–4, and Dark, now 0–1 as a base coach, said he would remain in the dugout for the rest of the year.

Dark proved to be a colorful manager, but more importantly, he moved the Giants up two places in the standings with a six-win improvement over his predecessors in 1961, and paved the way for the Giants' 1962 pennant-winning year over the Dodgers.

While the Giants might not want to admit it, there must have been something about Dodgers baseball that attracted them when it came time to shop for a manager starting in the 1980s. From 1981 to 2002, with the exception of 200 games, the Giants were led by a former Dodger. Roger Craig, who pitched for Brooklyn and Los Angeles from 1955 to 1961, took over at the end of the disastrous 100-loss 1985 season, and continued in the role through 1992. Craig was involved in one of the Giants' wildest brawls, though he wasn't a member of the Giants or Dodgers when it occurred. In 1962, while pitching for the expansion New York Mets, Craig got into a fight with Giants first baseman Orlando Cepeda after hitting him with a pitch. While that was going on, Willie Mays got into a wrestling match at second base with Mets infielder Elio Chacon.

Craig guided the Giants to two NL West titles and a World Series appearance.

Frank Robinson, who played for the Dodgers in 1972, managed the Giants from 1981 to 1984, when he was fired during the season. Former Dodgers coach Danny Ozark replaced Robinson as interim manager. Dusty Baker, a Dodger from 1976 to 1983, managed the Giants from 1993 to 2002. Baker led the club to two NL West titles, a wild card and one World Series berth. The Giants finally went with one of their own, Felipe Alou, to manage the club from 2003–2006. Alou inherited a strong team during the Barry Bonds-mania era, and guided the club to 191 wins and a division title in his first two years. After back-to-back losing seasons, including a dismal 2006 in which the Giants lost 13 of 19 to the Dodgers, the Giants looked to Southern California once more for leadership.

Bruce Bochy, the manager of the San Diego Padres for 12 years with successive NL West titles in 2005 and 2006, was hired to replace Alou in

2007. Three years later, Bochy did what no other San Francisco manager had been able to do—win a World Series. And he did it again in 2012 and 2014. Bochy, a former catcher, became one of baseball's best game-strategy managers, with an uncanny skill to play the hot hand on offense, while masterfully getting the best out of a strong rotation and bullpen. Bochy's three World Series championships make him San Francisco's all-time manager.

The Dodgers would go from having two managers in 43 years to nine in the following 21 seasons. One of those was a mega-baseball figure, Joe Torre, who ran the club from 2008 to 2010, and won the NL West in his first two seasons.

But while the names Alston, Torre, Baker, Craig, Dark, Bochy, and others will be forever linked to the rivalry and West Coast baseball, Lasorda remains king of the hill.

The year 1996 would turn out to be a significant one for the Dodgers, as well as for the rivalry, because of the midseason retirement of Lasorda. The skipper was hospitalized on June 24, and underwent an angioplasty procedure on his heart two days later. On July 29, the 68-year-old Lasorda, fighting back tears, reluctantly announced he was stepping down because of his health problems. Lasorda left with 1,599 wins in his 20-year managerial career with the Dodgers. He led his teams to two world championships, four pennants, and eight division titles. Lasorda was a combination coach and cheerleader, easily excitable and 100 percent ecstatic about the Dodgers organization he had been part of for 47 years. It was his passion for the Dodgers that fueled his volatile relationship with San Francisco Giants fans. Lasorda was an incendiary device at Candlestick Park through the years, angrily berating the stadium's legendary unruly spectators, and taunting them with smiles, waves, and a tip of the cap. But in the end, even the most hardened Giants fans would probably admit that his departure as manager took some of the fun out of Dodgers-Giants games. The salutes to Lasorda were many, including this one given at the time from Carl Erskine, who pitched for the Dodgers in Brooklyn and Los Angeles: "Tommy was like Jackie Robinson in that he was bigger than the team he played for. He was true blue for the Dodgers."

14

—◦∞◦—

DREAM TEAMS

I f there could be one mythical West Coast game between the Dodgers and Giants, who should be on the roster? The teams could be chosen based solely on statistics, but that approach would ignore the spirit of the rivalry. The following selections include many of the stars, but there are some who make the squad because of just one incident or memorable moment or for their special proven ability to heat up tensions with their words or deeds. Where should the game be played? Some might push the Giants' majestic downtown ballpark on a sunny Sunday afternoon with a slight breeze blowing out to right to give Snider a shot at McCovey Cove. Others might favor an 80-degree, balmy Southern California day at Dodger Stadium. The Los Angeles Coliseum would be an interesting venue, as 100,000 would pack the place to see if Barry Bonds altered his swing to take advantage of the 250-foot left-field screen. Those who bask in nostalgia would summon the clubs to 16th and Bryant in San Francisco for an intimate gathering at tiny Seals Stadium. All those sites have arguments in their favor, but is there really any debate that this game must be scheduled on a chilly Friday night at Candlestick Park? The edgy crowd and the unpredictable elements were the backdrop for the bareknuckle era of the rivalry.

So let the game begin, as the spectators settle in to watch Mays battle the fiery Gagne, Will Clark take his best shot against Hershiser, Drysdale brush back Barry Bonds and Ramirez try to get in synch with Marichal's high leg kick. So many thrills would come in this All-Time Rivalry contest, perhaps the Greatest Game Never Played.

Giants starters

1B Willie McCovey: Drysdale vs. McCovey remains one of the great match-ups.

2B Joe Morgan: 1982 Dodger-killing homer made him a rivalry legend.

3B Jim Davenport: Batted .429 against Dodgers in inaugural 1958 season.

SS Rich Aurilia: Good Karma. S.F. finished ahead of L.A. in his first six years as a starter.

OF Barry Bonds: Thrived on adversity, and the Dodgers dished out plenty of it.

OF Willie Mays: The game wouldn't count if he didn't play.

OF Bobby Bonds: Debuted with slam vs. Dodgers.

C Brian Johnson: Broke Dodgers' hearts with Bobby Thomson-like homer in 1997.

P Juan Marichal: Beyond bat incident, Marichal vs. Dodgers were classics.

Dodgers starters

1B Steve Garvey: Perfect image didn't go over well at imperfect Candlestick.

2B Jeff Kent: Giants hero became overnight S.F. enemy after joining Dodgers.

3B Ron Cey: Part of classic infield that made life miserable for Giants.

SS Maury Wills: Even Giants' grounds crew joined effort to slow down speedster.

OF Mike Marshall: Started riot at Candlestick all by himself.

OF Manny Ramirez: An instant, larger-than-life villain for San Francisco fans.

OF Reggie Smith: Led the league in getting doused with beer at Candlestick.

C John Roseboro: Only Dodger to sue a Giant player.

P Don Drysdale: No player did more to bring intensity to the rivalry.

Giants reserves

P John Montefusco: He hated the Dodgers. They hated him. A perfect match.

P Gaylord Perry: Dodgers accused him of throwing spitter. Gaylord was amused.

P Sam Jones: Didn't hate Dodgers, but not too crazy about their official scorer.

P Tim Lincecum: Brought an extra buzz to the game whenever he started.

P Ramon Monzant: Involved in first West Coast beanball battle with Dodgers.

P Rod Beck: Eddie Murray DP ball in 1997 his finest moment.

P Robb Nen: Premier closer helped get Giants to 2002 Series.

P Madison Bumgarner: Confrontations with Yasiel Puig are like the good old days.

C Buster Posey: Young star appears poised to be big factor in rivalry's future.

C Tom Haller: Caught for both teams in heyday of rivalry.

INF Will Clark: Dodgers weren't thrilled by his enthusiasm.

INF Matt Williams: Strike deprived him of chance to catch Maris in 1994.

INF J. T. Snow: Spectacular defense could showcase this game.

OF Felipe Alou: Went head to head with Dodgers as Giants player and manager.

OF Orlando Cepeda: Big bat was fixture in most of epic rivalry games in early years.

OF Michael Tucker: Part-timer had altercations with two Dodgers pitchers in two days.

Dodgers reserves

P Sandy Koufax: His 1965–66 excellence was enough to kill Giant pennant hopes.

P Orel Hershiser: Bulldog tried to love S.F., but it was only a one-year fling.

P Clayton Kershaw: Ace dominates Giants; Bochy snubs him for All-Star game.

P Brian Wilson: Had postgame showdown with Giants' owner over not getting his World Series ring.

P Andy Messersmith: Once observed, "People aren't the best of friends on these clubs."

P Steve Howe: Confrontation with hard-nosed F. Robbie is a rivalry favorite.

P Eric Gagne: Ripped out S.F. dugout phone; Giants billed him for new one.

C Mike Sciosia: You expected a brawl every time he blocked the plate.

INF Davey Lopes: All members of Fab 4 infield must be on team.

INF Bill Russell: Founding Father of Fab 4 as he was first of group to be a regular.

INF Kevin Elster: Went from unknown to rivalry legend with 3-HR day at PacBell opener.

OF Yasiel Puig: Most booed Dodger in SF, had stare downs with Bumgarner.

OF Steve Finley: Crushed Giants with Dodgers' biggest home run of West Coast rivalry.

OF Roger Cedeno: Dodgers youngster stole second in ninth with L.A. leading S.F. 11-2.

OF Duke Snider: Willie and The Duke on the same field for one more sweet time.

Giants managers/coaches

Manager: Dusty Baker: Carried around chip on his shoulder after Dodgers let him go.

Coaches: Roger Craig: Former Dodger battled hard against his old club.
Coaches: Alvin Dark: Led team over Dodgers in classic 1962 playoff.
Coaches: Bruce Bochy: Just kept piling up championships.

Dodgers managers/coaches

Manager: Tommy Lasorda: Earned his boos by merrily teasing, scolding rowdy Giants fans.
Coaches: Walter Alston: Steady style could provide calm when Lasorda gets unhinged.
Coaches: Don Mattingly: Mound debacle in 2010 is one of rivalry's craziest highlights.
Coaches: Joe Torre: Could restore order in case things really got out of hand.

YEAR-BY-YEAR RESULTS: 1890–2016

(Dodgers, Giants yearly overall results, head-to-head results; postseason results; 1890 was the first year the teams were together in the National League.)

YEAR	TEAM	W	L	GB	PLACE	TEAM	W	L	GB	PLACE	HEAD-TO-HEAD
1890	Brooklyn	86	43	-	1	New York	63	68	24	6	Brooklyn 10, N.Y 8
(Brooklyn split championship series 3–3–1 with Louisville Colonels)										
1891	New York	71	61	13	3	Brooklyn	61	76	25.5	6	N.Y. 11, Brooklyn 8
1892	Brooklyn	95	59	9	3	New York	71	80	31.5	8	Brooklyn 7, N.Y. 7
1893	New York	68	64	19.5	5	Brooklyn	65	63	20.5	6	N.Y. 6, Brooklyn 6
1894	New York	88	44	3	2	Brooklyn	70	61	20.5	5	N.Y. 7, Brooklyn 5
1895	Brooklyn	71	60	16.5	5	New York	66	65	21.5	9	Brooklyn 9, N.Y. 3
1896	New York	64	67	27	7	Brooklyn	58	73	33	9	N.Y. 8, Brooklyn 4
1897	New York	83	48	9.5	3	Brooklyn	61	71	32	6	N.Y. 9, Brooklyn 3
1898	New York	77	73	25.5	7	Brooklyn	54	91	46	10	N.Y. 11, Brooklyn 3
1899	Brooklyn	101	47	-	1	New York	60	90	42	10	Brooklyn 10, N.Y. 2
(No postseason)										
1900	Brooklyn	82	54	-	1	New York	60	78	23	8	Brooklyn 10, N.Y. 10
(No postseason)										
1901	Brooklyn	79	57	9.5	3	New York	52	85	37	7	Brooklyn 11, N.Y. 6
1902	Brooklyn	75	63	27.5	2	New York	48	88	53.5	7	Brooklyn 10, N.Y. 10
1903	New York	84	55	6.5	2	Brooklyn	70	66	19	5	N.Y. 12, Brooklyn 7
1904	New York	106	47	-	1	Brooklyn	56	97	50	6	N.Y. 19, Brooklyn 3
(No postseason)										
1905	New York	105	48	-	1	Brooklyn	48	104	56.5	8	N.Y. 15, Brooklyn 7
(New York Giants defeat Philadelphia Athletics in World Series 4–1)										
1906	New York	96	56	20	2	Brooklyn	66	86	50	5	N.Y. 13, Brooklyn 9

YEAR	TEAM	W	L	GB	PLACE	TEAM	W	L	GB	PLACE	HEAD-TO-HEAD
1907	New York	82	71	25.5	4	Brooklyn	65	83	40	5	N.Y. 12, Brooklyn 10
1908	New York	98	56	1	2	Brooklyn	53	101	46	7	N.Y. 16. Brooklyn 6
1909	New York	92	61	18.5	3	Brooklyn	55	98	55.5	6	N.Y. 15, Brooklyn 7
1910	New York	91	63	13	2	Brooklyn	64	90	40	6	N.Y. 14. Brooklyn 8
1911	New York	99	54	-	1	Brooklyn	64	86	33.5	7	N.Y. 16. Brooklyn 5

(New York Giants lose to Philadelphia Athletics in World Series 4–2)

1912	New York	103	48	-	1	Brooklyn	58	95	46	7	N.Y. 16. Brooklyn 6

(New York Giants lose to Boston Red Sox in World Series 4–3–1)

1913	New York	101	51	-	1	Brooklyn	65	84	34.5	6	N.Y. 14. Brooklyn 8

(New York Giants lose to Philadelphia Athletics in World Series 4–1)

1914	New York	84	70	10.5	2	Brooklyn	75	79	19.5	5	N.Y. 13. Brooklyn 9
1915	Brooklyn	80	72	10	3	New York	69	83	21	8	Brooklyn 12, N.Y. 8
1916	Brooklyn	94	60	-	1	New York	86	66	7	4	Brooklyn 15, N.Y. 7

(Brooklyn loses to Boston Red Sox in World Series 4–1)

1917	New York	98	56	-	1	Brooklyn	70	81	26.5	7	N.Y. 13. Brooklyn 9

(New York Giants lose to Chicago White Sox in World Series 4–2)

1918	New York	71	53	10.5	2	Brooklyn	57	69	25.5	5	N.Y. 12, Brooklyn 8
1919	New York	87	53	9	2	Brooklyn	69	71	27	5	N.Y. 12. Brooklyn 8
1920	Brooklyn	93	61	-	1	New York	86	68	7	2	Brooklyn 15, N.Y. 7

(Brooklyn loses to Cleveland Indians in best-of-nine World Series 5–2)

1921	New York	94	59	-	1	Brooklyn	77	75	16.5	5	Brooklyn 12, N.Y. 10

(New York Giants defeat New York Yankees in best-of-nine World Series 5–3)

1922	New York	93	61	-	1	Brooklyn	76	78	17	6	N.Y. 14, Brooklyn 8

(New York Giants defeat New York Yankees in World Series 4–0–1)

1923	New York	95	58	-	1	Brooklyn	76	78	19.5	6	N.Y. 11. Brooklyn 11

(New York Giants lose to New York Yankees in World Series 4–2)

1924	New York	93	60	-	1	Brooklyn	92	62	1.5	2	N.Y. 14, Brooklyn 8

(New York Giants lose to Washington Senators in World Series 4–3)

1925	New York	86	66	8.5	2	Brooklyn	68	85	27	6	N.Y. 12. Brooklyn 10
1926	New York	74	77	13.5	5	Brooklyn	71	82	17.5	6	N.Y. 13, Brooklyn 9
1927	New York	92	62	2	3	Brooklyn	65	88	8.5	6	N.Y. 12. Brooklyn 10
1928	New York	93	61	2	2	Brooklyn	77	76	17.5	6	N.Y. 13. Brooklyn 9
1929	New York	84	67	13.5	3	Brooklyn	70	83	28.5	6	Brooklyn 14, N.Y. 7
1930	New York	87	67	5	3	Brooklyn	86	68	6	4	Brooklyn 13, N.Y. 9
1931	New York	87	65	13	2	Brooklyn	79	73	21	4	N.Y. 10, Brooklyn 10
1932	Brooklyn	81	73	9	3	New York	72	82	18	6	Brooklyn 15, N.Y. 7
1933	New York	91	61	-	1	Brooklyn	65	88	26.5	6	N.Y. 14, Brooklyn 8

(New York Giants defeat Washington Senators in World Series 4–1)

1934	New York	93	60	2	2	Brooklyn	71	81	23.5	6	N.Y. 14, Brooklyn 8
1935	New York	91	62	8.5	3	Brooklyn	70	83	29.5	5	N.Y. 13, Brooklyn 9
1936	New York	92	62	-	1	Brooklyn	67	87	25	7	N.Y. 13. Brooklyn 9

YEAR	TEAM	W	L	GB	PLACE	TEAM	W	L	GB	PLACE	HEAD-TO-HEAD
(New York Giants lose to New York Yankees in World Series 4–2)											
1937	New York	95	57	-	1	Brooklyn	62	91	33.5	6	N.Y. 16, Brooklyn 6
(New York Giants lose to New York Yankees in World Series 4–1)											
1938	New York	83	67	5	3	Brooklyn	69	80	18.5	7	N.Y. 14, Brooklyn 8
1939	Brooklyn	84	69	12.5	3	New York	77	54	18.5	5	Brooklyn 12, N.Y. 10
1940	Brooklyn	88	65	12	2	New York	72	80	27.5	6	Brooklyn 16, N.Y. 5
1941	Brooklyn	100	54	-	1	New York	74	79	25.5	5	Brooklyn 14, N.Y. 8
(Brooklyn loses to New York Yankees in World Series 4–1)											
1942	Brooklyn	104	50	2	2	New York	85	67	25.5	3	Brooklyn 14, N.Y. 8
1943	Brooklyn	81	72	23.5	3	New York	55	98	49.5	8	Brooklyn 14, N.Y. 8
1944	New York	67	87	38	5	Brooklyn	63	91	42	7	N.Y. 12, Brooklyn 10
1945	Brooklyn	87	67	11	3	New York	78	74	19	5	Brooklyn 15, N.Y. 7
1946	Brooklyn	96	60	2	2	New York	61	93	36	8	Brooklyn 15, N.Y. 7
1947	Brooklyn	94	60	-	1	New York	81	73	13	4	Brooklyn 14, N.Y. 8
(Brooklyn loses to New York Yankees in World Series 4–3)											
1948	Brooklyn	84	70	7.5	3	New York	78	76	13.5	5	Brooklyn 11, N.Y. 11
1949	Brooklyn	97	57	-	1	New York	73	81	24	5	Brooklyn 14, N.Y. 8
(Brooklyn loses to New York Yankees in World Series 4–1)											
1950	Brooklyn	89	65	2	2	New York	86	68	5	3	Brooklyn 12, N.Y. 10
1951	New York	98	59	-	1	Brooklyn	97	60	1	2	Brooklyn 14, N.Y. 11
(New York Giants defeat Brooklyn 2–1 in three-game playoff)											
(New York Giants lose to New York Yankees in World Series 4–2)											
1952	Brooklyn	96	57	-	4.5	New York	92	62	4.5	2	N.Y. 14, Brooklyn 8
(Brooklyn loses to New York Yankees in World Series 4–3)											
1953	Brooklyn	105	49	-	1	New York	70	84	35	5	Brooklyn 15, N.Y. 7
(Brooklyn loses to New York Yankees in World Series 4–2)											
1954	New York	97	57	-	1	Brooklyn	92	62	5	2	N.Y. 13. Brooklyn 9
(New York Giants defeat Cleveland Indians in World Series 4–0)											
1955	Brooklyn	98	55	-	1	New York	80	74	18.5	3	Brooklyn 13, N.Y. 9
(Brooklyn defeats New York Yankees in World Series 4–3)											
1956	Brooklyn	93	61	-	1	New York	67	87	26	6	Brooklyn 14, N.Y. 8
(Brooklyn loses to New York Yankees in World Series 4–3)											
1957	Brooklyn	84	70	11	3	New York	69	85	26	6	Brooklyn 12, N.Y. 10
(Teams move to California following the 1957 season)											
1958	S.F.	80	74	12	3	Dodgers	71	83	21	7	S.F. 16, Dodgers 6
1959	L.A.	88	68	-	1	S.F.	83	71	4	3	L.A. 14, S.F. 8
(Los Angeles Dodgers defeat Milwaukee 2–0 in 3-game playoff for NL pennant)											
(Los Angeles Dodgers defeat Chicago White Sox in World Series 4–2)											
1960	L.A.	82	72	4	13	S.F.	79	75	16	5	S.F. 12, L.A. 10
1961	L.A.	89	65	4	2	S.F.	85	69	8	3	S.F. 12, L.A. 10
1962	S.F.	103	62	-	1	L.A.	102	63	1	2	S.F. 11, L.A. 10

YEAR	TEAM	W	L	GB	PLACE	TEAM	W	L	GB	PLACE	HEAD-TO-HEAD
(San Francisco Giants defeat Dodgers 2–1 in 3-game playoff for NL pennant)											
(San Francisco Giants lose to New York Yankees in World Series 4–3)											
1963	L.A.	99	63	-	1	S.F.	88	74	11	3	L.A. 9, S.F. 9
(Los Angeles Dodgers defeat New York Yankees in World Series 4–0)											
1964	S.F.	90	72	3	4	L.A.	80	82	13	6	S.F. 12, L.A. 6
1965	L.A.	97	65	-	1	S.F.	95	67	2	2	L.A. 10, S.F. 8
(Los Angeles Dodgers defeat Minnesota Twins in World Series 4–3)											
1966	L.A.	95	67	-	1	S.F.	93	68	1.5	2	L.A. 9, S.F. 9
(Los Angeles Dodgers lose to Baltimore Orioles in World Series 4–0)											
1967	S.F.	91	71	10.5	2	L.A.	73	89	28.5	8	S.F. 13, L.A. 5
1968	S.F.	88	74	9	2	L.A.	76	86	21	7	S.F. 9, L.A. 9
1969	S.F.	90	72	3	2	L.A.	85	77	8	4	S.F. 13, L.A. 5
1970	L.A.	87	74	14.5	2	S.F.	86	76	16	3	L.A. 9, S.F. 9
1971	S.F.	90	72	-	1	L.A.	89	73	1	2	L.A. 12, S.F. 6
(San Francisco Giants lose to Pittsburgh Pirates in NL championship series, 3–1)											
1972	L.A.	85	70	10.5	2	S.F.	69	86	26.5	5	S.F. 9, L.A. 9
1973	L.A.	95	66	3.5	2	S.F.	88	74	11	3	L.A. 9, S.F. 9
1974	L.A.	102	60	-	1	S.F.	72	90	30	5	L.A. 12, S.F. 6
(Los Angeles Dodgers defeat Pittsburgh Pirates in NL championship series 3–1)											
(Los Angeles Dodgers lose to Oakland A's in World Series 4–1)											
1975	L.A.	88	74	20	2	S.F.	80	81	27.5	3	L.A. 10, S.F. 8
1976	L.A.	92	70	10	2	S.F.	74	88	28	4	S.F. 10, L.A. 8
1977	L.A.	98	64	-	1	S.F.	75	87	23	4	L.A. 14, S.F. 4
(Los Angeles Dodgers defeat Philadelphia Phillies in NL championship series 3–1)											
(Los Angeles Dodgers lose to New York Yankees in World Series 4–2)											
1978	L.A.	95	67	-	1	S.F.	89	73	6	3	L.A. 11, S.F. 7
(Los Angeles Dodgers defeat Philadelphia Phillies in NL championship series 3–1)											
(Los Angeles Dodgers lose to New York Yankees in World Series 4–2)											
1979	L.A.	79	83	11.5	3	S.F.	71	91	19.5	4	L.A. 14, S.F. 4
1980	L.A.	92	71	1	2	S.F.	75	86	17	5	L.A. 13, S.F. 5
(Los Angeles Dodgers, Houston Astros tie in regular season; Dodgers lose one-game playoff)											
1981											
First half	L.A.	36	21	-	1	S.F.	27	32	10	5	
Second half	S.F.	29	23	3.5	3	L.A.	27	26	6	4	L.A. 7, S.F. 5
(Los Angeles Dodgers defeat Houston Astros in NL West playoff 3–2)											
(Los Angeles Dodgers defeat Montreal Expos in NL championship series 3–2)											
(Los Angeles Dodgers defeat New York Yankees in World Series 4–2)											
1982	L.A.	88	74	1	2	S.F.	87	75	2	3	L.A. 9, S.F. 9
1983	L.A.	91	71	-	1	S.F.	79	83	12	5	S.F. 13, L.A. 5

YEAR	TEAM	W	L	GB	PLACE	TEAM	W	L	GB	PLACE	HEAD-TO-HEAD
(Los Angeles Dodgers lose to Philadelphia Phillies in NL championship series 3–1)											
1984	L.A.	79	83	13	4	S.F.	66	96	26	6	L.A. 10, S.F. 8
1985	L.A.	95	67	-	1	S.F.	62	100	33	6	L.A. 11, S.F. 7
(Los Angeles Dodgers lose to St. Louis Cardinals in NL championship series 4–2)											
1986	S.F.	83	79	13	3	L.A.	73	89	23	5	S.F. 10, L.A. 8
1987	S.F.	90	72	-	1	L.A.	73	89	17	4	L.A. 10, S.F. 8
(San Francisco Giants lose to St. Louis Cardinals in NL championship series 4–3)											
1988	L.A.	94	67	-	1	S.F.	83	79	11.5	4	L.A. 12, S.F. 6
(Los Angeles Dodgers defeat New York Mets in NL championship series 4–3)											
(Los Angeles Dodgers defeat Oakland A's in World Series 4–1)											
1989	S.F.	92	70	-	1	L.A.	77	83	14	4	L.A. 10, S.F. 8
(San Francisco Giants defeat Chicago Cubs in NL championship series 4–1)											
(San Francisco Giants lose to Oakland A's in World Series 4–0)											
1990	L.A.	86	76	5	2	S.F.	85	77	6	3	S.F. 10, L.A. 8
1991	L.A.	93	69	1	2	S.F.	75	87	19	4	S.F. 10, L.A. 8
1992	S.F.	72	90	26	5	L.A.	63	99	35	6	S.F. 11, L.A. 7
1993	S.F.	103	59	1	2	L.A.	81	81	23	4	L.A. 7, S.F. 6
1994	L.A.	58	56	-	1	S.F.	55	60	3.5	2	L.A. 5, S.F. 5
(Season canceled by strike)											
1995	L.A.	78	66	-	1	S.F.	67	77	11	4	L.A. 8, S.F. 5
(Los Angeles Dodgers lose to Cincinnati Reds in NL division series 3–0)											
1996	L.A.	90	72	1	2	S.F.	68	94	23	4	L.A. 7, S.F. 6
(Los Angeles Dodgers lose to Atlanta Braves in NL division series 3–0)											
1997	S.F.	90	72	-	1	L.A.	88	74	2	2	S.F. 6, L.A. 6
(San Francisco Giants lose to Florida Marlins in NL first round series 3–0)											
1998	S.F.	89	74	9.5	2	L.A.	83	79	15	3	S.F. 6, L.A. 6
1999	S.F.	86	76	14	2	L.A.	77	85	23	3	L.A. 8, S.F. 5
2000	S.F.	97	65	-	1	L.A.	86	76	11	2	L.A. 7, S.F. 5
(San Francisco Giants lose to New York Mets in NL division series 3–1)											
2001	S.F.	90	72	2	2	L.A.	86	76	6	3	L.A. 11, S.F. 8
2002	S.F.	95	66	2.5	2	L.A.	92	70	6	3	S.F. 11, L.A. 8
(San Francisco Giants defeat Atlanta Braves in NL division series 3–2)											
(San Francisco Giants defeat St. Louis Cardinals in NL championship series 4–1)											
(San Francisco Giants lose to Anaheim Angels in World Series 4–3)											
2003	S.F.	100	61	-	1	L.A.	85	77	15.5	2	S.F. 13, L.A. 6
(San Francisco Giants lose to Florida Marlins in NL division series 3–1)											
2004	L.A.	93	69	-	1	S.F.	91	71	2	2	L.A. 10, S.F. 9
(Los Angeles Dodgers lose to St. Louis Cardinals in NL division series 3–1)											
2005	S.F.	75	87	7	3	L.A.	71	91	11	4	S.F. 10, L.A. 9
2006	L.A.	88	74	-	1	S.F.	76	85	11.5	3	L.A. 13, S.F. 6

YEAR	TEAM	W	L	GB	PLACE	TEAM	W	L	GB	PLACE	HEAD-TO-HEAD
(Los Angeles Dodgers, San Diego Padres tie; San Diego wins title based on series record)											
(Los Angeles Dodgers lose to New York Mets in NL division series 3–0)											
2007	L.A.	82	80	8	4	S.F.	71	91	19	5	L.A. 10, S.F. 8
2008	L.A.	84	78	-	1	S.F.	72	90	12	4	L.A. 9, S.F. 9
(Los Angeles Dodgers defeat Chicago Cubs in NL division series 3–0)											
(Los Angeles Dodgers lose to Philadelphia Phillies in NL championship series 4–1)											
2009	L.A.	95	67	-	1	S.F.	88	74	7	3	L.A. 11, S.F. 7
(Los Angeles Dodgers defeat St. Louis Cardinals in NL division series 3–0)											
(Los Angeles Dodgers lose to Philadelphia Phillies in NL championship series 4–1)											
2010	S.F.	92	70	-	1	L.A.	80	82	12	4	S.F. 10, L.A. 8
(San Francisco Giants defeat Atlanta Braves in NL division series 3–1)											
(San Francisco Giants defeat Philadelphia Phillies in NL championship series 4–2)											
(San Francisco Giants defeat Texas Rangers in World Series 4–1)											
2011	S.F.	86	76	8	2	L.A.	82	79	11.5	3	S.F. 9, L.A. 9
2012	S.F.	94	68	-	1	L.A.	86	76	8	2	S.F. 10, L.A. 8
(San Francisco Giants defeat Cincinnati Reds in NL division series 3–2)											
(San Francisco Giants defeat St. Louis Cardinals in NL championship series 4–3)											
(San Francisco Giants defeat Detroit Tigers in World Series 4–0)											
2013	L.A.	92	70	-	1	S.F.	76	86	16	3	S.F. 11-8
(Los Angeles Dodgers defeat Atlanta Braves in NL Division Series 3–1)											
(Los Angeles Dodgers lose to St. Louis Cardinals in NL championship series 4–2)											
2014	L.A.	94	68	-	1	S.F.	88	74	6	2	L.A. 10-9
(Los Angeles Dodgers lose to St. Louis Cardinals in NL Division series 3–1)											
(San Francisco Giants defeat Pittsburgh Pirates in NL wild-card game)											
(San Francisco Giants defeat Washington Nationals in NL division series 3–1)											
(San Francisco Giants defeat St. Louis Cardinals in NL championship series 4–1)											
(San Francisco Giants defeat Kansas City Royals in World Series 4–3)											
2015	L.A.	92	70	-	1	S.F.	84	78	8	2	S.F. 11-8
(Los Angeles Dodgers lose to New York Mets in NL division series 3–2)											
2016	L.A.	91	71	-	1	S.F.	87	75	2	4	S.F. 11-8
(San Francisco Giants defeat New York Mets in NL wild-card game)											
(San Francisco Giants lose to Chicago Cubs in NL Division series 3–1)											
(Los Angeles Dodgers defeat Washington Nationals in NL Division series 3–2)											
(Los Angeles Dodgers lose to Chicago Cubs in NL championship series 4–2)											

ACKNOWLEDGMENTS

One of the favorite pastimes of my childhood was playing wiffle ball with my friends in the garage at my house. It would be two on two. One team would be the Dodgers and the other team the Giants, and we'd have full lineups. The rules were that you had to mimic the player whether you were pitching or batting. It was from this kids' play where I began being a student of the rivalry. I entered this project being able to recall many of the intimate details of the clubs and the rivalry from more than a half-century of following the games. That familiarity with the topic helped immensely in assembling this book. However, I am indebted to the sources I used to get the specifics need to fully tell the story. I enjoyed searching through *The Sports Encyclopedia of Baseball* and the *Giants Encyclopedia*, two marvelous reference books. Baseballreference. com and baseballalmanac.com were good places to check the numbers. The Associated Press and UPI accounts of some games were helpful. *The Sporting News* annual baseball magazine helped me dig up details on the preseason outlook for both teams. The Dodgers and Giants media guides, and the team websites also have been valuable. I am very grateful to Ward Bushee, executive editor of the *San Francisco Chronicle*, and his photo/ library staff for providing *Chronicle* photos. The most special treat of my research was to go back and read the beat work over the years of the baseball writers of the *San Francisco Chronicle*, *San Francisco Examiner* and *Los Angeles Times*. Their writing and reporting are works of art that are worthy of any museum. But in all due respect, of all the sports writing I came across in my hundreds of hours of research, my favorite report came from the *New York Times* of May 4, 1890. In its account of the first ever regular season game between Brooklyn and the New York Giants, the writer said of the victorious team, "The Brooklyns were out for blood. They hit smiling Mickey Welch hard." The writer wrapped up the contest played at Washington Park before one of its largest crowds at 3,774 this way: "The game was a splendid one and everyone enjoyed it."

INDEX